DATE DUE

OCT 4 1972			
1976			
1			
1982-1			
GAYLORD			PRINTED IN U.S.A.

Fifteen Men on a
Powder Keg

Fifteen Men on a Powder Keg

A History of the U.N. Security Council

Andrew Boyd

STEIN AND DAY/*Publishers*/New York

First published in 1971
Copyright © 1971 by Andrew Boyd
Library of Congress Catalog Card No. 70-160354
All rights reserved
Printed in the United States of America
Stein and Day/*Publishers*/7 East 48 Street, New York, N. Y. 10017
ISBN 0-8128-1397-9

To Lindsay

Contents

List of Illustrations

ix

Maps

Acknowledgements

I should like to express my warmest thanks to the United Nations for supplying all the plates, and to W. H. Bromage for allowing me to use a selection of his maps from the sixth edition of my *An Atlas of World Affairs*.

Foreword

The Security Council of the United Nations has been entrusted by most of the world's governments with primary responsibility for the maintenance of international peace. Our governments have thereby shown greater faith even than Kipling's in the beneficent properties of wood. For the Security Council is, essentially, a table shaped like a lucky horseshoe.

Around this table, on average once a week, gather fifteen men, each of whom is employed by a national government to promote its interests. By gathering around the table, these men do not cease to be so employed. On the contrary, when they are at the table it is their duty to do their best for their employers – whatever their employers may have been up to. If they fail in this duty they will, of course, be replaced. The primary responsibility of each man in the Council is, then, the maintenance of his government's interests. At times, fortunately, those interests coincide with the maintenance of international peace. When they do not, an awful lot of primary responsibility for peace rests with the table. (Do not be deceived by the sight of the Secretary-General sitting at the table. He is not a member of the Council, and the Council does not concede him any primary responsibility – except when the UN runs into trouble; then he can take all the responsibility he likes.)

A remarkable thing about this system of maintaining peace is that it sometimes works. Another thing about it is its uniqueness. These men (and their table) are the only group that the world's governments have ever entrusted with primary responsibility for maintaining peace. Nor, in our time, is there any prospect of our governments entrusting it to anybody else. It seems this is the best we can do.

They have been at it now for a quarter of a century. Times have changed: so have they. How have they changed? What were they originally supposed to be and do? Were they ever, and did they ever do, these things? Who are they, anyway? This book is not a comprehensive history of the Security Council. It does not pretend to cover the whole range of the Council's activity since 1946. But it seeks to provide, if not complete answers to all the questions, at least some clues to the answers; to shed some light on both major and minor aspects of the Council's origins, actions and possibilities.

I have tried to avoid unduly detailed treatment of some parts of the Council's record that have been extensively described and discussed elsewhere; on the other hand, I have picked out some of the more interesting but less well known episodes. The story of the Council does not lend itself very easily to chronological, geographical or any other really systematic arrangement, and I must ask the reader to forgive me for rushing him around the world and hurling him backward and forward in time. A number of cross-references are given in the hope of limiting the confusion.

Fifteen Men on a
Powder Keg

Chapter One

The horseshoe

Fifteen men. Nothing in the Charter says they have to be men; but they are. Like a Pall Mall club in London, the Security Council, sitting in the Turtle Bay area of Manhattan, is a masculine redoubt. And this at once tells you something – not so much about what the Council is, as about what its members think it is.

Women are to be found in the other committees and assemblages that proliferate all over the UN headquarters building; in the Secretariat, the press corps and the ranks of the attendant lobbyists. But they have not yet left their imprint on the seats around the Security Council's horseshoe table.

Angie Brooks, the lady from Liberia who presided over the 1969 General Assembly, was not the first of her sex to hold this high office. By established custom, women appear in many states' delegations to the Assembly and in their permanent missions at the UN. They may be politicians, like Vijayalakshmi Pandit or Lady Tweedsmuir; well-known figures like Myrna Loy, with a wide appeal that may help to promote non-political UN enterprises; something of both, like Shirley Temple Black; or career diplomats. In this last and largest category, Agda Rössel of Sweden was the first woman to become, in 1958, her country's permanent representative at the United Nations. As chief of its mission, with ambassadorial rank, it would have been normal procedure for her to take over the seat that Sweden was then occupying in the Security Council, to which it had been elected for the two years 1957 and 1958. But the seat continued to be filled by her predecessor at the UN, Gunnar Jarring, who had moved on to become the Swedish ambassador in Washington. Perfectly relevant explanations for this were given. Yet the effect was that the Council's masculinity remained undefiled.

1

It is not difficult to detect an underlying idea that the Security Council's work is man's work − unlike all that idle chatter that goes on in other UN gatherings; that there is something about the Council that separates the boys from the girls. I am sure no such conscious thought goes through the head of the representative of, say, Burundi, Nepal or Nicaragua (all currently councilmen*) as: 'Look at *me*, sitting here with the *great powers*, settling matters of *war and peace!*' And yet there is a mystique of sorts attached to that horseshoe table, in the eyes of some British elder statesmen as well as in those of young hopefuls among the smallest states' representatives.

For twenty years the Council was a 'team' of eleven. Now it is one of fifteen. These are not particularly auspicious numbers. True, one old English song † recalls 'the eleven who went to heaven'; but at times of midnight stress in the Security Council such words are liable to evoke thoughts of thermonuclear holocaust, or at least death from exhaustion, rather than of a happy release. Another song, 'Fifteen men on the dead man's chest', is more apt; often somebody has to be killed before the Council is called upon to tackle a dispute. But, as R. L. Stevenson reminds us, this favourite ditty of the infamous pirates Flint, Bones and Silver terrified all who heard it, and its associations are with treachery and kegs of rum rather than pacific settlement. Only in the context of team games is there a more cheerful significance to eleven and fifteen. And coincidence must have been at work here. The Council's original number was first proposed by officials in Washington, where cricket is seldom played, while in American football the words First Eleven are less heroically evoca-

---

* 'Councilman' is not a word in common usage at Turtle Bay. I use it here, simply for brevity, to mean the permanent representative of a state that is a member of the Security Council. To sprinkle this book with the initials 'PR' for permanent representative would seem inappropriate, both because the abbreviation PR conveys confusing undertones and because, while all councilmen are PRs, only 15 of the 126 PRs are councilmen at any one time.

A word about ambassadors. All PRs, and so all councilmen, rank as ambassadors unless they have higher rank (as in the case of Caradon, who was a Minister of State). But so do many of their deputies. In 1970 the American and Dominican UN missions each included five ambassadors; the Russian and Venezuelan missions had three each; 13 other missions boasted two each. During Assembly sessions ambassadors are as the sands of the sea in Turtle Bay.

† 'Green grow the rushes O'.

tive than they are in soccer. The enlargement to fifteen reflected pressure from the Asian and African member states, which do not specialise in rugger. But even these accidents of arithmetic tend to strengthen the Council's male image.

In a rational world, one feels, no government in its right mind would ever volunteer to fill an elective Council seat. To do so means that for two years a small state, which presumably has no wish to get into needless quarrels, is liable to have to take a public stand on various awkward questions that are of no direct concern to it, thereby risking the anger of one or more of the great powers and perhaps of other states too. But it seems that the only people who have grasped this point firmly are the Mexicans. Mexico served on the Council in its first year, and thereafter showed little enthusiasm for doing so again. It would be nice to think that governments who offer themselves for the hazards of Council service are moved only by a sense of duty to the world community. In fact, as has been repeatedly shown during the Assembly's annual election of non-permanent members, candidates are often motivated by something more like what the Latin Americans call *machismo* – an urge to demonstrate some sort of masculinity by courting danger.

A relevant case is surely that of Finland. Tenaciously maintaining its independence under Russia's looming shadow, it held to the idea that discretion was the better part of *sisu* for at least a decade after it had joined the UN in 1955. By the end of the 1950s Denmark, Norway and Sweden had each taken a turn on the Council, and it might have seemed logical for Finland to be the next choice among the Nordic group. But the Finns showed no immediate eagerness to occupy what for them was bound to be a hot seat. So Norway again filled the slot in 1963–4, and Denmark in 1967–8. Towards the end of the 1960s, however, President Kekkonen and his ministers were clearly persuaded that it was time for their country to abandon its 'low posture' and cut more of a figure on the international stage. Finland became a Council member for 1969–70; and in that capacity it calmly proceeded to oppose the Russians on several quite substantial issues. I am not suggesting for a moment that the Finns sought election to the Council just to throw their weight about. Their representative, Max Jakobson, has been an outstandingly valuable

3

member of the Council, skilfully putting his weight behind many constructive moves. My point is that the Council is no place to go if you want to lead a quiet life, and that it might be difficult to make up its numbers at all if governments did not have some basic drive to international self-assertion.

There are certain UN member states which, under the existing arrangements, are unlikely ever to be elected to the Council. They include Albania, Cuba, Israel and South Africa. In the category of distinctly doubtful starters may be placed, at least for the time being, Jugoslavia, Malawi, Mongolia and Portugal. (True, among these Cuba and Jugoslavia have already had Council terms; but circumstances have changed since then.) However, inability to get elected does not necessarily mean that a member state's representative is never seen or heard in the Council chamber. The Security Council is a hospitable body. When it discusses a dispute or conflict the states directly concerned (if they do not happen to be Council members) usually ask to be, and are, allowed to sit at the ends of the horseshoe table and join in the speechmaking – but not, of course, in the voting. Over the years Israel, which has never been a member of the Council, must have taken as large a part in its debates as most of its elected members.

On occasion, the Council's hospitality has also extended to states whose connection with the matter in hand was somewhat less than direct. The capacity of the horseshoe table has sometimes been exceeded, and additional seating has had to be provided. At times the 'visiting firemen' have outnumbered the members of the Council itself. In December 1964 there were 14 of them at the 'Stanleyville' debate; in November 1965 there were 17 at the debate on Rhodesia immediately after its illegal declaration of independence (see pages 178 and 234). In using the expression 'visiting firemen', which in New York usage can be applied to almost anybody who gets in on an act that strictly speaking belongs to others, I do not mean to suggest that the Council's guests invariably help to extinguish the flames of controversy. Most often, the exact opposite is true. Only a few of the guests have come to act as conciliators. As to the others, more often than not their purpose in seeking permission to speak is to state a strongly partisan case – on their own behalf or on that of another

4

country. Their presence is likely to raise the temperature of the Council chamber rather than to lower it; and it might be more descriptive to call many of them visiting fire-raisers, or at least fire-eaters.

I think it will already be clear that the atmosphere of the chamber itself does not, in fact, closely resemble that of a Pall Mall man's club. True, the seats are comfortable, the thick carpet silences footsteps; the male figures seated around the heavy table are mostly sober-suited, mostly middle-aged; it is unthinkable that any of them would spring into sudden movement; for long periods, motionless and expressionless, they may seem close to coma. (If you enter the chamber during a typical speech it may take you some time to find out who is making it. The speaker, seated like the others, talking quietly into a microphone, may seem merely to be looking down at the papers laid out before him. Indeed, he is doing so; he is reading from them.) But that is as far as the resemblance to an old-established club goes.

The chamber has no intimacy. It is not one of those smoke-filled rooms in which a few men around a table really thrash things out. It has the dimensions of a theatre. As a matter of fact, its layout is mainly that of a theatre – with the Elizabethan characteristic that there are a lot of privileged spectators sitting on the 'stage' itself. Steeply tiered rows of seats – the public gallery, the press seats and, below them again, more seats for delegates and officials who may want to watch the show – descend from a level two floors above that of the chamber itself. Occupants of these seats see before and below them the horseshoe table, its open end towards them (bad luck?), and on the lofty wall beyond it a huge Norwegian mural which can very fairly be described as replete with symbolism.

Centrally placed in the mural's confusion of images is another horseshoe table; this encircles what looks like a phoenix rising (but leaving its ghost behind) from a fire that never got lit. All around, suffering humanity gropes upward out of the murk of war, bondage and more obscure unpleasantness towards garishly bright scenes full of dancing children, cavorting horses and Adam and Eve in not quite modern dress. This backdrop at least gives the audience plenty to

5

look at when, as is normal, nothing much seems to be happening at the table.

The Secretary-General, the Russian Under-Secretary concerned with Security Council affairs, and the Council's president for the month sit together at the mid-point of the horseshoe (which, although I have spoken of fifteen seats, really has seventeen if you count the two occupied by the Secretariat men). They are spared the sight of the mural, which is behind them; but they have to face the audience in the banked rows of seats – when there is one. At times the Council plays to an almost empty house. In the best showbiz tradition, the councilmen never let this discourage them. But they do tend to reserve their bravura bits for moments when the galleries are packed and they know the television cameras are also lapping up every word and gesture. And they can usually be counted on to maintain an unruffled phlegm on the rare occasions when tumult breaks out in the public gallery.

Sitting around their horseshoe, they gaze at each other over the heads of a Secretariat team which, at a smaller table in the sunken central well, scribbles away industriously and gives each speaker the reassuring feeling that, no matter how tedious and repetitive his words, somebody is following every one of them. Behind each of the fifteen sit his assistants and advisers, also in light blue chairs. But theirs are clamped to the floor. This is presumably (though not, perhaps, always successfully) intended to prevent an adviser from edging in close behind a councilman other than his own, and whispering fiendishly ill-advised advice into the poor innocent's ear. Behind the advisers' blue seats, at both sides of what one may well think of as the Council's stage, are more seats for more assistants, observers and spear-carriers. These (the seats) are bright red. The horseshoe table itself being almost yellow, the walls blue and the big doors on each side of the chamber the same near-yellow as the table, the whole scene – what with that mural – is fairly kaleidoscopic.

It is not quite as static as I may have suggested. The councilmen themselves just sit, and perhaps think. But there is usually a ripple of movement somewhere in the chamber. Aides and officials come and go, delivering notes or murmured messages to the men in the blue seats, pausing on the way out for a word with a friend in the red. A report that tanks have crossed the frontier? Miss Otis regrets she's unable to lunch, but is free for dinner? Your foreign minister says your last speech stank, and your replacement will arrive in New York tomorrow? Whatever the content of the communications, their privacy makes them interestingly mysterious. But occasionally the informed observer sees a movement that tells him something. The Japanese adviser who slips round the table for a word with the Brazilian may look inscrutable; but those in the know have been waiting for the moment when the Latin Americans' draft resolution would pick up enough support to be worth putting to the vote, and this could be it.

There are, of course, moments of high drama when word goes round the building that a Council member is going to make a really important statement, or that a crucial vote is about to be taken without any certainty which way it will go. Then, especially if the Assembly is also in session, the delegates of non-Council states will come swarming into the chamber so that every available seat is filled and a highly distinguished and highly interested crowd is standing tightly packed around the horseshoe. But the visitor who hopes for something spectacular can still be disappointed, with nothing to hear but another speech, nothing to see but a raising of hands. The air may be full of tension, but there is a lack of eye-catching movement. It is rare indeed for some visual novelty to be introduced, as it was in the 1962 Cuba crisis when the Americans brought blown-up photographs of missile launching pads into the chamber; or when the Russians staged their dramatic walkouts in the Council's early years.

True, as recently as December 1969 the chamber witnessed a walkout. Francisco Bonifacio de Miranda, representing Portugal, indignantly withdrew from a debate on a complaint made by Guinea against his country. But this left no conspicuous gap in the horseshoe, for Portugal was participating not as a Council member but as one of the visiting firemen. Indeed, Miranda's protest was against the admission of Samar Sen of India as another of these. By an untimely chance, this happened to be the eighth anniversary of what Miranda angrily recalled as India's 'unprovoked aggression' against Goa. Portugal, he said, 'does not accept in any slightest degree the moral status of that representative, and will withdraw'. To which Samar Sen

7

retorted that 'any day when we can displace the Portuguese representative from this body' was a good day, and that in fact: 'This is the
best day of my life.' For the audience, it was at least a day with a
touch of theatre about it.

I have described them as fifteen men sitting on a powder keg. Kegs
apart – whether of gunpowder or rum – the Security Council is not
sitting anywhere, most of the time. It averages one formal meeting a
week. The Charter (Article 28) lays down that the Council 'shall be
so organised as to be able to function continuously', and that each of
its member states shall therefore 'be represented at all times at the
seat of the Organisation'. Over the years the practice has grown up
that every UN member state keeps a permanent mission in New
York; so there is no longer anything very distinctive about the
Council members in this last respect. They have only to be rather
more on the *qui vive* than the mass of UN members. At a time when
all seems quiet, an ordinary member's UN mission can be left in the
hands of a junior official, or, at a pinch, somebody from a
Washington embassy can commute to and from New York and deal
with routine business there. A Council member's mission, however,
must at all times be adequately manned; its chief can escape only if
he leaves behind a responsible deputy. Yet the fact that the Council is
organised for continuous work does not mean that it works continuously.

Several months can pass without a Council meeting being called at
all. And this does not necessarily mean that the world is enjoying a
period of universal calm. War may be looming in one place and
actually raging in another. In such circumstances the Council's
apparent inertia naturally exposes it to criticism. But the criticism
is not always justified. There are times when most of the councilmen are thoroughly alarmed at the way things are going in one or
another of the world's trouble spots; but they are also aware that no
purpose would be served by starting a public debate. In words that
the British representative, Lord Caradon, used in the Council in
1969:

> Those of us who have long served on the Security Council know that
> perhaps the first unwritten rule of the Council is that it is unwise to call

the Council until and unless there is a plain prospect that agreement can be reached . . . To call the Council with no such confidence can often do more harm than good. It can sometimes embitter controversy and even intensify conflict.

That is a good rule of thumb. It is a sad sight to see an unready and unwilling Council dragged to its table when it is clear to all that a public exchange of familiar accusations will merely 'embitter controversy' and cannot possibly help to improve matters. However, like all good rules, this one has exceptions. The chief exception may be stated as follows: 'an apparently quite unproductive debate can be justified when its net effect is not to inflame but to temper passions'.

A government may be under strong pressure from an angry public opinion to 'do something'. The only alternatives may be to resort to military action against another state – or to take the matter to the UN. The government probably knows perfectly well that it will not get anything like full satisfaction from the Council; but an airing of its grievance in New York may still gain time, permitting passions to subside, and enable the government to claim something of a moral victory – or at least to shift some of the blame for its own failure to get results on to the UN. The important thing, in cases of this kind, is to handle the approach to the Council properly. As examples of good handling, one might cite the 1968 *Pueblo* and 1969 Northern Ireland proceedings (pages 299 and 318); and, as an awful warning of 'how not to do it', the Stanleyville debates in 1964 (page 234).

But the Council's whole life is not played out on its garish stage, in full view of the television cameras. Symbolically as well as usefully, an extensive suite of private rooms adjoins its public chamber. These rooms are one of the few parts of the UN building in which it is really impossible for the unauthorised to set foot. In their privacy, Council members can often do much more useful work than they could possibly accomplish round that horseshoe table. Not that these rooms provide their only refuge. There are other possibilities for private rendezvous. The rooms adjoining the chamber are most valuable when, with time pressing, the Council breaks off public debate for urgent consultations. On the day that the 1967 'six-day war' broke out, for example, most of the members ended up by spending

9

most of their time in these rooms, which include an office for the Council president. That month's president, Hans Tabor of Denmark, had one group or another of the members closeted with him virtually throughout that long day. But when time permits, and especially when the Council is not holding any formal meetings, its members will usually prefer to do their private consulting elsewhere, if only because a gathering in the Council's own rooms inevitably sets off speculation.

Consultation need not involve all members coming together at the same place and time, and indeed it seldom does. When the members have ample warning of what must be done, and there is an underlying consensus about it, the Council president can dispense with the need for furtive rendezvous altogether and, having simply satisfied himself that no member is going to kick up a fuss, he can present an informally agreed draft for approval at a formal meeting.

This is the routine into which the Council has slipped for the more or less 'regular' meetings at which it has renewed, two or three times a year, the life of the United Nations force in Cyprus. When the president has opened one of these Cyprus meetings he announces that: 'As a result of the consultations held among members of the Council before this meeting, a draft resolution has been prepared.' The anonymous–unanimous* draft is duly voted on and adopted unanimously. If all goes well it will be safely in the bag before members get their familiar grouses off their chests. No power on earth, it seems, can stop them speaking 'in explanation of vote' (or stop the Cypriot, Greek and Turkish visiting firemen from having their usual say). But the routine has worked so smoothly at most recent Cyprus sessions that the essential resolution has gone through before the public back-biting between members even begins.

So the fact that the Council is not visibly sitting does not always mean that it has lapsed into a deep sleep. It may mean that its members, bright eyed and bushy tailed, have been hard at work and have successfully staved off the holding of public meetings that would have proved futile or even harmful.

---

* During one recent Assembly it took me some time to get used to hearing what sounded like 'The General Assembly has decided anonymously to ...' being announced by a president who shall, of course, be nameless.

10

The Council has a polite custom that, at its first formal meeting in any calendar month, its new president compliments his predecessor on his work (whether the man had earned compliments or not). At its first meeting in June 1969 the new president had two predecessors to say something nice about, for there had been no May meetings. Responding, the April president threw in an extra word of thanks to the May one for 'a leadership that was so effective and excellent that the Council managed to dispense with the need for any meeting whatever'. This was not entirely fluff; he spoke with some feeling, having himself been obliged to preside in April over a bitter meeting at which the Council had adopted one of its less helpful resolutions. But unfortunately it cannot be taken for granted that the councilmen are always doing good work when they are invisible. As another chapter of this book shows, their inability to get together for useful consultations in the early months of 1967 may be seen as one of the factors that contributed to the new outbreak of war between Israel and its Arab neighbours; and between July and October of that year they signally failed to respond to an urgent call on their attention made by the Assembly – a call which nearly all the Council's members, in their capacity as Assembly members, had backed with their votes.

One of Franklin D. Roosevelt's dreamier early ideas about the new world organisation that he did much to shape, but did not live to see, was that the Security Council might best be sited on some fairly remote island (while the Assembly roamed the world like a nomadic horde). Variations on this theme are recurrent: it has been suggested that the Council should sit in Jerusalem, in Berlin or some other area of tension where, believe it or not, it is supposed that its presence would act as a tranquilliser; or that it should be marooned somewhere obscure and uncomfortable, and left there to concentrate its mind wonderfully, well away from the fleshpots of Manhattan. Those fleshpots are almost the least of the reasons why New York is not the ideal location for the whole UN as well as the Council. But there is no ideal location. And whatever New York's drawbacks, it is a stimulating city. If the Council were to be dumped in Bermuda, Tahiti or the Galapagos islands one could well believe that its lapses into seeming inertia reflected a real lotus-land inertia among the

11

members. In its New York setting, it is less easy for people to get the idea that they have simply given up trying.

Only at one period in its twenty-five-year history has the Security Council appeared to grind to a complete halt: that was in the first half of 1950. On January 13 of that year Yakov Malik, then as now the chief Soviet representative at the UN, not only walked out of the Council but declared, on leaving, that Russia could not recognise any Council decisions as being legal until 'the representative of the Kuomintang group had been removed'. Just in case people thought they were not serious, the Russians withdrew in the course of the next few weeks from no less than twenty-one other UN committees and bodies. Many of those other bodies were in fact able to tick over quite comfortably despite the Russians' absence; but this hardly seemed possible for the Council.

Twenty years later, China's Council seat is still occupied by a representative of the Kuomintang government that had fled to Taipeh in Formosa (Taiwan) in 1949; and Malik, like all the Soviet representatives who appeared at the UN in between his two terms there, has not contested the legality of the many decisions the Council has taken over the years with the participation of Taipeh China. But back in the early months of 1950 no one could have foreseen the outcome of the crisis that Malik had sparked off. It had been widely expected that the UN would shortly accept the new Peking government as representing China. Five out of the ten other Council members (Russia, Britain, India, Norway and Jugoslavia) had already recognised the communist government proclaimed in 1949. Before the walkout the United States announced that it would not seek to block UN acceptance of the Peking men if any seven Council members voted for it. France, Egypt and Ecuador were all seen as potential reinforcements for the existing five favourable members, given a few months' calm.

But – as Trygve Lie told the Russians without mincing words – they were, by boycotting the Council and refusing to recognise the validity of any decisions it took in their absence, not only making it more difficult for Peking to win its seat; they were also violating Article 28 of the Charter, which, as we have seen, requires that

12

Council members should always be represented at UN headquarters and should thus enable the Council to 'function continuously'. Perhaps it was in order to make this violation less conspicuous, rather than in hope that his condition for a return to the Council might be met at any moment, that Malik stayed in New York long after Soviet participation in all UN activity there had ceased.

All this was overlaid by the outbreak of the Korean war in June. The Council, ignoring Russia's absence, rose to the challenge. Then, five weeks after the war began – and while the North Korean invaders still seemed likely to overrun the whole of the south – Malik blandly reappeared in the Council, claiming as his due its presidency for the month of August, and making as much use as he could of that office to foul up the workings of the UN in regard to the war. Russia has stayed in the Council ever since. No comparable threat of total breakdown has appeared since 1950; not even in the 1962 Cuba crisis, when the two nuclear super-powers seemed for a moment so perilously close to the brink. The Council then took itself out of the picture rather abruptly; but its existence was in no more apparent jeopardy than that of everybody else.

For the Council, however, the rare danger of a complete breakdown is less preoccupying than the recurrent problems that arise whenever it enters a period of what may be called bloody-mindedness: when relations between its members, and particularly between the great-power members, are particularly tense. At such times the Council may still be able to meet, but its meetings are liable to prove so envenomed and sterile that its more prudent members will try to hold down the time spent in debate to the minimum. And these tensions may not necessarily arise from matters with which the Council itself is dealing.

In 1961, a year throughout which the Council-authorised UN operation in the Congo remained in a painfully bright spotlight, the Council itself tackled the Congo problem only twice, in February and in November. From February onward the Russians' objections to the handling of the operation by Dag Hammarskjöld brought them to the point of imposing a total boycott on the Secretary-General. The November Council session followed Hammarskjöld's death and the failure of the first UN attempts to resolve the Katanga problem.

After November 1961 the Council faded completely out of the picture while, for more than a year, the new Secretary-General was left to wrestle with the Katanga problem without any further support or guidance from Council or Assembly – which did not, however, prevent him from disposing of it in January 1963.

For the UN as a whole, the later months of 1964 and the earlier ones of 1965 were darkened by the struggle that arose from the refusal of Russia, France and several other members to pay their assessed shares of the cost of UN peace-keeping operations. Under Article 19 of the Charter the defaulters' right to vote in the Assembly was challenged by America, Britain and many other member states, and the nineteenth annual Assembly session became almost paralysed. No debate leading up to a vote could be held during that session; such decisions as were taken were based on unanimity or informal 'consensus'. This period of deadlock in the Assembly did not wholly disrupt the work of the Security Council, which contrived to meet and carry on some essential business, such as extending the life of the force in Cyprus, while the Article 19 storm raged all about it. But the mood of the moment was an ugly one; and it was a fortunate non-coincidence that the Council's basic decision on the Cyprus operation had been taken earlier in 1964, and that it did not have to face the outbreak of war between India and Pakistan until September 1965, when the Article 19 dispute was already being composed.

Even the Council's most uncontroversial routines were affected to some extent. For instance, it met on 9 October 1964 to recommend to the Assembly the admission to the UN of Malawi, which had just become an independent state. There was no dispute or even doubt about this recommendation, which duly and swiftly went through. But the Soviet member of the Council, Nikolai Fedorenko, was unable to refrain from announcing, in the middle of the purely formal proceedings about Malawi, that 'the Soviet Union is not prepared to pay one single kopek, one single cent, for the illegal operations of the United Nations in the Middle East and the Congo'.

I have deliberately dwelt on the Council's long periods of inactivity, the soporific quality of many of its formal proceedings, and the

14

difficulty often experienced in getting any quick results from it even in emergency situations, because there still seems to be a recurring notion that it is an 'executive' body – a compact, united group that can swiftly take hold of a crisis and then maintain control of a fast changing situation. It is important to disabuse oneself of the idea that this can be done, as a matter of regular routine, by a group of representatives of national governments whose attitudes to any given dispute or conflict are likely to vary widely. The nearest thing to a real 'executive' that the UN has acquired is the Secretary-General's office; and there are visibly many limitations to that office's authority and scope. However, as I have tried to show in an earlier book,* it has become the UN's 'unforeseen executive'. The great powers who founded the UN did not intend anything of the kind to happen, and they are still reluctant to see any more of it happen. But they have been unable to make a reality of their own original vision of the Security Council as an instrument for joint great-power direction of world affairs.

On the other hand, I do not want to suggest that a Council seat is a sinecure. The councilmen do not constitute an ever-busied 'cabinet of the world' – for weeks on end, they may not even see their horseshoe table; when they do get to it the tempo of their speechmaking may seem leisurely to the point of sluggishness – but all this does not mean that they can afford to be idle. Public debate in the Council, when it occurs, is only the visible tip of an iceberg of unseen activity – and sometimes even the top tenth of this iceberg sinks out of sight.

The work is mainly of a discouraging kind. Not often can the Council end a session with any sense of solid achievement. Still less often can a councilman feel that he has really made his own government's view prevail. He is more usually forced to concentrate on a 'no-lose' objective. His situation resembles that of Admiral Jellicoe during the First World War, when it was said of the Grand Fleet's commander that he could not win the war, but he could lose it: the destruction of the German fleet in the 1916 Battle of Jutland would not have decided the outcome of the war, but the destruction of the British fleet might well have done so. The councilman can turn no magic key that will win him a great diplomatic victory; but he can,

_____

* *United Nations: Piety, Myth and Truth*, London, 1962, revised edition 1964.

15

by one incautious word or move, seriously damage his country's position and perhaps the prospects for peace too. Which is one reason why he is apt to churn out innocuous platitudes.

And there are times when he will need great stamina if he is to keep a cool head and steady touch during long-drawn-out Council sessions held in a context of general alarm. While many a Council debate merely meanders through swamps of repetitious oratory, there are moments of spasm when the members find themselves sitting late into the night, having to vote in the small hours of the morning, or dispersing thankfully at midnight, only to be called back to their table before dawn. In recent years such moments occurred, for example, during the 1965 war between India and Pakistan, during the 1967 Israel–Arab war and after the Russian invasion of Czechoslovakia in 1968 (pages 142, 213 and 309). These are the times when a weary councilman fully earns his pay, for he must not merely keep going but must also remain fully alert – both to seize fleeting opportunities to make the moves he himself has in mind, and to fend off other members' attempts to lead the Council the way they want it to go while it is having difficulty in keeping its eyes open.

Chapter Two

People or puppets?

Are the occupants of the seats around the horseshoe table to be regarded as real people, or as mere puppets? The answer must be: a bit of both, the puppet factor being variable but almost always strong. The councilman may or may not be a personality in his own right; but he is unquestionably his government's official mouthpiece. If he was not, he would not be there. You cannot strike out on a line that your government disapproves and continue to fill its seat in the Security Council, or anywhere else in the United Nations.

Some representatives enjoy relations with their governments that leave them an unusual amount of elbow room for manoeuvre and negotiation, and may even enable them to influence their country's policy instead of merely executing it. But even these must work within certain defined limits. All the councilmen twitch at the end of strings that are pulled in the capitals whose official views they must voice. Nor are these necessarily their only strings. They may also feel sharp pulls from other directions: from great powers, from their own countries' immediate neighbours, from regional caucus groupings. In this respect the UN is not essentially different from any other diplomatic meeting place: just more complicated.

It may sound as if all a councilman has to do, when approaching a debate, is to report to his government how the land lies (what pressures are being brought to bear by other members; what kind of resolution, if any, is likely to be adopted; how the various alternative outcomes may affect relationships at the UN), and then wait to receive from his foreign ministry the text of the speech it wants him to make and instructions about how to vote. It is seldom so simple. The situation the Council is discussing may be rapidly changing. At a late hour unexpected amendments or new draft resolutions may be

17

proposed. Alignments may suddenly start to shift, but not so conspicuously that the councilman can be sure that his foreign ministry will accept his diagnosis of what is happening.

So the 'puppet', while faithfully following the prescribed policy, may have to make many personal decisions about tactics. And this is not just a matter of deft timing and ingenious choice of words. His primary need is to retain the confidence of his own government. But, second only to that, it is also his business to cultivate the best possible working relationships with his Council colleagues. Not that even the warmest personal friendship is likely to swing any of the councilmen right over from one policy to another. In a complex setting like the UN, however, it is very important to know as much as possible of what is going on in other people's minds, to vibrate to their unspoken feelings, to detect shifts in their positions at the earliest possible moment.

As a rule, it is therefore important to show oneself to be approachable, patient and understanding. Even when relations between two governments are going through a bad phase, it is one of the great advantages of the community life of the Turtle Bay kibbutz that the members of the two missions will constantly be brought together by force of circumstances; even if it has been ordained that they must not so much as exchange greetings, there will still be willing go-betweens to convey discreet messages from one side to the other. And when better relations prevail, it is a vital part of all UN representatives' duty to keep fully informed of one another's thoughts and intentions – which may not be at all accurately reflected in the formal statements that have been made 'on the record'. Tactical decisions need to be firmly based on this kind of information, which can be garnered only by continuous informal exchanges.

These points have a direct bearing on a member state's choice of a councilman. It is nice to have a man who comes over well on television; a man with enough charismatic quality to improve the chances that his speeches will be attentively heard and widely reported; a man of substantial reputation outside the UN. But it is primarily necessary to have a man who can be trusted not to embarrass his government by making a fool of himself. And it is highly desirable to have a man experienced in the ways of diplomatic consultation and negotiation. If your councilman lacks this skill, other members of your mission at the UN will have to do the most important part of his job for him, which is an unsatisfactory state of affairs.

It is not surprising, then, that most councilmen have been professional diplomats. The most conspicuous exceptions to that rule have been the representatives of the United States, most of whom, until very recently, have been prominent figures drawn from the world of politics. But for these exceptions there have been various exceptional reasons.

American custom still dictates that very few high diplomatic posts are held by diplomats. In part, this is an extension of a traditional distrust of all permanent bureaucracy. Americans never quite went as far as electing their ambassadors; but they long took it for granted that, under the 'spoils system', a party's electoral victory entitled it to put new men of its own choice into a large number of official posts, including ambassadorships, which even in recent years have sometimes been openly bestowed as rewards on men who have made large contributions to party campaign funds.

When the first UN representatives were appointed in 1946 the British felt they were showing that they took these appointments seriously when they named Sir Alexander Cadogan. He had led their team at Dumbarton Oaks in 1944, when the great powers shaped the UN Charter; he had also, as Permanent Under-Secretary, been the Foreign Office's official head. But Americans would have thought it derogatory to the United Nations to make an appointment from the ranks of their career diplomats, who were still low men on the American totem pole.

Particularly at that formative stage, it was also felt to be very important to retain bipartisan support in Congress for the whole UN enterprise. The Senate had consented to ratification of the Charter in July 1945, and there was thus no risk of the kind of catastrophe that Woodrow Wilson had encountered when he failed to bring the United States into the League of Nations. But the memory of Wilson's failure still lingered. The Democratic Administration had taken great care to associate leading Republican senators with the

19

preparatory work for the new world organisation. And the problem was not only one of bipartisanship. Congress as a whole, and the Senate in particular, had learnt to keep a sharp-eyed watch for opportunities of asserting its right to share control of foreign policy with the Administration; and this looked like being such an opportunity. Moreover, beyond all these tactical considerations, there was in the American air a certain amount of rather illusory thinking about the ideal status of the councilmen, which was linked to the prevalent notion that the Security Council was going to be a very powerful instrument through which the great powers would jointly direct the course of world events.

In a book published in 1946 Sumner Welles, the former Under-Secretary of State, wrote:

> It was clearly the obligation of every one of the governments ... to choose the ablest men available. ... The contrast between the hopes and anticipations, and the reality, was shocking. ... With but a few exceptions, the members of the Security Council failed lamentably to meet those standards.*

This judgment may have been rather strongly coloured by the fact that the United States' first UN representative was Edward Stettinius, who had just served a brief term as Secretary of State, during which his diplomatic inexperience had become as apparent as his lack of any really strong influence in Washington itself. (Although Stettinius had headed the American team at the great-power talks at Dumbarton Oaks, he had left no noticeable mark on the draft UN Charter that was prepared there; he had been working under Cordell Hull's direction, and with Leo Pasvolsky and other professionals to hold his hand.)

After only a few months Stettinius was replaced at the UN by Senator Warren Austin, who carried heavier guns. As a prominent Republican serving a Democratic Administration, Warren Austin was able to bring President Harry Truman – whom he served until 1952 – an impressive amount of bipartisan support in Congress. As a former influential member of the Senate Foreign Relations Committee, he could often get a respectful hearing for his own views

* *Where Are We Heading?*, New York, 1946.

A Council session as seen from the public seats

Fifteen hands raised in a unanimous vote

From left: Yost, Bérard, Solano-Lopez and Caradon (pages 23, 30, 33, 40)

Urgent huddle over a new draft for a resolution. The group includes American, French and Russian representatives

from Truman and from his successive Secretaries of State, James Byrnes, George Marshall and Dean Acheson.

Even so, Warren Austin remained an executor, not a shaper, of American policy in the UN. Senator Henry Cabot Lodge, who succeeded him in 1953, did not have the same bipartisan support in Congress, but enjoyed a somewhat higher standing within the Administration. Lodge attended the meetings of President Eisenhower's Republican cabinet as a 'minister without portfolio', and the Secretary of State, John Foster Dulles, allowed him a wider scope than Austin had been permitted. Lodge's immediate successor, when he resigned in 1960 to be Richard Nixon's running mate in the Republican candidate's unsuccessful campaign for the presidency, was his long-time deputy, James Wadsworth, who was widely respected and liked at the UN but had no great aspirations about influencing American policy. Then the idea of an American councilman with great personal influence was revived by President Kennedy's appointment of the former Democratic contender for the presidency, Governor Adlai Stevenson.

Long before Stevenson's death in harness in 1965 it had become apparent that even a personality of his standing could not make any substantial impact on his country's UN policies from the post he held at the UN itself. His many admirers sought in vain to produce any evidence that his views had prevailed over Washington's in regard to issues of real importance. Adlai Stevenson was able to add a touch of his celebrated style and wit to the proceedings in New York, and his high international reputation was of obvious value to the United States in many of the matters that came up in the Council or elsewhere at the UN. But even he could not make much more of the job than that.

His successor, Arthur Goldberg, although coming to the UN without Stevenson's background in international affairs (or his oratorical talents), brought remarkable qualities of his own. President Johnson's powerful persuasiveness had induced Goldberg to take the post at the cost of relinquishing, after only three years, the seat on the Supreme Court bench to which Kennedy had appointed him in 1962 in succession to Felix Frankfurter. For Johnson it made political sense to find a new permanent representative in a man who

21

commanded much of the same liberal Democratic backing that Adlai Stevenson had enjoyed. As Kennedy's Secretary of Labour before he became a Supreme Court Justice, Goldberg had proved a vigorous champion of minority rights. And if he lacked broad international experience he showed every intention, at the age of 56, of remedying this as fast as he could – with the aim, it was widely assumed, of following Dean Rusk as Secretary of State. Whereas Stevenson had taken the post after being disappointed in his hopes of both the presidency and the State Department, Goldberg was thus a man with ambitions and a fair hope of fulfilling them. His long experience of shrewd bargaining as a labour lawyer (in the 1950s he had been a brilliantly successful advocate for the American trade union federation) was quickly, and often very effectively, applied to the negotiating tasks he faced at the UN. And he proved to be better placed than Stevenson for obtaining White House and State Department approval of the tactical initiatives he wanted to take in New York. But 'tactical' was still the key word. The policies that 'USUN' – the American mission at the United Nations – had to try to put through in the 'big glass house', which faced the mission's offices across First Avenue, were still policies shaped in Washington, not by Arthur Goldberg. In 1968 he resigned, saying that he hoped to be able to work for a speedy ending of the Vietnam war from a position outside the Administration.

To be the permanent representative of a permanent Council member does not, at the UN, imply any permanency. This was most signally demonstrated in the months between June 1968 and January 1969, which saw four men, in swift succession, serving as 'permanent representative' of the United States: Arthur Goldberg, George Ball, James Russell Wiggins and Charles Yost. Ball held the post for only three months, Wiggins for three and a half. This brisk turnover was a reflection of the harried state of President Johnson's Administration in its final year. And one noteworthy link between three of the four successive councilmen in that year was that they all played a part in Hubert Humphrey's unsuccessful campaign for the presidency – Goldberg and Ball after ending their terms at the UN, Yost before beginning his.

22

Wiggins had responded to Johnson's appeal that he should stop editing the *Washington Post* in time to fill out the last months of 1968 in the UN post; he did so without any expectation of retaining it beyond the new year, whatever the result of the presidential election. With Ball and Yost, however, a new phenomenon became apparent, for these were the first State Department men to become permanent representatives. Both had retired from government service in 1966; but their successive recalls, and particularly Yost's, showed an American trend towards alignment with the other powers' policy on the choice of councilmen.

George Wildman Ball, a still muscular six-foot-two figure when he did his brief stint at the UN at the age of 58, was no career diplomat but one of those remarkable men, without whom the American governmental mechanism would be sadly incomplete, who reach high office without either working their way up a departmental ladder or going through the mills of political elections. An able lawyer from Des Moines, a New Deal veteran from the 1930s, he came to the State Department as one of the Kennedy men in 1961 and served there as Under-Secretary for nearly six years. During those years his forceful personality left its mark not only in Foggy Bottom but also in the various places he visited on trouble-shooting missions – including Cyprus. Decidedly a Europe-firster, he made no secret of his dislike of America's involvement both in southeast Asia and in the multifarious African and Asian preoccupations of the UN. (There was an extraordinary aptness about the fact that the debate on Russia's invasion of Czechoslovakia – see page 303 – was the outstanding feature of Ball's three-month tenure of a Security Council seat.) And there was little doubt in most minds that he, like Goldberg, accepted the New York post with the idea that it might be a stepping stone towards the goal of becoming Secretary of State.

In sharp contrast, Charles Yost had a background of nearly thirty-five years as a career diplomat, and had spent a good part of that time in the UN orbit. As far back as 1944 he had been at Dumbarton Oaks; as lately as 1966 he had been deputy permanent representative in New York. Showing no sign of political ambitions, he had retired from the service at the age of 60 and, while largely occupied in academic work in 1968, had entered a published debate about the American UN mission with this comment:

> I should strongly urge that there be, at this time at least, no change in the arrangement which has existed for so many years whereby the United States representative to the United Nations is a member of the President's Cabinet and an outstanding domestic political figure.*

Ironically, a few weeks later President-elect Nixon named Yost as the new permanent representative. Nixon announced that Yost would attend meetings of the National Security Council and such Cabinet meetings as were concerned with foreign policy. And Nixon also took pains to reveal that he had previously offered the job to his defeated rival, Hubert Humphrey; to Humphrey's defeated rival among the Democrats, Senator Eugene McCarthy; to Nixon's own defeated rival among the Republicans, Governor Nelson Rockefeller of New York; and to Sargent Shriver (a member of the Kennedy clan), who was then ambassador in Paris.

It was remarked at the time that, if Nixon really agreed with Yost that the job should go to 'an outstanding domestic political figure', he might have stretched his list of invitees a bit further and tried somebody other than the men who were least likely to accept any kind of appointment from him. In practice, it appeared that, after going through the motions of seeking a politician, Nixon had done what he really meant to do all the time: appoint a professional diplomat. He did not go quite so far as simply to assign a serving official from the State Department to the New York post, or to promote the current deputy in the UN mission to be its chief; but he got remarkably close to that, for Yost had been serving as the mission's second in command only two years earlier.

There were those who, without questioning Charles Yost's undoubted abilities (or the value of preserving continuity at a change of Administration by sending back to the UN a man who knew its ropes and was himself well known and respected there), saw the Yost appointment as a deliberate downgrading of the UN in Washington's order of foreign policy priorities. No doubt Nixon himself thought that the move would mollify many Republicans who felt that successive Democratic presidents had let the UN loom far too large in their

* *Vista* (the journal of the UN Association of the United States), November 1968.

scale of values. But I am not at all sure that, in itself, the break with the American tradition of political appointments amounted to a downgrading. It needs to be considered in the wider context of changing circumstances, which I will try to set out later in this book.

*   *   *

In contrast to the American tradition of political appointments, it has been France's custom – and until 1964 it was also Britain's – to send a senior diplomat to head the mission in New York. It has sometimes been complained that this in itself implies a certain lack of interest in the United Nations. Undoubtedly, when Harold Wilson formed his Labour government in 1964 and sent Caradon to be permanent representative with the rank of Minister of State (which, in the Foreign Office hierarchy, is intermediate between the Secretary of State and the junior ministers, who are Parliamentary Under-Secretaries), his immediate intention was to make a gesture, to up-grade Britain's visible concern with the UN.

The British system requires every minister to be a member of Parliament, and thereby subject to parliamentary questioning in one House or the other. A minister who does not hold a seat in the House of Commons must therefore be ennobled. So Sir Hugh Foot became Lord Caradon, and his familiar face reappeared in New York with his new label. Inevitably there was some gentle chuckling.

Ever since 1946 Britain had been represented at the UN by a series of knights – Sir Alexander Cadogan, Sir Gladwyn Jebb, Sir Pierson Dixon, Sir Patrick Dean. Not that the post was reserved for the aristocracy (as it would surely have been forty years earlier); this chivalrous succession consisted of hard working career diplomats whose professional abilities had enabled each of them to 'get his K' – and Cadogan and Jebb had both won their spurs in UN work before they became Britain's permanent representatives. But there were those in New York whose vision of a socially stratified Britain led them to suppose that Wilson's gesture of esteem for the UN actually consisted of sending it a baron instead of the usual knight. It seemed to follow that successive British governments, if they wished to go on raising the bidding, would endow the Security Council with, in due

25

order, a viscount, an earl, a marquess, a duke and, eventually, a prince of the blood royal.

The order of knighthood, however, did not vanish from the British UN mission offices on Third Avenue, where Caradon was still buttressed about by such trusty knights as Sir Roger Jackling, Sir Edward Warner, Sir Leslie Glass and Sir Keith Unwin. And in 1970, when the new Conservative government reverted to the practice of choosing a career diplomat as its councilman, it sent Sir Colin Crowe to the UN.

There is room for doubt whether the fairly vigorous British role in the Council drama in recent years had much to do with the appointment of a Minister of State to the New York post. One of the other relevant factors was the (far from welcome) prominence thrust upon Britain by circumstances such as the Council's recurrent preoccupation with Cyprus and Rhodesia: since 1965 the Rhodesian problem has led two British Foreign Secretaries to make personal appearances in the Council. A second factor was the Labour government's explicit wish to play a more constructive part in UN affairs than its Conservative predecessor, which Wilson and his ministers regarded as having retreated into a strictly defensive position. A third was Caradon's own vigorous and extrovert personality.

It would appear to be true that his standing, as a minister by political appointment, enabled him to manoeuvre a little more freely at the UN than his official predecessors, and to put a little more weight behind his moves; but it is difficult to calculate the exact margin of difference that the ministerial appointment, in itself, made. A first-class official representative might, for instance, have been able to equal Caradon's undoubtedly impressive feat in getting a unanimous Council vote for the famous November 1967 resolution on the Israel–Arab conflict. Such an official might not, on the other hand, have been able to draw on the reserve of personal respect among the African representatives that helped Caradon through several tight spots during the series of Council meetings on Rhodesia. Caradon's public performance contrasted sharply with that of most of his predecessors; but, significantly, not of all. Telegenic and voluble, he 'came over' – whether speaking in Council, giving filmed interviews or lecturing to a wide variety of audiences –

26

in a way that would have been impossible for Cadogan, Dixon or Dean. However, it must not be forgotten that Gladwyn Jebb, whose arrival in New York as a councilman coincided with the communist invasion of South Korea in June 1950, then became almost overnight an astonishingly successful television star. Although Senator Warren Austin made a bold play for the attention of the American viewing audience by suddenly producing, from under the horseshoe table, a Russian-made machine-gun which had been taken from the North Korean invaders, Jebb's urbane manner and commanding presence won him a vast number of fans during his series of debating duels with Yakov Malik of Russia in the Council chamber.

Jebb's effortless mastery of UN procedure and practice, which helped to make his public performances so impressive, reflected the fact that he had been executive secretary of the preparatory commission for the United Nations in 1945–6, had handled the servicing of the first Assembly and Council meetings in London, and had thereafter run the Foreign Office department concerned with UN affairs. But what won him particular attention during his four years as councilman was the zest with which he threw himself into the new role of a performer in front of a mass audience – a role previously thought to be quite alien to any British career diplomat. If each of the four knights who filled Britain's Council seat between 1946 and 1964 had ridden into the lists with sharpened lance and streaming banners as Gladwyn Jebb did, and if these professionals had then been followed by a Minister of State of less colourful vigour than Caradon, the change might well have given the impression that Britain was backing away from the Council table rather than seeking to loom larger at it.

Extrovert personalities have not been favoured in France's selection of diplomats as councilmen. The first of these, Alexandre Parodi, came to New York after playing a distinguished part in the wartime Resistance; he left it to become the Quai d'Orsay's official head, thus reversing Alexander Cadogan's sequence. The taciturn Parodi never failed to keep his emotions well under control, though his position was often a painful one. France had not even shared with China the privilege of limited participation in the Dumbarton Oaks talks; it had

27

played a secondary role at San Francisco; now here it was, by the grace of the other powers, a privileged permanent member of the Security Council, but still with very little sinew to back this status – yet with vivid memories of the leading role France had played at Geneva in the days of the League.

Things went rather better for Parodi's successors, Jean Chauvel and Henri Hoppenot, at least in the Council, which consistently refused to discuss complaints brought against French actions in Tunisia, Morocco and Algeria in the early 1950s; and where, in 1953, Hoppenot had the gratifying opportunity of breaking the deadlock over the appointment of a new Secretary-General by proposing the name of Dag Hammarskjöld. But there followed the traumatic experience of the 1956 Suez conflict, which envenomed France's relations with the UN even more than Britain's. The last days of October 1956 were particularly painful for the French representative, Bernard Cornut-Gentille, who found himself virtually ostracised by all the other members (except Pierson Dixon) of a Council over which he had to preside that month. On the 30th he and Dixon vetoed first an American and then a Russian draft resolution, each of which would have called for a cease-fire and an Israeli withdrawal and would have asked all UN members to refrain from threatening or using force in the area. Next day they failed to prevent the Council summoning an emergency Assembly session. Cornut-Gentille then collapsed, from heart trouble brought on by nervous exhaustion. Such was the tension of the moment that it was even thought necessary to hush up the gravity of his condition.*

Less than two years later General de Gaulle was back in power in Paris and, while working away bravely to liberate France from Algeria, was skilfully exploiting for nationalistic ends the anti-UN feeling that had been caused in France by the organisation's attempts to end the Algerian war. At the start of the 1960s the odd position developed that the UN, while being denounced by British Tories because it was controlled by the Afro-Asians, was denounced by de Gaulle because it was controlled by the Anglo-Saxons.

* Only once, to my knowledge, has a representative actually died while addressing the Council. This was an Egyptian, Mahmoud Azmi, who suffered a heart attack while inveighing against Israel.

To the French president, the United Nations was an American-run *machin* (thingummyjig). His campaign against it, like his later campaign against Canada, was primarily a part of his struggle to destroy America's 'hegemony'. He knew little about the UN, and did not want to know any more. To the smaller member states he offered sometimes a contemptuous patronage, sometimes just contempt. It was much remarked that when no less than fourteen ex-French African states joined the UN in 1960, France failed to take advantage of this sudden accretion of influence. De Gaulle could not forgive Hammarskjöld for his attempt to stop the 1961 fighting between France and Tunisia over Bizerta. So he denounced Hammarskjöld for having tried to end the Katanga secession in the Congo; yet the man who actually ended it, Thant, won de Gaulle's praise – because of his attitude to America's actions in Vietnam.

De Gaulle insisted (like the Russians) that UN peace-keeping operations must be authorised only by the Security Council, never by the Assembly. But he paid France's share of the cost of the Assembly-authorised UN force in Egypt (Unef), while refusing to help pay for the Council-authorised Congo operation. His peculiar logic, which was Gaullist rather than Gallic, brought France into such ludicrous postures as the coupling of its refusal to sign the 1968 nuclear non-proliferation treaty with its solemn announcements, made in both Assembly and Council, that it would behave exactly as if it had signed. France, in fact, welcomed the treaty; but America had promoted it, so France had to reject it.

Under de Gaulle, France equipped itself with an airborne *force d'intervention*, and repeatedly used it, not only in places like Djibuti but even in sovereign states like Gabon and Chad. Yet de Gaulle proclaimed himself the apostle of the purest non-intervention. The UN Assembly, he insisted, must renounce all rights of intervention, in favour of the Security Council, as a matter of principle. The Council must abstain from intervention as a matter of practice. One might have thought that this 'logic' would lead France to use its veto whenever the Council contemplated a move that France opposed because it meant intervention. Strangely, France never did.

The French councilman's basic instructions during these years seemed to run something like this: Do not take initiatives. If somebody else does, say that the action contemplated is illegal or at least improper. But do not vote against it. As a rule, abstain. If abstention would make you look particularly silly you may occasionally vote for a resolution; but even then, state reservations; and if possible get a separate vote on the operative paragraph, and abstain on that.

Roger Seydoux was the councilman who had to maintain this aloof performance in the mid-1960s. A hereditary diplomat – his father, grandfather and great-grandfather had all served the Quai d'Orsay before him – and an old UN hand who had been at San Francisco in 1945, Seydoux was well equipped to keep his distances with punctilious style. Like one of W. S. Gilbert's peers, he 'did nothing in particular, and did it very well'.

France abstained in the Council votes on the Congo in 1960–1 and 1964; on Palestine in 1962; on the South African arms embargo in 1963–4; on Rhodesia each year until 1967; on non-proliferation in 1968. In the case of Cyprus it used the abstain-on-the-operative-paragraph gambit. It opposed Council discussion of Vietnam in 1966. Alone among the major powers, it declined to take a position in the Israel–Arab conflict of 1967, on the crucial question whether the Arabs had the right to blockade the Gulf of Aqaba. At the time of the Indo-Pakistani war of 1965 Seydoux was able to go along with the unanimous calls for a cease-fire, but felt obliged to state a cautious (and remarkably abstract) position of principle in regard to Thant's deployment of observers, without which the cease-fire could not have been made effective.

All this stately aloofness began to crumble in 1968, when Seydoux had been succeeded by Armand Bérard (another old UN hand). For the first time, Bérard cast a French vote in support of a resolution on Rhodesia sanctions. He repeated some of the legalistic arguments that Seydoux had used to justify previous French abstentions, but he conceded that France must now acknowledge the strength of African feeling. This shifting of ground immediately followed the outburst of protest in France in May 1968 that had cracked the self-confidence of the Gaullist regime.

It was Andrei Vishinsky who personified Russia at the UN during the organisation's first decade – until his sudden death in 1955, in

30

New York. His was not, of course, the only Soviet face the UN saw during those years. Yakov Malik was the permanent representative from 1948 to 1953, the last five years of Stalin's life, during most of which time Vishinsky was serving as foreign minister; Andrei Gromyko was in at the start, and had the distinction of staging the first walkout from the Council; Semyon Tsarapkin, who had been with Gromyko at Dumbarton Oaks, later took a particular hand in disarmament questions; Dimitri Manuilsky of the Ukraine was another who made his mark. But Vishinsky was the symbolic figure, and something more, in the Stalin years.

He used Russia's first veto in the Council, on 16 February 1946, and used it in a way that was even more disturbing than the mere resort to this weapon within a month of the Council's birth. Syria and Lebanon had asked the Council to prod Britain and France into removing their troops from the two countries. Seven Council members backed a draft resolution in this sense; Britain and France took it well, and complied – but Vishinsky blocked the resolution, simply because its language was not strong enough to suit Moscow. Instantly it became clear that there was not going to be any nonsense about Russia wielding its veto only in cases where its vital national interests were threatened.

Vishinsky was to cast other vetoes, including the one in October 1948 that blocked the move by the Council's six 'neutral' members to break the great-power deadlock over Berlin and end Russia's blockade of the city's western sectors. But this tense little man gave the impression that, while he enjoyed being obstructive well enough, what he particularly relished was a virulent onslaught. Some of his polemical feats in New York gave his audience the chilling reminder that he had served Stalin as chief prosecutor in the rigged show trials of the great pre-war purges. At that time he had endowed the Soviet legal system with the convenient principle that a 'confession', however obtained, was the only evidence needed to prove guilt. He often seemed to be wishing he could enforce this principle at Turtle Bay. He was not entirely humourless. James Wadsworth (a large man) has recorded how one evening, in a tight-packed lift, he heard a strangled cry: *'Au secours! Je suis accablé par un éléphant!'*, and looked round, and down, to find 'little Vishinsky' crushed into the

31

corner behind him, 'grinning wickedly'. But the image most familiar to the UN was that of a Vishinsky seated grim-faced in his place, or speeding through the lobbies at the head of an equally grim-faced flying wedge of aides. A year after Stalin's death, Vishinsky for the first time accepted a drink in the delegates' lounge. A year later, at the age of 72, he was dead.

The Russians have clung tightly to the privilege, which they won in a private deal made between the great powers in London in 1945, of providing the head of the Secretariat's department for Security Council affairs. The other powers have contended that this was never meant to be more than a temporary initial arrangement; Trygve Lie certainly regarded it as applying only to the UN's first five years. But nobody has mounted a frontal attack on it, for it has long been apparent that it is simpler to by-pass the Soviet occupants of the post than to dislodge them.

In 1950 Lie had no choice but to form a 'Korea club' of Secretariat officials who handled the UN's end of the Korean operations without reference to Constantin Zinchenko, who was then assistant secretary-general for Security Council affairs. When Hammarskjöld took over he appointed under-secretaries for special political affairs and used them to handle peace-keeping operations and other delicate matters, leaving the Security Council department with little more than routine procedural and servicing activities. He tried the experiment, for a while, of assigning his senior Russian assistant, Ilya Chernyshev, to special political work. The predictable failure of this experiment seemed to convince even the Russians that a Soviet official could not be used in such work; and since then a succession of Russians have headed the Security Council department and have, in effect, condoned the separation from it of all Secretariat activity of a really sensitive kind.

Moscow has not allowed these Russians to remain with the Secretariat very long (they might, in time, actually develop a loyalty to the UN); their stays in New York have averaged less than three years. Their quality has proved variable, but only one, Georgy Arkadyev, has openly indulged in improper conduct. One night in 1960 he left the UN building to attend a party at the Soviet mission without informing Hammarskjöld that an urgent Council meeting for the next day had been initiated by Valerian Zorin, who was then Russia's councilman. One day in January 1962, during a Council meeting, Arkadyev was seen to be passing a series of notes to Zorin, clearly giving him advice about how to raise obstructive points of order. Soon after that, Arkadyev was back in Moscow.

At one early stage it looked as if the Russians meant to use the Secretariat post as a training ground for their councilmen. Arkady Sobolev had been the first Soviet assistant secretary-general, serving in that capacity until 1949. He returned to New York to spend the latter half of the 1950s there as Russia's permanent representative. He made a competent councilman, and this was doubtless the result, at least in part, of his previous UN experience. But there was some unease in New York at the prospect of a whole succession of Russians coming back to the horseshoe table as councilmen after having previously sat there as Secretariat officials.

There is no objection, in principle or in practice, to the idea of a councilman having had earlier Secretariat experience of one kind or another. There have been many such councilmen: Gladwyn Jebb might be counted as one of the first among them, while in more recent years several new member states have been well served by permanent representatives who had learnt the UN ropes during previous service with the Secretariat. It was felt, however, that so long as Russia kept a permanent lien on the Security Council department post, it would not be very congenial to other Council members to find Russians who had held that post repeatedly reappearing as councilmen. Moscow seemed to take the point, and the Sobolev experiment was not repeated. Anatoly Dobrynin, who in 1957–60 proved an unusually valuable Secretariat official, returned to America in 1962, but not to New York; instead he became ambassador in Washington, a post in which he has since performed as skilfully as he did at the UN.

*   *   *

It is rare for the Council to include such a combination of 'old hands' as appeared in the spring of 1970, when this label could be applied to

33

each of the four great-power councilmen. Yakov Malik was their unchallenged doyen, having already been Russia's permanent representative in New York more than twenty years earlier. During that first term of service, from 1948 to 1953, he had carried out the famous Soviet walkout from the Council early in 1950, and the Soviet return to the Council six months later, after the communist invasion of South Korea. When he came back to New York in March 1968 for a second term there he brought with him the rank of deputy foreign minister and a somewhat mellowed manner; this seemed to survive even the bitter exchanges in the Council that followed the Russian invasion of Czechoslovakia in the fifth month of his new term of service at the UN.

Charles Woodruff Yost, whom President Nixon had appointed to serve from January 1969, had retired from the American diplomatic service less than three years earlier. His last five years in that service had been spent in New York as deputy permanent representative, a role he filled throughout Adlai Stevenson's years at the UN and during Goldberg's first months there. But Charles Yost had had early, as well as recent, UN experience. He was on the American team at the Dumbarton Oaks and San Francisco conferences in 1944 and 1945, and at the 1946 Assembly.

Jacques Koscziusko-Morizet came back to New York in April 1970 as France's permanent representative, after spending the late 1950s and early 1960s there as the member of the French mission specialising in colonial and post-colonial questions and filling the seat on the Trusteeship Council. This background gave him some affinity with Caradon, who, having been British permanent representative for over five years, ranked in early 1970 as the senior of the four in terms of continuous recent service at the horseshoe table. For Caradon, under the appellation of Sir Hugh Foot, had previously been the colonial and trusteeship man on the British UN team in 1961–2. In his own words, in taking that earlier appointment he had been responding to a suggestion by the then prime minister, Harold Macmillan, that 'as a colonial governor who had run out of colonies, I might follow my sheep to the United Nations'. In 1962 he had resigned, feeling that he could not in all conscience defend in New York the policy that the Conservative government had adopted on

34

Rhodesia. But the Labour government that came to power in October 1964 sent him back to the UN as permanent representative, with the rank of Minister of State – and with the peerage necessitated when a minister does not happen to be a member of the House of Commons.

One episode during his 1961–2 spell at Turtle Bay must have come back to him when he received that peerage. His Russian 'opposite number' in the UN committee concerned with colonial questions, Valentin Oberemko, once referred to the then Sir Hugh Foot with withering scorn as 'Mr Foot, a subordinate colonial official'. He replied that it was fascinating to see the Soviet communists becoming snobs and putting such emphasis on rank and status; and he encouraged the Russian with the thought that, 'one day, if he sticks carefully to the party line, he will, I feel sure, become Sir Valentin Oberemko or even, perhaps, Lord Oberemko of Turtle Bay'.

He must also have recalled the circumstances of his resignation in October 1962. This followed the white-minority Rhodesian government's banning of the main African nationalist party, its detention of African leaders like Joshua Nkomo who had been in New York presenting their case only a few months earlier, and the British government's refusal to intervene. At his press conference on departure from New York, Foot had stuck carefully not to the 'party line' but to the rule that an official does not betray confidences. He had refused to be drawn into criticising Britain's Rhodesia policy or elaborating on his reasons for resigning. But his departure had inevitably caused a sensation both at the UN and in London, and it was clearly perceived at the time that he had quit because he could not argue the case for a policy of inaction that he saw as leading straight towards a disastrous conflict.

Such a gathering as that of early 1970 might lack something in youthful vivacity – with Yost and Caradon aged 62 and Malik 64 – but it could hardly be faulted on experience. However, one should not be led to visualise even this particular concentration of 'old hands' as a group of men who had known each other and continuously worked together (or worked against each other) over a period of many years. There had been only a few overlappings, and only brief ones, between their previous spells of UN service. None of them had spent, in all, more than about seven of the organisation's twenty-five years in New York. For real personal permanence there one had to look to such long enduring Secretariat men as Ralph Bunche, not to the permanent members' permanent representatives.

There is a good side to this as well as a bad one. Rapid turnovers admittedly mean that time, and opportunities, are lost while newcomers master the ropes; and that slowly nurtured personal relationships of mutual confidence are abruptly broken. But a man who is left too long in a Council seat not only gets stale and fidgety; he is also a living symbol of the policies and attitudes his government has adopted during his years in New York, and it may be eager to change some of these. Both it and he may feel a certain embarrassment if he is required to eat, publicly, words that he uttered in the Council in earlier years. A change of government, of course, is likely to bring a change of man anyway. But a change of man can also be timely when it is only the policy, not the government, that has changed.

The Russians have tended to play their own variation on this theme. Their technique vividly suggests one of those barometers that are made to look like a little house with two doors, for rain and shine, through which, according to the weather, a figure emerges appropriately dressed – with or without umbrella. The little sunny man has most often, in recent years, been Vasily Kuznetsov. One cannot invariably be sure that the appearance in New York of this Soviet deputy foreign minister means that sweetness and light are breaking out all over; nor – fortunately – that his departure presages storm and stress. But the record is, at least, suggestive. In July 1960 Kuznetsov was in New York and taking a quite reasonable attitude to the UN's initial involvement in the Congo (Russia, unlike Britain and France, actually voted in favour of the first Council resolutions on the operation). By September Kuznetsov had vanished, and a barrage of angry Soviet protests against Dag Hammarskjöld's handling of the Congo affair was being laid down by Valerian Zorin, who popped out, on this as on other occasions, in the role of the foul-weather man. (Many people at the UN have learnt to grope for their umbrellas when they see Zorin coming.)

At the table in 1954. From top: Hammarskjöld, Vishinsky, Chernyshev (Under-Secretary), Pierson Dixon and Henry Cabot Lodge (pages 21, 25, 30–2)

Fedorenko takes a back seat, left, behind Kuznetsov (pages 36 and 49); on the right, Caradon

Bernardes of Brazil, helping out on Cyprus (page 41)

Alex Quaison-Sackey of Ghana, a visiting fireman (page 42)

In October 1962, when Khrushchev sent Kennedy his nick-of-time message agreeing to remove the Soviet nuclear missiles from their launching pads in Cuba, he said in the same breath that he was sending Vasily Kuznetsov to New York to take over from Zorin — who had been stonewalling in the Council with particular stoniness. So often was this pattern repeated that by 1968 it was almost being taken for granted at the UN that a Kuznetsov advent would help to ease any crisis. It didn't work out every time, but there was some justification for the light-hearted sally that Caradon made in the Council in June 1968, a week after the Assembly had approved the nuclear non-proliferation treaty — which was the result of a notable piece of Russo-American co-operation. Welcoming Kuznetsov's further co-operation over the Council resolution that accompanied the treaty (see page 335), the British representative ended a speech by breaking into verse:

> When prospects are dark and hopes are dim
> We know that we must send for him.
> When storms and tempests fill the sky
> 'Bring on Kuznetsov!' is the cry.
> He comes like a dove from the communist ark
> And light appears where all was dark.
> His coming quickly turns the tide
> The propaganda floods subside
> And now that he has changed the weather
> Lion and lamb can vote together.
> God bless the Russian delegation.
> I waive consecutive translation.

A year later the Russians seemed to be endorsing Caradon's verdict when, 'all attempts at reconciliation proving barren' between them and the Chinese, they sent Vasily Kuznetsov to Peking to see whether he could spread a little sunshine even there.

But Kuznetsov's case may be taken to illustrate not only the existence of the personality factor but also its limitations, in the Council as in UN diplomacy more generally. Vasily Kuznetsov is not exactly a flamboyant personality: more of a well-tried workhorse. His name, a very ordinary one in Russia (the equivalent of, say, William Smith; *kuznets* is in fact the Russian word for smith), is in

37

itself emblematic. Now aged sixty-nine, he worked his way up the Soviet ladder for twenty-five years during Stalin's long reign, and became a member of the party presidium a year before the old dictator died. He was over fifty before he took up a diplomatic career. His earlier advancement had come by way of success in engineering – he was awarded a Stalin prize for work on high-quality steels – and in the Soviet 'trade union' system, which he headed during the Second World War.

Like Anastas Mikoyan, he had the useful experience of spending some time in America between the two world wars. He took a degree in engineering at Pittsburgh in the early 1930s and, in connection with his studies there, put in a spell of work at Detroit in a Ford plant. So, like Mikoyan, he became a trusted member of the party apparatus who also knew a thing or two about how to get on with Americans. He was sent to San Francisco in 1945, and to the first UN Assembly in London in 1946. Although he lost his presidium membership after Stalin's death, his new masters found him particularly useful whenever they decided to develop a practical working relationship with the Americans for some specific purpose.

As a deputy foreign minister, he was involved in work of this kind at the time of the 1954 Geneva conference on Indo-China, and in later years during disarmament negotiations in Geneva. During the 1960s he became an increasingly familiar face in New York. But he proved no more of a miracle-worker than anybody else at the UN. There was never any evidence that he could personally pull strings in the Kremlin that would cause a change in Soviet policy and lead to the settlement of some major problem. It was rather that, when Moscow had taken a decision to open up some new possibility of a settlement, Vasily Kuznetsov was a likely man to be charged with handling the new formula, because of the deftness with which he could make a deal – once he had been authorised to make one.

At the beginning of 1963 western hopes that the sight of a new Russian face in the Council meant a new and more co-operative Russian policy were centred not on Kuznetsov but on Nikolai Fedorenko, who was then appointed to succeed Valerian Zorin as permanent representative. Fedorenko seemed to have been picked because he made such a complete contrast with the old-guard hard-liner Zorin. Zorin's behaviour at the UN had done nothing to diminish the unpleasant reputation that had clung to him ever since he had played a sinister role in the 1948 communist *putsch* in Czechoslovakia. He had begun his two years in the Council by launching a venomous attack on Dag Hammarskjöld, and had ended it with a disastrous performance in the Cuba missiles crisis (page 175), which brought about his swift removal from New York after a much shorter spell there than Moscow usually accorded to its councilmen.

Any change would have been welcome in these circumstances; but the choice of Fedorenko seemed to indicate that Khrushchev wanted to emphasise what a big change he was making. Nikolai Fedorenko gave the impression that he had always led a quiet, scholarly and indeed bourgeois life. A bow-tied smoker of bendy pipes, he could surely have merged unnoticed into an arts faculty at a west European or even an American university. He was in fact a professional sinologist, and, at this stage in the emergence of the Sino-Soviet rift, his arrival in New York set off much speculation about its significance for Moscow's China policy.

At first his performance seemed to fit his outward appearance. He seemed relaxed, unbuttoned and amiable. But of course 1963, the 'post-Cuba' year, the year of the partial nuclear test ban treaty, a year that saw the quietest Assembly session of the 1960s, was not a real time of testing. Later, when the pressure mounted, Nikolai Fedorenko's limitations became painfully clear. His manner now seemed more arrogant than academic. His early attempts to woo Asian and African representatives were conspicuous failures, and after a time he seemed to stop trying. Once again Moscow found itself having to send the trusty Vasily Kuznetsov over to New York to regain the ground that Fedorenko had lost. Much as the musical play *1776* depicts John Adams at the Continental Congress, the unfortunate Fedorenko was simply 'obnoxious and disliked'. There was general relief when it was announced in January 1968 that he was to be replaced by Yakov Malik.

There were not by then many people at the UN who actually

remembered Malik from his earlier term there in 1948–53, but in a broad sense he was welcomed back as 'a devil we know', and a reasonable sort of devil at that. And things looked even brighter when, soon after his return, his team was drastically overhauled. The dogged Platon Morozov, who had been second in command to Fedorenko, and to Zorin before him, and had in fact been at the UN so long that even those who were glad to see him go felt a certain sense of loss, was replaced by Lev Mendelevich, one of the very few Jews to reach high rank in the Soviet diplomatic service. Another equally lively intelligence appeared among Malik's deputies (he was given no less than four, Mendelevich ranking first among them) in the shape of an Armenian, Victor Israelyan. The Soviet mission office on East 67th Street couldn't yet show an Italian, or an Irishman (though one of the attachés' names was widely rendered as Tim O'Keane), but, within its limits, it was taking on quite a New Yorky flavour.

*   *   *

Miguel Solano-Lopez of Paraguay, presiding over one of the Council's meetings in 1969, remarked at the end of the day:

> Generally speaking, the person assuming the office of president addresses those who ask to speak by using the words 'distinguished representative'. Since I have not addressed members as 'distinguished' representatives, I have shattered a long standing custom, and I have done so for a specific reason. Personally, I feel that all representatives sitting around the Council table fulfil the qualifications of being exceptionally distinguished.

With all due respect to Solano-Lopez's feelings, the truth must be told. Some councilmen are exceptionally undistinguished. Some are indistinguishable. Their courteous habit of describing each other as distinguished is, of course, as remote from reality as the parliamentary politeness which, in the House of Commons, represents all members as honourable members and some of them as right honourable. (But one should be grateful for small mercies. Since the councilmen are all ambassadors, they might easily have got into the way of addressing each other as 'excellency'.)

The undistinguished have included a number of representatives of great powers. The truly distinguished have included several spokesmen for lesser states. As a rule, however, it is not easy for a non-permanent member's representative to make a real mark in the Council. He cannot sit there for more than two years; immediate re-election is barred, and by the time his country's turn comes round again he will almost certainly have left New York for some other post. It must depend very largely on the fall of the cards whether any opportunity arises during his two-year term for him to distinguish himself in any real sense. A good many gifted men have served their time on the Council without finding any such opportunity. But other non-permanent representatives have had some degree of greatness thrust upon them. The record shows that this is most likely to happen to a councilman if, when a critical situation arises, he is presiding over the Council; if his country's (and his own) standing is such that the contending parties will accept him as a reasonably disinterested third party; and if the major powers are in some disarray, unable to settle matters among themselves and willing to tolerate, if not warmly welcome, an attempt by a spokesman for the smaller fry. From time to time this combination of circumstances, or something like it, propels an elective councilman into sudden prominence.

In the 1948 Berlin crisis Juan Atilio Bramuglia of Argentina, as Council president for October, took the lead in a sustained effort to break the deadlock which was mounted by the six so-called 'neutral' members – Argentina, Belgium, Canada, China, Colombia and Syria. Gunnar Jarring of Sweden was presiding in the Council when the Kashmir dispute came to a new head in 1957, and he was given a 'good offices' mission to India and Pakistan. In 1960 Mongi Slim of Tunisia, who was the only African Council member that year, played a major role in the Council's handling of the early stages of the Congo operation. Carlos Bernardes of Brazil worked hard and successfully to bring about agreement in the Council over which he was presiding when it was called upon to authorise the Cyprus operation early in 1964; and later he did good service in Cyprus as Thant's special representative there. Hans Tabor of Denmark was Council president in June 1967, the month of the Israel–Arab 'six-day war', and earned general respect for the way he acquitted himself during that strenuous period in the Council's life.

There have also, of course, been elective councilmen who made

41

their mark in a rather different way. A striking case in the UN's earliest years was that of Ales Bebler of Jugoslavia. By the time he took a Council seat in 1950, the breach between Stalin and Tito had gone so far that Bebler proved one of Russia's sharpest critics in the Council, and his performance there was often highly gratifying to the western members. But they still found it hard to forget that two or three years earlier Bebler had been 'distinguishing' himself, in the Assembly and various UN committees, by the unsurpassed bitterness of his diatribes against the western powers. When a member state's policies change, its man at the UN must obviously conform or quit; but it was felt at the time that Bebler's transmogrification had been somewhat grotesque. A more recent instance of the earning of unenviable notoriety may be seen in the story, summarised on pages 237 and 238, of the actions in April 1966 of Moussa Keita of Mali, who was then president of the Council but seemed unwilling to admit that he was.

And then there are the cases of 'visiting firemen' – representatives taking part in the Council's discussions without being members of it – who have stolen some of the limelight by giving performances that were, if not always distinguished, at least distinctive. Among these, the performances of Jamil Baroody of Saudi Arabia have been in a beyond-the-fringe class by themselves.* Impressive in a more substantial way, if not necessarily more fruitful for the Council, have been the weighty interventions by such titans of the talkathon as V. K. Krishna Menon of India and Sir Muhammad Zafrulla Khan of Pakistan,† who were notably well matched in the Kashmir debates of 1962. But there have also been valuable contributions by men who have proved exceptions to the common practice of invited participants behaving like 'visiting fire-raisers'.

A memorable example of this was provided in September 1960 by Alex Quaison-Sackey, the representative of Ghana, who was later to serve as a councilman in 1962–3 and as president of the 19th

* Samples may be found on pages 202 and 256. Baroody has long enjoyed the distinction, which in any other case would be a curious one, of heading a UN mission with the rank only of deputy permanent representative, the post of permanent representative being left vacant for years on end.

† In 1970 Zafrulla became president of the International Court at The Hague.

Assembly. Both behind the scenes and in public debate he played an important role in the handling by Council and Assembly of one of the early stages of the Congo crisis.

On 5 September 1960 President Joseph Kasavubu had dismissed his prime minister, Patrice Lumumba, whom he accused of plunging the Congo into civil war. Lumumba at once retorted that he was deposing Kasavubu. Lumumba's men took over the Leopoldville radio and broadcast fiery appeals for support. Andrew Cordier, whom Hammarskjöld had temporarily placed in charge of the UN Congo operation, feared that full-scale civil war was about to break out and sent UN troops, including Ghanaians, to close the capital's radio station and airport.

In form the UN action was impartial; in practice, it prevented Lumumba from whipping up his supporters and from flying troops loyal to him into Leopoldville in the Soviet-manned transport planes with which Russia had just supplied him. A week of confused political manoeuvre followed, and then on the 14th the army chief of staff, Colonel Joseph Mobutu, announced that the army was 'neutralising' the contending factions, installing a caretaker government of technicians – and expelling the Soviet ambassador and his staff.

The Russians had already launched their attack on Hammarskjöld's tactics in the Congo, and the action taken by Cordier – an American – led Nikita Khrushchev to join personally in even more bitter accusations against the Secretary-General. Hammarskjöld called for a Council debate. A series of meetings began on September 9, when the first Russian move was to propose, unsuccessfully, that the Council should go to the Congo in a body and meet in Leopoldville. Rival representatives – Justin Bomboko sent by Kasavubu, Thomas Kanza sent by Lumumba – arrived in New York, and the Council, unable to decide between them, refused to seat either.* Valerian Zorin presented a violently worded draft resolution which, among other things, demanded the removal of the existing command of the UN force in the Congo. Mongi Slim of

* It was when Bomboko and Kanza were seen warmly embracing each other outside the Council chamber that several councilmen decided they would never get to understand Congolese politics.

43

Tunisia, the only African Council member, defended the Secretary-General.

Alex Quaison-Sackey, speaking as a non-voting participant on the 16th, told the Council that the UN should work for a compromise between the Congolese rivals, and should demand the ending of all bilateral external aid whether Russian or Belgian. Ghana, he said, 'had not been very happy over certain matters in connection with the application of the resolution'; but President Nkrumah had asked him to appeal to Council members 'to refrain from all personal attacks on Mr Hammarskjöld':

> The clear vision of this man, 'his merited rank, his superior eloquence, his splendid qualities, his eminent services, the vast place he fills in the eyes of mankind', must embolden us to pay tribute to him for his great services in the cause of peace.

This apt invocation of Edmund Burke made Hammarskjöld blush, while Zorin went red with anger.

With this voice from black Africa echoing in the Council chamber, Mongi Slim and Sir Claude Corea of Ceylon were encouraged to propose a resolution supporting Hammarskjöld's position. In the small hours of the morning on Saturday the 17th, eight votes (including America's and Britain's) were cast in favour of the Ceylon–Tunisia resolution; but Zorin vetoed it. Almost incredibly, just at a moment when many Asian and African governments were decidedly worried about the effects of UN actions in the Congo, Russia had pushed its vendetta against the Secretary-General to the point where it came out in open opposition to the Afro-Asians and forced them to line up in defence of Hammarskjöld with the western powers (except the ever-abstaining France).

Quaison-Sackey had defended in the Africans' name a man whom Khrushchev had just denounced as the conscious instrument of an 'imperialist conspiracy'. And Khrushchev himself was due to arrive in New York on September 19. By the time the Soviet leader landed, the wretched Zorin had sustained further wounds from the emergency Assembly session which, like a sword of Damocles, was dropped on to him as soon as he vetoed the Slim–Corea resolution in the Council.

44

It was again the Ghanaian representative who presented in the emergency Assembly a resolution that differed from the vetoed one only in being more explicit and asked Hammarskjöld 'to continue to take vigorous action'. All the African member states, and eight of the Asian ones, joined in sponsoring it. Zorin was obliged to withdraw his own resolution because there was no support for it outside the Soviet group. Early on the morning of Tuesday the 20th (with Khrushchev already in New York and due to star later that same day at the opening of the regular Assembly session) the Afro-Asian resolution was carried by a squelching majority of seventy votes to none. Every African and Asian member of the UN supported it. Zorin dared not even record a vote against it, despite the violent objections he had voiced. The Soviet group merely abstained, along with France and, this time, South Africa. The Congo operation had been saved.

*   *   *

The point should be noted that, although a substantial power may rate its UN mission rather low among its diplomatic posts, there are other states that regard the UN as a pivotal point in their diplomacy and try to appoint a really good envoy there. When great states combine, the small must associate (as that Burke fan Quaison-Sackey might put it). At the UN the little fellows may not often be able to unite their little strengths and stand up effectively against the big boys; but they can at least keep in touch with each other there. For a small state with a small diplomatic service the UN may be just about the only place where it can maintain continuous contact with many of the other small states.

So, however limited the lesser members' diplomatic talent may be, some of the best of that talent is sent to New York. (This applies not merely to Afro-Asian 'new nations' but also to quite a few European and other states.) But, since the Council's ten elective seats accommodate only one-twelfth of the UN's member states at any one time, and they follow each other into those seats in a lurching sort of succession that would baffle the cleverest computer yet born, the average level of competence of the elective councilmen is unlikely to rise much above that of the mass of permanent representatives as a whole. A foreign ministry will not normally wait until it is sure of getting a Council seat and then send one of its particularly bright boys to New York; for that would mean being represented in the Council by a man who had not had time to learn the UN ropes.

Sometimes (but, unfortunately, not very often) the fact that a particular representative has already won general respect among his colleagues may contribute to his country's election to a Council seat. Sometimes the knowledge that a representative is inept will tip the balance enough to keep his country out of the Council for the time being. This, too, happens less often than it should; and, bearing in mind the present state of the law of libel, it might be imprudent to cite any examples.

However, when a temporary councilman achieves a special prominence the brevity of his tenure of a Council seat is often offset by the fact that he was a valued member of the corps of permanent representatives in New York before he moved into that seat. For example, Mongi Slim was recognised as a pivotal figure at the UN long before he took his place at the horseshoe table (the year after leaving the Council he was elected president of the Assembly). And in other cases a man who has only recently joined the resident corps in New York will prove to have mastered the ropes very quickly, because he has previously served on Assembly delegations; has worked in his foreign ministry's department for UN affairs; or has experience of other international bodies.

No two international organisations are quite alike. But, as is increasingly recognised in the training of diplomats, there is a certain sameness about the techniques of 'conference diplomacy', 'parliamentary diplomacy', multilateral negotiation or whatever you like to call it, wherever these methods are in use. It is hardly surprising that a growing number of councilmen should have some experience of working with international bodies other than the United Nations; and this can be very useful, so long as the man does not get muddled and behave at Turtle Bay as if he was in some quite different international forum.

A good many of the African representatives in the Council have had previous experience with the Organisation of African Unity, in

Addis Ababa or elsewhere. There is no corresponding class of graduates from the Council of Europe, because its assembly consists of parliamentarians, while the European states are almost always represented in the Security Council by career diplomats. But there are plenty of other links of the same general kind. George Ignatieff, for instance, was Canada's councilman in New York in 1967–8 after having represented it in the North Atlantic Council; and he went on from the UN to replace General Burns as the Canadian representative at the Geneva disarmament negotiations.

The case of Gunnar Jarring was in striking contrast to these patterns. He had entered his country's diplomatic service at a fairly late age (and almost accidentally), after making his mark in the academic world as a specialist in the Turkic languages of central Asia. He came to the UN without any particular experience in the work of multi-national bodies. Only a few months after his arrival in New York Sweden became a Council member. By March 1957 – the third month of his Council service – Jarring had already been launched into orbit as the Council's choice for a special mission to India and Pakistan. A very quiet man with qualifications that speak loud, Jarring won high praise for his performance during this plunge into the intricacies of the Kashmir conflict. He had been chosen for the task partly because of his Asian experience (apart from his linguistic work, he had already been ambassador to Teheran and New Delhi); partly because, as Council president for a month when the Kashmir dispute once again loomed large in New York, he revealed a willingness to involve himself deeply in it, and was seen to be acceptable to both the disputing parties.

Ten years later, at the end of 1967, Jarring accepted another and not dissimilar mission on behalf of the UN, when the Council, in its British-sponsored resolution of November 22, asked U Thant to designate

a Special Representative to proceed to the Middle East to establish and maintain contacts with the states concerned, in order to promote agreement and assist efforts to achieve a peaceful and accepted settlement. . . .

At the time when this second, long-running, 'Jarring mission' began, Gunnar Jarring was Swedish ambassador to Russia; and he retained that post, returning to Moscow at intervals when it seemed he could do no more good by keeping up a circuit of the Arab and Israeli capitals. He had left the UN as far back as 1958, when he became ambassador in Washington, and had been moved to Moscow in 1964 – an appointment that gave him a rather special pleasure, since, twenty years earlier, the Russians had refused to accept him as an attaché, evidently because he knew too much about their central Asian territories.

Jarring had long been known for his *Wanderlust*, a quality that doubtless enabled him to sustain, longer than most other people would have done, the unrewarding round of visits to Jerusalem, Cairo and Amman – not Damascus: Syria would not play – on which he embarked from the 'base' he chose at Nicosia in Cyprus. (Because of Arab refusal to allow direct travel to or from Israel, Cyprus has long served as a convenient place for UN and other envoys to change planes when in transit from one side to the other. Since 1964 there has also been the ironic convenience that Nicosia, being the headquarters of the UN force in Cyprus, can provide good facilities for communication with New York and other useful services.)

However, as the months passed, even Jarring's enthusiasm for the nomadic life became satiated. And, although Moscow is not a post to which diplomats usually cling, once they have experienced the ghetto-like isolation to which the Russians subject foreign residents, it had for Gunnar Jarring the attractions that he could there pursue his Asian linguistic studies and that it was near enough to Sweden to permit holiday visits to his seaside home.

*   *   *

Each councilman is both more and less than a councilman. He is more, because as a permanent representative he is the chief of a mission that must play its part in many different UN activities. If his mission is a large one his deputies will handle most of the work that involves attending meetings other than those of the Security Council and of the Assembly and its First Committee; but he must still supervise the whole show. He may also be required to attend UN conferences at Geneva or elsewhere. If a Council meeting is suddenly called while he is away from New York his deputy will, of course, appear in his stead at the horseshoe table. He himself will usually come winging back to it if anything like a real international crisis has arisen; but there are times when the whole thing fizzles out before he can get back, even in the jet age.

He is less than a councilman in the sense that he must back away from the table, and sit more humbly in one of those seats for advisers that are bolted to the floor, if and when his government chooses to be represented in the Council at a higher level. Only once, and that as recently as 1969, has a head of government personally taken a member's seat in the Council; and that was a distinctly odd occasion (page 338). But foreign ministers have appeared on quite a number of occasions; and there have also been instances of a seat being taken by a special representative who, while junior to the minister, still outranks the regular councilman. It is in these latter cases that, I fear, the regular man may feel a certain humiliation.

When, for example, Vasily Kuznetsov, who ranks as a deputy foreign minister as well as a trouble-shooter, makes one of his appearances at the UN, his coming is usually hailed by other nations' representatives as an encouraging portent; but I am not so sure that it is welcomed with equal warmth by the incumbent Russian representative. Communist society being the stiffly hierarchical thing it is, the mere thought of (literally) having to take a back seat must be painful enough, to say nothing of the realisation that the Kremlin has found you wanting and has felt it necessary to send another man to do a councilman's job. When Khrushchev sent Kuznetsov, at the breaking point in the 1962 Cuba missiles crisis, to take over at the UN from Valerian Zorin, the fact that Zorin too held the rank of deputy foreign minister did not save him from having to move down one place in the pecking order, for Kuznetsov, being a *first* deputy foreign minister, was his superior in protocol as well as in diplomacy.

It is the non-voting participants in Council debates who are most often represented by their foreign ministers or by other special envoys: naturally enough, for while the subject of discussion may seem of mere marginal interest to most of the councilmen, the visiting firemen have come to the table precisely because they think this subject is of vital concern to them. If debate stretches out over a period while tension continues to mount, or actual armed conflict rages, the parties directly involved may send to New York a whole series of special representatives, each bringing a fresher brief and possibly a higher rank than his immediate predecessor. A pattern of this kind evolved in the 1965 Indo-Pakistani conflict. At the start the two belligerents were represented at the Council table by their resident New York men; then waves of new emissaries came winging in from their two capitals; by the seventh week, both foreign ministers were in New York and locking horns in the debates.

The appearances of the Council members' own foreign ministers are, in contrast, very rare occasions. Back in 1946 the foreign ministers of America, Britain and France – James Byrnes, Ernest Bevin and Georges Bidault – took part in some of the Council's earliest meetings. The unforeseen sharpness of some of the exchanges that marked these first meetings doubtless helped to bring this personal participation by ministers to a quick end. Ten years passed before there was any really impressive gathering. At the 735th meeting, held on 5 October 1956, the Suez Canal crisis brought together at the Council table the foreign ministers of four permanent members, two other Council members and one invited participant. Christian Pineau of France presided over a Council that included John Foster Dulles of the United States, Selwyn Lloyd of Britain, Dimitri Shepilov of Russia, Paul-Henri Spaak of Belgium, Koca Popovic of Jugoslavia and, as a very interested non-voting participant, Mahmoud Fawzi of Egypt. Whether there are likely to be similar gatherings in the future is a question to be pursued in the last chapter of this book.

Chapter Three

The dead men's chest

Once upon a time (in the early 1960s) there was a permanent member of the Security Council who, for the purposes of this story, may be known as Britain.* Britain had a Foreign Secretary who, at the time, was known as Home.† Home had a rather special attitude to the UN and the Council. He may not have been quite as ignorant as he seemed about who really founded the UN and what the real founders' real intentions had been. But, whether deliberately or not, he propagated a misleading version of the organisation's origins.

He had a way of uttering, in such centres of international diplomacy as Berwick on Tweed (giving due notice to *The Times*, in case the whole thing should go unnoticed), rousing calls for 'a great new effort to bring the United Nations back to working the Charter as it was meant to be'. And what was it meant to be? 'The founder members,' said Home, had set up a Security Council and 'named the Great Powers as permanent members, in the expectation that they would deal together with any breach of the peace by the smaller powers'. But now, alas, 'a large part of the organisation which is dedicated to peace openly condones aggression. . . . This evidence of a serious falling away from the principles of the Charter places Britain in an appalling dilemma.'

Stirring stuff like this, although – as we shall see – it was actually nonsense, helped to bring him to Downing Street within two years. (They had not even 'intended him to be the next prime minister but

---

* At the UN it is known as the United Kingdom. Tactfully, the full name, with its mention of Northern Ireland, is seldom used.

† Lord Home, as he then was, has since become the Rt. Hon. Sir Alec Douglas-Home, KT, MP. The Home part still rhymes with fume. And, in 1970, he is once again Foreign Secretary, as he then was.

51

three'.) His career as a foreign policy specialist having been marked by such milestones as Munich 1938 and Suez 1956, it was no great surprise when, as prime minister, he promptly led his party into its first electoral defeat in fourteen years. Undismayed by the loss of both office and party leadership, he remained a stern chastiser of the UN as it ploughed on through one 'dreadful mistake' after another. Given his rather special experience of disasters, it was perhaps surprising that more respect was not paid to his views at the UN, where people even tended to recoil from his insistence on the need to sustain the South African regime as a strategic bastion of liberty.

And what about the restoration of the UN 'as it was meant to be', with a proper respect for the concepts of Britain, Home and great-power glory? For some years after Sir Alec's fall from power the banner of the Douglas-Homes was upheld by General de Gaulle. *Grandeur* being even grander than British 'greatness', the French President was not content to demand a strict 'return to the Charter'. He pushed his claim that only great powers should handle great affairs to the point of pulling France out of the Geneva disarmament talks when the intolerable decision was taken to let a few small states participate in them. But now de Gaulle, too, has fallen. The Geneva conference has brazenly seated eight more non-great powers. And there are even more of these pesky small fry in the Council than there were when Home so boldly faced his 'appalling dilemma'.

The anti-UN feeling among British Tories that Home was exploiting and promoting at the time of his celebrated Berwick speech in 1961 had largely been aroused by the UN's efforts to frustrate the attempt to keep the Katanga as a satellite of the white-run southern African regimes. But this was a sticky wicket for the Foreign Secretary to bat on. So he pinned his 'crisis of confidence in the United Nations' mainly on to a remarkably tortuous suggestion that the Council had 'approved' India's occupation of Goa; and proceeded to link this, still more strangely, to a charge that 'democracies, because their stock in trade is reason and compromise', got a raw deal from the UN. His widely applauded speech was in fact a masterpiece of misrepresentation. If Portugal had been democratic, reasonable and ready to compromise (as France had been about its enclaves in India), things would have gone differently over Goa. As to the Council, the only thing that prevented it calling upon India to withdraw its forces from Goa immediately was a Soviet veto of the draft resolution that seven members had backed.

'Crisis of confidence'? 'Appalling dilemma'? 'An organisation which was founded to sustain law and order encourages policies which must endanger it'? This was Russia's 99th veto. It can hardly have come as a shock, even to Home. Nor could he have forgotten that his own government, in 1956, had vetoed an almost identical draft resolution calling upon Israel to withdraw its forces from Egypt. Indeed, he had not forgotten. The one thing missing from his long list of charges against the UN was any reference at all to the great-power veto. Instead he tried to give the impression that the Council's Goa resolution had been blocked by its three Asian and African members.

The truth that lay, and lies, behind all the 'Home truths' about 'a serious falling away from the principles of the Charter', about getting back to 'working the Charter as it was meant to be', and about the alleged founders' alleged expectations, can be understood only if we contrast this verbiage with the realities of the UN's origins.

The question is not whether mankind has fallen short of perfection since 1945, much as it tended to do before that date. The shining ideals proclaimed in the Charter are, of course, flouted every day, just like those in the Decalogue, the *Bhagavad Gita* and Thomas Jefferson's Declaration of Independence. The real questions are: What practical results did the practical men who devised the United Nations – Charter, Council and all – expect it to produce? And how have the actual results differed from the expectations of the devisers? It is best to begin by recalling what the world was really like when the Charter was adopted and the UN came into being. This will at least help us to see very quickly who the real founders were.

The world into which the UN was born strongly resembled Julius Caesar's Gaul in one respect. It was virtually divided into three parts. Never before had there been a moment when such a small number of great powers dominated almost the entire globe. You needed only three flags to mark the distribution of power on the world map.

In the northern hemisphere one border line between American and

Russian power lay in Korea and China, the other one on the other side of the world in the heart of Europe. The Russians, as well as stretching out their domain to east and west, had moved southward too, into Iran and the Balkans. The Americans' newly increased sea power made them masters of the Pacific and gave them a strong position in the Mediterranean. As for the third power, Britain, although the strains of world war had brought it to a marked degree of economic dependence on the United States, its flag flew, more widely than ever before in all its imperial history, over vast regions in the south. From the West African coast to the South China Sea, by way of the Middle East and southern Asia, the British with their great imperial armies raised during the war in India and Africa were, for the moment, in control of the greater part of what we now call the Afro-Asian world.

The Axis powers lay prostrate; civil war loomed over an already ravaged China; France and other countries just freed from Axis occupation were only beginning to pick themselves up again. Although the war had accelerated the drive to independence of many countries in Asia, Africa and elsewhere, the immediate situation at the time of the UN's birth did not reflect this new development very clearly. The direct pressures of war had worked to enhance the great powers' standing. Lesser allies had accepted their predominance as a wartime necessity. Their advancing armies had been widely hailed as liberators. Here and there, they had had to make a few concessions to subject peoples and small states who had contrived to exploit the old formula that 'England's difficulty is Ireland's opportunity'. But, for the most part, their ears had even been shielded from troubling sounds of dissent. (Nehru of India and Vorster of South Africa had alike been incarcerated when they looked like impeding the war effort. Stalin's regime had deported and decimated whole peoples.) And the great allies themselves had had every reason to resolve rapidly, or at least play down, such differences as threatened to divide them.

Against this background, it would have been naïve to expect that the delegates from fifty countries who came to San Francisco in 1945 would be in any position to draw up a Charter that cast down the mighty from their seats. The San Francisco 'founders' were, in fact, summoned to that Californian city to approve a basic structure for the UN that had already been privately agreed between the Big Three. The 'Charter as it was meant to be' was what the great powers meant it to be. It did not exactly come as a surprise to them that the supposed 'founders' at San Francisco 'named' them as permanent Council members 'in the expectation' that they would take charge of all the peace-keeping. They had so named themselves. They bluntly told the smaller fry that they had already decided on a UN security structure which would be entirely controlled by the great powers. They over-rode protests; and the 'founders' had no choice but to counter-sign the great powers' plan.

A central feature in that plan was that it gave each of the great powers the right to do precisely what Russia did when the Council discussed Goa in December 1961. When Russia vetoed the Goa resolution it was 'working the Charter as it was meant to be' – as it was meant to be by the British and American governments as well as by Russia's.

*   *   *

There had been full agreement between Roosevelt, Churchill and Stalin that the proposed United Nations organisation was to be an instrument for the execution of decisions jointly made by the Big Three (with China and France as their privileged associates). This agreement was first given shape at the 1943 Moscow talks. True, the declaration signed on 30 October 1943 by the three foreign ministers and the Chinese ambassador in Moscow said that they aimed to create an organisation on the basis of 'the sovereign equality of all peace-loving states, large and small'. In direct line of descent from this statement, Article 2 of the Charter proclaims that the UN is 'based on the principle of the sovereign equality of all its members'. But some sovereign equals are more equal than others, both in the Charter as it was meant to be and in the practice of the UN today. There was, in fact, 'a serious falling away' from this principle in the Charter itself. But neither then nor later was this seen as presenting 'an appalling dilemma' by Home or by other devotees of great-power privilege.

In the Charter great-power privilege loomed far larger than it had done in the Covenant of the League of Nations. This was all the more remarkable because the Covenant had been quite openly a great-power product; it was never reviewed and revised by anything like the fifty-member San Francisco conference. The Covenant included certain references to 'the Principal Allied and Associated Powers' (which, in the absence of the United States, came to mean Britain, France, Italy and Japan). But the only privilege it gave them was that of sitting permanently in the League Council. They had no privileged veto power. In the Council every member had the same power of veto, in that all important decisions had to be unanimous (except recommendations about a dispute, which could be approved by a majority vote, but would then carry less force than a unanimous recommendation). Permanent Council members were given no such special rights as the UN Charter gives them ('transitional security' rights, power to block admissions and Charter amendments, control of the Military Staff Committee).

The ratio between permanent and other Council members fluctuated wildly during the League's lifetime, the elected members multiplying from an initial four to an ultimate eleven, while, among the permanent seat-holders, Germany and Russia came and went, and Italy and Japan just went. But this fluctuation was of little significance in view of the unanimity rule. One oddity in the League's history was Brazil's withdrawal from it in 1926 after being refused a permanent Council seat. Since the seat conferred no special rights, this was one of the purest instances on record of obsession with the mystical prestige of the 'top table'.

Only to a marginal extent was the privileged great-power position set out in the Charter the result of a particular Soviet insistence on it. Long before Roosevelt and Churchill discussed these matters with Stalin in late 1943 they had been in basic agreement. Roosevelt started out in 1942 with the idea that no state in the post-war world should be allowed any heavy armaments except America, Britain, China and Russia, who would undertake to act as the Four Policemen. Some alarm spread among America's smaller allies when they got wind of the Four Policemen concept.

Churchill had no objection to the general idea, but he didn't like the thought of the fourth policeman, China. ('There would be a faggot vote on the side of the United States in any attempt to liquidate the British overseas empire.') He also wanted to see regional Councils of Europe and Asia, with their own armies for enforcement of their decisions and prevention of aggression within their respective baili-wicks. Roosevelt thought Churchill was pushing this idea too far, especially when he produced his 'Morning Thoughts' about a European federation of federations 'which will embody the spirit, but not be subject to the weakness, of the former League of Nations'. But by mid-1943 Churchill had agreed that his regional councils would be subordinate to Roosevelt's world council, and that Roosevelt could have a Chinese policeman if he wanted one.

About the same time the first proto-Security Council took shape on a State Department drawing board. It was to have eleven mem-bers; and its substantive decisions would need the unanimous sup-port of the permanent members. Only in three significant respects did it differ from the Council that was to come into being in 1946. Decisions would require a two-thirds majority (as against the requirement of seven favourable votes in the eleven-member Security Council of 1946–65, and the requirement of nine in the present fifteen-member Council). Non-permanent members would be form-ally chosen from regional groupings. (Since 1966 the Council has adopted this practice, or rather the Assembly has done so in its elections of Council members; thus the Council now conforms more closely to the 1943 Washington model than it used to do.) And there were to be only four permanent members. France still lay hull down beyond the State Department's horizon.

At Dumbarton Oaks, a delightful mansion in Washington's Old Georgetown, the UN's three real founders met in August and September 1944 to do the real founding. France was still ineligible for their club, and China could not sit with the Three, because Russia, being neutral in the Japanese war, feared that such a gather-ing would be compromising. But the Americans and British had the Chinese in to a little party at Dumbarton Oaks immediately after their main talks with the Russians, so that was all right. Anyway, there was agreement by now that both China and France should be privileged permanent members (which from now on I may abbreviate

57

to PPs) of the proposed Security Council. The Americans even toyed with the idea of adding Brazil to the PPs, but the Russians and the British (not wanting to start that League business all over again?) held them to the firm line that the Council should consist of five PPs and six other members, and that these numbers could be changed only by going through the difficult process of amending the Charter – which a PP veto could prevent. The Three (indeed, the Four; China challenged none of the Three's points) were entirely agreed that each PP should have veto power in the Security Council, and that the Council should have the real responsibility for maintaining peace.

Seven months before anybody went to San Francisco, the essential guts of the Charter security system were thus agreed and put on paper in a quiet corner of Georgetown by Edward Stettinius, Sir Alexander Cadogan, Andrei Gromyko and their respective official teams. Of course, unlike San Francisco, this was supposed to be a conference behind closed doors. But the American press, with James Reston of the *New York Times* well in the lead, saw to it that the Dumbarton Oaks story was immediately made known to the world in almost complete detail.

So the fifty delegations that went to San Francisco in 1945 had had plenty of time to get adjusted to the idea of what they were going to be asked to accept. And for the most part they had to accept it. They accepted the enforcement provisions that are contained in Chapter Seven of the Charter virtually as these had emerged from Dumbarton Oaks. On paper, these provisions looked mightily impressive. For the first time in history an international organisation would be equipped to bring overwhelming force to bear on an aggressor, or on any situation in which peace was being broken or even merely threatened. The Security Council would control a Military Staff Committee, which in turn would direct the actions of the armed forces that all member states undertook to contribute for the maintenance of peace. There had never been anything like it. (As a matter of fact, there still isn't anything like it. But that comes later.)

What became plain, on a closer look, was that this Goliath of peace enforcement could be defied with impunity not only by any one of the five PPs but also by any state that could count on a PP to use its veto as a shield. Only with the consent of all five PPs could the Security Council determine that peace was being threatened or broken. Only with their consent could it decide to resort either to force or to 'measures not involving the use of armed force' (economic and other non-military sanctions). Only with their consent could it make agreements with member states that would bind these states to contribute armed forces for use by the Council. And who would direct these armed forces? A Military Staff Committee manned by the five PPs.

So, if Lilliput and Blefuscu agreed to have a battle, and one of them had a powerful PP patron who would block UN enforcement action against him, the mighty machine at the disposal of the Military Staff Committee and the Security Council would stand idle while the two little fellows fought their war. If a patron PP was for some reason reluctant to use a veto in open Council it might still be able to use its position in the Military Staff Committee to ensure that UN armed force was not applied effectively.

Things could work out more painfully, of course, for any little state that had no friend among the PPs. But, by and large, the fifty states that were invited to come to San Francisco and become UN 'founder' members were invited because they did have friends among the PPs. And those that were admitted to membership later had to be so generally acceptable that no PP would veto their admission. In this light, the 'security system' that the Three thrust upon the San Francisco 'founders' is seen to be less impressive.

It was justified by the plausible argument that hard reality made it unthinkable for UN enforcement action to be attempted in the teeth of the opposition of a great power. If a veto-free UN undertook to discipline little Ruritania for attacking a neighbour, and mighty Megalomania then announced that it would fight anybody who touched a hair of the little chap's head, the UN would either have to plunge into something unpleasantly like a world war or be forced to back down. That is perfectly true, as far as it goes. But it doesn't go all the way. As Herman Kahn would surely point out, there are many other 'scenarios'.

To start close to the bone, it is another 'hard reality' that among the PPs, as among UN members as a whole, some are more equal

59

than others. It is militarily unthinkable for the UN to contemplate enforcement action that could bring it up against the full might of one of the two super-powers. Is it quite so unthinkable that it might act against some state which only Britain, or only France, felt like defending? It is thinkable, I think, that a Ruritania that was shielded from UN action only by a veto wielded by Taipeh China, or by a Brazilian veto (assuming, for a moment, that Brazil had been given PP status at Dumbarton Oaks), would be regarded as escaping chastisement not because of any 'hard reality' but because of an artificial impediment resulting from an accident of history. (Taipeh China has used its Council veto once, in 1955 – to block, temporarily, the UN's admission of Mongolia.)

It is also a fact – which the wartime Three were in no mood to acknowledge – that even great powers, like other people, spend much of their lives in a quandary. And one of the points about which they often feel uncertain is, precisely, how far they should commit themselves to go to the help of smaller states. Patron states rarely enjoy lasting popularity among their client states; and the converse is also true. It is a recurring situation for a major power to find a smaller state that has some sort of claim to its protection, or at least its benevolence, acting in alarming ways that can easily bring it into a conflict with a neighbour. The patron, nervous and irritated, suspecting that the quarrel is mainly or entirely the client's fault, may not really be enthusiastic about defending the little nuisance against all comers, or convinced that its own interests require it to do so. So Ruritania cannot, in fact, always be sure that Megalomania would rush to protect it with armed might against any UN action for peace enforcement. But it may feel reasonably sure that the Megalomaniac veto will be wielded on its behalf in the Council; and that assurance may encourage the Ruritanians to provoke their neighbours a little more.

All the UN's experience has indeed shown that a system that assumes that a great power will be either wholly for or wholly against every proposal for action is absurdly simplistic. This is why so much of the Security Council's activity in regard to peace-keeping has been along the lines of the famous chapter that the Three never put into the Charter at all, 'Chapter Six and a Half'; whereas the elaborate military enforcement provisions of Chapter Seven still do not seem likely ever to be put into full effect.

Over-simplified, too, is the often repeated statement that the founders of the UN blithely assumed that the great powers were going to maintain their wartime unity. There still seems to be a legend to the effect that the Three at Dumbarton Oaks and the Fifty at San Francisco shared this complacent vision of enduring great-power harmony, and therefore made the serious mistake of shaping the new organisation in a way that took it for granted. Yet the record shows that the Russians, at least, never for one moment during the negotiations lost sight of the need to secure their position against the all too likely prospect that they would find the other great powers opposing them. As for the British, it should be enough to recall the fears that Churchill voiced in his 1943 comment, already quoted, about the other great powers' designs on his empire. (Churchill championed France's right to PP status less out of a warm affection for General de Gaulle than out of a wish to have another colonial power in the group alongside Britain.)

If there ever was a phase of real American confidence about postwar great-power unity it was all over long before San Francisco. And if there had not already been the ominous wranglings, at and after Yalta, about the future of Poland and quite a few other matters, the San Francisco conference itself would have put paid to such complacency. What is sometimes forgotten is that when that conference ended and the Charter was signed, in June 1945, the war was over in Europe but not in the Far East. What Russia intended to do in its new East European sphere, and particularly in Poland, was becoming painfully clear. But the United States (which had not yet even tested its atomic bomb) was anxious to get Stalin to fulfil his promise to move troops eastward, enter the war with Japan and help bring it to an early end. It is not surprising that the tone of many American public statements at this time should have suggested greater hopes of continuing great-power harmony than were privately entertained. Given the additional need to depict the new international organisation as having a brighter prospect before it than the League of Nations, it is not difficult to see how the legend was born. It is less easy to understand its survival.

61

The Three did not shape a UN security system that depended on great-power unity because they were sure this unity would continue. They did it because they had no other idea how such a system could operate without endangering their own interests. Obviously, a system shaped by the Three themselves was not going to be one that involved them in surrendering any part of their vast military might to the control of the whole body of smaller states; or to that of the UN Secretary-General (they saw him as their creature, and a timid creature at that); or to the International Court or anybody else. But, equally obviously, the Three did not trust each other. The veto was to be their shield against each other as well as against the nose-count power of the lesser states. 'The Charter as it was meant to be' did not reflect any confident 'expectation' that the great powers 'would deal together with any breach of the peace by the smaller powers'. It reflected an expectation that the great powers were likely to quarrel.

According to the legend of expected unity, the Security Council was going to be 'the Cabinet of the world' – a phrase used by Harold Macmillan in 1962 when, as prime minister, he endorsed and even extended the theories that Home had propounded on his big day in Berwick in December 1961. Macmillan complained that: 'The whole foundation on which the UN was built has been undermined', because

> the effective operation of the Council has been made impossible by the Russian veto. . . . The Council has been made impotent, due to conditions having developed wholly contrary to what was thought likely at San Francisco in 1945.

If this farrago meant anything, it could mean only that the British at Dumbarton Oaks and San Francisco would have been horrified by any suggestion that there would be quarrels between great powers in the future. Which is obviously nonsense. But what else could Macmillan have meant? That the British in 1944–5 thought it likely that a veto-free UN would emerge from the San Francisco conference? That they thought it likely that great powers (including Britain) who had rammed the veto down the other states' throats, insisting that without it there would be no UN at all, would then suddenly renounce it? That the veto right to which the great powers had attached such vast importance would prove to be of no importance after all? None of these extraordinary 'conditions' would have been 'thought likely at San Francisco in 1945' by the British or anybody else.

The 'foundation on which the UN was built' – by the great powers – *was* the great-power veto. Whatever Russia had done, it hadn't exactly been undermining this foundation. Russia (and other powers, including Britain) had been using a right which all the great powers had depicted, at San Francisco, as their new foundation's one foundation. ('Thou art Veto, and upon this Rock I will build my church.') If the Council had been 'made impotent', this was done jointly by the Three when they laid the foundation stone in Georgetown in 1944.

*   *   *

Arguing with the Three at San Francisco meant standing up against a group of powers whose armies had already occupied, re-occupied or liberated twenty-eight countries in Europe, Africa and Asia – countries ranging from Norway to Greece to Ethiopia to Iraq to Burma to the Philippines – and were still on the move. Their forces were in Berlin, Rome, Vienna, Warsaw, Athens, Cairo, Baghdad, Rangoon, Manila, Asmara, Tripoli, Iceland, the Azores and more strategic islands and positions than you could find on an ordinary world map. Of the governments that were invited to take part in the San Francisco conference, a dozen had only recently returned to their capital cities in the wake of the great powers' advancing armies. Some of the conferring governments had been effectively constituted or reconstituted by one or more of the Three.

Poland was unable to obtain an invitation to San Francisco because the powers were at that moment disputing about how its new government should be constituted. Later, when Russia had won the dispute (by citing the nine points of the law conferred by possession), Poland was to be formally listed among the UN's fifty-one 'founders', although it had not even had a chance of commenting on the Dumbarton Oaks draft on which the Charter it signed had been based. These 'founders' also included the governments of two out of the Soviet Union's sixteen federated republics, Ukraine and

Byelorussia. As UN member 'states', these two have often been represented in the Assembly by their 'foreign ministers', whose method of occupying their time in between Assembly sessions remains a mystery to this day; and the Ukrainian SSR was even foisted on to the Security Council in 1948, despite the fact that this Soviet move evoked widespread indignation. (The Ukraine was unable to collect the necessary two-thirds majority in the Assembly voting until India withdrew its rival candidacy.)

As 'founders', the two Soviet republics sent delegations to San Francisco in 1945 and enjoyed the same formal status in the conference as, say, Canada or Brazil or Norway. The fact that these two subordinate Soviet entities were going to be 'founders' was another little thing that had been agreed between the Three (at Stalin's insistence) and presented to the conference as a virtual *fait accompli*. There was a confused dust-up about it at first, with Russia horse-trading its demand for additional 'founder' places against the admission of Argentina; but the Ukrainian and Byelorussian delegates were seated less than a week after opening day, and by the time the Charter was signed two months later they had taken root.

Anybody who got a close view of proceedings like these was left in little doubt about who were the real founders of the United Nations and the real writers of the Charter. And to no part of the Charter does this apply more particularly than to the sections bearing on the Security Council.

When the San Francisco conference opened on 25 April 1945 the Three had formally become the Four. China had co-sponsored the conference and the invitations to it, which were sent to all states that had declared war on the Axis powers.* But France had declined the honour of becoming a fifth sponsor. General de Gaulle resented the failure of the Three to invite him to join them at the Yalta meeting in February. *En principe*, admittedly, de Gaulle's government had declared itself willing to be a San Francisco sponsor; but only on condition that the conference should consider not only the

---

* There was a slight irony in the fact that the Charter provided for later adhesion by 'all other peace-loving states', whereas the original members qualified by virtue of their all being at war.

Dumbarton Oaks proposals but also France's suggested amendments to them. This condition was not acceptable to the Four. Presumably it was not meant to be acceptable to them: for at that point France had not yet suggested any amendments. However, a week after the opening of the conference France began to take part in the sponsoring powers' private talks at San Francisco. Though the French might, technically, still consider themselves to be 'observers' in the group, the Big Five had in fact made themselves manifest. At their biggest, the Five were the foreign ministers who attended the first few weeks of the conference: Edward Stettinius, Vyacheslav Molotov, Anthony Eden, T. V. Soong and Georges Bidault. When the Russian, British, Chinese and French ministers left San Francisco during May their places in the group were filled by Andrei Gromyko, Lord Halifax, Wellington Koo and Joseph Paul-Boncour; and the set-up was completed by the 'little five' – the team of deputies who maintained continuous contact in between meetings of their principals.

Neither France nor China showed any inclination to upset the great-power apple-cart. It rolled steadily through the conference's first month. One by one, the Dumbarton Oaks provisions relating to the Security Council were apple-polished into Charter articles. Nearly all the minor changes that were made concerned points that the Big Five did not consider important (though they were not always right about this: see, for instance, pages 87 and 88).

A good deal of haggling developed, however, over the proposed subordination to the UN of regional security arrangements. The Three had agreed at Dumbarton Oaks that

> no enforcement action should be taken under regional arrangements or by regional agencies without the authorisation of the Security Council.

This duly went into the Charter's Article 53. But an exception was tacked on, at the particular insistence of Russia and France, to permit for the time being action taken against a Second World War enemy state under arrangements directed against possible further aggression by such a state (meaning the treaties, directed against a renewed German threat, that Russia had concluded with Britain, France and several East European states). This amendment was jointly proposed by the sponsoring powers themselves, and with their

65

weight behind it it was soon accepted. But the Latin Americans now sought a similar exemption from Council control for action taken by the regional agency that was shortly to take the name of the Organisation of American States (OAS). The United States was sympathetic but worried; for it was clear that the Latins' demand was liable, in the American phrase, to open up a whole new can of worms. An exemption in favour of one regional group would almost inevitably bring a series of similar demands from other groups.

A British compromise formula was eventually accepted. A new Article 51 was inserted in the Charter, providing that

> Nothing in the present Charter shall impair the inherent right of individual or collective self-defence if an armed attack occurs against a Member of the United Nations, until the Security Council has taken the measures necessary to maintain international peace and security. . . .

It was not foreseen how, within a few years, Article 51 was to become an important juridical justification for the creation of the North Atlantic Treaty Organisation (Nato) and other defensive alliances that were neither strictly regional nor subject, under Article 53, to the risk that a Council veto might prevent them from taking action.

Much more spectacular, but much less productive, was the fight that developed at San Francisco over the great-power veto itself. Behind the sound and fury loomed the hard fact that the PPs had designed their whole Dumbarton Oaks plan around their veto privilege, and there was never the slightest chance that the smaller states could crack this foundation stone of the proposed world organisation. The American Senator Tom Connally has left his own account of how he dramatised the central issue:

> You may go home from San Francisco, if you wish, I cautioned the delegates, and report that you have defeated the veto. . . . But you can also say 'We *tore up the Charter'*. At that point I sweepingly ripped the Charter draft in my hands to shreds and flung the scraps upon the table.*

Rather than give here a detailed account of the abortive attempts to reduce the scope of the veto that were made at San Francsico by a

* *My Name is Tom Connally*, New York, 1954.

valiant group of delegates from smaller states, I have preferred to mention elsewhere in this book some aspects of the 1945 proceedings that were to prove relevant to actual situations later encountered by the Security Council. What should be recorded here, however, is the one outstanding feature of the San Francisco exchanges. While no headway was made by those who sought to whittle the veto down, there was at one stage the alarming prospect that its scope was going to be extended still further.

The 'Yalta formula' agreed by the Three, which became Article 27 of the Charter, stipulated that non-procedural Council decisions would require seven affirmative votes 'including the concurring votes of the permanent members'; but that a party to a dispute should abstain from voting on a Chapter Six decision about pacific settlement of that dispute. (It was not foreseen at San Francisco that the Charter ink would soon fade at the words 'concurring' and 'dispute' – pages 85 and 88.)

On May 23 the sponsoring powers were presented with a questionnaire, in which the other states posed a large number of questions that might be summarised by a single one: 'What do you mean by non-procedural?' The Five (France having, for practical purposes, joined the sponsoring four) started to prepare their joint reply. They managed fairly well until they came to Question 19, which was the sixty-four-dollar one, bearing on the 'double veto', as it was to become known:

> 19. In case a decision has to be taken as to whether a certain point is a procedural matter, is that preliminary question to be considered in itself as a procedural matter, or is the veto applicable to such preliminary question?

The veto was applicable, said the Russians, to the dismay of the other PPs. These others pointed out that Russia had already agreed to the inclusion in the draft of the Five's joint reply of a paragraph that read:

> 3. Since the Council has the right by a procedural vote to decide its own rules of procedure, it follows that no individual member of the Council can alone prevent a consideration and discussion by the Council of a dispute or situation brought to its attention. . . .

Thus, under Paragraph 3, a veto could not be used to prevent discussion. But, according to Russia's response to Question 19, it could.

The 'little five' deputies passed the problem up to their masters. Halifax asked Gromyko point blank whether he accepted Paragraph 3. Gromyko hedged. Obviously he needed to get instructions from Moscow. The other four could only wait till he got them.

On June 2 Senator Arthur Vandenberg wrote in his diary:

> The *big* crisis broke last night. Gromyko was ready with his answer from Moscow. . . . The answer: Russia demands her 'veto' even on *free speech* in the Council. . . . When Gromyko made his report to us in the Penthouse, we all knew that we had reached the 'zero hour' of this great adventure. . . . Did it mean the immediate break-up of the Conference? Did it mean going on to a Charter without Russia? . . . Stettinius adjourned the meeting until tomorrow. Meanwhile he phoned Truman and Hull, both of whom said we must irrevocably reject the Soviet position.*

At the next meeting of the Five Stettinius told Gromyko that the conference would never accept, nor would the American Senate ratify, a Charter that included a veto on mere discussion. Gromyko undertook to consult Moscow again. Meanwhile Stettinius, at Truman's suggestion, also got in touch with Moscow – with the American ambassador there, Averell Harriman, and Harry Hopkins, whom Truman had sent to Russia as a special envoy. He told Harriman and Hopkins that the Soviet demand would 'make a farce' of the United Nations, and instructed them to see Stalin personally and urgently:

> Please tell him in no uncertain words that this country could not possibly join an organisation based on so unreasonable an interpretation. . . . We will have to take the necessary steps to wind up the conference here if we have nothing favourable from you in this regard.

On June 6 Harriman and Hopkins saw Stalin and Molotov. Stalin gave the impression that the whole thing was news to him. When it had been explained he said it was an unimportant matter; and he told Molotov that the American position was quite acceptable. Next day at San Francisco, Gromyko duly gave way. On June 8 Stettinius was

* *The Private Papers of Senator Vandenberg*, Boston, 1952.

able to present to the conference the five PPs' agreed 'San Francisco Statement' on Council voting procedures.

The Statement made discussion veto-free all right. It included the original wording of Paragraph 3 on this point. But, that having been said, it gave Russia the rest of the game in regard to Question 19. The answer to that question was that

> . . . the decision regarding the preliminary question as to whether or not such a matter is procedural must be taken by a vote of seven members of the Security Council, including the concurring votes of the permanent members.

In the *New York Times* James Reston commented that the original dispute over the veto, between great powers and smaller states, 'has been overwhelmed by the Big Five dispute . . . the crisis over this has been just serious enough to persuade the small powers to take the "discussion" and forget about the rest'. This was true in the sense that freedom of Council discussion was as much as the complaining states could get the PPs to permit in their joint Statement. But the game wasn't quite over. The smaller states managed to keep it open-ended. They simply refused to let the conference accept or endorse the five great powers' Statement. With the redoubtable Herbert Evatt of Australia in the lead, Belgium, Canada, Chile, Mexico, the Netherlands, New Zealand and Norway all voiced their objections.

Tom Connally did his paper-tearing act, and the Five issued what in effect was an ultimatum to the conference: accept Article 27 as it stands, or there will be no United Nations at all. Australia's amendment was voted down, but only by 20 votes to 10, with a significant 20 abstentions or deliberate absences. On June 20 Article 27 was reluctantly approved. But the interpretation of it given in the five powers' Statement bound only those five. It had no binding force for the other states represented at San Francisco in 1945; and it has none for any of the Council's elected members today.

The UN's experience has shown that the relationship between the Council (especially its PP members) and the Secretary-General is of the first importance. But the Three seemed unaware of this at Dumbarton Oaks and only dimly aware of it at San Francisco.

Which was decidedly fortunate. Happily busied with their grand scheme for military enforcement through the Military Staff Committee, which in the end proved to be wasted labour, they never even glimpsed the possibility that the new world organisation's chief official would have to run its international forces. (At one point, in 1964, U Thant was responsible for three UN forces at the same time, not to mention two important observer operations.) This unawareness on the great powers' part made it possible for other states to gouge out a greater scope, and a wider independence, for the Secretary-General than the Three would have permitted if they had seen what was coming.

The draft that emerged from the Stettinius–Cadogan–Gromyko sessions at Dumbarton Oaks in 1944 said very little about the Secretary-General, and nothing at all about the Secretariat. It contained nothing that remotely resembled the Charter's Article 100, which very bluntly asserts the Secretariat's international loyalty and forbids governments to seek to influence the UN's staff. The only positive point the Three put into their draft was the wording that was duly reproduced in the Charter's Article 99, giving the Secretary-General the right to

> bring to the attention of the Security Council any matter which, in his opinion, may threaten the maintenance of international peace and security.

Article 99 has turned out to give the Secretary-General a remarkable amount of leverage, particularly in regard to the Council. The article was not to be explicitly applied until Hammarskjöld used it in 1960 to bring the Council into urgent activity and launch the Congo operation. But it was often wielded as a sheathed weapon before that. As early as 1946 Trygve Lie invoked it to support his assertion of a right to investigate a potentially dangerous situation, even when the Council itself could not agree to authorise an inquiry.

Because the scope of the Secretary-General's work has been so strikingly enlarged since 1946, it has become natural for people to recall, for instance, how Roosevelt, at an early stage in his thinking about the UN, had thrown in the idea that a 'World's Moderator' should head the organisation; or how Herbert Evatt of Australia, who as foreign minister led his country's delegation at San Francisco, argued that 'the Secretary-General is intended to be far more than an administrative officer'. It is perfectly clear that Article 99 gave him a political role. It is equally clear, however, that when the Three put the Article 99 wording into their Dumbarton Oaks draft the last thing they had in mind was to launch the UN's chief official into a far-ranging political orbit. What they were mainly thinking about was the League's discovery that, all too often, no member government was willing to earn illwill by asking the Council to discuss a threatening problem. The British, who got the Article 99 bit into the Dumbarton Oaks proposals, wanted a lightning-conductor, a device that might make it unnecessary for any state to take on the responsibility of drawing attention to something nasty in somebody else's woodshed. They got this device – but they also got more than they had bargained for.

At San Francisco the great powers' concern about the Secretary-Generalship was concentrated on making sure that it would be filled by a man of their own choice. Vyacheslav Molotov opened the bidding with a proposal that the post should be filled by a national of one of the five PPs, that there should be four 'elected' deputies who would in practice be provided by the other four PPs, that all five men should be limited to two-year terms and that they should not be eligible for immediate reappointment. This formula for total domination of the Secretariat by the Five struck the other four of them as just a little too obvious. So the proposal that the Five jointly made to the conference was for three-year terms, with eligibility for re-election. But the great powers held firmly to the idea that the Security Council should choose the candidates, who would then be put to the Assembly for approval; and that the great-power veto would operate when the Council made its choice. They beat down the objections to this procedure that were voiced by other states, notably Australia, Belgium, Canada and the Netherlands. These four all saw the Secretary-General's independence as being jeopardised by the great-power formula. The Dutchman went so far as to say that he feared only a nonentity would accept the job on such terms. His protests at least had the effect that the conference agreed not to fix the length of the term of office at all.

At this stage it was still widely assumed that the UN's top official post, and most if not all of the deputies' posts, would be filled by PP nationals. Canada and New Zealand spearheaded the attack on the great powers' proposals about the 'election' of deputies. If the Secretary-General could not choose his own deputies, the Canadian complained, he could hardly perform his duties properly; the set-up would mean 'the practical domination of the Secretariat by the great powers'. The New Zealander warned that the great powers' scheme would ensure instability and 'produce a crisis in the Secretariat at the beginning of its work'.

The British gave way; then the Americans; Russia held out on the question of deputies to the last, but was voted down once the PP front had cracked. The Charter was worded with no mention of deputies at all. Following through after this victory, Canada and New Zealand secured the inclusion in the Charter of the Article 100 wording on the Secretariat's international loyalty. Once this article had been approved, it was impossible to revive any idea of the great powers filling the Secretariat's top ranks with men openly serving their own governments' interests. But Russia, at least, did not give up once the Charter had been signed.

Later in 1945, when the UN's Preparatory Commission met in London, Andrei Gromyko proposed that there should be not one Secretariat but several – one for each of the main UN organs (Assembly, Security Council, Economic and Social Council, Trusteeship Council). This was scarcely compatible with what had already been written into the Charter. But Gromyko's proposal gave him a bargaining position that enabled him to obtain the other powers' agreement that the department servicing the Security Council would be headed by a nominee of the Soviet government. And so it has been, ever since, except for one brief interlude.

Chapter Four

When the chest was opened

I have described the setting in which the Security Council has staged its meetings for nearly twenty years: a purpose-built, roomy, comfortable and, in its way, very impressive setting. But it was not always thus. The Council's first five years of life were spent in extemporised accommodations in London, Paris and several parts of New York.

The first horseshoe-shaped table around which the members gathered was in Church House, Westminster – not much more than a stone's throw from the Houses of Parliament. No stones were thrown during the first purely ceremonial meeting that was held on 17 January 1946. But two days later they began to rain in through the Church House windows. It had been optimistically thought that the Council would not face any serious work until it had left London. As things turned out, by the time it ended its month in London with the meeting of February 16 it had tangled with four acutely controversial cases, witnessed some doughty duelling between Ernest Bevin and Andrei Vishinsky (both of whom were begged by Trygve Lie to moderate their language), and seen Vishinsky, on the last of the London days, use the first veto.

On moving to New York in February, the Council at first found itself homeless. It met in the Henry Hudson Hotel; it met at 610 Fifth Avenue; and then it (and the Secretariat) found refuge in the Bronx, at Hunter College. The young ladies of Hunter did not have to be turned out so that the Council could have the use of their gym, for the College had been taken over during the war by the US Navy, which had only just finished with it. The Council first met there on March 25; and two days later Hunter College had the doubtful privilege of seeing Andrei Gromyko stage the first Soviet walkout from the Council.

The Council has an Elizabethan habit of blending elements of fairly coarse farce into moments of heavy drama. Trygve Lie has left a felicitous account of how, on March 27, only the keen eye of a Secretariat man saved Gromyko from stalking sternly out of the Hunter gym and into the crowd of press photographers who were waiting to record this historic Soviet gesture, with his zipper open. On April 9 Gromyko returned to the Council; but on the 23rd he withdrew for the second time from its objectionable debates about the presence and activities of Russian troops in Iran. This time, however, he had adjusted his dress before leaving.

In August 1946 the Council was able to move again, to the more spacious Sperry Gyroscope plant at Lake Success, forty-five minutes away from Manhattan on Long Island, where an air-conditioned chamber had been specially and speedily built for it. And at Lake Success it enjoyed some respite from its wanderings, for there it stayed through most of the next four years, experiencing, among other things, Yakov Malik's January 1950 walkout and the high drama of the first days of the Korean war.

'Nothing succeeds Lake Success' became an all too hard-worked pun. What actually succeeded Lake Success was the present permanent headquarters at Turtle Bay, between Manhattan's First Avenue and the East River. But the Long Island years were interrupted in 1948 when the Assembly, showing a sensitivity about an American presidential election year which was later to wear off, chose to hold its session at the Palais de Chaillot in Paris. The Security Council was drawn into its wake.

So it was in Paris that the Council learnt of the murder of the United Nations' first Mediator in Palestine, Count Folke Bernadotte. In Paris it ratified Lie's appointment of Ralph Bunche to continue Bernadotte's work. And Paris saw the first attempts to dissolve the deadlock over West Berlin, which the Russians had begun to blockade during the summer of 1948. But the Council had been back at Lake Success for some weeks when Philip Jessup of the United States, finding an opportunity to speak privately with Malik in the delegates' lounge just before a Council meeting in February 1949, thereby opened the dialogue that slowly developed, through a series of less casual conversations, into the shaping of the agreement that ended the blockade in May.

*   *   *

In London on 10 January 1946 the United Nations General Assembly met for the first time. One of the first formal actions it took at this session in the Central Hall, Westminster, was to elect Australia, Brazil, Egypt, Mexico, Netherlands and Poland as the first non-permanent members of the Security Council. A formal action, because these six elections had been agreed in advance, on the basis of the private understanding about regional distribution between the five privileged permanent members (PPs) that was to become known as the 'London agreement'.

What had not been fixed in advance was the choice of the first Secretary-General. The PPs had kept this choice in their own hands. At Dumbarton Oaks they had agreed that the Assembly should be allowed to go through the motions of 'electing' a Secretary-General, but should in practice vote only on the candidate whom the Council 'recommended'. And this recommendation was made subject to the great-power veto. So there was no point even in consulting the whole Council until the PPs had chosen their man. While the newborn Council, from January 17 onward, began its meetings at Church House, the Five got together privately.

The pre-eminence among the Five of the Big Two emerged quite clearly in this first week of the Council's existence. Edward Stettinius and Andrei Vishinsky put forward the names of, respectively, Lester Pearson of Canada and Stanoje Simic, the Jugoslav ambassador in Washington. Vishinsky knew that Simic would not be acceptable, and he soon made clear that Pearson would not be. Privately, the Americans and the Russians indicated to Trygve Lie, then foreign minister of Norway, that he would be acceptable to both of them. (Both had embarrassed Lie, only two weeks earlier, by the way they involved him against his will in a contest for the Assembly presidency, which was won by Paul-Henri Spaak of Belgium.) There were, in the end, no other serious candidatures. Earlier, General

75

Eisenhower, who had seemed to be the candidate of Philip Noel-Baker and the *Daily Express*, had declined to be considered. Stettinius called a PP meeting on January 28 and formally proposed Trygve Lie. Andrei Gromyko, substituting for Vishinsky, at once agreed. The Chinese agreed. Joseph Paul-Boncour agreed provisionally and squared it with his foreign minister, Georges Bidault, on the telephone that evening. As Trygve Lie recorded,* 'my wartime friend and old trade union colleague, Ernest Bevin, was finally brought around' a little after midnight, in Stettinius's suite at Claridges Hotel. On the afternoon of the 29th the full Council, at Stettinius's proposal, made it a unanimous recommendation. Norman Makin, the Australian who had become the Council's first president, wired to Lie, who had returned to Oslo, and got his acceptance. On February 1 the Assembly voted 46 to 3 for the appointment; and Lie was sworn in on the 2nd, to serve a five-year term.

The right to fix the length of the Secretary-General's term was one little thing that had been left to the Assembly – thanks to the Dutchman who had made a hole in the great powers' dyke at San Francisco (page 71). A few years later Russia, for one, was going to regret that it had failed to plug the Dutchman's hole.

By June 1950 Trygve Lie had so frankly stated the case for giving the UN China seat to the government that controlled China that he was branded as a communist 'partisan' by some 'China lobby' Americans. Ting-fu Tsiang, the Taipeh China councilman, announced on the eve of the Korean war that he would veto any move to reappoint Lie for a second term after his first expired in February 1951. (He ignored the fact that Lie had already said that he would not seek reappointment.) But Tsiang said he would consent to a one-year extension of Lie's original term. (He also ignored the fact that his consent was not necessary for this.) Within a few weeks, Russia had unleashed a violent campaign against Lie because, in *Pravda*'s words, he had become an 'active accomplice of American intervention in Korea'. When the Council held several private meetings about the secretary-generalship in October it was Yakov Malik who vetoed the proposal (backed by nine members) to reappoint Lie

* *In the Cause of Peace*, London and New York, 1954.

for a new term, while Tsiang merely abstained. By now it was plain that Russia had the simple aim of 'punishing' Lie for his attitude to the Korean war. Conversely, America, Britain and France seemed bent on ensuring his continuation in office, despite his own doubts, in order to deny Russia a political victory. Their foreign ministers, Dean Acheson, Ernest Bevin and Robert Schuman, had each personally assured Lie in September that they wished him to stay on. Lie, with real reluctance, agreed to remain available, but not for more than another three years.

After Malik's veto on October 12 the American-led group pressed for an Assembly debate on a draft resolution that would extend Lie's original term for three years. The Russians tried every kind of delaying device, calling a series of further private Council meetings, issuing warnings that if Lie remained in office they would not recognise him to be Secretary-General, and eventually announcing quite frankly that they would accept any nominee whatsoever so long as it was not Lie.

In the Council on October 18 Sir Benegal Rau of India suggested that each Council member should put forward two names, from which the PPs would extract a 'short list' by retaining only those who would not be vetoed. The effect, of course, would be to rule out Lie; so Malik was enthusiastic. But Arne Sunde of Norway, bluntly accusing Russia of seeking 'to punish Mr Lie' and pointing out that nine Council members had already voted for him, argued that 'his elimination would thus be tantamount to a victory for North Korea'. Ales Bebler of Jugoslavia likewise flatly opposed the Indian plan, and Rau withdrew it. Cuba then suggested that the Council call on the PPs to meet and try to agree on a candidate. This could hardly mean agreement on Lie, so Sunde, Bebler, Sir Gladwyn Jebb and Senator Warren Austin received the suggestion coldly; but it was approved by the necessary seven votes, and two private PP meetings were held. In the course of these meetings Tsiang proposed General Carlos Romulo of the Philippines; Yakov Malik proposed Charles Malik of Lebanon (no relation), Benegal Rau and Luis Padilla Nervo of Mexico; and Warren Austin created quite a stir by announcing that, since Russia had vetoed Lie, America would if necessary veto any other candidate.

No American veto was needed in the end. Rau and Padilla declined to be candidates. When Romulo and Charles Malik were voted on, at Yakov Malik's insistence, in the private Council meeting on the 25th, each was backed only by Russia, Taipeh China, Egypt and India. On the 30th Yakov Malik was voted down in the Council seven to one when he tried to stave off the Assembly vote by calling for further Council talks.

Vishinsky, who was then attending the Assembly as foreign minister, held a press conference in the Security Council chamber at which he accused Lie of wanting to keep his job simply for the money, and Rau of backing out simply because of Austin's veto threat ('Sir Benegal waved his arms and maybe his feet, he was so scared'). When a correspondent asked if he had any more candidates in mind, Vishinsky replied: 'I would be glad to nominate you.'

A few hours later the Russians made a last desperate bid and approached Lester Pearson – whom they had turned down in 1946, and whom they would veto in 1953. This time it was he who turned them down. On November 1 the Assembly gave Lie a three-year extension by a 46–5 vote, after hearing Pearson deliver a cutting exposure of the real motives behind the Russian witch-hunt.

'There shall be established a Military Staff Committee. . . . It shall be responsible, under the Security Council, for the strategic direction of any armed forces placed at the disposal of the Security Council. . . . [It] shall consist of the Chiefs of Staff of the permanent members of the Security Council, or their representatives'.

So the Three had agreed at Dumbarton Oaks. So ran Article 47 of the San Francisco Charter. So it still runs. But the Military Staff Committee itself has proved one of the great non-runners. With professional punctilio, it has been marking time on the spot for twenty-four years.

Second only to the sacred veto itself, the MSC had been the apple of the great powers' collective eye. Or perhaps the apple of their teeth. They were not only going to give the UN the 'teeth' that the League had lacked; they were also going to make sure that the actual biting was done by themselves. Any enforcement action under

Chapter Seven would be handled by this team of senior officers appointed by the five PPs.

To be fair to the Russians, they had proposed at Dumbarton Oaks that the MSC should represent not just the Five but the whole membership of the Security Council. It was the British who argued most firmly that the UN's top brass should be provided only by the permanent members. On this point Alexander Cadogan prevailed over Andrei Gromyko. At San Francisco the British once more emerged victorious, this time over the Philippines. The furthest the great powers were willing to go was that the MSC might set up 'regional sub-committees', in which the lesser states might take their modest places; and that it would invite such states 'to be associated with it' when it decided to take command of their forces or to order other forces into their territory.

In January 1946 the Security Council, in only the second week of its own existence, conjured up the Military Staff Committee. The Five sent a dazzling array of generals, admirals and air marshals to London for the first meetings of what was surely going to be a uniquely impressive series. At the last of the Council's London meetings, on February 16, it directed the MSC to go to work on the shaping of the agreements by which, under Article 43, UN member states were to make armed forces available to the Council.

General Matthew Ridgway of America, Air Chief Marshal Sir Guy Garrod of Britain, General Pierre Billotte of France, Generals Vasiliev and Sharapov of Russia, General Ho of China and numerous other officers of exalted rank and great distinction embarked on their labours, and laboured mightily all through 1946 and on into the next year. In December 1946 the Assembly, unanimously and a little tetchily, asked the Council to 'accelerate as much as possible' the organising of the forces that were to be at its disposal. In February 1947 the Council passed the buck along to the MSC, setting an April deadline for it to report how far it had got. On April 30 the soldiers duly reported: they were deadlocked on sixteen points.

Boiled down, the main conflicts of military opinion were two. The Russian generals insisted that the Five must all make exactly matched contributions of armed forces to the Security Council's 'teeth'; the other powers held that the contributions should be generally comparable, but that the proportions could vary as between the different arms – land, sea and air. As to the size of the forces that the Council was thought to need, the Americans held out for much larger figures than the others. If the Council was to keep the peace the Americans thought there should be 3,800 military aircraft at its disposal; the other powers would settle for around 1,200. The Americans wanted 20 army divisions, the French 16, the Russians 12 and the British 8 to 12.

Perhaps somebody forgot to tell the generals, admirals and air marshals that – as already noted on page 59 – the Chapter Seven type of 'enforcement' was going to be applied only to those few and not very formidable countries that would not be protected by a PP veto. In the circumstances, if the Council had merely been provided with, say, three or four more divisions than the Pope it could probably have done all that it was likely to be asked to do. The problem the generals could not solve was a quite unreal one. But the deadlock, unfortunately, was real. It reflected the great powers' rapid loss of faith in the grandiose security structure that they had shaped at Dumbarton Oaks and imposed on their doubtful fellow members at San Francisco. In 1948 both the MSC and the Council gave up even pretending that they were still trying to make Article 43 a reality. For some strange reason, however, the great powers did not give up the pretence that the Military Staff Committee was still a reality. For more than twenty years the Five (including Taipeh China) have annually appointed shining phalanxes of generals and admirals and air marshals to the MSC, and have maintained the military–legal fiction of its existence by solemnly staging regular fortnightly meetings. If you think Lewis Carroll was over-indulging in fantasy when he invented the Mad Hatter's tea party you should see what the governments of the great powers require their military men to do every two weeks in New York.*

But of course the slightest suggestion that anything should be done to carry out the basic intention of the Charter drew from

* In 1970 the members of the five-power Military Staff Committee included two air force generals, one air vice-marshal, five army generals, one vice-admiral, two rear-admirals, and a small platoon of colonels, group captains and naval captains.

the great powers' tea table a ringing cry of 'No room! No room!'. In 1948, when the killing in Palestine was going merrily ahead despite a series of appeals from the Security Council, Trygve Lie tentatively floated the idea that a very small 'United Nations guard force' might be recruited to help out, in Palestine and elsewhere, until the great powers could get around to providing the Council with something more in keeping with all their big talk at San Francisco. Far from welcoming this suggestion, the great powers treated it with deep suspicion. When, in May 1950, Lie made a last personal effort to interest Stalin and Molotov in the idea, they simply dismissed it as an 'Anglo-American' proposition. This at least gave Lie the rueful satisfaction of being able to assure the Russian leaders (and Vishinsky, who was also present, was obliged to confirm his assurance) that the Americans, far from backing his proposal, were only too likely to share the Soviet objections to it.

'The Security Council, with the assistance of the Military Staff Committee ... should have the responsibility for formulating plans for the establishment of a system of regulation of armaments. . . .' Another precept solemnly agreed by the Three at Dumbarton Oaks, and solemnly embodied in the Charter's Article 26. But in real life the Council ceased even to affect an interest in the problem after some ten years of sporadic effort, and left it in the hands of the Assembly. This was neither the intention of the UN's real founders, nor that of its alleged ones. At Dumbarton Oaks the Three assigned to the Council a mandatory duty to tackle the disarmament problem; to the Assembly, they merely accorded a rather vague permission to discuss, if it wished to, 'the principles governing disarmament and the regulation of armaments' (Article 11). If the Assembly wanted to waffle about principles, very well, let it do so; the real job was to be the Council's responsibility, and the Council, in carrying out its duty to draw up plans for a regulatory system, would have the hard-nosed help of those magnificent men in that high flying machine, the five-power MSC. But the MSC never got off the ground.

If it hadn't been for Andrei Gromyko the Assembly would not even have been given a specific right to discuss armaments. At Dumbarton Oaks, Stettinius and Cadogan thought it would be unnecessary and confusing to give it any such right; but they yielded to their Soviet colleague. At San Francisco there was no sign of interest among the mass of member states, and the Three saw their draft wordings go into the Charter virtually without discussion.

A few weeks later an atomic bomb was dropped on Hiroshima. The Assembly, finding itself born in the first months of the new age of nuclear weaponry, took the first possible opportunity of using its rights under Article 11. The first resolution adopted during the first Assembly session, on 24 January 1946, established the UN Atomic Energy Commission. But the Assembly showed no desire to oust the Council from its constitutional primacy in this field. The new commission was instructed to report to the Council; and in point of fact it virtually *was* the Council, for it consisted of all members of the Council, with the addition of Canada when Canada was not a Council member.

A year later the Council, at the Assembly's urging, endowed itself with a second *doppelgänger*, the Commission for Conventional Armaments – consisting of the same members as the Council. The Council's two shadows ran vainly alongside it until Russia withdrew from both of them in 1950 – ostensibly as part of the Soviet protest at Taipeh's retention of the China seat – after which they were faded out and replaced in January 1952 by a single Disarmament Commission intended to combine their two tasks. Its members were, of course, the same as those of the Security Council, plus Canada. At this point the Assembly began to show signs of impatience. It told the new Disarmament Commission to report not only to the Council (i.e. to itself) but also to the Assembly. In 1953 the Assembly urged the still deadlocked commission to try setting up a small sub-committee. A five-member sub-committee was duly formed, comprising America, Britain, Canada, France and Russia, and between 1954 and 1957 it held an extensive series of private meetings at Lancaster House in London.

But now the first Soviet sputnik arrived; and the Security Council quietly departed. The Russians would no longer talk about armaments in a body as heavily tilted westward as the Council, its 'shadow' commissions or the five-power sub-committee. The 1957 Assembly enlarged the Disarmament Commission to twenty-five

82

members, but Russia still refused to play. The 1958 Assembly expanded the commission to include all UN members – who by then numbered eighty-two. Instead of shadow Councils, there was now a shadow Assembly.

Actual negotiation soon passed to the Geneva disarmament committees, first of ten, then of seventeen and now of twenty-five members. But the Geneva groups' activities and reports have been debated at the regular annual Assembly sessions, where the disarmament items have become prominent features in the agenda. The Council has disengaged. So much for Article 26 and the original intentions of the Three.*

*   *   *

I have quoted a British prime minister as saying (in 1962) that 'the effective operation of the Council has been made impossible by the Russian [sic] veto'. How much truth, if any, is there in this fairly sweeping generalisation?

An admirable analysis has been made by Sydney Bailey of the 109 vetoes that were used in the Council's first twenty-two years, 1946–67.† I cannot do justice to many of the nice points in his study; but it is impossible to resist the temptation to try to summarise some of his most revealing findings. Only three of the cases listed by Bailey are 'double vetoes' (in which a veto is used to ensure that the main resolution is not classed as procedural and veto-free). The *last* of these concerned the 1948 communist coup in Czechoslovakia. In the first of the three cases (in 1946, concerning Spain) France joined Russia in preventing 'procedural' treatment.

The list includes the two vetoes used jointly by Britain and France in October 1956 against calls for a cease-fire in Egypt and an Israeli withdrawal; France's veto over Indonesia in 1947, China's over Mongolia in 1955 and Britain's over Rhodesia in 1963 (pages 28, 99, 118 and 227). All the other vetoes listed are Russian. (America's

---

* But see pages 335 to 339 for intimations of the Council's prospects of solving its re-entry problem.

† *Voting in the Security Council*, Indiana University Press, 1970. Also *Veto in the Security Council*, Carnegie Endowment for International Peace, 1968 (an earlier version of a relevant part of the same book).

first veto was not used until 1970; see page 260.) Of the 104 Russian vetoes, 51 were used to block admissions to UN membership. Of the seventeen candidates who were thus temporarily blocked, all but two (South Korea and South Vietnam) got in later. Russia vetoed the reappointment of Trygve Lie in 1950 – but the Assembly then extended his term (page 78): it vetoed a move to replace the resigning Lie with Lester Pearson in 1953, but, two weeks later, Russia accepted Hammarskjöld. Russia vetoed five resolutions on arms control, the last of these being in 1949. It used nine vetoes on East European questions; except in the 1956 Hungary case, these were all before the end of 1948 (as to Czechoslovakia 1968, see page 309). It used 4 vetoes over Spain in 1946, 3 over Indonesia between 1947 and 1949, 5 over the Congo in 1960–1 and 5 on Israel–Arab questions between 1954 and 1966. In the first 5 of Bailey's 22 years there were 47 Soviet vetoes; in the last 5 years, only 4.

Russia has unquestionably abused the right of veto. It has not limited its use to matters of real substance and of direct concern to Russia itself, but has vetoed drafts which it claimed were too weak for its taste; others which it said were too strong, but which in fact were utterly innocuous; others, again, that were merely distasteful to states Russia wished to placate.

But, as Bailey shows, if you set aside cases where a veto merely caused delay (as with most of the admissions of states to the UN), cases where a majority Council vote had pretty much the same effect as a formal resolution, cases that were taken over by the Assembly and so on – including certain exquisitely ineffective vetoes (e.g. vetoes of amendments to resolutions that then failed to get adopted) – there would then appear to be only 26 vetoes, in 22 years, that actually prevented something happening. Of these, 24 were Russian, 1 British and 1 French. And even these vetoes, in most cases, merely prevented the placing on record of a resolution that was not going to produce any action.

The UN was not prevented by the veto from organising international forces in Egypt, the Congo and Cyprus, from placing observers in Indonesia, Greece, Palestine, Lebanon, Yemen, India and Pakistan, from conducting investigations, calling for cease-fires and helping to bring about cease-fires or withdrawals in most of the

84

conflict situations it was asked to tackle over these years. And there is no recorded case in which a failure to achieve a real settlement of a dispute or conflict can be attributed simply to the use of the veto.

Let us now look at some ways in which, since 1946, the great powers have both widened and narrowed the scope of the veto in practice.

In 1951 the Security Council stopped discussing international disputes. This was one of the fairly numerous things that the far-sighted governments of the great powers had failed to foresee. At Dumbarton Oaks in 1944 the teams led by Stettinius, Gromyko and Cadogan had set out the Council's duties and powers, along the lines that the Charter would duly follow, under two main heads. Under one head came the action to be taken when international peace was threatened or broken: these elaborate provisions for 'enforcement', involving the Military Staff Committee, made up the Charter's Chapter Seven and, as we have seen, were almost all fated to lapse into innocuous desuetude. The other head, which stands over the Charter's Chapter Six, was: 'Pacific Settlement of Disputes'.

What could not be agreed at Dumbarton Oaks was the great powers' voting rights in the Council when they were parties to a dispute. The Three agreed that each power must be able to veto any enforcement action; but the Americans and British held that a PP should not have the right to veto a mere Council recommendation about a dispute in which it was itself involved. The Russians held out for a comprehensive right of veto over everything except procedural decisions. Stalin, Roosevelt and Churchill came back to this problem at Yalta in February 1945. On February 6 they seemed to be dead-locked. On the 7th Stalin and Molotov did one of their volte-faces and accepted the Anglo-American formula which now appears in the Charter's Article 27: that 'in decisions under Chapter Six . . . a party to a dispute shall abstain from voting'. This became part of the 'Yalta formula' on Council voting which the lesser members of the San Francisco conference, after voicing a good deal of indignation, were obliged to accept.

The great powers, of course, made much of their virtuous renunciation of the veto in disputes that involved them. Some of the other states' spokesmen, and particularly the blunt Herbert Evatt, then foreign minister of Australia, were sceptical about this as about other aspects of the Yalta formula. Less than a year after San Francisco, their scepticism was to prove amply justified.

In the first weeks of the Council's life Britain and France denied that the complaint by Syria and Lebanon about British and French troops was a 'dispute'; and Russia acted on the assumption that Iran's complaint about the presence and activities of Soviet troops in Iran did not make Russia a party to a 'dispute'. Syria, Lebanon and Iran had all described the matters they brought to the Council as disputes. But the first months of 1946 seemed to be witnessing the establishment of a rule that might be stated as follows: When a small state has a dispute with a great power, and brings that dispute to the Council, the great power will say it is not a dispute, and will thus retain its right to vote on the dispute, whatever the small state – or the Charter – may say. Which leaves one to wonder what all the pulling and hauling that went on between Dumbarton Oaks and Yalta had been about.

Things picked up a bit in 1947. When Britain brought to the Council its complaint against Albania arising from the damaging of two ships by mines laid in the Corfu Channel, the British frankly called the dispute a dispute, and refrained from voting except on procedural points. Then two non-permanent members of the Council set examples worthy of emulation by the PPs. In 1950, 1951 and 1952, when the Council voted on the Indo-Pakistani dispute while first India and then Pakistan was an elected member, both countries refrained from voting.

But meanwhile the when-is-a-dispute-a-dispute question came to a frothy head when Israel complained to the Council in 1951 about Egypt's action in restricting the passage of merchant shipping through the Suez Canal. A good many governments of maritime nations had already complained to Egypt about these restrictions. Egypt contended that the matter was quite clearly a dispute, and that any state that had complained to Egypt was a party to that dispute; and therefore the obligation under Article 27 to abstain from voting applied to no less than five members of the current Council – America, Britain, France, Netherlands and Turkey. There was a

86

chorus of protest from the five councilmen who were thus involved in a dispute about whether they were involved in a dispute. They pointed out, quite accurately, that if they were barred from voting the Council would be 'paralysed'. Of its eleven members, only six would be left who were qualified to vote at all, and it would be impossible to muster the seven votes needed to adopt any resolution. The indignant five proceeded to use the votes which Egypt had sought to deny them; and with the aid of these votes the Council duly adopted a resolution on 1 September 1951, which called upon Egypt not to obstruct the passage through the Suez Canal of ships carrying cargo to or from Israel. Egypt took no notice of the resolution. But we should not follow the Egyptian example. Apart from its actual content, this resolution deserved attention in at least two other respects. Adopted only two years after Russia's enthusiastic welcoming of Israel to UN membership, it belonged to a period when the Arabs could not yet count on Russia to veto any Council resolution they disliked. The Council that adopted this one was not 'paralysed by the Russian veto' − yet its call to Cairo went unheard, and that was even in the days before Colonel Nasser came to power and to the presidency.

The second significant aspect of the September 1951 resolution was that the councilmen would not accept the view that they were bound by the Article 27 ban on disputants voting. They rejected also Egypt's suggestion that the International Court should be asked to give an opinion on the point. And since then the Council has shuddered away from all idea of describing the disputes brought before it as disputes.

Does this mean that Chapter Six of the Charter has followed Chapter Seven into near-oblivion? Not quite. Fortunately some of the smaller member states showed more foresight than the great powers in the UN's formative stages. In the draft that the Three had worked out at Dumbarton Oaks the Council's power to 'recommend appropriate procedures or methods of adjustment' applied only to disputes. The Council could 'investigate' any potentially dangerous situation, but only if there was a dispute could it make any recommendations. At San Francisco, in response to a blunt Australian objection, this was changed to enable the Council to make recom-

87

mendations not only about a dispute but also about 'a situation of like nature'. So it is a Situation of Like Nature that is usually in question when the Council meets, debates and adopts resolutions – except on the very rare occasions when it dips a cautious toe into Chapter Seven (see Chapter Seven). And if it hadn't been for Bert Evatt and his team of long-sighted men (doubtless accustomed to peering at the far horizons of the great Australian outback) the combined wisdom of the great powers would not have sufficed to keep the Security Council in business for more than six years. Since 1951 it has survived on a diet of Australian-labelled Situations of Like Nature.

And, of course, in such Situations there is nothing to prevent votes being cast (and vetoes being used) by a Council member who, if the thing was deemed to be a dispute, would be identified as a party to the dispute and thus barred from voting. So there is little left of the principle, to which the Americans and British had once claimed to attach importance, that a state should not 'vote in judgment on itself'. This principle had been somewhat more successfully upheld in the League of Nations.

Great powers, like children (and many adults), often want to dodge the responsibility for decisions, especially when it is a case of a choice between two evils. It took the great powers only three months to discover that the veto, which they had insisted on awarding themselves despite all the protests about it, was going to be a grave embarrassment to them in such cases. Aptly, it was the Russians who made the discovery first. On 29 April 1946 Andrei Gromyko informed a Security Council which had only begun work in January that he was faced with a draft resolution (on Spain) that he didn't like; but that he liked the idea of its not being adopted even less. So, he said, he would not veto it; he would abstain from voting. Within a year his American colleague had imitated him.

Now what the Charter says, in Article 27, might be thought to be quite clear. Council decisions, other than procedural ones, require 'the concurring votes of the permanent members'. To the plain man that would seem to mean that all five of them must vote for a resolution if it is to go through. But councilmen are not plain men.

As early as 1 August 1947 the president of the Council (a Syrian) was able to look them all straight in the eye and say, without being challenged:

> I think it is now jurisprudence in the Security Council, and the interpretation accepted *for a long time*, that an abstention is not considered a veto; and the concurrent votes of the permanent members mean the votes of the permanent members who participate in the voting. Those who abstain intentionally are not considered to have cast a veto.

Nearly twenty years were to pass before there was anything like a serious challenge to this pronouncement. In April 1966 Alberto Franco Nogueira, the indignant foreign minister of Portugal, wrote to U Thant challenging the validity of the Council resolution of April 9, which authorised the British navy to prevent tankers bringing crude oil to Beira for transmission by pipeline to Rhodesia (page 239). Russia and France had abstained in the vote on this resolution. Franco Nogueira contended that these abstentions by permanent members had prevented the Council from making a valid decision. Thant pointed out that only the Council itself could give an authoritative interpretation of the relevant texts. The Portuguese put in two formal requests that the Council should ask the Secretary-General to 'express his views on the matter', but the Council did not respond. Perhaps it was better for Portugal that it didn't. Sydney Bailey, who misses nothing, has noted in this connection that two permanent members had abstained in the Council vote that permitted Portugal to become a member of the United Nations in 1955 (page 100).

Meanwhile, two decades had rolled smoothly by, and the Council had adopted a couple of hundred resolutions, and at least a third of them had been adopted despite the abstention of one or more of the five permanent members. The plain man might well wonder why, if everybody agreed (except, very belatedly, Portugal) that 'concurring' didn't really mean concurring, they hadn't amended Article 27 to make this clear. Ah, he would be told, amending the Charter is very difficult − because the great-power veto applies to that too. But, he might ask, surely the great powers had all agreed about this point? Only in practice, he would learn; amending the Charter is a matter of principle, and quite different. Hasn't it ever been amended, then? Well, yes, admittedly it has. And which article was amended? Not Article 27 by any chance? Er, hum, well, actually, yes.

The whole ponderous business of Assembly debate, resolution and ratification by member governments (including all the five PPs) was in fact carried out between 1963 and 1965 to amend this and two other articles so that the Council could be enlarged (page 110). But they omitted to take the opportunity of doing something about that little word 'concurring'. It still stands in the amended Charter.

Meanwhile again, the great powers had been given (or, rather, had given themselves) added reason to make less use of the veto right to which they had originally attached such enormous importance. On 3 November 1950 the Assembly passed the 'Uniting for Peace' resolution. This embodied Secretary of State Dean Acheson's contingency plan to meet the possibility that, if a second Korea-type communist invasion came elsewhere in the world, a Russian veto would prevent the Council from urging member states to act jointly to resist the aggression. The nub of the resolution was the proposal that the Assembly should meet within twenty-four hours, if so requested by a majority of member states or by any seven Council members, when a veto had prevented the Council from acting to meet a threat to the peace. For all Vishinsky's and Malik's furious protests at the time, there was nothing 'illegal' in this. The Assembly was not awarding itself any such 'mandatory' powers as the Council enjoyed under Article 25. The Assembly was merely equipping itself with a specific procedure for exercising its own undoubted right, under Article 11, to *recommend* action – which was all that the Council had done in response to the Korean invasion in June 1950.

No 'second Korea' came. Who can say whether the adoption of the 'Uniting for Peace' procedure helped to prevent it coming? Unfortunately, the success of peace-keeping devices can seldom be proved; it is only their failure that is conclusively demonstrated by the outbreak of war. But the resolution of November 1950 had a further effect that could be demonstrated, and eventually was.

I have described the visible décor of the Security Council chamber on the East River waterfront. There is also an invisible but important feature which was installed in the chamber – a short time before the Norwegian designer's work was completed and the Council was able to move in – not by any Norwegian hand but by that of Dean Acheson. Over the head of each great-power representative sitting at the horseshoe table hangs a sword of Damocles. In the case of Damocles himself, you will remember, having a naked sword suspended above him by a single hair completely destroyed his appetite. He had asked his princely patron to let him experience the privileges of power; which, to his simple mind, meant unlimited access to wine, women, song and *cordon bleu* cookery. Dionysius provided him with all the goodies – and the sword, as a reminder that power involves peril as well as privilege. And the wretched Damocles sat there paralysed, not daring even to reach out for any of the temptations that were spread before him.

What hangs over the heads of the privileged five at the Council table is the prospect that a rash veto may bring an emergency Assembly session crashing down upon them. This happened to Sir Pierson Dixon of Britain and Bernard Cornut-Gentille of France when, in October 1956, they vetoed two calls for a cease-fire and Israeli withdrawal from Egypt. It happened to Russia's Valerian Zorin in September 1960, when he vetoed a resolution, presented by Mongi Slim of Tunisia and Sir Claude Corea of Ceylon, which upheld Hammarskjöld's handling of the Congo crisis. It has not yet happened to any representative of the United States, which did not find it necessary to use a veto until 1970. But all the PP councilmen have had reason, for many years now, to glance up at the lofty ceiling of the Council chamber whenever they were minded to oppose an important resolution in a critical situation. Although other factors have been involved, the dangling sword has had some bearing on the fact that, whereas in the Council's first five years vetoes were being used at the rate of ten a year, the annual rate fell to 6, 3 and 2 in the second, third and fourth five-year periods.

After Zorin's painful experience in September 1960 (page 44) there were several later points in the Council's Congo activity at which Britain, France and Russia might each have used a veto but for the *memento mori* effect of Dionysius Acheson's sword. Zorin did in fact veto a few amendments to Congo resolutions; but he did not dare

to block the Council resolution of 21 February 1961, which strengthened the hand of a Secretary-General whom Russia had just denounced as a murderer. Nor did either Britain or France dare to veto
the resolution of 24 November 1961, although they had voiced
strong objections to it. In both cases it was plain that the sword was
hanging only by a hair.

Vishinsky had denounced the 'Uniting for Peace' resolution, and
the whole idea of bringing in the Assembly when the Council got
stuck, as 'a crude violation of the Charter' and a 'usurpation of the
Council's privileges'. Long after November 1950 Moscow was still
rumbling out these charges. They have never been withdrawn. On the
record, it remains the Russians' view – as stated, for example, in a
memorandum presented in July 1964 – that

> under the Charter, the only body authorised to take action in the mainten-
> ance or restoration of international peace and security is the Security
> Council.

Another Soviet memorandum, circulated to Council members in
April 1967, recalled that

> in 1950, under pressure from the United States, the UN adopted the
> notorious 'Uniting for Peace' resolution, under the terms of which
> measures for the maintenance of peace with the use of armed forces
> could be taken by the General Assembly. . . . The Soviet Union will not
> be able to remain a detached observer of breaches of the Charter which
> would enable certain Western Powers to impose on the General
> Assembly decisions likely to impair the basic interests of Member States.
> If Member States were to embark on that course, a situation would arise
> in which the Soviet Union would be obliged to reconsider its attitude to
> UN activities.

Fighting talk. But what about Russia's deeds, as opposed to its
words? Russia has refused to agree to any formal arrangement giving
the Assembly a 'residual' right to meet and take over in threat-to-
peace cases which the Council has failed to tackle. Yet, in successive
cases of this kind, what the Russians have actually done has been in
flagrant violation of their own declared principles.

On 31 October 1956 Jugoslavia proposed that the Council should
call an emergency special session of the Assembly under the Uniting

for Peace procedure. Did Russia vote against this 'crude violation of the Charter'? It did not. The 'illegal' Assembly session ran from November 1 to 10. Did the Russians boycott it? No. They were there in their places; they spoke; they asked this 'illegal' Assembly to demand British, French and Israeli withdrawals from Egypt; they acted as if they had never said a word about 'usurpation of the Council's privileges'. On November 4, 5 and 7 the 'illegal' Assembly adopted resolutions that authorised the setting up of a UN international force. Did Russia even vote against these 'measures for the maintenance of peace with the use of armed forces'? It did not. The Russians even sent their then wholly docile Rumanian and Czechoslovak colleagues up to the 38th floor of the UN building to offer Ralph Bunche troops for this 'illegal' UN force (Unef). They even put up a Pole in the Assembly to ask that a member of the Soviet group should be included in the advisory committee on Unef. Both bids were rebuffed. But they showed that Russia, far from being a mere passive accomplice in all the 'violation of the Charter' that was going on, was eager to plunge still deeper into crime.

When, on November 3, Uniting for Peace was again invoked in the Council to call an emergency Assembly on the Soviet invasion of Hungary, the Russians voted against this move in the Council and then, in the Assembly, on the 4th, protested that an Assembly debate on the Hungarian question would amount to a violation of the Charter. Rather understandably in the circumstances, they were laughed out of court. They did not, of course, show any sign of complying with the resolutions passed by this emergency Assembly, which among other things called for a Soviet withdrawal from Hungary. But even in this case they incurred complicity in a further 'crime' merely by attending the 'illegal' session.

It is widely known that the Russians later refused to help finance Unef on the ground that it had been 'illegally' created by the Assembly. But it seems to be less generally realised that they were equally categorical in refusing to help pay for the UN forces in the Congo and in Cyprus, although both of these were authorised by the Council; and although the Council resolutions authorising these two forces had both been backed by Soviet votes.

October 1956 was only the start of Russia's life of 'crime' – by its own definition. In August 1958 Nikita Khrushchev in person assumed responsibility for the move by which the Council called the Assembly into emergency special session for the third time. Not a word was heard from Moscow about 'usurpation' or 'illegality' or 'violation of the Charter'. Khrushchev performed this extraordinary word-eating feat under intense pressure from Peking. He had called for a 'summit' conference about the Arab crisis which had led Lebanon and Jordan to call in American and British troops in July. In reply, America and Britain had proposed that the heads of government should meet in the Security Council – which had already discussed Lebanon, and in which Russia had just vetoed a proposal to permit Hammarskjöld to enlarge the UN observer group (Unogil) that had been sent to Lebanon in June. (Hammarskjöld enlarged it anyway, but that is another story.)

Apparently Khrushchev simply forgot Mao. Some say that it was this episode that made the Chinese leader decide that the Soviet one could never be trusted again. The Peking press violently denounced the 'deceptive plan' to stage a summit meeting in the Council, scathingly commenting that 'most of the Council members are American-controlled, including the Kuomintang man who represents nobody except the moribund Chiang Kai-shek'. It was indeed more than Mao could be expected to swallow quietly. But Khrushchev neither foresaw this nor bothered to have anybody keep him informed about Chinese reactions. A few hours after the Peking newspapers had blown their tops, he cabled to Eisenhower accepting the Council summit idea and saying that he himself was ready to be in New York the following Monday morning.

The thought of Khrushchev sitting down that Monday at the horseshoe table alongside Chiang in person must have mortified Mao beyond words. In public, the Chinese did what they could to save the Sino-Soviet alliance's collective face. The Peking press went into reverse with a grinding of gears and hailed the idea of a Council summit as eagerly as it had denounced it two days earlier. The world was informed that: 'The peace-loving peoples of the world welcome and support this proposal.' In private it was rather different. Mao in effect summoned Khrushchev to Canossa. After three days in Peking

during which he must have heard its ruler's views somewhat forcefully expressed, Khrushchev returned to Moscow a wiser and perhaps sadder man and, dropping the Council summit idea as if it had
stung him (which it had), demanded instead an emergency special
Assembly. He could not quite bring himself to cite the Uniting for
Peace resolution. And the Americans – who were greatly relieved by
the vanishing of the 'summit' plan – tactfully omitted to mention it in
so many words. But in fact the unanimous Council call for an
emergency Assembly which was made on August 7 at Russo-
American behest was the third invocation of the 'illegal' and
'Charter-violating' device which Dean Acheson had hung from the
ceiling of the Council chamber in 1950.

By the time the sword fell on Zorin in September 1960 the
Russians seemed to realise that they were no longer in a position
even to protest about it. Zorin went into the fourth emergency special
session of the Assembly like a lamb to the slaughter; and was duly
slaughtered by Alex Quaison-Sackey.

The fifth time round, Alexei Kosygin and Leonid Brezhnev did not
merely go farther up Acheson's garden path than Khrushchev had
done; they went farther than Acheson. The Assembly's fifth emergency special session was called in June 1967 at the direct request of
the Soviet government, a request made in a letter to U Thant from the
Soviet foreign minister, Andrei Gromyko. Gromyko asked for an
emergency session within twenty-four hours, not on the basis of
Uniting for Peace but on that of Article 11 of the Charter.

Now Article 11 says flatly that the Assembly must not make any
recommendations about a situation while the Council is exercising its
functions in respect of that situation. Over the years, UN practice
had somewhat eroded this rule, but the erosion had mainly occurred
against, not because of, Russia's wishes. Again and again, as in the
memoranda of July 1964 and April 1967, Moscow had insisted on
the Council's absolute primacy in regard to the maintenance of
peace. But here was Gromyko specifically insisting that the
Assembly should meet urgently and 'should adopt a decision
designed to bring about . . . the immediate withdrawal of Israel forces
behind the armistice lines'.

Had the Council ceased to concern itself with the situation arising from the 'six-day war' at the time when Gromyko wrote to Thant on June 13? It had not. It was actually meeting that day – a meeting that went on until near midnight; it met again next morning, the 14th, and yet again later on the same day. Had the Council found itself unable to proceed because of the use of a veto? Or for any other reason? On the contrary, it had already adopted no less than five resolutions – unanimously; it still had several proposals before it which had yet to be put to a vote; nothing had been vetoed. Had the Council, by a procedural vote, itself called for an emergency Assembly? It had not. It had not been invited to do so, by Russia or by anybody else. Russia had arbitrarily chosen to appeal from the Council to the Assembly at a moment when the Council was very visibly engaged on a question of the maintenance and restoration of peace. Russia had not even sought to get the Council to vote for the transfer of debate to the Assembly (indeed, it was quite clear that a Council majority could not have been mustered to vote for a transfer). Where did this leave the Soviet gospel of absolute Council primacy in peace-keeping? In shreds.

In summary, of the five emergency special Assembly sessions Russia opposed (but took part in) two; accepted one (and only later, after choosing not to oppose its decisions, denounced them as illegal); and itself initiated two – the third and fifth. The present Russian rulers might feel able to dismiss Khrushchev's enthusiasm for the third session, as they dismissed Khrushchev. But they could not disclaim direct responsibility for the fifth, at which Kosygin himself played the star role (page 215). Whether their successors could scrabble back to the original doctrine of strict Council primacy is a matter which, presumably, would depend on the circumstances in which Kosygin and Brezhnev were removed from power.

*   *   *

As we have seen, to become an original member of the UN you had to be at war; to join later, you had to be 'peace-loving'. The test of whether you were peace-loving was quite clear. If one of the five PPs in the Security Council voted against your admission, you weren't.

Of the first hundred vetoes used in the Council, 51 were used to block admissions to the UN. And this, of course, was only one side of the coin. While all but one of these 51 vetoes were used by Russia to block candidates whom the western powers backed, those powers repeatedly mustered majorities in the Council to block the admission of Russia's protégés. It took the great powers nearly ten years to kick this little habit. At the time, tremendously plausible reasons were given by all the PPs for their blocking actions. These were all the more plausible because they kept changing. Admirable flexibility was demonstrated on both sides. When Russia abandoned its first arguments and took over those used by America and Britain, these two powers abandoned them and adopted the ones that had originally been Russia's. There seemed no reason why this delicious diplomatic quadrille should not go on for ever. The Council was only seven months old, and had just moved into the Sperry Gyroscope building, when the wheel began to spin. Eight putative peace-lovers had already applied. Of these, Afghanistan, Iceland and Sweden were acceptable to all the PPs. But Russia objected to Ireland, Jordan and Portugal; and the other powers didn't think much of Russia's two little friends, Albania and Mongolia. Herschel Johnson, who was then acting as America's councilman, offered a package deal. 'To accelerate the achievement of universality of membership', he proposed that all eight candidates be admitted. Trygve Lie made one of his earliest interventions in the Council immediately after Johnson had submitted his resolution, reminding the councilmen that

> all the great powers have agreed, on numerous occasions, that the United Nations must be as universal as possible. . . . In my capacity as Secretary-General of the United Nations, I wish to support the admission to membership of all the states which are applying today.

Andrei Gromyko thought this was all highly improper. Each candidate, he argued, must be judged separately and strictly on its own merits. So Johnson withdrew his package proposal; Gromyko used three vetoes against Ireland, Jordan and Portugal; Albania and Mongolia failed to get seven of the Council's eleven votes, and only the Afghans, Icelanders and Swedes were passed and raised to the rank of peace-lovers.

A year later it was Gromyko's turn to propose a package deal, and Warren Austin's and Alexander Cadogan's turn to reject it. Peace treaties had been concluded with Bulgaria, Finland, Hungary, Italy and Rumania. The western powers' insistence that each must be considered separately meant that not one of them got into the UN in 1947; nor did Austria, whose application also ran into a Russian veto. By 1949 there were thirteen candidates vainly beating on the doors of the Sperry plant – the 5 losers from 1946, the 6 from 1947, and Ceylon and Nepal. Yakov Malik proposed a 13-nation package; America and Britain again insisted on separate votes; and in one September week Malik used up eight vetoes, while the five communist candidates failed to get seven Council votes. Just three years later, in 1952, another September week saw Malik again shedding vetoes like autumn leaves, this time on Cambodia, Japan, Laos, Libya and South Vietnam.

When Malik left his UN post in 1953 he became ambassador in London, and from 1954 on he took part in the Lancaster House sessions of the five-power sub-committee on disarmament. At the age of 48 his heart began to give him trouble, and at one point the Lancaster House talks had to be halted for two weeks because of this apparently quite undiplomatic illness. Later, while in New York again at the time when the long deadlock on UN admissions was at last broken, he was observed by James Wadsworth to be looking unusually happy. (Stalin and Vishinsky were dead and it was now permissible for a Russian to look happy at the UN.) Malik told Wadsworth that the breaking of the deadlock gave him real joy; that having to veto all those admissions in earlier years had made him feel physically ill, and that he thought his heart trouble had been directly attributable to this.

By 1953 the great-power deadlock on admissions had aroused such impatience that the Assembly formally appointed a Good Offices Committee to try to soften up the intransigent PPs. Britain was somewhat softened, but the others held out until December 1955. Then a Canadian initiative secured the adoption of an Assembly resolution asking the Council to let in 18 out of the total of 22 applicants – setting aside the particularly difficult cases of the two Koreas and the two Vietnams. Britain and Russia voted for this resolution, America and France abstained, and Taipeh China voted against it. At that moment the Chinese vote was not taken too seriously. The Council went hopefully to its horseshoe, in the belief that this time it would be lucky. It did not foresee that it was about to run head-on into the drama of The Mongolian Candidate.

Taipeh China and Peking China are united in resenting the way Russia has made Mongolia into a Soviet protectorate and then claimed that it is an independent state. Most Chinese tend to feel that Mongolia ought to be part of China anyway. In the Council on 13 December 1955 the Taipeh man skilfully finessed the Russians by first insisting on the inclusion of South Korea and South Vietnam in the 'package' – which thereby became more of a Chinese box. Yakov Malik, probably already groping for his heart pills, was trapped into using two vetoes. The Taipeh man then vetoed Mongolia.

This was the first, and so far it is the only, Chinese veto. The occasion was well chosen for dramatic effect. The entire package came apart. Malik used up another 13 vetoes on Austria, Cambodia, Ceylon, Finland, Ireland, Italy, Japan, Jordan, Laos, Libya, Nepal, Portugal and Spain. Nobody got through that day; Albania, Bulgaria, Hungary and Rumania were again blocked; and the unlucky 13th came to a sad end with rage and frustration and risk of heart attacks all round – except, of course, for the blandly smiling representative from Taipeh, who looked fulfilled.

A hard night's work was put in at the UN by Paul Martin and other Canadians, Krishna Menon and Arthur Lall of India, and, among the members of the Council itself, Victor Belaunde of Peru. Most members of the Assembly were set on getting the admissions deadlock broken before their 1955 session ended. The Council was giving them two kinds of pain simultaneously. Already they had had to extend the Assembly session because, after 29 inconclusive ballots, neither Jugoslavia nor the Philippines had won enough votes to fill the last Council vacancy (page 106). Now they wondered how long they might have to wait in New York to endorse the Council's recommendations on admissions, if it ever managed to make any.

Nikita Khrushchev and Nikolai Bulganin were then making a tour of southern Asia, including India. Menon cabled to Nehru urging him to tell the Russian visitors about the mood of angry frustration at the

UN. By next morning Malik had received new instructions from his government. The Soviet representative called the sullen Council back to its table and explained that he had authority to propose a smaller package. Japan would have to stay in the ante-room with Mongolia, the Koreas and the Vie·nams; but the 16 other candidates could enter the UN *en bloc*. The Council voted them in (America, Belgium and China abstaining); and that night the Assembly endorsed the admissions. As from 14 December 1955, the membership of the United Nations rose from 60 to 76. A curious feature of this outcome was that such countries as Italy, Portugal and Spain had been admitted with Russia's support in the Council but without America's. And a curious sequel was that Russia agreed to (indeed, voted for) Japan's admission only a year later; yet it was not until 1961 that Mongolia at last squeezed in (America abstaining, and China ostentatiously not taking part in the Council vote).

The rejection of candidates did not entirely cease after 1955. In 1960 Russia held up Mauritania's admission for a year, and in 1961 it did the same to Kuwait; the Koreas and Vietnams remained, and remain, blocked. West Germany and East Germany are still non-members, the former having shown no wish to enter the UN as long as the price set by Russia was the simultaneous entry of the latter. But, with these few exceptions, the general rule since December 1955 has been that the Council no longer impedes admissions, and 50 more states have entered the UN, all of them, except for Cyprus and Malta, being African, Asian or Caribbean countries.

*   *   *

The very existence of the Security Council has more than once been jeopardised by difficulties encountered in filling its non-permanent seats. The states occupying these seats, normally for two-year terms, are elected by the Assembly, which annually proceeds to secret balloting for this purpose. The Charter requires that a candidate must be elected by a two-thirds majority of all states participating in the vote. So, if two candidates for a seat are more or less evenly supported, there is no question of one of them winning by a nose: instead, there is a deadlock. As early as the second Assembly, in 1947, such a deadlock developed between India and the Ukrainian Soviet republic. The Assembly voted eleven times without giving either of them the necessary two-thirds majority, and the problem was resolved only when India withdrew.

This proved to be a mere foretaste of worse trouble to come. At the 1955 Assembly 36 successive ballots were needed to break a deadlock of the same kind, and at the 1959 Assembly 52. In both these cases balloting dragged on over a period of two months, the Assembly was forced to extend its sessions into late December, and the New Year deadline loomed alarmingly near. Only eleventh-hour compromises averted the extinction of the Council.

Evidently the great powers did not foresee these difficulties either at Dumbarton Oaks, at San Francisco or even in the UN's first year of life. Their only specific proposal on the subject, which emerged from a British initiative and went into the Charter (Article 23) without encountering opposition, was that the Assembly, when electing Council members, should pay 'due regard' firstly to states' contributions to the maintenance of peace and other UN purposes, 'and also to equitable geographical distribution'. Neither of these criteria has been fully satisfied throughout the first quarter century of the Council's existence.

When the Council was first constituted in London early in 1946 the permanent members privately agreed among themselves on a pattern of geographical distribution for the elective seats. Their 'London agreement', which was never officially published, gave two seats to Latin America (which then comprised two-fifths of the UN's membership), one each to Western and Eastern Europe, one to the Middle East and one to the Commonwealth. At the time these categories covered all the UN's member states except Liberia and the Philippines. This great-power formula enjoyed some degree of respect, or at least lip service, until 1956. In reality, however, it had lasted for only four years. From 1950 until 1965 – the last year of the eleven-seat Council – the annual electing process in the Assembly was bedevilled by two unresolved problems. One concerned the 'East European seat', the other the mounting demand for more representation of Asia and Africa as more states in these regions became UN members. The table on page 102 may shed some light on both.

ELECTED MEMBERS OF THE SECURITY COUNCIL

	Latin America		'Old Commonwealth'	West Europe		East Europe
1946	Brazil	*Mexico*	Australia	*Netherlands*		Poland
1947	Brazil	Colombia	Australia	Belgium		Poland
1948	Argentina	Colombia	Canada	Belgium		Ukraine
1949	Argentina	Cuba	Canada	Norway		Ukraine
1950	Ecuador	Cuba		Norway		Jugoslavia
1951	Ecuador	Brazil		Netherlands	Turkey	Jugoslavia
1952	Chile	Brazil		Netherlands	Turkey	Greece
1953	Chile	Colombia		Denmark		Greece
1954	Brazil	Colombia	New Zealand	Denmark	Turkey	
1955	Brazil	Peru	New Zealand	Belgium	Turkey	
1956	Cuba	Peru		Belgium		*Jugoslavia*
1957	Cuba	Colombia	Australia	Sweden		
1958	Panama	Colombia	Australia	Sweden		
1959	Panama	Argentina	Canada	Italy		
1960	Ecuador	Argentina	Canada	Italy		*Poland*
1961	Ecuador	Chile			*Turkey*	
1962	Venezuela	Chile		*Ireland*		*Rumania*
1963	Venezuela	Brazil		Norway		
1964	Bolivia	Brazil		Norway		*Czechoslovakia*
1965	Bolivia	Uruguay		Netherlands		
1966	Argentina	Uruguay	*New Zealand*	Netherlands		Bulgaria
1967	Argentina	Brazil	Canada	Denmark		Bulgaria
1968	Paraguay	Brazil	Canada	Denmark		Hungary
1969	Paraguay	Colombia		Finland	Spain	Hungary
1970	Nicaragua	Colombia		Finland	Spain	Poland

Year	Arab	Other Asian	Other African
1946	*Egypt*		
1947	Syria		
1948	Syria		
1949	Egypt		
1950	Egypt	India	
1951		India	
1952		Pakistan	
1953	Lebanon	Pakistan	
1954	Lebanon		
1955		Iran	
1956		Iran	
1957	Iraq	*Philippines*	
1958	Iraq	Japan	
1959	Tunisia	Japan	
1960	Tunisia	Ceylon	
1961	Egypt	Ceylon	*Liberia*
1962	Egypt		Ghana
1963	Morocco	*Philippines*	Ghana
1964	Morocco		Ivory Coast
1965	Jordan	*Malaysia*	Ivory Coast
1966	Jordan	Japan	Mali Nigeria *Uganda*
1967		Japan India	Mali Nigeria Ethiopia
1968	Algeria	Pakistan India	Senegal Ethiopia
1969	Algeria	Pakistan Nepal	Senegal Zambia
1970	Syria	Nepal	Burundi Zambia Sierra Leone

Italics indicate a one-year term.

	Americas	West Europe, 'Old Commonwealth', &c.	East Europe
Permanent Council members	*United States	*Britain (UK) *France	*Russia (USSR)
States that have been elected to the Council	*Argentina *Bolivia *Brazil *Chile *Colombia *Cuba *Ecuador *Mexico *Nicaragua *Panama *Paraguay *Peru *Uruguay *Venezuela	*Australia *Belgium *Canada *Denmark Finland *Greece Ireland Italy *Netherlands *New Zealand *Norway Spain Sweden *Turkey	Bulgaria *Czechoslovakia Hungary *Jugoslavia *Poland Rumania *Ukrainian SSR
Other UN member states	Barbados *Costa Rica *Dominican Republic *El Salvador *Guatemala Guyana *Haiti *Honduras Jamaica Trinidad	Austria Cyprus Iceland Israel *Luxemburg Malta Portugal *South Africa	Albania *Byelorussian SSR

* Original Members.

UNITED NATIONS

Arab	Other Asian	Other African	
	*China (Taipeh)		
Algeria	Ceylon	Burundi	
*Egypt (UAR)	*India	*Ethiopia	
*Iraq	*Iran	Ghana	
Jordan	Japan	Ivory Coast	
*Lebanon	Malaysia	*Liberia	
Morocco	Nepal	Mali	
*Syria	Pakistan	Nigeria	
Tunisia	*Philippines	Senegal	
		Sierra Leone	
		Uganda	
		Zambia	
Kuwait	Afghanistan	Botswana	Lesotho
Libya	Burma	Cameroon	Madagascar
*Saudi Arabia	Cambodia	Central African	Malawi
South Yemen	Indonesia	Republic	Mauritania
Sudan	Laos	Chad	Mauritius
Yemen	Maldives	Congo–Brazzaville	Niger
	Mongolia	Congo–Kinshasa	Rwanda
	Singapore	Dahomey	Somalia
	Thailand	Equatorial Guinea	Swaziland
		Gabon	Tanzania
		Gambia	Togo
		Guinea	(Upper) Volta
		Kenya	

The contortions that developed turned out to be almost solely to the benefit of Turkey, which held a seat for no less than five of the fifteen troubled years. As an exceptionally agile 'odd man in', Turkey first appeared in the Council in 1951 as a 'Middle Eastern' member; then, after an interval of only one year (non-permanent members are not eligible for immediate re-election) it was back as an 'East European'; the third time round it had tenure for only one year, but the shortness of time was compensated in other dimensions, for in this year (1961) Turkey could fairly claim to be the sole representative of both Western and Eastern Europe.

The East European difficulty first came to a head when the 1949 Assembly, to Russia's loud indignation, gave a seat in the Council to Jugoslavia, which had just broken away from Soviet domination. From then until 1956 the 'East European seat' was filled by either Greece, Jugoslavia or Turkey. The Russians complained publicly that this was a breach of the great powers' 1946 private understanding. The American response was that the 'London agreement' had been meant to apply only to the 1946 elections; that the geographical requirement in Article 23 was being fully respected; and that this article's other touchstone, the bit about helping to maintain peace and to serve other UN purposes, actually disqualified those East European states that were toeing Moscow's line, since they weren't contributing any such help to the organisation. The Russians got little sympathy from non-aligned member states when they wheeled out their claim about the 1946 understanding. India, in particular, insisted that the Assembly could not be bound by any secret deal made between a few major powers.

In 1957 the Philippines took the 'East European seat' and the 1946 formula was broken beyond repair. The Philippines and Jugoslavia had been the main contenders in the 36-ballot deadlock during the 1955 Assembly. When that Assembly session reached its agreed closing date in mid-December, there had already been 34 ballots, and neither candidate had obtained the necessary two-thirds majority. The Assembly president, José Maza of Chile, who had repeatedly warned the delegates that all this was discrediting the organisation, called the two candidates to his private office and got them to agree to split the two-year term between them. They drew

106

lots in his office to see who should take the first year; and the lot fell on the Jugoslav. Maza then announced to the Assembly that the Filipinos had withdrawn their candidature in the Jugoslavs' favour, with a 'gentlemen's agreement' that Jugoslavia would resign the seat after one year and that the Philippines would then be elected to complete the term. There were loud protests. Seventeen delegates voiced objections or reservations. The Russians said that Maza's plan would violate the principle of equitable geographical distribution. (They were just in the process of making friends with Jugoslavia again, so they were not entirely disinterested.) Sir Leslie Munro of New Zealand, who was the Security Council president at the time, could not approve of what he called a 'disturbing' proposal. Rodriguez Fabregat of Uruguay also disapproved. He disclosed that the idea of drawing lots had been raised in the Latin Americans' Assembly caucus on an earlier occasion when two rival Latin candidates were seeking the group's support for a Council seat, and that he had opposed the suggestion then, as he did now. On the other hand, Sir Pierson Dixon argued that 'abnormal situations need abnormal remedies'. He and Henry Cabot Lodge contended that there was nothing unconstitutional about Maza's plan.

Maza had to let the Assembly start balloting again; and the session had to be extended for another four days. But then, somehow, Jugoslavia picked up a two-thirds majority on the 36th ballot. Somehow, a year later, Jugoslavia felt that it must resign from the Council. Somehow, the Philippines was promptly elected – on the very first ballot – to fill the vacancy for one year.

Maza had assured the Assembly that it would not be setting a precedent if it approved his proposal. The Turkish delegate (who was surely not a disinterested party) had remarked that 'this most peculiar procedure . . . would be a precedent whether we want it to or not'. His comment was a perceptive one. In fact, Maza had given the Assembly a lead that was to help it out of the same difficulty several times. When the 52-ballot deadlock came in 1959 a weary Assembly was induced to give its approval, quite openly, to a deal by which Poland and Turkey split a two-year term. The next few years saw three similar deals – clinched after much less balloting.

One effect of this was that the 'East European seat' was occupied by a member of the Soviet group every second year. Another effect was that the by now rather mystical succession to the 'Commonwealth seat' was kept almost, but not quite, intact. In one year, 1964, there was no Commonwealth state among the Council's elected members. However, for the faithful, there was even then the assurance that Malaysia would get its turn in 1965.

The Filipino phenomenon of 1957 had marked not only the overt abandoning of the 'London agreement' in regard to Eastern Europe but also the first appearance in the Council of an Asian state that could not be classed as either Middle Eastern or Commonwealth. Another such state, Japan, followed immediately. But the appearance of the first black African Council member was preceded by a fierce struggle at the 1960 Assembly. The danger of deadlock was so clear that year that no balloting was even attempted until mid-December. With inspired ill-timing, the West Europeans had put up Portugal as their nominee for a Council seat, just at the moment when the black Africans' voting strength in the Assembly had been multiplied from four to twenty. This bit of old-world European diplomatic finesse ensured that the Africans would concentrate on gaining ground at the expense of Europe, not of Latin America. By December the antagonists had dug in so deeply that it really looked as if there would be no Council at all on 1 January 1961.

Just before Christmas a bargain was struck that brought Liberia into the 1961 Council, with Ireland – a much more widely acceptable European candidate than Portugal – slated to inherit the seat in 1962. So in 1961, for the first time, the Council had no elected member from Western Europe – unless you counted those rather nomadic Turks. And there was no longer any doubt that the Council would have to be enlarged if it was to be made at all reasonably representative of the main groups in the whole UN membership.

It was not now just a question of somehow making room for the Africans. They were in from 1961 onward (Ghana followed Liberia the next year), and they had acquired enough leverage in the form of Assembly votes to ensure that they could stay in.* It was much more

* There were rueful smiles around Turtle Bay in 1964 when Barry Goldwater, during his campaign for the American presidency, warned his followers that things were getting so bad at the UN that there would soon be an African on the

a question of the impossibility of an eleven-member Council continuing to provide the Latin Americans and Europeans with as many seats as they had been accustomed to hold. The Latin Americans had had a strong claim to two out of six elective Council seats in 1946, when they numbered 20 out of only 46 original UN members (excluding the Big Five). Now they numbered 20 out of a membership of more than a hundred; and they could see themselves losing one of their two Council seats at any moment. As for the West Europeans, they were almost as worried as the East Europeans; and the 'Old Commonwealth' states hadn't had a Council seat since 1959.

But none of the great powers liked the idea of enlarging the Council. And no enlargement was possible without an amendment of the Charter, which could be blocked by any great power's veto. America, Britain and France did not want to oppose enlargement categorically. They preferred to suggest that nothing should be done without a great deal of careful thought, and that in any case the enlargement should be a very small one. For the time being, however, they did not need to incur much of the odium involved in blocking enlargement, because Russia took a more categorical attitude of opposition.

In the early 1960s the Sino-Soviet rift had become an open one, but it had not yet reached the point at which the Russians gave up even going through the motions of trying to get the UN China seat for Peking. So they committed themselves, publicly and repeatedly, to the position that they would not permit any Council enlargement until the Peking men were seated in the Council. This gambit was meant to force those members who wanted enlargement to vote for Peking. It had no such effect. It merely earned the Russians unpopularity – and, very soon, humiliation too, for communist China proceeded to pull the rug out from under their feet.

At the 1963 Assembly a very widely supported proposal for enlarging the Council was presented for debate. Russia's response

---

Security Council. The Ivory Coast was a Council member at the time; Liberia and Ghana had already occupied Council seats – and so had Egypt, Tunisia and Morocco, though, even if Goldwater had known about these latter, they might not have been quite what he had in mind.

was to put forward a new formula for the distribution of the existing six elective seats: one each for Western and Eastern Europe, only one for Latin America, one for the Middle East and one each for the remaining parts of Asia and Africa. As things stood in the Council at that moment, three seats were already occupied by Asian and African members, one by Norway and two by Latin Americans. So the new Russian plan amounted to little more than reasserting the old claim to an 'East European' (i.e. Soviet group) seat at the expense of the Latin Americans. It found no takers. The pressure for enlargement continued to mount.

Fedorenko said his familiar piece about the impossibility of enlarging the Council until the Chinese seat had been transferred. Two days later an official statement was issued in Peking accusing Russia of misrepresenting the Chinese attitude to this question. Peking declared that it strongly supported the Asians' and Africans' claims to greater representation in the UN. It insisted that the China seat question was a quite separate one; and it regretted that Fedorenko had tried to use this question as a pretext for opposing the enlargement plan.

The recommendation for enlargement was then adopted by a massive Assembly majority which left the great powers virtually isolated. Of the then 112 members, 97 voted for the resolution. Only France, Russia and nine other Soviet-group delegations voted against it. Only America, Britain, Portugal and South Africa abstained. The resolution called for Charter amendments that would give the Security Council ten elected members instead of six, and increase the number of votes required for its resolutions from seven to nine.

For the first time, the 1963 Assembly resolution also placed on the formal record a proposed pattern of geographical distribution for the ten elective seats in the Council. Latin America was assigned its customary two seats, while no less than five were accorded to the Asians and Africans. One seat was assigned to Eastern Europe (though the Assembly resolution said nothing about this being earmarked for states of the Soviet group), and two to West European 'and other' states – which took care of the 'Old Commonwealth', and, in theory, of such outliers as Israel and South Africa, though there was no practical prospect of South Africa, at least, picking up the

110

two-thirds majority needed for election. The new pattern corresponded well enough (as the tables on pages 102 to 105 show) to the numerical balance among UN member states; and also to the general balance of population among the regions of the world.

None of the great powers hastened to toe the line that nearly all the other members had laid down. But in June 1964 Fedorenko circulated a note to Asian, African and Latin American representatives at the UN in which he indicated that Russia had now decided to accept and ratify the Charter amendments which it had voted against only six months earlier. During 1965 the Russians, followed by the other great powers, completed ratification, and the amendments came into force in August of that year. From 1 January 1966 the Security Council therefore had fifteen members instead of the former eleven; and, although the geographical formula recommended by the Assembly was not inserted into the Charter or otherwise given any binding force, it has been faithfully respected in all the elections to the Council since 1966.

Since then, the Assembly has been spared its former agonies of endless balloting and deadlock. However, elections to the Council have not become wholly uncontroversial. At the 1966 Assembly, for example, there was some lively in-fighting within the Afro-Asian group. Syria was eager to succeed Jordan in the seat that had previously been occupied by a succession of Arab states. But Syria was not a popular candidate, even among its fellow Arabs; India entered the field, and defeated Syria on the first ballot – as a result of which there was no Arab Council member in the year of the 'six-day war'. Next year the Arabs found a stronger candidate in Algeria, which could bring in more African backing.

The smarting Syrians at last got themselves nominated as one of the Afro-Asian group's agreed candidates in October 1969. They won their Council seat this time, but in unhappy circumstances. Resentment of their candidature was not confined to warm supporters of Israel. Syria's Article 23 rating was unquestionably low. It had refused to have anything to do with the Council's efforts to bring about an Israel–Arab settlement after the 1967 war. And at the time of the 1969 Assembly's election of new Council members Syria was still detaining two Israelis who had been passengers on board an

111

American airliner that Palestinian Arabs had hijacked to Damascus several weeks earlier. On October 20, the day of the elections, there were demonstrations against Syria outside the UN building in New York, and Israel's foreign minister, Abba Eban, gave warning that his government might boycott the Council if Syria joined it in January 1970 without releasing the two detained men.

'It begins to look,' said Eban, 'as if one place on the Council is permanently reserved for states that shelter hijackers of planes and restrain people who have been abducted by force.' (He was referring to the fact that Syria was replacing Algeria, which had played a similar role in earlier hijacking affairs.) In the event, however, Syria freed its two prisoners before taking its seat in the Council.

The 1966 enlargement has not in itself brought about any really significant change in the balance of forces within the Council. The table on pages 102 and 103 shows how, as a result of the growth of UN membership, that balance had swung quite a long way before the enlargement. Compare, for example, the 1952 and 1962 compositions. Setting aside the Latin Americans, the other elected members in the first of these years were the Netherlands, Greece, Turkey and Pakistan; in the second, Ireland, Rumania, Egypt and Ghana. The numerical preponderance of Council members associated with the western powers by alliance or otherwise could not be maintained when the 'electorate' in the Assembly came to include a large number of non-aligned Asian and African states.

True, it is now possible for nine or ten elected Council members to carry a resolution without the support of any of the five permanent members – providing that each of these five is content to abstain, rather than cast a contrary vote that would have the effect of vetoing the resolution. In the pre-1966 Council the necessary seven votes could be made up only if at least one permanent member joined the six elected ones in voting for a resolution. But even this change is of less significance than would appear at first sight. Back in 1965 there was a quietly historic occasion (page 225) when a resolution was adopted despite the abstentions of America, Britain, France and Russia, the four 'substantial' permanent members; the six elected members had the support of Taipeh China, and that sufficed them.

And, as was then evident, a Council resolution that has no real great-power backing has no great reality either. This underlying fact has not been changed by the 1966 enlargement.

Less remarked, but somewhat more disturbing, has been the increasing tendency for regional groups to resort more openly to the 'Buggin's turn' principle of simply giving each dog its day. Miniature poodles can be charming pets, but the Council is not going to win more respect if it is seen to contain whole packs of them. Since its enlargement, a certain trend to miniaturisation has set in, with the result that the 1970 Council includes not only Syria but also Nicaragua, Nepal, Burundi and Sierra Leone. One would not wish to see the smallest and weakest states dogmatically excluded from the Council, but one may question its ability to 'carry' too many of them. Picture a Council whose elected members were Barbados, Nicaragua, Luxemburg, Cyprus, Byelorussia, Kuwait, the Maldives, Burundi, Chad and Gambia. Who would take any of its fiats seriously? How far would the great powers be encouraged to treat their Council colleagues with respect?

Chapter Five

From the case-books

When the Security Council moved into its first American home in the Bronx, in March 1946, it was provided with a newly made ballot box. It has little use for a ballot box except when it plays its part in the election of judges to the International Court at The Hague. But this box at Hunter College won some fame, because there was found in it a note that read:

> May I, who have had the privilege of fabricating this ballot box, cast the first vote? May God be with every member of the United Nations organisation, and through your noble efforts bring lasting peace to us all – all over the world.
>
> – Paul Antonio, Mechanic.

Paul Antonio was probably a bit disappointed and more than a bit perplexed if he learnt later that, during its Bronx months, the Council had adopted only four substantive resolutions, while four other proposed resolutions were vetoed; and that two of the former and all of the latter concerned the Spanish Question.

In April 1946 Poland asked the Council to call upon all UN members to break off diplomatic relations with General Franco's regime, and to declare that regime's existence a threat to peace. The Council was unwilling to go that far. But on April 29 it agreed to set up a sub-committee to look into the Spanish Question. It took this decision by a vote of ten to none, Andrei Gromyko abstaining.

Gromyko wasn't trying to protect Franco. Years had yet to pass before Franco's ministers would start to visit Moscow and Russian votes would be cast in the Assembly in support of his claims on Gibraltar. Gromyko thought the Council was not being tough enough. However, the Polish councilman was happy to vote for the resolution, so the Russian didn't want to veto it. 'My voting against

... would make its adoption impossible,' he acknowledged; and he abstained, thus making the first historic puncture in the veto by denying the resolution the 'concurring' PP votes to which he had attached such vital importance a year earlier at San Francisco.

The sub-committee went to work, and on June 6 it reported that the Franco regime's activities represented a 'potential' but not an actual threat to peace. It suggested that the Assembly should recommend severance of diplomatic relations if political freedom was not restored in Spain. On June 18, when a draft resolution along these lines was voted on, Gromyko could hold himself in no longer. He vetoed it. On the 26th he used up three more vetoes, letting only one resolution get past him (it was adopted without a vote), and making a little more history by wielding the 'double veto' for the first time. His contention was that the Spanish threat to peace was real and earnest and not by any yardstick 'potential'; and that breaking off relations with Madrid was a thing to be called for by the Council, not the Assembly. The Assembly disagreed with him. In December it called for a general withdrawal of ambassadors from Madrid.

But four years later, in November 1950, the Assembly faced up to the annoying fact that General Franco was still there (as indeed he still was in 1970); and it revoked its recommendation of December 1946. Time rolled on, and in 1955 Spain entered the UN – with Russia's support in the Council. In 1969 it became a member of the Council. The Soviet councilman, Yakov Malik, then found himself sitting at the horseshoe table next to a representative of the same regime that Gromyko (now Russia's foreign minister) had denounced as an active threat to peace twenty-three years earlier. Malik and Jaime de Pinies seemed to get along rather well. Perhaps the Spaniard, glancing at the Russian who sat beside him, occasionally reflected on the mutability of things. Perhaps the Russian, looking back, wondered what all that vetoing, veto-puncturing and double-vetoing in 1946 had achieved.

*   *   *

It was as early as 1947, when the Security Council was only one year old, that it first put into the field what could be regarded as a modest

INDONESIA

United Nations 'presence' – though that term was not to become a familiar one for another decade.

In the first months of the year a commission of investigation sent by the Council was at work in northern Greece, producing a report on the help that Albania, Jugoslavia and Bulgaria were giving to the Greek communist guerrillas in the frontier zones. When Russia blocked moves in the Council to follow up this report the problem was turned over to the Assembly, which by the end of 1947 had created a Special Committee on the Balkans (Unscob). Military and civilian Unscob observers were active in northern Greece for several years, but the matter was out of the Council's hands.

Meanwhile, however, the Council itself had approved the creation of a group of military observers in Indonesia. The group's initial strength was twenty-five, and in the course of four years of activity this rose to over sixty.

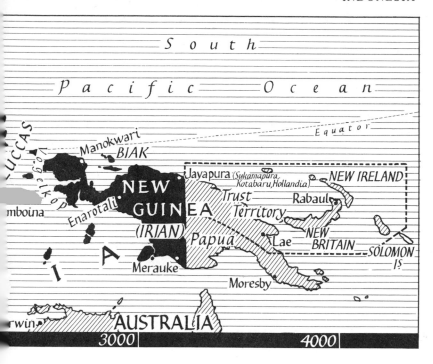

When Japan's surrender ended the Second World War in 1945 the Dutch had not been in a position to reimpose their control over the whole huge archipelago of the Netherlands East Indies. An independent Republic of Indonesia was proclaimed, and negotiations between its leaders and the Dutch eventually produced an agreement in early 1947, in which the Dutch recognised the Republic's *de facto* authority over Java and Sumatra, while both sides agreed to help form a sovereign United States of Indonesia, in which the Republic would be federated with Borneo and 'the Great East' (Celebes, the Moluccas and other islands east of Java). But in July 1947 the Dutch accused the Republic of failing to fulfil the terms of the agreement, and launched an armed attack against it. Australia and India asked the Council to intervene. (India was itself only on the eve of independence at that moment, but it had been an original member of the UN since 1945.) The Australian councilman used particularly strong

117

language, declaring that there was a 'threat to international peace' within the meaning of the Charter's Chapter Seven, and presenting a draft resolution which cited that chapter's Article 39.

On August 1 the Council called for a cease-fire and a peaceful settlement. When the fighting was seen to be continuing the Council met again. On the 25th Russia, which only a week earlier had vetoed proposals for UN observation in Greece, proposed that a commission representing all Council members should supervise compliance with the cease-fire call in Indonesia; but this was vetoed by France. This was the first time that a substantive Council decision was blocked by a veto other than Russia's. (But a year earlier France had joined Russia in vetoing a presidential ruling that a draft resolution about Spain – for which France had voted – was procedural, and thus valid despite Russia's vote against it. The president concerned was a Mexican, and it may have been too much of this kind of thing that soured Mexico on the Council.) The French councilman, a taciturn type, did not trouble to say why he had used his veto. Britain and China had abstained on the Soviet proposal; America and the two Latin American Council members had actually voted for it. But the Frenchman then joined the majority (while Britain and Russia abstained) in carrying a Sino-Australian resolution under which Council members' consuls in Batavia (now Jakarta) would be charged with observation duties. This tactful device saved Dutch face and kept the Russians out of the field of activity, for only six Council members had consuls in Batavia – America, Australia, Belgium, Britain, China and France. Their six governments supplied military observers at the consuls' joint request.

The Council also set up a Good Offices Committee of three – Australia, chosen by the Republic; Belgium, chosen by the Dutch; and the United States, chosen by Australia and Belgium. At its first meetings they were represented by Herbert Evatt, Paul van Zeeland and Frank Graham – an American who was later to serve the Council, in the 1950s, as its representative for India and Pakistan. The committee got Dutch and Republican delegates to meet on board the USS *Renville* off the Java coast, and to sign in January 1948 the '*Renville* agreement', which provided for a truce and set out a basis for a settlement.

During 1948 the Dutch grew more impatient. In December they denounced the truce and, in a swift 'police action', overran much of the Republic, capturing its President Achmed Sukarno and other political leaders. Meeting in emergency session, the Council called for a cease-fire and the freeing of the detained leaders. Up to this point it had dealt tenderly with Dutch susceptibilities about UN intervention in a 'domestic jurisdiction' affair. Now the Americans in particular felt that strong pressure must be applied. Their council-man, Philip Jessup, demanded that the Netherlands should 'end its defiance of the Security Council' and stop obstructing the Good Offices Committee. In Java, meanwhile, the committee's current Australian chairman, Thomas Critchley, was pressing the Dutch to permit renewed activity by the UN military observers, who were by now serving the committee.

On 28 January 1949 the Council (France and Russia abstaining) adopted a resolution transforming the committee into the UN Com-mission for Indonesia and directing it to help the parties to bring about a transfer of sovereignty over Indonesia, which, the Council recommended, should be completed not later than July 1950.

Caught between the increased international pressure and the con-tinuing resistance of guerrillas in the areas they had seized, the Dutch had to give ground. They had alienated British sympathy; France would not now use its veto on their behalf, and America was even threatening to suspend its economic aid. The transfer of sovereignty was completed by December 1949 after negotiations, first at Batavia and then in The Hague, in which the UN Commission played an active part, while the UN observers watched over the withdrawals of Dutch troops. The commission and the observers remained in Indonesia until 1951 to complete their supervisory work. Then the Council was able to close this chapter. True, West New Guinea (West Irian) was left in Dutch hands for the time being. Its eventual fate was to trouble the UN Assembly nearly twenty years later, in November 1969; but the Council was no longer involved.

*   *   *

In 1948, the first year of its long involvement with the Palestine problem, the Security Council adopted no less than sixteen resolutions on the subject. Not one veto was used, by Russia or by any other PP. America, Britain and Russia each abstained on one or more of the resolutions; and in one case Yakov Malik resorted to the rather comic device of showing an extra coolness by having his Ukrainian stooge cast a negative vote in the Council while he himself abstained – because he did not really want to block the cease-fire call of November 4. The great powers' silent retreat from Article 27 'concurrence' was already accomplished. Whatever it was that prevented the Council from acting more effectively on Palestine in 1948, it was not the much bemoaned 'paralysis because of the Russian veto'.

What was it, then? A head-on collision between conflicting American and Russian policies? Hardly. One of the outstanding features of the situation was the close alignment that America and Russia had shown in their join promotion of the plan for Palestine partition; an alignment they were to continue into 1949, when they jointly backed Israel's admission to UN membership. The ugly truth is that the Three who, three years earlier, had obliged other nations to accept a UN structure that left peace-keeping authority in the great powers' hands, between them dragged the UN into the Palestine crisis and then promptly ratted on it when things got tough.

In 1945 they had said, in effect: 'Stand back, small fry. You may count on us to deal with any breach of the peace by any of you. We Tarzan.' Beating their chests, the great apes of the international jungle had swung away through the trees with loud cries about 'primary responsibility for the maintenance of peace and security', 'plans for the application of armed force shall be made by the Security Council . . . to ensure prompt and effective action', and so forth (Articles 24 and 46 of the Charter).

Where had all the big talk gone? By 1948 the great powers were looming so small that a desperate Secretary-General felt obliged to send out special emissaries to see if they were still there, and if so whether they could be coaxed into doing anything. In May one of Lie's envoys was conveying his feelings to a great-power councilman in these terms:

> The Secretary-General believed that it was imperative that the Security Council should take quick and effective action. . . . If the Great Powers accepted that this situation in the Middle East could best be settled by

leaving the forces concerned to fight it out among themselves, while at the same time those Great Powers sat in the Security Council, they would be tacitly admitting that the Security Council was a useless instrument in attempting to preserve peace. . . .

Trygve Lie was really being rather kind to the great powers. They were not just lamentably failing to do their Tarzan thing in the hour of need. They were failing to cope with a situation for which they were themselves directly responsible. The Three, between them, had set it up, pinned it on to the unfortunate UN – and tiptoed away.

First, Britain dumped the whole Palestine problem in the UN's lap. One of the world's great primary peace-maintainers announced that it could not maintain peace in little Palestine; that it was pulling out in a year's time; and that it was confidently (but not, of course, irresponsibly, for it was a *great power*) handing over the whole problem. To the Assembly. To that babbling, inchoate, ineffective talk-shop, the United Nations General Assembly. What had happened to all the stern British insistence in 1945 on the primacy of the Security Council in peace-keeping? The Council, said the British government, was 'an imperfect instrument' for this particular peace-keeping job. What this meant, it was explained, was that in the Council Russia would veto everything.

How strange that in the end Russia vetoed nothing, when, in spite of Britain's care, the problem landed in the Council after all. But was it really so strange? In the Assembly Russia joined wholeheartedly with America in pushing through the 33–13 vote for a partition plan (with economic union between the projected Arab and Jewish states, and an international regime for Jerusalem). It was Britain that abstained. Indeed, the Russians earned Trygve Lie's praise for proving 'more steadfast' than the Americans – a tribute that Lie paid them in the memoirs he wrote after Moscow's venomous attacks on him had left him with no reason to pay it undeserved compliments.

The Jewish leadership in Palestine accepted the Assembly's partition plan. The Arabs rejected it, and it was entirely clear that only 'the application of armed force' by the UN could bring the plan into effect or avert full-scale Arab–Jewish war once the British troops left. On Russia's initiative, the Assembly asked the Council to take the necessary steps to carry out the UN plan; to consider whether the situation already constituted a threat to peace (and thus necessitated enforcement action under Chapter Seven); and to decide whether any attempt to upset the plan by force would constitute such a threat. It was clear that the answer to both these questions was yes.

The Council did nothing. Only in late February 1948 – three months after the adoption of the Assembly resolution – was the Council reluctantly obliged to interrupt its leisurely discussion of such problems as Trieste and actually hold a meeting about Palestine – and then only because the Palestine Commission appointed by the Assembly had reported that it would be helpless unless the Council provided it with armed force. None of the great powers showed any wish to provide anything of the kind. They acted as if they had never heard of 'primary responsibility' or 'prompt and effective action' – or indeed of Dumbarton Oaks or San Francisco.

In March (Britain abstaining) the great powers, in a Council resolution, requested themselves to consult together about what fresh instructions they might give to the helpless Commission. In April (Russia abstaining) the Council issued a mild call – which was ignored – for a halt to the fighting that was already going on, and set up a three-member Truce Commission (America, France and Belgium). It also called the Assembly back into special session; which implied that the Council PPs were yelling for the help of the despised small fry.

Meanwhile the unhappy Warren Austin had been obliged to announce that America no longer supported the partition plan for which it had fought so hard, and twisted so many arms, in the Assembly only five months earlier; and to make instead a totally unrealistic proposal that a UN trusteeship should be imposed on Palestine. To impose trusteeship, which would be resisted by both Jews and Arabs, would require more UN armed force than to impose partition. There was no sign of any such force emerging, and Trygve Lie was not alone in assuming that the Americans were simply ducking out. But Lie found that he was alone when he suggested to Austin that, in the circumstances, they should both resign. (It was Gromyko who persuaded Lie not to.)

On 14 May 1948 the British pulled out of Palestine, the Jewish authorities there proclaimed the new state of Israel, and, to the visible surprise and acute embarrassment of Warren Austin and his American colleagues in the Assembly, President Truman instantly gave the new state *de facto* recognition. The shattered Assembly appointed a Mediator, Count Folke Bernadotte of Sweden, and faded away. The armies of Egypt, Syria, Iraq, Jordan, Lebanon and Saudi Arabia invaded Palestine, with the proclaimed intention of suppressing the Jewish state and establishing Arab rule over the whole territory.

The Security Council met on Saturday the 15th – and dispersed to spend a peacefully inactive Sunday. Trygve Lie spoiled the permanent members' sabbatical repose by bombarding them with reminders that

> this is the first time since the adoption of the Charter that Member States have openly declared that they have engaged in armed intervention outside their own territory. Moreover, this armed intervention has taken place in a territory which has been the special concern of the United Nations. . . . In Article 24 of the Charter, the Members conferred on the Security Council primary responsibility for the maintenance of international peace and security 'in order to ensure prompt and effective action' . . .

Even so, it was not until the next Saturday, May 22, that the Council managed to call for a cease-fire. Its call had no visible effect on the combatants.

On the third Saturday of the war, the 29th, the Council produced its first resolution that conveyed a slight baring of 'teeth'. It called for a four-week truce, and warned that refusal would lead it to reconsider the situation 'with a view to action under Chapter Seven'. But it still took some furious shuttling between the belligerents' capitals by Bernadotte and his chief assistant, Ralph Bunche, before the truce was brought into effect on June 11.

As the four-week truce neared its end, the Council appealed for an extension. The Israelis, who had done well in the first month of the war, were agreeable. The Arabs, who had done less well, rebuffed the Council and resumed fighting on July 9. On the 15th the Council (Russia now abstaining, and Syria understandably voting against) at last adopted a resolution in which the 'teeth' were quite visible. It determined that the situation already constituted 'a threat to peace within the meaning of Article 39', and declared that

> failure by any of the governments or authorities concerned to comply . . . would demonstrate the existence of a breach of the peace within the meaning of Article 39 . . . requiring immediate consideration by the Security Council with a view to such further action under Chapter Seven of the Charter as may be decided upon by the Council . . .

The second truce came into effect on the 18th. Before the end of the year the Council had been obliged to issue four more cease-fire calls, each of which echoed its warning of July 15. But the labours of Bernadotte and, after his murder by a Jewish terrorist gang, of his successor Ralph Bunche, gradually had their effect, and armistice talks began in January 1949 under Bunche's chairmanship.

Why, when the Council faced its first great challenge on Palestine, did the great powers give such a vivid imitation of five elephants sitting in a ring, paralysed by the sight of two mice slugging it out? It took them as much as two months after the overt internationalising of the war to get out a Council warning with any real teeth in it. Nor had this war flashed out upon them suddenly from some mysterious, neglected, remote corner of the world. The slow approach of its thunder had been growing louder for more than a year. Direct responsibility for the trouble spot had been thrust upon the UN by one of the Five with the consent of the others. Appeals for them to act rained upon them from all sides. But, in Lie's words, 'those Great Powers sat in the Security Council . . . leaving the forces concerned to fight it out'.

The British abandonment of responsibility was open and un-ashamed. Britain pulled out, and gave the UN no help in getting in. France was at least willing to provide truce observers, the chief of whom, Colonel Serot, was killed with Bernadotte; but in general the French held to their habitual view that Britain's Middle East policies were mad, bad and sad, and bound to lead to wrecks which the British could not expect others to salvage. Roosevelt's Fourth Policeman, China, was having a civil war, and losing it. The Russians and Americans were hamstrung by their own insistence that UN peace-keeping was a job only for great powers. When Lie begged in

124

vain for authority to raise a small UN guard force, which the Council might use for truce preservation until the great powers managed to make something of Article 43 (page 81), he was rebuffed with particular sharpness by the Russians, who had until then seemed at least more serious than the other powers about trying to stop the bloodshed.

The Americans became hypnotised by the alarming idea of Russia 'getting into the Middle East' – an idea that arose, of course, directly from the insistence of the Three in 1944–5 that it should be strictly the great powers' privilege to police the whole world. The veering inconsistency of America's Palestine policies in 1947–8 reflected the pulling and hauling between the keep-Russia-out strategists, bent on retaining Arab goodwill, and the Zionists and their sympathisers, bent on ensuring the creation of a Jewish state. Poor Warren Austin was the yo-yo. One could hardly blame the distraught Senator for letting his anguish lead him to cry out one day in the Council that all would be well in Palestine if only the Jews and Moslems would act like Christians.

This incident might have become an enlivening feature of the Council's undistinguished 1948 record. But it is not on the record. For all Senator Austin's air of apple-cheeked Vermont innocence, he was a shrewd old politician who knew very well that such an outburst, however understandable at the time, is better not set down in cold print. So he exercised his right to amend the official record of his speech. Copies of the unamended provisional record are still prized possessions of some old UN hands to this day.

*　　　*　　　*

General Wu Hsiu-chuan had the distinction of addressing the Security Council in 1950 as the representative of the one-year-old communist People's Republic of China. This first and, hitherto, last appearance of Peking man in the Council was the brief result of a long and complex process that occupied three months.

On 24 August 1950 the Council received a cable from the Peking foreign ministry which complained that the United States was committing aggression against China by sending armed forces to Taiwan

125

(Formosa). An American response was immediately presented to the Council. The United States, it said, had acted in order to keep the peace and to protect the security of the troops who were at that moment fighting in South Korea under the United Nations flag. But the American government would welcome consideration of the matter by the Council.

Yakov Malik had not only returned to his seat at the beginning of August, after the six-month Soviet boycott of the Council; he had returned as Council president for that month. In that capacity he had used every procedural device he could find to prevent the Council from playing an active part in regard to the Korean war that had begun in June. In particular, he had fought a running battle throughout the month to prevent South Korea's representative from participating in the Council's discussion of the war. (When Sir Gladwyn Jebb succeeded Malik as president on September 1 the representative from Seoul was at once installed at the Council table, with such lightning speed that the Russian could do no more than record a belated protest.) Malik now proposed that a Peking representative should be invited to New York to attend a Council debate on Peking's charge of aggression in Taiwan.

In the case of states that are members of the UN but not of the Council, it is a matter of course that, under Article 31 of the Charter, they are allowed to join in Council debates (without voting) if they have an interest in a specific subject of discussion. A state that is not a UN member has the right, under Article 32, to be invited to join in the discussion of any 'dispute' to which it is a party, subject to whatever conditions the Council may 'lay down'. In practice, the Council has tended to shy away from Article 32. It has never been very good at the job of laying down conditions; and it positively hates having to define the matter it is discussing as a 'dispute' – a definition that debars any Council member which is a party to the dispute from voting (page 85). Sometimes invitations to non-members are issued without the citing of any formal basis for them at all. Sometimes they have been issued under Rule 39 of the Council's rules of procedure. This rule permits it to invite 'persons, whom it considers competent for the purpose, to supply it with information or to give other assistance in examining matters within its competence'. It is a handy sort of rule, for it frees the Council from any need to decide that it is dealing with a 'dispute'; or that the invitee is a 'party' to that dispute; or that the invitee represents a 'state'. But, of course, an invitee may think it somewhat demeaning to accept an invitation in these terms. Hence the Council's usual preference for inviting non-UN states just to come along without worrying about their precise status.

In August 1950 the Council rejected its Russian president's proposal that a Peking representative should be invited under Article 32. This would have implied recognition of communist China as a state; and the Council, by a slim majority, was committed to the view that China was still legally represented by the government that had fled to Taipeh in 1949. Next it was proposed to send an invitation to Peking without any mention of Article 32. The five Council members that had recognised the new Peking government (Britain, India, Jugoslavia, Norway, Russia) voted for this, and so did France; but seven votes were needed to approve the invitation, so it was not issued.

The plot thickened with the arrival of a second complaint from Peking, which claimed that American aircraft had dropped bombs on Chinese territory on August 27. Peking now asked the Council both to condemn the United States as an aggressor and to secure the immediate withdrawal of American forces from Korea. (At this time the South Korean, American, and other allied forces were holding out in a small area around Pusan in the southeast. The rest of South Korea had been overrun by the North Korean invaders who had struck south on June 25.) A Council majority supported a proposal that Peking's charges should be investigated on the spot by representatives of India and Sweden. On September 12 Malik vetoed this proposal. Further complaints of American bombing arrived from Peking later in September, but at Malik's request these were referred to the Assembly.

At the end of September, with Sir Gladwyn Jebb still presiding, the Council staged one of its most exotic procedural jousts. On the 28th two separate proposals to invite Peking representatives to New York were voted on, and each failed to muster seven votes. Jebb had ruled that the invitations should be put to the vote without a previous vote about whether the matter was procedural (and thus veto-free) or

KOREA

not; he said that 'after we have taken it, we can argue this question out as to whether the vote is valid or not'. The American councilman had promptly announced that, in that case, he would vote against the invitation to Peking, regarding it as a procedural question; but that he reserved the right to change his vote to an abstention if the Council subsequently accepted the Taipeh representative's view that the question was substantive. In other words, he was not going to veto it.

Next day, September 29, the Council tried again. One of the two resolutions was submitted again, by Ecuador, and this time it was backed by seven members. The American, Cuban and Taipeh

128

Chinese councilmen voted against it. Gladwyn Jebb's ruling that the resolution had been duly adopted was challenged by the Taipeh man, who argued that the question was substantive and that his own vote thus constituted a veto, whatever the American might think about his. Jebb asked for a vote on whether the question had been procedural, and nine members voted that it had been; the Cuban abstained, and the Taipeh man again cast a negative vote. Jebb then gave a second and somewhat crisper ruling that the proposal had been duly adopted. The Taipeh China representative continued to protest vigorously, and even suggested that the International Court at The Hague should be asked to give an advisory opinion. Jebb treated this as a further challenge to his ruling, and asked the Council to vote on the challenge. It seemed, however, that the councilmen had had all the procedural voting they could take; even the Taipeh man gave up. It had to be solemnly recorded that there were no votes in support of the challenge; no votes against it; and no formal abstentions. Jebb calmly (and not unreasonably) claimed that his ruling had been upheld by this somewhat historic 0–0–0 vote.

The Taipeh man's objections had in fact been totally unfounded. There has never been any doubt, from the start of the Council's life, that invitations are procedural and veto-free matters. This point was specifically covered in the San Francisco Statement that the Big Five – including China – issued in 1945; it was reaffirmed in a 1949 Assembly resolution, which China co-sponsored. However, October brought the Taipeh representative temporary relief, for no envoy from Peking appeared in New York. Then, in November, communist China sent a large army into Korea and inflicted a heavy defeat on the United Nations forces – which by now had pushed far into the North.

The first clash between the Chinese troops and the UN forces, on November 5, was only a limited one. But the shock effect on the Council was considerable. At Jebb's urging, the Council agreed on th 8th to send a further invitation to Peking. This was a Rule 39 invitation, not to participate in, but 'to be present' during the Council's discussion of the UN Command's report on the Chinese intervention in the Korean war. In practice, the president and most members of the Council recognised that there would be no way of

129

preventing a Peking representative from airing his views about Korea in general. Most members were also not surprised when Peking rejected the invitation.

Attempts were made to reassure Peking that the UN action in Korea posed no threat to China itself. On November 10 six Council members put forward a draft resolution which, while calling upon Peking to withdraw its soldiers from Korea, would have declared that it was the UN's policy 'to hold the Chinese frontier with Korea inviolate, and fully to protect legitimate Chinese and Korean interests in the frontier zone'. On the 27th the Council agreed that it would combine the further discussion of the complaints about communist aggression in Korea and American aggression against China. The intention behind this move was to make it possible for a Peking representative to attend the combined debate. This aim was achieved, to the extent that at the end of November a Peking delegation led by General Wu Hsiu-chuan flew to New York by way of Moscow, Prague and London. General Wu announced that he had come only to present the Council with Peking's case about alleged American aggression. But it was hoped, by Council members and other representatives at the UN, that Wu could be drawn into informal discussion of a settlement of the Korean conflict.

Unfortunately, it was the last week of November that saw the launching – possibly in reaction to a new forward movement ordered by General Douglas MacArthur, commander of the UN forces – of the massive Chinese offensive that was to drive MacArthur's shattered forces southward even beyond Seoul. And in the Council on November 30 Malik vetoed the six-power draft resolution that had been presented on the 10th. General Wu addressed the Council for two hours, in utterly uncompromising Chinese, on the subject of American aggression against Taiwan. He produced his own draft resolution, which would have condemned the United States' aggression against China and intervention in Korea and demanded the withdrawal of its forces. Malik had this voted on – and found that he was the only Council member prepared to vote for it.

General Wu and his entourage settled into the Waldorf-Astoria Hotel and stayed in New York for three weeks. But Wu, who despite his own forceful manner seemed to defer at crucial moments to his nominal deputy, Chiao Kuan-hua, behaved in such an odd way that nobody could quite understand why he had come to New York at all, let alone why he lingered there so long. He met repeatedly and willingly with Trygve Lie, disregarding completely the fact that Russia had unleashed a furious campaign of personal abuse against the Secretary-General because of his support for the UN action in Korea. In all, Wu met Lie nine times. Lie got him to meet Ales Bebler of Jugoslavia, the Council president for December, and Nasrollah Entezam of Iran, president of the 1950 Assembly. Wu came to a dinner party at Lie's house in Forest Hills and there met Sir Gladwyn Jebb, Sir Benegal Rau of India, Sir Muhammad Zafrulla Khan of Pakistan and Moshe Sharett of Israel.

On December 9 – eight days after his first talk with Lie – Wu came to see Lie for the fifth time, declared that Peking wanted a cease-fire in Korea, and, making no mention of any conditions on his side, asked Lie to help him learn what the UN's conditions would be. But a few days later Wu was telling Lie, first, that his government had no interest in the Chinese 'volunteer' army that was fighting in Korea; and then that it would negotiate only on the basis that Malik had already stated: that is, there must be simultaneous negotiations for a cease-fire in Korea, for the transfer of the UN China seat and for acknowledgment of the Peking government's right to take over Taiwan.

After Malik's use of the veto in the Council on November 30 the Assembly added the question of China's intervention in Korea to its own agenda. On December 14 the Assembly appointed a three-man Cease-Fire Group consisting of its president, Entezam, Benegal Rau and Lester Pearson of Canada. Wu refused to meet this group. He had further talks with Rau (at which, it was said at the time, 'Rau did all the wooing, and Wu did all the rowing'), but stuck to the same line as he was now taking with Lie. On the 19th Wu and his party left for Peking – politely thanking Lie for all his help, but flatly rebuffing his pleas that they should extend their stay in New York even by just a few days.

Throughout December 1950 and January 1951 the Chinese army pressed its southward offensive in Korea. On January 31 the

131

Security Council admitted that it could no longer hope to reach any useful agreement, and unanimously decided to remove the Korea question from its agenda. Next day the Assembly convicted China of aggression in Korea. Then the tide of war began to turn, and the communist forces were driven out of South Korea for the second time. In June, when the UN Secretariat invited Malik to make one of a series of broadcasts it had arranged, he used the occasion to propose that talks about an armistice should start; and two weeks later they started – but it then took two years and two weeks before the armistice was signed.

In September 1954 communist China started to beat a lot of drums and gongs and announced that it was about to 'liberate' Taiwan (Formosa). Rather more ominously, it began to bombard the offshore islands, Quemoy and Matsu, which were (and are) still held by the forces of Taipeh China. The United States signed a mutual defence treaty with the Taipeh government, and President Eisenhower sought authority from Congress to use American forces in the defence of Taiwan and related areas.

Tension mounted, and it was compounded in November when Peking announced that it still held captive fifteen American airmen who had been shot down during the war in Korea, and that it had just staged a 'trial' and sentenced eleven of them to long terms of further imprisonment for alleged espionage. This was a gross breach of the 1953 Korea armistice terms, and there were angry demands in America for a blockade of the China coast. Eisenhower and his Secretary of State, John Foster Dulles, preferred to try an approach by way of the UN. On December 10 the Assembly adopted a resolution declaring that the detention of the airmen was a violation of the armistice agreement and asking Dag Hammarskjöld, as Secretary-General, to seek their release 'by the means most appropriate in his judgment'.

Hammarskjöld embarked on his first major venture in 'vacuum-filling', setting off for Peking in person and spending four days there in early January 1955. His talks with Chou En-lai were to open the door to the release of the airmen later in the year. But after he had returned to New York from China with nothing immediate to show

132

At Hunter College in 1946 (page 73). At left, Evatt (page 69); at right, Trygve Lie

At Lake Success in 1950. To the right from Russia's empty chair, Gladwyn Jebb and Warren Austin (pages 20, 27, 74)

In Paris, 1948, the Council stands in tribute to the murdered Bernadotte (page 74)

Count Folke Bernadotte, in Jerusalem while serving as UN Mediator in Palestine (page 123)

for his pains, the tension in the Formosa straits continued to mount. On January 28 New Zealand, which was then a member of the Security Council, asked the Council to consider the question of the fighting in the area of the offshore islands between the forces of the two Chinese regimes. On the 30th Russia asked for a discussion of 'American aggression' in the area. The Council decided to take the New Zealand item first.

On 31 January 1955 the Council sent Peking an invitation to take part in the debate on the New Zealand item. On February 3 the Peking foreign minister replied that the Council was violating the Charter in discussing the question, since the liberation of China's own territory was a purely domestic Chinese affair. He added that his government would not participate in any Council discussions until its representative had occupied the Chinese seat at the UN.

The Council adjourned in mid-February after an inconclusive preliminary discussion, and with the general impression that the distance between New York and Peking was as great as ever in spite of Hammarskjöld's personal breakthrough.

*   *   *

The 1965 war between India and Pakistan was one of the biggest conflicts the Council has ever grappled with. Compared with, say, the 1967 Arab–Israel war, the 1965 one involved fighting over a larger area, for a longer period, between the forces of much larger nations – quite apart from the concurrent threat of armed intervention by communist China. As in the 1967 case, the major powers were unhappily involved in the conflict in a variety of ways, including the fact that the war was fought largely with arms that they had supplied; and, also as in 1967, the crisis brought about a brief display of unity between the two super-powers.

The war began in Kashmir, the Himalayan territory whose fate had recurrently preoccupied the Council since 1948; as a familiar problem it was, for the Council, of the same vintage as that of Palestine. In January 1948 India had asked the Council to demand that Pakistan should cease to support the invasion of Kashmir by Pathan tribesmen from Pakistan's North-West Frontier province.

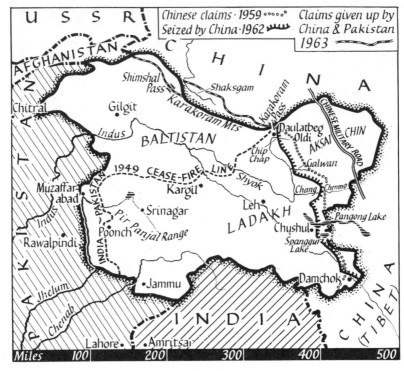

KASHMIR

The Council sent out a five-member commission (America, Argentina, Belgium, Colombia, Czechoslovakia) to mediate. A cease-fire was arranged – by now Pakistan's regular forces were also fighting in Kashmir – and took effect in January 1949. Since then the territory (which is formally named Jammu and Kashmir) has in fact remained partitioned, the west and northwest being under Pakistani control, while India holds the central Srinagar valley – the real bone of contention – as well as Jammu and Leh.

To watch the 500-mile cease-fire line, most of which runs through difficult mountainous terrain, the commission, with Council approval, installed an observer group whose strength varied between thirty and forty-five over the years. The first observers were provided by America, Belgium, Canada, Mexico and Norway; later contributors included Australia, Chile, Denmark, Finland, Italy, New

Zealand, Sweden and Uruguay. General Maurice Delvoie of Belgium, as the commission's military adviser, was initially in charge of the operation; he handed over to General Angle of Canada, who became the first Chief Military Observer of the UN Military Observer Group in India and Pakistan (Unmogip). After Angle had been killed in an air crash, General Robert Nimmo of Australia took over and commanded Unmogip from 1950 until his death in 1966, when he was succeeded by General Luis Tassara Gonzalez of Chile.

While the observers kept their long watch, and did a great deal to prevent petty frictions from building up into serious clashes along the cease-fire line, the Council experimented with a variety of approaches, all unsuccessful, to the task of shaping a political settlement. At the start it had seemed to be agreed that the Kashmiris should decide their future by a plebiscite; but the conditions in which this should be staged were never agreed. In 1949 Admiral Chester Nimitz of the United States was appointed by Trygve Lie as plebiscite administrator. In 1950 General McNaughton of Canada, as the Council's president, tried and failed to get India and Pakistan to agree to a plan for the demilitarisation of Kashmir as a step towards a plebiscite. The Council dissolved its commission and instead appointed, as UN Representative for India and Pakistan, first Sir Owen Dixon of Australia and then, in 1951, Frank P. Graham of the United States. In 1953 Graham got the two parties as far as holding ministerial talks in Geneva under his chairmanship, but neither then nor during his later efforts was agreement reached on terms for military withdrawals and the holding of a plebiscite. In 1957 the Council asked Gunnar Jarring of Sweden, who was its president at the time, to visit the two countries and examine any possibilities of achieving a settlement. Jarring was no more successful than his various predecessors in finding a magic key to the problem; but his skilful performance in a very delicate situation did much to reduce tensions that had been ominously rising.

The mid-1950s had seen several developments that made the Kashmir problem seem even more intractable than before. Pakistan had eagerly joined the western-sponsored Seato and Baghdad Pact (later Cento) alliances. Although these were explicitly intended to shield southeast Asia against China and the Middle East against

135

Russia, India had some reason for its belief that Pakistan had joined them largely with the aim of getting arms and allies that would strengthen its position *vis-à-vis* India.

Jawaharlal Nehru, perhaps over-zealously advised by V. K. Krishna Menon, came to lean heavily on the support that Nikita Khrushchev now offered for India's claim that the Kashmir issue had been settled by the legal incorporation of the whole state into India. In November 1956, when the UN Assembly called for internationally supervised elections in Hungary, India was alone in siding with the Soviet group to vote against the resolution. Nehru's attitude to the Russian invasion of Hungary was sharply criticised in the Indian parliament, but he won applause there when he said that he particularly opposed the idea of UN supervision of elections, which would set a dangerous precedent − a reference, of course, to Kashmir.

In January 1957, at Pakistan's request, the Council broke a four-year silence on Kashmir by embarking on a series of debates during which Krishna Menon distinguished − and nearly extinguished − himself by delivering a succession of marathon speeches. One of them lasted for eight hours. (Even the austere and eloquent Menon's oratorical ability was not limitless, and one of his Kashmir speeches in the Council ended with an alarming, though brief, collapse. This inspired a rather cynical jest, which enjoyed a long life in the UN corridors, to the effect that Menon could always be revived by waving a microphone under his nose.) The filibustering did not prevent the Council from passing a resolution which restated the original agreement that Kashmir's ultimate fate should be settled by a UN-supervised plebiscite. Ten of the eleven Council members voted for this resolution. Arkady Sobolev, instead of using Russia's veto, merely abstained. This seemed strange, for in the debate he had backed India up to, indeed beyond, the hilt, insisting that 'the question of Kashmir has been settled by the people of Kashmir themselves'. One explanation offered at the time was that Sobolev feared that a veto might bring an emergency Assembly session down upon him; another was that the Russians, in these post-Suez months, did not want to alienate Moslem opinion and see Moslem eyes turn instead to America.

When Jarring had made his journey and delivered his uncomforting report the Council resumed debate on Kashmir in September 1957, and was confronted with a new proposal made by the Pakistan foreign minister, Malik Firoz Khan Noon. Since India would not agree that a UN force should replace both countries' troops in Kashmir, Noon offered a unilateral Pakistani withdrawal from Azad Kashmir (the Pakistani-held 'free Kashmir' west of the cease-fire line) if the UN would place a force there. But India strongly opposed this idea too, and there was little support for it among Council members. In December the Council ended by asking Frank Graham to have one more go. During 1958 Graham's latest suggestions, which included the proposal to put a UN force into Azad Kashmir, were rejected by India; and the military coup in Pakistan brought in a regime led by Field Marshal Ayub Khan, whose first years in power were marked by a temporary improvement in Indo-Pakistani relations.

Early in 1962 Pakistan succeeded, despite Indian objections, in getting the Council to hold another series of meetings on Kashmir; but these ended inconclusively after Russia had vetoed a draft resolution, sponsored by Ireland and very mildly worded, that would have asked the two countries to resume negotiations. The mere introduction of this draft was denounced as 'a hostile act' by Krishna Menon, by now India's defence minister, who was making what was to prove something of a farewell appearance in the Council. Later in that year the Chinese invasion of India cost him his office and plunged him into political eclipse. It also led to a fresh attempt at bilateral negotiation of the differences between India and Pakistan. But this petered out, while a new Pakistani orientation towards China now emerged, its chief architect being Ayub Khan's volatile young (35) foreign minister, Zulfikar Ali Bhutto. A further series of Council meetings on Kashmir were held, at Bhutto's request, between February and May 1964. At the end of them the Council's president, Roger Seydoux of France, was able only to read out a very vague consensus. All that really emerged was that no Council member actually objected to the idea that the two disputants should 'resume their contacts in the near future'. Even this supremely cautious statement was received with supreme caution both by Bhutto and, for India, by M. C. Chagla. (Chagla, a Moslem and former judge, was then minister for education, but, as his presence in New York indicated, was doing much of the work of the foreign ministry, which he later took over.)

The background to the 1964 meetings was that the Kashmir state government installed by India had collapsed amid anti-Indian rioting. Nehru had once again released from detention Sheikh Abdullah, the popular Kashmiri leader who had become increasingly pro-Pakistani. For a moment it looked as if Nehru and Ayub were going to meet and at last make a real attempt to settle the Kashmir dispute; but Nehru's sudden death removed this possibility. Early in 1965 the two countries became embroiled in a new territorial conflict over the Rann of Kutch; and Abdullah was arrested on his return to India from a tour during which he had found Chinese as well as Pakistani backing.

In the first week of August, 1965, large numbers of armed Pakistanis in civilian clothes began to infiltrate across the cease-fire line at many different points. They sought to cut the communications of the Indian army in Kashmir and to set off a popular rising. Pakistani troops launched supporting attacks; by the end of August Indian troops, too, had advanced across the cease-fire line in several places. On September 1 U Thant sent urgent appeals to President Ayub Khan and to the new Indian prime minister, Lal Bahadur Shastri. On the 3rd he presented the Council with a report in which he said that the cease-fire agreement had 'collapsed'.

Thant reported that there had been a disturbing increase in the number of violations of the cease-fire line during 1965; that during August the violations had become unprecedented in scale; that he had been appealing to both sides for restraint since August 9, without effect; and that he had summoned General Nimmo to New York, but that India and Pakistan had made difficulties when he proposed to send Ralph Bunche out as his personal representative to discuss the restoration of the cease-fire. He summarised for the Council the detailed information provided by Nimmo's men.

The Council met on Saturday September 4, at the urgent request of Arthur Goldberg, its current president. The representatives of India and Pakistan were, as usual, invited to take part in the meeting.

Gopalaswami Parthasarathi asked the Council to condemn Pakistan as an aggressor and order it to withdraw its forces from the whole of Kashmir. Syed Amjad Ali denied all the Indian allegations, but, saying that he had received no instructions, left it at that. The six non-permanent Council members (Bolivia, Ivory Coast, Jordan, Malaysia, Netherlands and Uruguay) sponsored a resolution calling for an immediate cease-fire and withdrawal of each country's forces to its own side of the 1949 cease-fire line. This was adopted unanimously.

On Monday the 6th, however, the Council was called together again to hear a new and even more alarming report from Thant. Nimmo, who had returned to Kashmir, had reported that the fighting was 'broadening and intensifying'. (It was, in fact, on the 6th that the war spread beyond Kashmir, when Indian forces struck across the Punjab border towards Lahore. Two days later they also invaded Pakistan 500 miles farther south, in Sind.) Neither government had responded to the Council's cease-fire call.

Amjad Ali had by now got some instructions. He proceeded to tell the Council that India had always wanted to annex Pakistan, and was now invading it on a flimsy pretext; this 'brazen aggression' was comparable to Hitler's actions. The Council should use enforcement measures under Chapter Seven of the Charter to halt the aggression, and then enforce the original agreement on a UN-supervised plebiscite in Kashmir. Chandra S. Jha (Parthasarathi's predecessor as India's UN representative) now took over the Indian case, in the first of what was to become a bewildering series of substitutions on both sides during these meetings. Jha produced his government's response to the Council's appeal of the 4th. This appeal, it said, should have been addressed only to Pakistan, which had clearly prepared a large-scale offensive against India. India had been obliged to invade Pakistan to prevent attacks in Kashmir being launched from bases there. Once again the Council heard both parties out in almost complete silence and then unanimously adopted a resolution sponsored by its six elected members. This repeated the call for cease-fire and withdrawal, and asked Thant to 'exert every possible effort' to restore peace and to 'take all measures possible' to strengthen Unmogip.

Thant immediately flew to India and Pakistan and saw Ayub and Bhutto, Shastri and his foreign minister, Sardar Swaran Singh. Shastri told Thant he was ready to order a cease-fire; but Ayub's response, which Thant received on the 14th, said only that Pakistan would welcome any cease-fire that provided a 'self-executing arrangement' for a settlement of the Kashmir dispute. The Council's resolution of the 6th, said Ayub, merely meant that India's grip on Kashmir would be restored. There should be a complete Indian and Pakistani withdrawal from Kashmir; a UN force drawn from Asian and African countries should be sent to keep order there, and a plebiscite should be held within three months. Thant got back to New York on September 16 and at once gave the Council a forceful report in which he asked it to consider ordering India and Pakistan to stop fighting, under Article 40 of the Charter, and warning them that failure to comply would show that there had been a breach of the peace within the meaning of Article 39. This was a strong hint that the Council would have to consider enforcement action of the Chapter Seven type.

In the Council on the 17th India was represented by Chagla, who described Ayub's conditions for a cease-fire as 'preposterous' and accused Pakistan of trying to set off a religious war that would involve the fifty million Moslems in India. And Chagla also brought into the debate news of a most ominous development. That day an ultimatum had reached New Delhi from Peking. Chagla's immediate reaction was to argue that Pakistan had clearly attacked India in the expectation that China would join in the war. 'She wants China to stab us in the back and force us to fight on two fronts,' he said.

The Chinese ultimatum was undoubtedly an attempt to intervene in the Indo-Pakistani war. On paper, of course, it had nothing to do with that war. Peking accused the Indians of violating its border in the neighbourhood of Sikkim, more than 600 miles east of Kashmir. It demanded a withdrawal within 72 hours, and the restitution of various things allegedly misappropriated by the Indians, the most memorable item on its little list being fifty-nine yaks. But its tone was one of immediate menace. In effect, Peking was saying: kowtow at once, or we shall invade you, just as we did in 1962.

The ultimatum posed a dilemma for America and Britain as well

140

as India. It had already proved sufficiently embarrassing for the Americans that Pakistan was fighting this war with arms they had provided in the belief that they were stiffening southern Asia against the communist powers. Now the Pakistanis were rejoicing at Peking's move and almost begging it to invade India. After the 1962 invasion America and Britain had given India general assurances that they would support it against any further Chinese attack. How could they do this when India was already at war with Pakistan, and they had suspended arms shipments to both the warring countries?

Debate ground on in the Council under this dark new shadow. On Saturday the 18th Pakistan's law minister, S. M. Zafar, restated Ayub's conditions and claimed that to ask for a simple cease-fire and withdrawal was to ask Pakistan to accept dishonour and to sacrifice its Kashmiri brothers. Chagla declared that China was fighting India through Pakistan. The Council members themselves, who had hitherto kept a remarkable silence and (perhaps thereby) preserved a remarkable unanimity, began to speak and to differ. Zaid Rifai of Jordan came out frankly on Pakistan's side. The representative of Malaysia, Radhakrishna Ramani, refuted Rifai's arguments and insisted that the Council should acknowledge that India had accepted the cease-fire call, and should address its next call to Pakistan alone. (One suspects that, at some point during these jousts, the thought occurred to Ramani – the representative of predominantly Moslem Malaysia, but himself of Hindu origin – that life would have been easier for him if Malaysia had not fought so hard to get a Council seat.) Roger Seydoux of France inclined to the Jordanian view, Fedorenko to the Malaysian.

Throughout Sunday the 19th the Americans and British worked hard mustering support for a new draft resolution. In the early hours of the morning of Monday the 20th the Dutch representative, J. G. de Beus, introduced it in the Council and, over Zafar's protests, it was adopted by a 10–0 vote, Jordan abstaining on the ground that the Council ought to address itself directly to the underlying issues – that is, to Pakistan's grievances. Ramani of Malaysia voted for it although he deplored the fact that it made any reference at all to a political settlement. The resolution demanded a cease-fire by the 22nd; called for the 'subsequent withdrawal of all armed personnel to the positions held by them before 5 August 1965' (which meant that the Pakistani infiltrators must leave Kashmir); asked Thant to ensure supervision of the cease-fire and withdrawals; and said that after the withdrawals the Council would consider steps to 'assist towards a settlement of the political problem underlying the present conflict'.

There was no doubt that India could again accept this call. Would Pakistan comply? To do so meant its having to eat a lot of newly uttered words. Bhutto caught a plane for New York, and the Council waited anxiously for his arrival on the evening of Tuesday the 21st. There were hasty midnight talks as soon as he reached the UN, and then the Council was called to a second early morning session. Shortly before dawn on Wednesday the 22nd, just beating the deadline the Council had set, Bhutto informed it of his government's acceptance of the cease-fire.

By then another deadline had already expired – the one in the Chinese ultimatum to India. And the Chinese had not launched an invasion. They muffled their inaction in a cloud of confused words, some still threatening, others almost comic: thus, they claimed that India had bowed to their demands by pulling its troops back and dismantling fortifications it had allegedly built on the Chinese side of the border, but the Indians said they had neither entered Chinese territory nor withdrawn from it, and had neither built nor dismantled anything. However, it was clear that there was not going to be a War of the Fifty-nine Yaks.

This exposure of Peking's bluff added to the bitterness of Bhutto's position. He had many words to eat, but there was no alternative. Peking had failed him, Pakistan's army and air force were now being grievously mauled by the stronger Indian forces, no more American arms were arriving and the whole flow of economic aid from western countries was in jeopardy. He vented his anger on the Council in his pre-dawn speech, charging it with 'lethargy and indolence' ('For eighteen years you have played and toyed with the future of Kashmir'); and he added that if the Council failed to solve the Kashmir problem this time Pakistan would withdraw from the United Nations. 'Then, sir, you will have one third or more of the world outside your organisation.' (It should be remembered that this was the year in which Indonesia had withdrawn from the UN and joined China in calling for the creation of a 'rival UN' based on Peking.)

But Bhutto's harsh words could not rob the Council members of their sense of relief and of achievement. A large and spreading war had been halted, just eighteen days after the Council first tackled the new crisis. A large tidying-up operation admittedly lay ahead, but Thant was losing no time in tackling it. The day after the cease-fire he announced that, as well as enlarging Unmogip, he was forming a second group, the UN India–Pakistan Observation Mission (Unipom), to supervise the cease-fire and withdrawals in areas other than Kashmir. On the 24th he appointed as Chief Officer of Unipom General Bruce Macdonald of Canada, who was already on UN peace-keeping duty with the force in Cyprus. By mid-October Nimmo had ninety observers at work in Kashmir, and Macdonald ninety on the Punjab, Rajasthan and Sind borders.

Thant was also, discreetly but strongly, urging Shastri and Ayub to meet somewhere in 'neutral' territory – one obvious possibility being that they might accept the invitation already issued by the Soviet prime minister, Alexei Kosygin, to meet at Tashkent and make use of his good offices. But there was still a long road to travel before they got to Tashkent; and for Shastri, tragically, that was to be the end of the road.

Meanwhile there was the mess to be cleared up. The two armies still stood eyeball to eyeball at many points along a line more than 1,000 miles long; and each was still occupying hundreds of square miles of territory on the wrong side of that line. By September 27 the Council was back at its table to hear Thant report serious violations of the cease-fire and to adopt without dissent (indeed, without voting) a resolution demanding compliance with the cease-fire and prompt withdrawals. During October Nimmo's and Macdonald's men kept up a flow of warning reports about further violations and about both armies' attempts to gain ground by edging forward.

On October 22 Pakistan asked for an urgent Council meeting on the ground that India was planning a new offensive in the Rajasthan sector and was also intensifying repression in Kashmir. When the Council met on the 25th Bhutto accused India of letting loose a

143

'reign of terror' in Kashmir. Hector Paysse Reyes of Uruguay, president for October, asked Bhutto to confine himself to the matter on the agenda. Muhammad El-Farra of Jordan and Arsene Usher of Ivory Coast urged that Bhutto should be allowed to speak about the situation in Kashmir because this, as well as the ending of the war, was a matter covered by the resolution of September 20. The Indian foreign minister, Swaran Singh, intervened on a point of order, asking the president to restrain Bhutto from discussing matters within India's domestic jurisdiction. Paysse Reyes said that, strictly, only Council members could raise points of order. He appealed to Bhutto not to refer to such matters, but did not stop him when he promptly resumed his allegations of atrocities. Swaran Singh then said that he could take no further part in the discussion, and he left the table, amid a good deal of procedural squabbling.

It was a bad day in the Council, October 25, and it got worse. Fedorenko broke the solid front that the great powers had shown ever since September 4, by attacking Thant's action in deploying more observers. Out of thin air, the Russian conjured up

> provisions of the United Nations Charter, in accordance with which only the Security Council is competent to adopt appropriate measures on concrete questions connected with observers of the United Nations, namely, with their functions, their numbers, the command, the method of financing their activities, and so on.

There are, of course, no such provisions in the Charter; and for fifteen years the Russians had tacitly accepted the obvious common-sense fact that, when the Council asked the Secretary-General to organise observation, it had to let him handle the job without undue interference if it was to be done at all. But now Fedorenko complained that the Council's resolutions 'do not give any basis for the actions that were taken'.

The debate was dragged out until November 5, when the Council adopted, by a 9–0 vote, another resolution calling on India and Pakistan to stop violating the cease-fire and co-operate with the UN observers. This time Russia as well as Jordan abstained. Meanwhile the correctness of Thant's action, and the need to let him get on with the job, had been upheld in chorus by the American, British, Dutch,

Ivory Coast, Jordanian and Malaysian representatives. Seydoux recalled the familiar French position of principle about Council control of all peace-keeping operations, but he emphasised that he was not challenging Thant's actions in this case. Fedorenko, however, repeated his arguments several times and insisted, in vain, that the Council should fix a three-month time limit for the expanded observer operation.

As to Thant's action in setting up the new group, Unipom, he had long since explained that he had had to do this simply because Pakistan would not agree to have Unmogip's scope extended beyond Kashmir; so how else was he to meet the Council's demand that he should ensure supervision of the cease-fire and withdrawals all along the fronts? Pained but not exactly surprised by feeling a Russian knife in his back, Thant quietly pressed on. During November he secured the agreement of India and Pakistan to appoint military representatives to discuss the problem of withdrawals with a special representative of the UN. For this purpose he sent General Tulio Marambio of Chile to both countries, and Marambio succeeded in bringing together their military representatives at a series of meetings, held alternately in Lahore and Amritsar, which began on 3 January 1966. A week later the long awaited Ayub–Shastri meeting at Tashkent produced a general agreement on withdrawal, and gave the green light for the soldiers to complete their plans, which they did by the 29th. By February 25 all the withdrawals had been carried out, under the watchful eyes of Macdonald's and Nimmo's men. (Nimmo himself, sadly, did not see this fulfilment of a mission. On January 4 he died suddenly in Rawalpindi, just after returning from a journey to UN headquarters in New York, having completed fifteen years of peace-keeping service at the age of 72.) Unipom was disbanded in March, while Unmogip soon reverted to its former size. At the time of writing, the UN observers in the Kashmir mountains are in their twenty-second year of uninterrupted activity.

*   *   *

Somewhere among the archives there is probably a bald and stoop-shouldered scholar who, by now, is the only man who could tell you without consulting the records that the Security Council first took up the problem of Indo-China as far back as 1954. The first days of May in that year had seen both the start of the Geneva talks on Indo-China and the end of France's long struggle to keep northern Vietnam out of the hands of the communist-led Viet Minh. The capture of the stronghold which the French had rashly established at Dien Bien Phu, in the jungly mountains that divide northern Vietnam from Laos, destroyed their will to fight on and also gave the Viet Minh easier access to Laos. On May 29 Thailand asked the Council to consider the Indo-China situation in general and the threat it posed to Thailand in particular. The Thais told the Council that there was evidence that the Viet Minh meant to take over both Laos and Cambodia and were carrying subversion into Thailand itself. They asked the Council to send out a team from the Peace Observation Commission which had been established, at least on paper, by the 1950 UN Assembly. They presented a draft resolution authorising this fact-finding move. On June 18 nine of the Council's eleven members voted for the resolution, but Russia vetoed it.

Under the arrangements approved in November 1950 by the Assembly, either Assembly or Council could activate the Peace Observation Commission. So on July 7 Thailand gave notice that it would ask for the Assembly to be reconvened to consider its request. But the Geneva conference, on July 21, reached agreements providing for the withdrawal of Viet Minh forces from Laos and Cambodia; and in August the Thais correspondingly withdrew their appeal to the Assembly.

Five years later the Council was drawn a little deeper into the Laotian jungle, which by then had thickened. Since 1954 the communist Pathet Lao movement had kept control of the northeastern part of Laos, which borders on North Vietnam. Prince Souvanna Phouma had failed in his attempts to bring the country together under a coalition government that included communist members. A right-wing government took over, and became increasingly dependent on American help in its struggle against the Pathet Lao. Dag Hammarskjöld saw trouble coming. He visited Laos in March 1959 and thereafter kept in constant touch with developments there. In August the Laotian government asked him to send out an observer

146

VIETNAM, LAOS, CAMBODIA

team which, it hoped, would discourage communist-ruled North Vietnam from intervening.

The Secretary-General took a cautious attitude. He explained that, without authority from Council or Assembly, he could not send a mission to watch over an international border unless both the countries concerned asked for one or, in this case, unless the request was backed by the 1954 Geneva conference's co-chairmen, Russia and Britain. (Russia was arguing that the Laos situation called for the reactivating of the Geneva machinery, not for UN action.) Hammarskjöld told the press that:

> If it were a case of one of these fairly new-fangled initiatives of the Secretary-General acting without authorisation, or without a formal decision of any of the other organs, he can never permit himself to act, so to say, in a legally ambiguous way.

The Laotian government then, on 4 September 1959, appealed specifically to the Security Council. Alleging aggression by North Vietnamese forces, it asked the Council to send out a UN emergency force to halt this aggression. Hammarskjöld, who was on tour in Latin America, returned hastily to New York, and on the 5th he asked the Council's president for September, Egidio Ortona of Italy, to convene it urgently in accordance with the Laotian request, though he made clear that he was not personally endorsing the charge of aggression.

A distinctly unhappy Council met on the 7th. Not only was it obvious that Russia would veto any move to send a UN force to Laos; the western Council members also disliked the idea – though their reasons varied, from the British feeling that the whole crisis was being overblown to the Americans' wish to be left alone to get on with their own action in Laos without any complicating action by the UN. By way of compromise, America, Britain and France proposed that the Council should set up an investigating sub-committee comprising four of its non-permanent members, Argentina, Italy, Japan and Tunisia. At one o'clock in the early morning of September 8, ten Council members out of eleven voted for this resolution. Russia opposed it, arguing that what was needed was a revival of the three-member (Canada, India, Poland) International Control Commission

148

General Nimmo (on left) with UN observers at their Kashmir headquarters
(page 135)

Observers signalling by flag to a Kashmir mountain post

Before debate on the 1965 Indo-Pakistani war: from left, Rifai, Ramani, the Netherlands' Quarles van Ufford (page 141)

Krishna Menon (page 136)

Zulfikar Ali Bhutto addressing the Council (page 142)

for Laos, which had been set up by the 1954 Geneva conference but had suspended its work in 1958. Arkady Sobolev, the Soviet representative, contended that his contrary vote constituted a veto. Ortona ruled that it did not, since the resolution was merely a procedural one; and the Council upheld its president's ruling by another 10–1 vote.

This was one of the most striking of the series of disputes in the Council about the 'double veto'. As usual in these cases, the argument harked back to the statement that the Big Five had issued at San Francisco on 8 June 1945 – a statement which the San Francisco conference never endorsed, but which might well be regarded as binding its five sponsoring governments (page 69). In the 'San Francisco Statement' the Five had sought to meet some of the other states' objections to the extent of the veto power. They stated that no veto could prevent the Council from discussing a dispute or situation; but they argued that 'beyond this point' Council decisions might set off 'a chain of events' that could bring the Council to invoke 'measures of enforcement' under Chapter Seven of the Charter. 'This chain of events begins when the Council decides to make an investigation . . . or makes recommendations to the parties. It is to such decisions and actions that unanimity of the permanent members applies. . . .'

Sobolev, not unreasonably, held that this formula exactly fitted the situation. The Council was deciding to make an investigation, which in the circumstances might very easily set off a 'chain of events' of the kind the 1945 Statement had described. America, Britain and France preferred to pick out another paragraph in the same Statement, which said that the Council would be able, by a vote of any seven of its members, to 'establish such bodies or agencies as it may deem necessary for the performance of its functions'. The subcommittee on Laos, they contended, was just such a body. Although the resolution authorised it 'to conduct such inquiries as it may determine necessary', these inquiries were to be somehow quite different from an 'investigation' of the kind mentioned in the 1945 Statement. The distinction might not have seemed very obvious to a layman's eye, but it apparently leapt to the eye of ten of the councilmen, and they lined up behind Ortona to squelch the protesting

149

Sobolev. This was not simply a matter of that year's Council membership being exceptionally solid in its antagonism to the Russians and their communist protégés in Indo-China. The elected Council members were at least partly influenced by an entirely different motive. Seeing that four of the five sponsors of the San Francisco Statement were prepared to give ground over its interpretation, they did not want to miss the opportunity to occupy that ground.

While Sobolev continued to insist that the whole thing was illegal, the sub-committee of four duly went to Laos. It spent a month there, which, although finding facts in a country like Laos is notoriously difficult, seemed a pretty adequate period for the conduct of its 'inquiries', and perhaps even permitted it to do some investigating too. When it reported on November 3 it made no recommendations for further action; and its findings indicated that there had been no invasion of Laos by North Vietnamese forces, though the Laotian communist guerrillas had received arms and other help from Hanoi.

The Council could do no more. Both Americans and Russians seemed to prefer that the UN should now keep out of Laos while a conflict developed there which each thought would be won by 'its' side. But Hammarskjöld believed there was still a chance of averting this. As he saw it, neither of the super-powers was wholeheartedly committed to ensuring the victory of its Laotian protégés, while there was widespread support – among other UN members, and among some Americans, as well as in Laos itself – for the idea of another attempt to shape a 'neutral' Laos and damp down the fighting. He got the Laotian government to invite him to visit Vientiane again. And, when informing the Council members that he was going to Laos, he also told them that he would install a personal representative there, whose presence would help him to fulfil his responsibilities 'regarding developments which might threaten peace and security'.

Hammarskjöld knew that neither Washington nor Moscow would welcome his initiative, but he rightly reckoned that neither of them would object too strongly to a move which in fact was intended to help them both get off the hook. There was no further Council meeting, so no further call for combative speechmaking. The only complaints were muffled ones. Sobolev protested (in a letter which he took care to leak to the press) that the Secretary-General's moves would 'further complicate' the situation. This was obviously just meant for the record, rather than as a serious objection.

A full year later, when the Russians had mounted a full-scale onslaught on Hammarskjöld and demanded the abolition of his office, they denounced his 1959 action in Laos in much stronger language than they had used at the time. He had 'exceeded his competence' in this as in other matters, they claimed. He gave them a crushing retort in front of the Assembly, restating the argument that Trygve Lie had used in 1946 in the Council – when Gromyko, of all people, had supported Lie (page 351). Hammarskjöld asked how the Secretary-General was to do his duty, under Article 99, of alerting the Council to threats to peace:

> Has he to rely on reports in the press, or from this or that government? Has he to take the word of Moscow or Washington? No, certainly not. He has to find out for himself. And that may mean, as in the case of the criticised journey to Laos last November, that he has to go himself. To deny the Secretary-General the right to such personal fact-finding is, in fact, to erase from the Charter Article 99.

Once more, five years passed before the Council again tangled with the problems of the Indo-Chinese countries. On 13 May 1964 Cambodia asked the Council to meet; to hear its complaint of 261 violations of its border by American and South Vietnam forces during the past year; and to send a UN mission to investigate these charges. Then and for several years afterwards, the Cambodian government headed by Prince Norodom Sihanouk denied that it was letting North Vietnam troops and communist guerrillas (Vietcong) use its territory in their attacks on South Vietnam. (Only in 1969 did Sihanouk admit that this had been happening; only after his overthrow in 1970 did Cambodia try to oust the Vietnamese communist forces which by then had taken effective control of large parts of the country.)

The American and South Vietnam representatives (the latter having been permitted to take part in the Council's debate, on the usual non-voting basis, although his country was not a UN member) said that any violations that had occurred had been unintentional, that apologies had already been made, and that the main trouble was the

151

inadequate marking of the border. They suggested that the UN should help to demarcate the border, and that it should be patrolled, either by the UN, or by joint Cambodian and South Vietnam patrols, or by a combination of these with UN observers.

Sihanouk had sought UN help, but this was more help than he wanted. Obviously, any effective border patrols would soon reveal, to his embarrassment, the extent to which North Vietnam's forces were using Cambodia for access to South Vietnam. His spokesman in the Council suggested that it would be better to have the border supervised by the International Control Commission for Cambodia that had been set up by the 1954 Geneva conference – and which had lapsed into almost complete inactivity. The Americans, and the British, feared that the ICC could not be expected to do the job effectively. The Council adjourned for consultations. To a good many people's surprise, it was able to meet again on June 4 and adopt, unanimously, a resolution providing for three Council members – Brazil, Ivory Coast and Morocco – to visit Cambodia and South Vietnam, inspect the sites of the alleged border violations, and propose measures to prevent their recurrence.

The missionary three reported their findings on July 27. They recommended that the Council should authorise the Secretary-General to send a UN observer group to Cambodia; and that it should appoint a person acceptable to Cambodia and South Vietnam who would get the two governments to tackle border demarcation and other causes of dispute. But Sihanouk didn't like any of this; so the Council did nothing about it. After all, it was he who had asked for its help. Now it seemed he had changed his mind, and the help could hardly be thrust upon him. Apparently he preferred to go on living with a situation in which his country was used by the North Vietnam forces as a corridor to South Vietnam, and intermittently subjected to incursions by American and South Vietnam forces in pursuit of their antagonists. And that was what he got, for another five years.

Almost at the same moment, the Council was asked – by the United States – to involve itself much more directly in the Vietnam war. At this stage the fighting was still confined to South Vietnam, and no American combat troops were involved. But in August 1964 the

Americans made a direct attack on North Vietnam from the sea. On August 4 Adlai Stevenson asked for an urgent Security Council meeting on the situation created by 'deliberate attacks of the Hanoi regime on United States naval vessels in international waters'. According to the letter he addressed to the Council president, there had been two unprovoked attacks, on the 2nd and the 4th, by North Vietnam torpedo boats on American destroyers in international waters off the North Vietnam coast in the Tonking Gulf. After the second attack the Americans had used naval aircraft to strike at the torpedo boats' coastal bases.

Council meetings were held on August 5 and 7. Roger Seydoux, echoing a proposal that General de Gaulle had made two weeks earlier, urged that it was now necessary to reconvene the 1954 Geneva conference on Indo-China. Stevenson did not comment directly on this suggestion, but he held to the line that President Johnson had taken in a statement made just after de Gaulle had spoken: that what was needed was to ensure compliance with the 1954 Geneva agreements, not to hold another conference. No resolution was proposed, but on the 7th the Council president, Sivert Nielsen of Norway, announced that consultations held in between the two meetings had produced a 'general understanding among the members of the Council'. The agreed text which Nielsen read out said that the Council would welcome any information relating to the American complaint that either North Vietnam or South Vietnam might wish to provide, 'either through taking part in the discussion' or in any other form. The Council then adjourned without setting any date for another meeting.

The Hanoi government rejected the invitation to send a representative to New York. It sent instead a lengthy statement of its case — yet this included, rather illogically, a firm statement that the Security Council had no competence to consider the Vietnam conflict, which was a matter for the Geneva conference. While thus giving the Council a cold shoulder, Hanoi also gave it a detailed and quite different account of the Tonking Gulf events. It claimed that on the 2nd it was the American ships that fired first; that the American report of a second engagement on the 4th was a 'myth'; that the American ships had been inside North Vietnam's territorial waters, and that since the end of July there had been repeated intrusions into those waters by American and South Vietnam warships which had shelled coastal islands and raided the mainland. A sharply contrasting statement reached the Council's members from the Saigon government, which offered the Council its full co-operation and any information the Council might need, and attached evidence of North Vietnam's having sent arms and military officers to support the communist guerrillas in the south.

Much, much later – early in 1968 – revealing light was shed on what had actually happened in the Tonking Gulf in August 1964. A hearing on the matter by the American Senate's foreign relations committee included a long interrogation of the Secretary of Defence, Robert McNamara. It emerged that in late July South Vietnam had begun a series of naval raids on North Vietnam's coast. The American warships were in the area of these raids, and although they did not, apparently, play any active part, one of them, the *Maddox*, was equipped to monitor North Vietnam radio transmissions. Whoever started the fight on August 2, the Americans won it, sinking one of the three torpedo boats and damaging the others, while the *Maddox* suffered little damage. On the 4th the Americans never actually saw any hostile craft, and the whole 'engagement' on that dark night might have been a succession of false alarms; if there was a fight, there were no reported hits.

Senator Fulbright, the committee's chairman, depicted its 1968 hearings as a sort of act of atonement for the role he himself had played in the Tonking Gulf affair. For, on 5 August 1964, in the high-tension atmosphere generated by the news of the naval clashes, President Johnson had asked Congress to pass a resolution expressing support for 'all necessary action to protect our armed forces and to assist nations covered by the Seato treaty'. (South Vietnam was not a member of the Seato alliance, but it was designated under the treaty as an 'Article 4' state, an attack on it being regarded by the allies as equivalent to an attack on one of themselves.) The Senate, in which Fulbright was the chief proponent of the resolution, adopted it by 88 votes to 2; the House of Representatives passed it unanimously. From then on, Johnson repeatedly silenced expressions of doubt about the constitutional propriety of the growing American involvement in an undeclared war in Vietnam by citing the 'Tonking Gulf resolution'.

In the disturbing light of later revelations, the American resort to the Security Council in August 1964 may be seen as little more than a part of the Johnson administration's swift exploitation of the Tonking Gulf affair for the purpose of rallying domestic support for its Vietnam policy. (It must be remembered that in July 1964 Barry Goldwater had been nominated as the Republican candidate for the presidency, one plank in his platform being a pledge of more forceful action in Vietnam.) The Council, in this somewhat miserable situation, acquitted itself well enough. It was not to be hustled; it did not get involved in a speechmaking marathon, or in abortive attempts to adopt resolutions; it made sensible use of the consensus technique; it gave North Vietnam a chance to state its side of the business – and the Hanoi version turned out to be not very far from the truth.

And, in the busy interval in between the two formal Council meetings, on August 6, a relatively inconspicuous event occurred, the significance of which was not to emerge for a long time. U Thant went to Washington to see Johnson. The appointment had been made long before the Tonking Gulf sensation burst upon the United States and the United Nations. Thant was known to have something to say to Johnson about the Asian tour he had made in July, during which he had taken soundings about possibilities of negotiation or mediation of the Vietnam conflict. But, at the time, nothing more than that was revealed.

February 1965 saw an ominous escalation of the fighting. The American base at Pleiku in South Vietnam was attacked on the 7th by communist forces. In swift retaliation, the Americans launched bombing raids against targets just north of the 17th parallel, the dividing line between north and south. Within the next few weeks the bombing was extended farther north and the first American combat units arrived in Vietnam.

On February 12 U Thant, frankly recognising that it was useless for him to call for a Security Council meeting – a move now opposed by all the permanent members – and that 'some of the large powers' also opposed the idea of a 'Geneva-type conference', urged instead that a start should be made with 'informal, private and confidential dialogues between some of the parties'. At a press conference on the 24th he said he had 'presented concrete ideas and proposals' to some of the 'parties directly involved'. He went on: 'I am sure the great American people, if only they know the true facts and the background . . . will agree with me that further bloodshed is unnecessary'; and he added: 'As you know, in times of war . . . the first casualty is truth'. These remarks gave great offence to President Johnson. His spokesman, George Reedy, said he was not at present contemplating negotiations and that 'there are no meaningful proposals for negotiation that are before our government'.

On March 8 the *New York Times* carried a report from 'reliable sources' at the UN that Thant had suggested in September 1964 that secret talks might be held at Rangoon between American and North Vietnamese representatives; and that Hanoi had accepted the suggestion, while the United States 'informally expressed interest' – whereupon Thant had invited the Americans to draw up terms of reference for such a meeting. In a version that James Reston gave in the same newspaper on April 3, it was stated that 'officials at the United Nations' (by implication, Thant and his staff) still hoped to see some private Washington–Hanoi talks, but were less hopeful than they had been in the autumn of 1964, when word that Hanoi was interested in talking had been 'passed on to Washington, which waited for two months before answering, and then, after the presidential election, indicated that it was not interested'.

For greater enlightenment about what all this had meant, the public had to wait until after the tragically sudden death of Adlai Stevenson on July 14. The American UN representative collapsed and died in a London street near the embassy in Grosvenor Square. Two days earlier he had had a long private talk at the ambassador's residence in Regent's Park with the American television news commentator, Eric Sevareid. According to Sevareid, Stevenson gave him in this late-night *tête-à-tête* a somewhat fuller version of the Secretary-General's efforts and experiences. Sevareid put the gist of it into a broadcast which he made for CBS some days later, but he gave no indication at that time that he had had it from Stevenson. In November, however, he published in *Look* a lengthy account of his last conversation with Stevenson, placing it in a decidedly emotional framework, but including a number of details.

By this account, Stevenson had said that Thant got Hanoi to agree, in the early autumn of 1964, to send an emissary to meet an American one in Rangoon. Washington demurred until the November presidential elections were over. (These, of course, were the elections in which Johnson crushingly defeated Barry Goldwater; so the Johnson administration emerged from them unchanged and strengthened.) After the elections, Thant found that Hanoi was still willing, but Washington was not – its objection being that any such talks would have a demoralising effect on the South Vietnam government, which was then in a very shaky state. Thant had then suggested a cease-fire, with a 'truce line' across both Vietnam and Laos, and had invited the Americans to propose the terms for it; but their response was again negative. (In the version published in *Look* it was Robert McNamara, the Defence Secretary, who was said to have been named by Stevenson as flatly opposing Thant's suggestions; but it soon came to be generally accepted that this was a confusion that had crept in somewhere along the line. It was certainly not the impression that Thant himself had got.) The State Department spokesman said on November 15 that Thant's suggestion of a Rangoon meeting had been declined because it was not felt that Hanoi had a serious interest in peace talks at the time; and that McNamara had taken no part in the decision. But the nub of the matter was that this was the first official American admission of the truth of the reports, which had circulated for eight months, about the fate of the proposals discreetly made by Thant a full year earlier, between August and November 1964.

It was not difficult to understand why the Johnson administration (meaning, in this context, primarily the Secretary of State, Dean Rusk) had shied away from the proposed Rangoon meeting in late 1964. At that time the communist forces were advancing with alarming speed, the Saigon government seemed close to a political collapse, and there were very few American troops in Vietnam. The Americans would have had little or nothing to bargain with at Rangoon; and merely by starting talks there, they might have brought about the collapse of the Saigon regime. Thant had argued that he was not urging an immediate American withdrawal, but that negotiation was the only approach that could eventually enable the United States to 'withdraw gracefully'. But Rusk, at least, had not seen it that way.

Between the events of late 1964 and the admissions about them a year later, much had changed. In April 1965 Thant had warmly praised Johnson's announcement, in a speech at Baltimore, that the United States was now ready for 'unconditional' negotiations. But as 1965 wore on it appeared that Peking's influence in Hanoi was growing, and that the North Vietnam leaders were close to joining the Chinese communists in an attitude of complete hostility to Thant, to the idea of the UN concerning itself with the Vietnam conflict, and even to the idea of trying to base a settlement on the agreements reached at the 1954 Geneva conference.

On 28 July 1965, when Arthur Goldberg had just succeeded Adlai Stevenson at the UN, Johnson sent to Thant, by Goldberg's hand, a letter asking that all the organisation's resources should be employed to bring peace in Vietnam. In the letter, which was made very public, Johnson voiced the hope that the member states, 'individually and collectively', would use their influence to bring all governments involved in the conflict 'to the negotiating table'. Thant responded appreciatively, while Goldberg embarked on a brisk round of consultations with other representatives. On the 30th Goldberg sent to Platon Morozov, who (in Fedorenko's absence) was acting president of the Security Council for July, a letter in which the United States said it would welcome the help of the Council members, and would 'collaborate unconditionally' with them in the search for a peace formula. But Goldberg did not ask for a formal Council meeting. The Americans agreed with Thant that such a meeting would do no good at that stage.

Sceptics at the UN assumed that Johnson was merely seeking to assuage domestic opinion. But the Council's six elected members – Bolivia, Ivory Coast, Jordan, Malaysia, Netherlands and Uruguay – embarked on an informal exchange of views. Later they asked Goldberg to meet them privately, and on August 6 he did so – coming almost directly from a weekend visit to Johnson's home in Texas. (New York, like Washington, had its absentees at this time of year. In addition to Fedorenko, Caradon and three of the non-permanent members' chief representatives were away, so Goldberg's talks were largely with deputies.) On the 10th, however, the six let it be known that they had decided to abandon their efforts, primarily because Morozov had told them that neither Peking nor Hanoi was ready to negotiate.

Soon after these inconclusive events, much of the attention of the UN in general and of the Council in particular became focused on the new Indo-Pakistani war. As well as diverting thoughts from Vietnam, this conflict and the UN response to it brought Russia into at least a temporary partnership with America, further widened the Sino-Soviet rift and did something to improve the standing of the Security Council.

The first weeks of 1966, in vivid contrast with those of 1965, were a time not of escalation but of restraint. Admittedly it was restraint at what might be called a higher level: by now there were almost 200,000 Americans in Vietnam, the bombing of the north had become massive in 1965, and the communist powers' support of Hanoi had become more open and extensive. But on December 24 the Americans had suspended all bombing of the north, and this Christmas pause lasted throughout January 1966. And 1965 had seen a variety of peace-making initiatives from many different quarters, including the Commonwealth conference and the Vatican. At the end of the year President Johnson sent Arthur Goldberg and five other special envoys to thirty-four capitals to ask for help in starting negotiations. Now the Americans' 'peace offensive' (Goldberg's words) brought them back to the United Nations again.

On 4 January 1966 Goldberg sent Thant a published letter which expressed the hope that all UN organs and states would consider what they could do to help restore peace. It reiterated that the United States stood ready for unconditional negotiations or discussions, in which a cease-fire might be the priority aim, while a scaling down of hostilities could also be envisaged; and that the Americans had no wish to keep troops in Vietnam, where the future of the south should be freely decided by its own people, and the question of reunification should be decided by the peoples of both north and south.

159

On the 20th Thant, at a press conference, made his first public appeal for an indefinite cessation of the bombing of the north. He said that all parties now agreed that a solution would best be sought through a Geneva-type conference (unfortunately he was wrong about this). He did not think a Security Council debate would help at this stage; but the UN could help in the carrying out of agreements reached at a peace conference. Thant was questioned about reports that, a week earlier, American and North Vietnam representatives had met in Rangoon. 'I was not instrumental,' he said in a very brief reply.

On the 31st bombing of the north was resumed, and simultaneously Goldberg, followed by a good many TV cameramen, went to the French mission's offices and gave Roger Seydoux, the Council's president for January, a letter urgently calling for it to meet. The letter said that North Vietnam had rejected all the American offers of unconditional negotiation; President Ho Chi Minh had made this quite clear in a statement broadcast from Hanoi on January 28, in which he had insisted that before there were any negotiations America must in effect accept Hanoi's terms. Goldberg also presented a draft resolution, in which the Council would call on the interested governments to start immediate and unconditional talks about holding a peace conference, with a view to the application of the Geneva agreements; the Council would also offer its own, and Thant's, help in ensuring the success of the conference, at which a supervised cease-fire should be the first objective.

The Council met on Tuesday, February 1, under the presidency of Akira Matsui of Japan. These were the first weeks after its enlargement, the ten elected members being Argentina, Uruguay, New Zealand, Netherlands, Bulgaria, Jordan, Japan, Mali, Nigeria and Uganda. There was at once some doubt whether the necessary nine votes would be mustered even to place the question of Vietnam on the agenda. This was opposed not only by Russia and Bulgaria but also by Seydoux, who said that the UN was not the proper framework and that 'its intervention at this stage would only add to the confusion'. Sori Coulibaly of Mali held that the Geneva conference was the most appropriate framework, and that a Council debate would be useless. Chief Adebo said that Nigeria would vote for a debate only if the participants included communist China and the communist National Liberation Front of South Vietnam, as well as the two Vietnam governments (whose participation had already been proposed by Goldberg). Apollo Kironde of Uganda welcomed the American draft, but urged that the Council must hear all the parties concerned. He suggested that it should adjourn at once and meet again some time later, perhaps in Geneva.

The pivotal man in the procedural tussle turned out to be the Jordanian. Muhammad El-Farra, Jordan's permanent representative, was not in the Council on February 1. At the request of his deputy, Waleed Sadi, Matsui postponed the voting on the agenda until the afternoon of the 2nd. Cynics were quick to note that Jordan's finance minister happened to be in Washington seeking aid. The American mission at the UN was sensitive enough about this coincidence to put out a denial that there was any question of any American–Jordanian agreement being concluded that had 'any relationship whatever with matters before the UN'.

When the Council reassembled on the Wednesday afternoon Jordan's representative said that his government thought a debate on Vietnam would be useless, but at the same time harmless. So he provided the ninth necessary vote. Russia and Bulgaria voted against a debate, while France and the three African members abstained. Having thus taken two days to decide to have a Vietnam debate, the Council immediately agreed not to have one. Matsui adjourned it indefinitely for private consultations. Four years later, the debate for which all this effort had cleared the way in February 1966 had still not taken place.

But during the procedural discussion Goldberg had effectively made his crucial point. He brought to the Council's attention the fact that the French, Russian and African representatives were arguing that Vietnam was a matter not for the Council but for the Geneva conference; and he showed that, far from quarrelling with this, the United States was proposing a resolution whose purpose was, precisely, to encourage the reconvening of the Geneva conference. He had Fedorenko and Seydoux over a barrel. Their governments had repeatedly urged America to return to Geneva. Now it was quite ready to do so. But the Peking government was not; and therefore

Hanoi was not; and therefore Moscow was rebuffing every suggestion from London that the conference should be reconvened by its
Russian and British co-chairmen.

The Council's performance on February 1 and 2 might have
seemed procedurally grotesque; but it had highlighted the
Americans' acceptance of the Geneva approach and the inability of
their critics, who had so long advocated this approach, to produce a
matching acceptance from Hanoi. With this, at least, achieved,
Goldberg did not press for any more formal Council meetings.

In the consultations between Council members that went on during February there was some discussion of the idea that the three
Africans, or some other group or sub-committee formed among the
elected members, might act as mediators, or might formulate a proposal pointing towards a Geneva conference in terms that Russia
could accept. But Russia and Bulgaria refused to take part in any of
the consultations, despite repeated approaches from Matsui. He was
therefore unable to produce any statement of agreed consensus in
even the vaguest of terms. So on February 26 Matsui sent all members a letter noting the continued divergences, and reporting only
what he called 'a certain degree of common feeling among many
members of the Council' – to the effect that further debate would
be inopportune, but also that peace in Vietnam 'should be sought
through negotiations in an appropriate forum' designed to implement
the Geneva agreements. This was not one of the most successful
attempts to use the partial consensus technique. Seydoux replied that
no conclusions about members' feelings should have been formulated
when there had been no debate. Sori Coulibaly of Mali echoed this
and said that Matsui's letter could not constitute a valid precedent in
Council practice. Fedorenko complained that Matsui had exceeded
his competence and violated the Council's rules of procedure and
established practice; his irresponsible and illegal statements were a
blatant attempt to help America in its 'manoeuvre' to conceal its
expansion of its aggressive war in Vietnam by bringing the matter to
the Council. Milko Tarabanov of Bulgaria refused to receive
Matsui's letter. On this jarring note, the Council's formal involvement with the Vietnam question ended; and that, for the next four
years, was that.

In the spring of 1970 the coup in Cambodia that removed Prince Sihanouk from power (while he was visiting Russia and China) opened a new chapter in the grim story of the Indo-Chinese conflict. Against the background of the subsequent conflict in Cambodia, Yakov Malik – who had succeeded Fedorenko as Russia's council-man in 1968 – told a press conference on April 16 that it appeared that only a new Geneva conference could resolve the problems of Indo-China. Since the Council proceedings in 1966 the Russians had tended to shy away from all talk of a Geneva conference; so Malik's remarks aroused keen interest. But two days later, in a television interview, he seemed to be backing away. 'To convene such a conference is unrealistic at present,' he said. The American councilman, Charles Yost, sought clarification from Malik and found him very reticent. On April 24 Peking's news agency, NCNA, put out a violent attack on the Russians for having suggested a conference, in which it said that although Malik had changed his tune and 'tried to hide his real face, the dirty soul of the clique of Soviet revisionists who have betrayed the Indo-Chinese peoples had already been revealed'.

This did not deter U Thant from appearing on television on May 5 to make a strong plea for the holding of an international conference by 'all the parties concerned' with the aim of restoring peace by returning to the Geneva agreements. Thant attributed the fact that the UN had not been able to play a decisive part in ending the conflict to the opposition of 'some permanent members of the Security Council' to any 'United Nations involvement'. Next day his appeal was welcomed by Secretary of State William Rogers. But it was sharply criticised by the Hanoi regime; and although the Russians seemed in no hurry to respond to it directly, their reactions were made clear by Moscow radio and Tass commentaries which – blandly ignoring Malik's April move – now denounced all idea of a conference as a device intended to allow 'American aggression' to continue.

*   *   *

'I hope I will never live to see the day when a small country comes to the United Nations to ask for protection against war, and is simply

163

greeted with the question, "What's the hurry?".' Thus spoke Senator Henry Cabot Lodge in the Security Council on 18 June 1954. He was waxing indignant at Russia's vetoing of a move to send UN observers to Thailand (page 146).

Two days later, Council members had the eerie sensation of having passed through Alice's looking-glass into a wonderland where everything was familiar but the wrong way round. On Sunday, June 20 the Council met at the urgent request of Guatemala, which complained that it was being invaded and asked the UN for its protection. And Lodge's reaction was, in effect, to ask 'What's the hurry?'

The Council, unanimously and on French initiative, did call for 'the immediate termination of any action likely to cause further bloodshed'. But there was no such termination; there was further bloodshed. Guatemala again appealed for protection: the Council met again on June 25. It held a 'procedural' discussion with bitter political undertones, and decided not to consider the matter. Four days later, Guatemalan resistance to the invasion collapsed. Early in July a new Guatemalan government informed the Council that it need not bother any more.

This was the Council's first serious tangle with a problem that involved the Organisation of American States (OAS), the regional grouping which, even before it was fully born, had exerted a pre-natal influence on the San Francisco conference (page 66). The leftward political trend in Guatemala had been alarming some of its small Central American neighbours, and its large North American neighbour. Between them, they encouraged and helped Colonel Castillo Armas and other right-wing officers who had left Guatemala to mount an invasion from Honduras, in which the decisive element was the bombing of Guatemala by aircraft apparently based in Honduras or Nicaragua or both. President Arbenz Guzman had allied himself too closely to his country's Communist party to be able to expect any protection from the OAS. Hence his appeal to the UN.

'Any member, large or small, has the right to have an urgent meeting of the Security Council called whenever it feels itself to be in danger,' conceded Henry Cabot Lodge. Nevertheless, the American councilman argued that it was for the OAS to deal with the Guatemalan conflict, at least in the first instance (i.e. 'what's the hurry?'). Brazil and Colombia proposed on June 20 that the Council should simply refer Arbenz's complaint to the regional organisation. Russia vetoed this move. Lodge's tone became almost apocalyptic. He warned the Council that if it gave the Guatemalan question any further consideration 'a chain of disastrous events' would be set in motion. There would be 'a catastrophe of such dimensions as will gravely impair the future effectiveness both of the United Nations itself and of regional organisations'. If the regional formula 'that made possible the adoption of the Charter' was not upheld, 'the United Nations will have destroyed itself in 1954'.

In 1954 American influence in the Council was at an unsurpassed height. The elected members were Brazil, Colombia, New Zealand, Denmark, Turkey and Lebanon. Even so, Lodge could muster little support for his argument that the Council should drop the whole business. At its second meeting, New Zealand, Denmark and Lebanon voted with Russia in favour of putting Guatemala on the agenda again. Britain and France abstained. Only the two Latin Americans, Taipeh China and Turkey joined the United States in voting against. But that sufficed. And it enabled John Foster Dulles to claim that the Council's decision to disengage had been 'a triumph for the system of balance between regional organisation and world organisation'.

'Stay out of this hemisphere, and don't try to start your plans and conspiracies here,' Lodge warned the Russians during the Council debate. In the *Manchester Guardian*, Alistair Cooke referred to 'the unmistakable yelp of the Monroe Doctrine when the Soviet Union stepped on its tail'. But, unless New Zealand and Denmark are to be considered as Soviet republics, it must be conceded that Russia was not exactly alone in arguing that the UN had a duty to 'meddle' in Pan-American affairs. In fact, the Russians' position was illogical; for they were asking the UN to override the 'Washington-dominated OAS' at the same time as, in other geographical contexts, they were fiercely denouncing the 'Washington-dominated UN'. Only seven months later they were to be completely flummoxed by another Central American episode. President Somoza of Nicaragua, having got himself a friendly neighbourhood right-wing authoritarian regime in Guatemala, promoted an attack on Costa Rica for the same purpose. The Russians hastened to tell the world that Washington was master-minding Somoza's move and that the OAS would once again bend to Washington's will. Surprise, surprise: this time the OAS moved swiftly, with strong backing from Washington, stopped Somoza in his tracks and saved Costa Rica's admittedly non-communist but distinctly left-of-centre government. Moscow's propagandists lost a good deal of face; and what face they had left was redder than ever.

Some 'unfamiliar problems' arose, to use U Thant's restrained words, when in 1965 the UN and the OAS came into uneasy juxtaposition in the Dominican Republic. This was the first time that the UN found itself operating a truce observer mission in an area where an international peace-keeping operation was simultaneously being carried out by a regional organisation.

On 29 April 1965 President Lyndon Johnson's Administration informed the Security Council that it had landed troops in Santo Domingo to protect and evacuate American citizens, in view of the outbreak there of what amounted to a civil war between left-wing and right-wing forces. On May 1 Russia asked the Council to meet urgently to discuss American armed intervention in Dominican affairs. On the same day the OAS, at United States prompting, decided to form a committee to help bring about a cease-fire. On the 6th, twelve Latin American governments joined the United States in voting for the establishment of an OAS international force in the little Caribbean republic. This force in fact consisted of the 22,000 American marines and soldiers who had been sent in (and had already completed the evacuation of civilians), plus, eventually, 1,250 Brazilians and a few Hondurans, Nicaraguans, Costa Ricans and Paraguayans.

The Security Council held sixteen meetings between May 3 and 25. It rejected Russia's demand that it call on the Americans to withdraw. But the Americans' actions were criticised by several councilmen, including those of France and, most tellingly, of Uruguay. Uruguay, with Chile, Ecuador, Mexico and Peru, had opposed (and Venezuela had abstained on) the OAS move to authorise an international force.

166

Adlai Stevenson found himself in much the same position as Henry Cabot Lodge had occupied in the 1954 debate on Guatemala, urging the Council to leave it all to the OAS. He had a stronger hand to play, in that OAS action was being taken; but a weaker one, in that the most visible feature of the landscape was the massive American intervention, which was noticeably resented by several of the more democratic Latin American republics. He was forced to give ground on May 14, when the Council learnt that the left-wing Dominican leader, Colonel Caamaño Deño, had complained that American troops had violated the truce that the OAS committee had arranged on the 5th. On the initiative of Ivory Coast, Jordan and Malaysia the Council unanimously adopted a resolution in which they called for a 'strict' cease-fire and asked Thant to send out a representative who would report on the situation to the Council. Thant sent José Mayobre, the Venezuelan executive head of the UN Economic Commission for Latin America, with what amounted to a small observer team led by General Indar Jit Rikhye, Thant's military adviser.

Fighting was continuing between Caamaño's forces and those of the right-wing military junta now headed by General Imbert Barreras. On the 18th Mayobre recommended that the Council should act to secure a new cease-fire in view of Imbert's refusal to adhere to the truce that the OAS had arranged. Mayobre also drew attention to the American forces' failure to prevent the movement of Imbert's, and to the way the Americans' deployment in Santo Domingo worked to the disadvantage of Caamaño's. Next day the OAS committee urged the UN to suspend its activities. Mayobre quietly disregarded this demand, and on the 21st he was able to bring about a new cease-fire. France proposed that the Council should call for this cease-fire to be made permanent. Stevenson objected to the French text because it made no reference to the OAS; but it was adopted on the 22nd by a 10–0 vote, America being the solitary abstainer – which meant that both Bolivia and Uruguay, as well as Britain, which had been trying to keep in line with the United States, had joined the majority. Stevenson complained that

> the purposes of the United Nations Charter will hardly be served if two international organisations are seeking to do things in the same place with the same people at the same time.

167

But the Council majority evidently felt that, in the circumstances, this overlapping was preferable to the UN leaving the OAS to work alone.

When the Council resumed debate on June 3 Russia, France, Jordan and Uruguay joined in urging that Mayobre's role should be enlarged. Since Russia and France, then as now, were normally stern opponents of any move to extend the role of the Secretary-General and his representatives in peace-keeping activity, it must be fairly deduced that Fedorenko and Seydoux were more concerned to add to Adlai Stevenson's embarrassments than to give Thant and Mayobre a real helping hand. Stevenson (who was to die only a few weeks later) was moved to speak rather waspishly about the new proposals. 'Isn't this a little childish?' he asked, adding that, 'We are not representing a petulant actress, jealous of her supporting cast.' Backed by Britain, Bolivia and Malaysia, he successfully resisted the Franco-Russian pressure, even when in mid-June Fedorenko was enabled to reopen the whole question after reports had come in of a new clash between Caamaño's forces and the Americans (or rather the Inter-Americans, as the OAS-labelled 'peace force' had become known).

At this stage the Council had evidently run out of consensus. On June 18 its Dutch president, J. G. de Beus, was able to relay Mayobre's report that the cease-fire had been re-established and the situation was again calm in Santo Domingo; but it was far from calm that day in New York. There was a lively exchange in the morning, during which Fedorenko solemnly proposed that the Council should hold a series of meetings in Santo Domingo. Around 1.30 the Uruguayan, Carlos Maria Velazquez, asked de Beus to try to summarise two points on which there seemed to be agreement at least in principle. The Dutchman tried to use this chance to present a broader summary of points on which he saw 'a certain degree of unanimity'. He quickly discovered that he had been rash to try. For when he presented a six-point statement at the afternoon meeting Fedorenko declared that it was 'inadmissible' for a president to make 'arbitrary summings-up' with which members did not agree; the president should have consulted all the members, but he had not. De Beus said rather plaintively that he had only had two hours between the morning and afternoon meetings, during which interval he had admittedly 'tried to eat one sandwich' but could hardly, sandwich or no sandwich, have held extensive consultations with all members. He had 'wanted to mention only a few points of agreement . . . which is something different from a consensus'. If the councilmen wanted him to try to draw up a proper consensus statement he would try 'to find a formula which is acceptable'.

That was a Friday evening. Under brisk fire from Seydoux, Rifai of Jordan and Velazquez, as well as from Fedorenko, de Beus retired to spend a fruitless weekend in search of more unanimity. On Monday the 21st he could tell the Council only that he would keep trying. The councilmen left their table on this inconclusive note; and their only further formal attention to the Dominican problem was given during four meetings held between July 20 and 26.

At these July meetings Platon Morozov presided. Speaking as Russia's representative, he again vainly urged the Council to go to Santo Domingo, where there had been fresh breaches of the cease-fire and reports of atrocities against civilians, both attributed to Imbert's forces. Then a remarkable unanimity suddenly emerged between the guest speakers who represented the two rival Dominican regimes headed by Caamaño and Imbert. Both of them asked the Council to secure the removal of the Inter-American force. But the councilmen themselves were not as agreed as the Dominicans about this.

It was now Morozov's turn to try to produce a presidential summary of the members' views, and – no doubt warned by de Beus's experience – he presented a very brief and minimal statement, carefully checked beforehand with all members (including, he took care to add, the Soviet 'delegation', which had made no objections). His one positive point of consensus was that members wanted Thant to go on reporting on the situation.

The Americans had by now lost some of their respect for the right-wing military junta and some of their alarm about the supposed communist domination of the left-wing regime. Their neutrality became more apparent, and this helped to bring the Dominicans to an 'act of reconciliation' in August, after which a compromise provisional regime was installed and elections were held. In the summer of 1966 both the Inter-American force and the UN mission were withdrawn. Mayobre's reporting function had continued to serve the

169

important purposes of reminding the Americans that they were being watched, and reassuring the Council that it was not being conned.

*   *   *

On Sunday 14 October 1962 American U-2 aircraft flying over Cuba photographed, near San Cristobal, what could only be a site being prepared for the installation of Russian nuclear missiles to be trained on the United States. On Tuesday the 16th, when this alarming evidence had been thoroughly cross-checked, President John F. Kennedy discussed it with his chief advisers. There were differing views about its real military significance. The question whether it would greatly increase Soviet power to devastate America could be answered only if the strength of the inter-continental missile force based in Russia itself was precisely known, and at that time it was not. But Kennedy and his advisers were fully agreed that the placing of Soviet nuclear missiles in Cuba was unacceptable. Nikita Khrushchev might mean to use them as a lever in his campaign to force the western powers out of Berlin; he would certainly, by installing them, score a major political victory in Latin America. From the start, the Americans were determined not to let him get away with it.

Adlai Stevenson was in Washington on the 16th, and Kennedy personally briefed his UN representative on the new threat. But he bound Stevenson, like all the others in the know, to strict secrecy; he did not want any disclosure of the crisis until he could announce exactly what he meant to do about it. Intensive photo-reconnaissance over Cuba was ordered, and by the 18th the expert opinion was that the first of the Soviet missiles in Cuba could be made ready for launching within twenty-four hours, while the full installation would enable the Russians to fire about forty missiles in one salvo, some of them with ranges of over 2,000 miles.

The Russian foreign minister, Andrei Gromyko, came to see Kennedy that day, by previous appointment. He put on a little more pressure over Berlin; and he assured Kennedy that what Russia was installing in Cuba was merely an anti-aircraft defence system, quite incapable of firing anything at the United States. The President did not tell Gromyko that he already knew better. He did not think the Russians would abandon their plan merely because it had been detected. He still felt he must decide what to do before he revealed his knowledge.

He decided on Saturday the 20th. Rejecting the idea of an immediate air attack on the missile sites, Kennedy chose to put a naval blockade around Cuba, in the belief that this would leave Khrushchev enough time and diplomatic elbow-room to permit him to disengage; but he envisaged the necessity of an air attack if the blockade did not stop the Russians from completing their installations. Warships were ordered to sea. Kennedy arranged to reveal the situation in a televised speech on the evening of Monday the 22nd.

He accepted Stevenson's suggestion that he should simultaneously call for an emergency meeting of the UN Security Council. But he turned down Stevenson's advice that he should consider the possibility that, in bargaining with the Russians, he might agree to abandon the American base at Guantánamo in Cuba or to remove American Jupiter missiles from Turkey – although there was by now no real military advantage to be got by preserving either this base or these missiles.

Before Kennedy broadcast on the Monday evening, the Americans had revealed the situation and their intentions to all their allies, and to the Russian ambassador in Washington, Anatoly Dobrynin (Gromyko had left for home earlier that same day, having completed his routine annual appearance at the UN Assembly). And John J. McCloy, the banker who had become one of America's international pinch-hitters (and had also served the UN, notably in the 1956–7 Suez Canal clearance operation), had been summoned back from Germany to reinforce Stevenson in New York. At 7 p.m. Kennedy told the world that his navy would turn back any ships bound for Cuba that were found to be carrying 'offensive weapons'; and he called upon Khrushchev, by name, to 'move the world back from the abyss of destruction' by removing the missiles. At 7.30 Stevenson delivered the request for an urgent Security Council meeting to Valerian Zorin of Russia, who happened to be that month's Council president. He simultaneously presented a draft resolution in which

171

the Council would call for the immediate removal from Cuba of both Soviet missiles and bombers; would authorise Thant to send UN observers to Cuba to verify the removals; would call for an ending of the American 'quarantine' once the observers had reported the weapons gone; and would urge America and Russia to negotiate about 'measures to remove the existing threat'.

In this case there was no question of the United States seeking to keep the matter within the framework of the Organisation of American States. On the contrary, the Secretary of State, Dean Rusk, spent much of the next day, Tuesday the 23rd, at an OAS council meeting in Washington with the aim of securing a Latin American endorsement that could be brandished in the UN Security Council. At 5 p.m. Rusk got a better score than he had hoped for. By a 19–0 vote (Uruguay abstaining) the OAS backed the United States position. At this moment Adlai Stevenson was already making his opening statement to the Security Council in New York; and he promptly knitted the good news from the OAS into his speech.

Mario García-Inchaustegui, who had been invited to join in the debate as representative of Cuba, asked the Council to condemn what he called the American 'act of war' in imposing the naval quarantine. He described it as the culmination of a series of American aggressive actions against Cuba. Since Fidel Castro and his followers had ousted the Batista regime and come to power in Havana, Cuba had thrice approached the Security Council with complaints of American aggressive designs against it. (Its complaint over the Bay of Pigs invasion by Cuban exiles and mercenaries in April 1961 had, however, been brought to the Assembly, not the Council.) Earlier in October 1962 President Osvaldo Dorticos, addressing the Assembly as a visiting head of state (and being repeatedly interrupted by heckling from anti-Castro Cubans in the public gallery), had moved Stevenson to protest at the way he departed from the usual style of distinguished visitors' speeches by violently denouncing American actions against his country. Dorticos' charges had included one to the effect that America was already imposing a 'naval blockade' on Cuba by using threats of reprisal to prevent other nations' ships from carrying cargoes to Cuban ports.

García-Inchaustegui's response to Stevenson's draft resolution included an impassioned declaration that Cuba would never admit any UN observers. Here the Cuban broke ranks with Valerian Zorin, who made no such objection – though the Russian generalised the point by suggesting that UN observers should verify the removal of 'all foreign bases on foreign territory'. On the second day of debate, Wednesday the 24th, Zorin presented the Council with a Soviet draft resolution condemning America for 'violating the United Nations Charter and increasing the threat of war', and insisting that it should abandon the quarantine. Only on one point did he visibly agree with Stevenson: that there was an exceptionally acute threat to the peace of the world. However, keen eyes seeking gleams of light in the murk spotted one common element in the American and Soviet draft texts. Each called for swift negotiations between the parties about means of removing the threat to peace.

By the morning of the 24th a line of twenty American warships was strung out east of the Bahamas (well away from Cuba; the idea being that interceptions would be made early enough to allow time for careful thought about the next move); and, farther east, more than twenty Soviet merchant ships were heading across the Atlantic for Cuba. The first interception was expected within a few hours. The Security Council resumed debate at 9 a.m., the floor of the chamber tightly packed with distinguished onlookers, many of whom had to stand. (At this stage in the annual Assembly timetable, many of the foreign ministers who had come to attend part of the session were, unlike Gromyko, still in New York.) Alex Quaison-Sackey of Ghana and Mahmoud Riad of Egypt, the Council's two African members – it had no Asian member that year, apart from Taipeh China – presented a third draft resolution. This would ask Thant to 'confer promptly with the parties directly concerned' about means of removing the threat and 'normalising' the situation in the Caribbean. It would also call on the parties to refrain from any action that might aggravate matters. This move found general support among many of the non-aligned UN members, and they called on Thant, privately but urgently, to intervene in the crisis.

That afternoon he sent messages to Kennedy and Khrushchev saying that the representatives of 'a large number of member governments' had asked him to appeal to them to refrain from aggravating the situation and to give time for negotiation. He urged 'the voluntary suspension of all arms shipments to Cuba and also the voluntary suspension of the quarantine measures . . . for a period of two to three weeks'.

Thant and his advisers had, of course, been considering some such appeal to both America and Russia since the crisis first broke. But they had started from the gloomily realistic assumption that the UN probably could not do very much in a case of head-on collision between the two super-powers. And if the Secretary-General tried to intervene in a situation where his effort was bound to fail, he would merely dissipate the prestige of his office. Yet Thant thought, at first, that this was going to be one of those cases in which, knowing quite well that he could not really affect the situation, he must nevertheless 'go on record' with some form of words that asserted the UN's basic concern for peace. When he was approached by the representatives of more than forty member states he recognised that he must go further than this. Even so, he expected nothing but rebuffs from both Moscow and Washington.

When he privately informed the Soviet and American representatives that he was sending an appeal to their heads of government he was assured by both of them that his requests for restraint would not be accepted. Zorin, at least, was as surprised as Thant himself when it began to emerge that Khrushchev was positively grateful for the Secretary-General's action, which provided the Soviet leader with a 'golden bridge' across which he could retreat without more loss of face than he could stand.

The morning of Thursday the 25th saw the first interceptions in the Atlantic. But the ships concerned were only a Soviet tanker and an East German passenger ship, and the Americans let them pass. Later in the day Thant received replies to his first message to the two heads of government. Khrushchev said: 'I agree with your proposals' – but he said nothing about turning his ships back. Kennedy said that the threat had been created by 'the secret introduction of offensive missiles into Cuba, and the answer lies in the removal of such weapons'; but he proposed that Thant should discuss his suggestions with Stevenson.

Thant sent off two further messages. He asked Khrushchev for assurances that his ships would keep away from the area of interception at least for a limited time. He asked Kennedy to ensure that his warships would 'do everything possible to avoid confrontation with Soviet ships in the next few days'. Meanwhile he appealed to Castro to halt work on the missile sites.

The Security Council assembled again that Thursday afternoon for what was to prove the last of its meetings during the crisis. At first Stevenson made an attempt to relieve the painfully tense atmosphere. In answer to complaints that the quarantine was an excessive reaction to the missile threat, he recalled an old Abe Lincoln story about a fierce boar on an Illinois farm that attacked a visitor. The man defended himself with a pitchfork, on which the boar impaled itself. Its angry owner asked why the visitor hadn't used the blunt end of the pitchfork, and got the reply: 'Why didn't he attack me with his blunt end?'

But a little later came one of the most dramatic exchanges on the Council's record. Zorin was rash enough to challenge Stevenson to produce any real evidence that Russia had placed missiles in Cuba. Stevenson had been waiting for this moment and was ready for it. He said:

We do have the evidence. . . . Mr Zorin, I remind you that the other day you did not deny the existence of these weapons. But today, if I heard you correctly, you now say that they do not exist. . . . Let me ask you one simple question. Do you, Ambassador Zorin, deny that the Soviet Union has placed and is placing medium and intermediate-range missiles on sites in Cuba? Yes or no?

Zorin, furious at realising that he had walked into a trap, flushed and replied:

I am not in an American courtroom, sir, and therefore I do not wish to answer a question that is put to me in the way a prosecutor puts questions. You will have your answer in due course. . . . Continue with your statement. You will have your answer in due course.

At which Stevenson, saying, 'I am prepared to present the evidence in this room,' proceeded to unveil enlarged air photographs of the Soviet missile sites which had been brought into the Council chamber and set up on easels behind his chair. Zorin was then forced to try to deny the damning evidence provided by the photographs. His efforts were remarkably unconvincing – and his performance that day undoubtedly hastened his departure from New York. Three days later Khrushchev was to send his recognised UN trouble-shooter, Vasily Kuznetsov, to take over from Zorin in the matter of Cuba. As soon as the Assembly was over, Nikolai Fedorenko was sent to the UN as the new permanent representative, while Zorin, although he held the rank of deputy foreign minister, vanished into a temporary limbo, no immediate announcement being made about his being assigned any new post.

The Council adjourned that evening without fixing any time or date for its next meeting on Cuba, on the understanding that its future actions would depend on the results of Thant's initiative. No move was made to press any of the three draft resolutions to a vote. Once again the Council's slogan was 'leave it to Thant', or, as some put it, 'over to U'. It had strutted its little hour upon the stage, catching a share of the limelight during the 'crisis week' that began on October 22. But, apart from Adlai Stevenson's picadoresque bout with Zorin and the veiled photographs, the world would little note nor long remember what the councilmen said or did during its mere three days of inconclusive activity. Stevenson had used the Council to dramatise the fact that the Russians had attempted a perilous gamble, lied about it and been caught out. Zorin had represented his country in the worst possible light. García-Inchaustegui had been swept aside. (His hysterical performance was apparently too much even for Castro's taste; he was replaced even quicker than Zorin.) Then the Council had hastened off the stage as if it was being pursued by a bear – at the height of the crisis, on the day of the first interceptions of Soviet ships, when the Americans' latest information indicated that the missiles in Cuba would be ready to fire a full salvo within a matter of hours.

It is not necessary here to record in detail the exchanges between Khrushchev and Kennedy during the following three days that culminated, on Sunday October 28, in the Soviet leader's public announcement that the launching bases would be dismantled and the missiles brought back to Russia. The world breathed more freely from that moment on. But the Cuba crisis was not instantly and completely liquidated. In fact, the chapter was not closed until January 1963. Thant was deeply involved in the two months' toilsome negotiation that followed October 28. The Security Council, on the other hand, remained inert. It was agreed, in the words used in late November by a well-informed American official at the UN, that all the Council could do was to wait until the whole thing was over and then perhaps meet for what he described as a 'requiem mass'.

Castro, somewhat understandably furious at the way Khrushchev had involved him in the crisis and then abruptly abandoned him, refused to permit any inspection of the removal of the missiles from Cuba. Thant, undeterred by the fact that the Council had given him no mandate to do anything, went to Havana and pleaded with Castro, but in vain. Khrushchev sent no less an envoy than Anastas Mikoyan to Havana to reason with Castro. Kennedy was eventually satisfied when the evidence of air reconnaissance showed that the launching bases had been dismantled, and American naval patrols had counted forty-two missiles being carried eastward across the Atlantic on the decks of Russian ships.

But this was not all. As well as missiles, Khrushchev had sent to Cuba a number of Ilyushin-28 bombers that were capable of delivering nuclear bombs on to the United States; and these, unlike the missiles, had technically become Castro's property. Not until November 19 did he give way over the bombers. Castro was far too angry, with Khrushchev as well as Kennedy, to be able to communicate this climb-down to either of them. But he could, and did, announce it in a message to Thant – in which he was able to save some face and work off some steam by not only denouncing American policies but also deriding the Russian bombers as 'antiquated'. Kennedy, who had been dropping heavy hints that he was about to tighten the blockade of Cuba, then announced that he was ending it. The Ilyushins were shipped back to Russia in December.

Thant had been able to remain on speaking terms with Castro because he had refused to act merely as the joint instrument of

177

Kennedy and Khrushchev in liquidating the crisis. But he had acted as an invaluable link between the Americans and the Russians. Kuznetsov, McCloy and Stevenson were able to meet in Thant's office and at his hospitable table; Mikoyan joined them there as soon as he had finished his three weeks' hard slog in Havana. On 7 January 1963 Thant received a joint letter from the Americans and Russians thanking him for his help in averting the threat to peace and telling him that they would not need to occupy the attention of the Security Council any more.

*　　　*　　　*

It is often assumed that a 'good' Council debate is one that produces a 'good' resolution. But the Council's record shows no such pattern. There have been instances in which the Council performed quite a useful service to the world without adopting any resolution. At the other extreme are cases of a surprisingly sensible resolution emerging from a debate that did not look like leading to anything but a shambles.

The most appalling debate in the Council's first quarter-century took place in December 1964. The general setting was a discouraging one. The Article 19 dispute had already forced the postponement of the 1964 Assembly session and was to make it impossible for that session to take anything like a normal course. Nerves had been shaken by the first Chinese atom bomb test, by the sudden overthrow of Nikita Khrushchev in Moscow and by rapid communist advances in Vietnam. But the Council's concern was with a matter unrelated to any of these things: with a brief episode that had just occurred in the very centre of Africa, at Stanleyville (now Kisangani) in the northeastern Congo.

The last elements of the United Nations force in the Congo had been withdrawn in June 1964. I will not try, in these pages, to go over the record of the four-year UN involvement in the Congo which ended at that moment. It has been examined quite extensively in a good many books, some of which are trustworthy; it is not easily encapsulated in a few paragraphs; and, although the operation was authorised by the Security Council, the Congo story as a whole was

178

less Council-centred than, say, that of the Cyprus operation, to which another chapter of this book is devoted. Here, I should only like to take issue with the still fashionable idea that the Congo (and the wider world) would have been better off if the UN had not made its effort there; and to support the view that Ralph Bunche expressed in a Dag Hammarskjöld Memorial Lecture given at Columbia University in March 1964:

> The United Nations Operation in the Congo, in the light of its mandates, has certainly had great success. It may even be considered the most successful operation the United Nations has undertaken, when measured in terms of what it was called upon to do and has in fact done. Striking evidence of the success of the operation is found in the almost complete cessation of organised attacks on it from whatever source, west or east.

Those 'organised attacks' left their mark, of course. For what it did in the Congo, the UN has not been forgiven either by the communist powers or by the southern African regimes and mining interests (with their associated 'Katanga lobbies'), neither of whom got the piece of pie they tried to snatch; it was part of the UN's achievement that they didn't. One of the more ironic features of the scene in early 1964 (as Bunche also pointed out in his Columbia lecture) was that some of those who had clamoured most loudly against the UN's activity in the Congo were then swivelling round to decry it for withdrawing its force. The withdrawal was in fact unavoidable. No financial authority had been given by the member governments for maintaining the force any longer. The Congo government, although facing several local rebellions, had not asked the force to stay on. And even if it had made such a request, the UN could not have responded affirmatively as long as the rebellions remained an essentially internal conflict.

No civil war or internal rebellion is, in itself, a matter in which the UN can intervene. It is not its business to prevent Congolese, or for that matter Nigerians, or Iraqis, or Spaniards, from fighting among themselves. The UN is not in Cyprus simply to stop the Cypriots killing each other: it is there because the Cyprus conflict involves a direct threat of a wider, internationalised, war. The

179

reason why the UN had been involved so long in the Congo was because of the pertinacious attempt by foreign interests to establish, by the use of armed force, an ostensibly sovereign state in the country's richest province, the Katanga (which then represented the northernmost extension of the southern Africa regimes' area of effective power – a role in which it has been succeeded by Rhodesia). In this light, Thant had been justified in reporting to the Security Council in 1963 that the aims of the Congo operation had been largely fulfilled and that the disengagement of the United Nations force should begin.

Soon after the last UN troops left in mid-1964 the Congo became the scene of more widespread fighting than had ever occurred during the UN's four-year presence. This was not simply due to the departure of the force. More immediately, it was a reaction to the fact that Moise Tshombe, the head (or at least figurehead) of the extinct secessionist regime in the Katanga, contrived in July 1964 to become head of the Congo government. Tshombe and his friends had somehow put over – both in Leopoldville (now Kinshasa) and in other capitals – the idea that he was the only man who could reconcile the country's feuding factions. The exact opposite proved to be the truth: when he took power, and hired South African and other white mercenaries to enforce his authority, rebellion flared across more than half of the Congo's vast area. And, because Tshombe with his white soldiers seemed once more to be serving as a white man's puppet, many white foreigners in the Congo became targets for the rebels' anger.

On November 21 the American and Belgian representatives at the UN called the Security Council's attention to the dangerous situation of about 1,000 foreigners (of eighteen different nationalities, but predominantly Belgian and American) at Stanleyville, who were being treated as hostages by the rebels there. Tshombe's troops were advancing on Stanleyville, and one of the rebel leaders, the visibly unbalanced Christopher Gbenye, was reported to have threatened to kill all the hostages if the town was attacked. On the 24th the same two representatives informed the Council that, their governments having despaired of saving the hostages in any other way, Belgian parachute troops had been dropped that day at Stanleyville from

180

American aircraft. The Congo government told the Council that it had authorised the operation; Britain said it had provided staging facilities at Ascension Island. By the 29th the Belgian troops had been withdrawn, after some 2,000 civilians – American, European, African and Asian – had been evacuated from Stanleyville to places of safety. The rescue operation itself, by all accounts, was almost surgically precise and effective, but there were two immediate consequences: a number of whites were killed, some by apparently panicky guards in Stanleyville, some in smaller places held by rebels, in apparent reprisal; and Tshombe's mercenaries, who occupied Stanleyville without difficulty once the Belgians had dispersed the rebel force there, treated the captured town with their customary brutality.

A wave of anger swept across Africa. On December 1 the Security Council was asked to meet urgently by twenty-two member states, mostly African (Algeria, Burundi, Central African Republic, Congo-Brazzaville, Dahomey, Egypt, Ethiopia, Ghana, Guinea, Kenya, Malawi, Mali, Mauritania, Somalia, Sudan, Uganda, Tanzania and Zambia; Afghanistan, Cambodia, Indonesia and Jugoslavia). They contended that the Belgo-American–British operation had violated the UN Charter and created a threat to peace.

The Council did not meet until December 9. But once it got going it found itself launched on a series of seventeen meetings which ran until December 30. Just before it met, the Congo government (Tshombe's) got in under the wire with a counter-demand that it should consider intervention in the Congo's domestic affairs by Algeria, communist China, Egypt, Ghana, Russia and the Sudan, which were allegedly aiding the rebels. The Council decided to consider this complaint too, after a 7–4 vote on this procedural question in which the two African and two communist members (Ivory Coast, Morocco, Czechoslovakia, Russia) were overruled.

No less than fourteen visiting firemen participated – Belgium, the Congo and twelve other African states, many of the guest speakers being foreign ministers. Most of the guest African representatives shared the basic argument that the airdrop had been an aggressive act, intended to sustain the Tshombe government by suppressing a

181

nationalist movement. They rejected the claim that it had been a humanitarian act, contending that it had been bound to jeopardise the lives of whites in other parts of the Congo; that in fact there had been more killings of whites after the airdrop than before it; and that the states responsible for it had shown no concern about the deaths of much larger numbers of Africans. They claimed that, in talks at Nairobi that had been started with a view to ending the Congo conflict, the Organisation of African Unity (OAU) had been assured by rebel representatives that the hostages would be safe as long as the talks continued. And they denied that there was any evidence of African states aiding the rebels. (This last was perhaps the weakest point in their case. There were few signs of much significant military aid reaching the rebels; but several African presidents had loudly proclaimed that they were providing military aid, or meant to provide it.)

It was the style rather than the substance of the charges that dragged the level of debate down to a nadir. The Congo–Brazzaville foreign minister set the tone by calling the airdrop 'the most ruthless and scandalous aggression of our era'. Louis Lansana Beavogui, foreign minister of Guinea, accused the 'self-styled civilised countries' of caring no more about Africans killed in the Congo than about 'American citizens with black skins murdered in Mississippi'. The Mali foreign minister, Ousmane Ba, said that Belgium, withdrawing from the Congo 'in black rage at losing the privileges of its imperialist exploitation, wished to leave behind only disorder, massacre and misery'. This kind of thing went on and on for two weeks, and got worse, until Charles Ganao, the Congo–Brazzaville minister, was accusing America and Belgium of deliberately keeping their citizens in rebel-held areas simply to provide a pretext for armed intervention; while the Czech, Jiri Hajek, compared the Stanleyville whites' appeal for rescue to the appeals that the Sudetenland Germans had made to Hitler in 1938.

Paul-Henri Spaak, the Belgian foreign minister, declared himself to be deeply shocked by the racial overtones of the debate. Spaak cited a message he had received on November 22 in which Gbenye threatened to burn the hostages alive. All those who had been saved, he said, told their rescuers that they had been sure they were going to be massacred if there was no airdrop. Caradon, who was making one of his earliest appearances in the Security Council (and, one imagines, hoping that it wouldn't always be like this), defended the operation as stoutly as Spaak, but showed rather more recognition that the situation was bedevilled 'by indignation and anger arising from race and colour feeling' and by 'the terrible burden of the bloody past'.

Adlai Stevenson was, in a sense, taking the worst brunt of the onslaughts, because it was the American public that was watching all this on television; because of the direct links some of the Africans were making with racialist oppression in the United States; and because his government, unlike those of Belgium and Britain, had earlier earned African goodwill by backing the UN against the sponsors of Katanga secession. He was quite visibly outraged by what he called 'the incessant parrot-like repetition of absurd charges . . . the ugly, abusive and dangerous polemics which have demeaned this hall'. The United States had been accused, among other things, of 'massive cannibalism'. 'I have served in the United Nations, from its inception, off and on for seven years,' said Stevenson, 'but never before have I heard such irrational, irresponsible, insulting and repugnant language in these chambers.'

Probably nobody had. In those ugly two weeks that ran right up to Christmas of 1964 the Security Council was dragged close to its limits in the toleration of both invective and futility. For those of the Africans who were indulging in the wildest talk had no purpose except to vent their spleen and vilify their supposed enemies. They were not banging away with the deliberate aim of goading the Council to do something; there was nothing they really wanted it to do – except give them emotional satisfaction. And at some point, their steam let off, it would appear that they eventually realised that there must be a return to sanity.

Quite early in the long debate, Jaja Wachuku, foreign minister of Nigeria, had introduced a more rational note with an appeal to both African states and major powers to stop interfering in the Congo. The two African Council members, Morocco and Ivory Coast, refused to be swept away by the polemical torrent that poured from the throats of the African visitors and the communist members. The

Ivory Coast representative, in particular, balanced his criticism of the airdrop against the fact that the Congo government was a legitimate and generally recognised one which had the clear right to ask for outside aid in a matter of this kind. After Christmas these two Council members presented a draft resolution – the first definite proposal that had been offered since the talkathon began – which, they said, represented a consensus reached among the African states after prolonged negotiations.

This resolution, after slight amendment, was adopted on December 30 by a 10–0 vote. France abstained, on the ground that it offended against the strict rules of non-intervention; but even the French representative took pains to show goodwill by recording support for the first paragraph, which asked all states to stop intervening in the Congo's domestic affairs. Otherwise the resolution was acceptable to Americans and Russians, British and Africans alike – and entirely sensible. It said that foreign mercenaries should be rapidly withdrawn from the Congo; encouraged the OAU to help the Congo government achieve national reconciliation; asked all states to help the OAU to do this; and appealed for an end to the fighting in accordance with an OAU resolution adopted in September. One would never have expected anything so reasonable to merge from that horror of a 'debate'.

There are times when the world at large takes little notice of the Council's speechmaking but does pay heed to its resultant resolution: as, for instance, in the case of the Middle East debate that produced the celebrated British-sponsored resolution of 22 November 1967. In the different circumstances of December 1964 the fact that a perfectly reasonable resolution had been agreed without opposition was scarcely noticed outside the Security Council chamber. What lingered on the world's retina was the lurid image of all that wild abuse.

From the Africans' point of view, moreover, the whole thing was sadly counter-productive. Just after the Stanleyville operation there had been lively doubts in Europe and America about the wisdom of such an action, and sympathetic understanding of African fears that it showed the western powers to be still habituated to meddling in African affairs. By the time Ba, Beavogui and company had

184

finished, most of that sympathy had been lost. It is arguable that the UN often has its uses as a forum where the aggrieved can simply let off steam without doing any great harm; but that game needs to be played within certain limits, and on this occasion those limits were disastrously exceeded.

Chapter Six

One week, one war

The 'Six-Day War' between Israel and three of its Arab neighbours, Egypt, Jordan and Syria, broke out on 5 June 1967. The new conflict rocked the UN on its heels and involved it in exceptionally intricate ways. The Security Council staged 21 meetings in 21 days. The Secretary-General made a spectacular peace-seeking dash to Cairo, played a conspicuous part in the whole drama and drew upon his own head much of the bitterness that it engendered. The Assembly was called into emergency special session, on the initiative of the Soviet government, whose head, Alexei Kosygin, attended the session and met with the United States president during it. Two UN peace-keeping formations were caught up in the whirlwind and torn from their positions; Unef, the force in Egypt and Gaza, being withdrawn under fire, while Untso, the truce organisation watching Israel's other borders, also found itself in the battle zone and emerged, when the dust settled, gamely watching over new dividing lines. Even more UN agencies and organisations were violently affected, most notably the Relief and Works Agency for Palestine Refugees (Unrwa). The whole UN climate was changed.

After so many years of ominous Middle Eastern rumblings, it may have been at least partly understandable that the signs of approaching conflict were not more widely recognised in the early months of 1967. Yet the portents were there for all to see. During 1966 Syria had passed into the hands of a regime bent on leading the Arab states into greater militancy towards Israel. Guerrilla raids into Israel across Syria's border were multiplied, with the open encouragement of the new government in Damascus headed by Noureddin Atassi, which nevertheless denied responsibility when Untso pressed inquiries. The Atassi regime also backed guerrillas who struck into

186

Israel from Jordan, much to the dislike of King Hussein's government in Amman.

In August 1966 Russia vetoed a Security Council resolution that would have asked both Syria and Israel to comply with the existing armistice agreement. In November Russia vetoed another Council resolution arising from a new Israeli complaint against Syria. But later in that month, after Israel had taken retaliatory action against Jordan, the Council (by fourteen votes to none, New Zealand abstaining) censured Israel and warned it that if there were more reprisals the Council 'will have to consider further and more effective steps, as envisaged in the Charter, to ensure against the repetition of such acts'.

The Israelis were left with the feeling that the Council was automatically unfair to them. The Syrians were encouraged to try again. At the start of 1967 the Syria–Israel border was tenser than ever. Thant urged both states to revive their Mixed Armistice Commission, which had not met for seven years. In form, they did so; but all the efforts of General Odd Bull, the Norwegian head of Untso, failed to get the commission to start any actual talking. On April 7 there was a brief but bloody battle on the frontier in which the Syrian government's own forces took part. In an atmosphere of growing tension, military preparations were stepped up by all parties, other Arab states responding to the Syrians' calls for solidarity. By the beginning of May things looked very nasty indeed.

During all this the Security Council clung to a policy of inactivity that could not be described as masterly. It held no meetings at all in January, February, March, April and the first three weeks of May. Now, it is arguable that formal Council debates, which almost inevitably include a lot of polemic if the situation is a tense one, are to be avoided unless there is some prospect of their yielding some useful result. But, as has already been emphasised, formal debate is only the outward and visible part of the Council's role. Article 28 of the Charter provides that

> The Security Council shall be so organised as to be able to function continuously. Each member of the Security Council shall for this purpose be represented at all times at the seat of the Organisation.

This does not mean that the members must, every day, take their seats in the Council chamber and drown each other in oratory. It means that they should be not only in New York but actively and alertly in touch with events and with each other. An ability to function continuously requires fairly continuous consultation. The Council's sin of omission in early 1967 was not a failure to orate but a failure to consult.

A heavy responsibility for this failure must rest on the members, who at the time, in addition to the permanent Five, were Argentina, Brazil, Bulgaria, Canada, Denmark, Ethiopia, India, Japan, Mali and Nigeria. And some must rest on the Council presidents for these lost months, the representatives of Argentina, Brazil, Bulgaria, Canada and China. The Canadian president for April, George Ignatieff, was later to admit in the Council (when it at last met, on May 24) that he had been perfectly well informed about the mounting tension:

> I was only too keenly aware of this, Mr President, when last month I had the responsibilities which you now have. Steady reports of deterioration along the frontier lines between Syria and Israel were reported in correspondence which I received and forwarded to my colleagues as President.

An unfortunate factor here was the way the working of the monthly change of presidency brought it in the crucial month of May to the representative of the Chinese government in Taipeh. Liu Chieh was an amiable fellow, but the intimacy of his relations with other Council members was reduced by the fact that only five of them, out of fourteen, recognised his government. Those that did not included Britain, France and Russia. And Nikolai Fedorenko, the Soviet representative, who happened to be a sinologist (he had translated some of Mao's poems into Russian, and liked to quote obscure Oriental proverbs), was particularly loth to be seen taking any notice of the representative of 'the stinking corpse of the Kuomintang'.

Liu told the Council on May 24 of his deep regret that 'circumstances did not permit me to have fuller consultations with my colleagues personally and individually, as I should have liked to do'. But of course his particular difficulty was not the only reason why the Council's whole membership had been so remiss. It must be recorded that several of its Latin American, African and Asian members showed no conspicuous concern about the Middle Eastern crisis either before or even during the war. This did not reflect an automatic siding with the Arabs against Israel on the part of the Asians and Africans. (At the 1966 Council meetings Japan, Nigeria and Uganda had voted for the resolutions that Russia vetoed in order to protect Syria.) It reflected a certain lack of real interest, which did no credit to members of a body entrusted with a special responsibility for world peace. It also reflected a feeling among smaller UN members that, at this period and in these circumstances, little could be achieved until the major powers found enough common ground to enable the organisation to function positively in regard to the Israel–Arab problem.

The depressing results of the Council meetings in the later months of 1966 had strengthened this feeling. The Americans had no wish to go through all that again, with the one-sided censure of Israel not being balanced by any Council condemnation of Arab offences against the armistice terms. The Russians were plainly going to go on vetoing any resolutions that would have warned off the Syrians. Most other Council members saw little purpose in working up drafts that would be vetoed.

The sadly ironic thing was that the 1967 Council was a good one, in the important sense that its elected members included a high proportion of 'middle powers', substantial states which were active contributors to UN enterprises. For contrast, compare the 1970 list of elected members: Burundi, Colombia, Finland, Nepal, Nicaragua, Poland, Sierra Leone, Spain, Syria, Zambia. Article 23 of the Charter lays down that, in elections to the Council, 'due regard shall be specially paid, in the first instance, to the contribution of Members of the United Nations to the maintenance of peace and security and to the other purposes of the Organisation'. In the 1970 list it is not easy to recognise this criterion as applying to any of the members except Finland. In 1967 it could reasonably be applied to Brazil, Canada, Denmark, Ethiopia, India, Japan and Nigeria: no less than seven out of the ten. Four of these – Brazil, Canada, Denmark and India – actually had troops serving in Unef at the time. Ethiopia and Nigeria had provided troops for the UN Congo operation; both loomed large among the African states and had often been looked to for a lead by smaller members of that group. Japan, then on the point of achieving the world's third largest gross national product, was making large and fast-growing contributions to UN development aid programmes. Moreover, the 1967 Council was almost unique in not having any Arab member. This was a particular blessing in that, if an Arab had been elected to replace Jordan at the end of 1966, it could well have been Syria, whose presence would hardly have improved the Council's manner of handling the new crisis.

But Nigeria, in early 1967, was increasingly preoccupied with the regional split that flamed up later that year into Biafran secession and civil war. Argentina and Brazil had passed into military hands and were not well placed to make constructive contributions to the solving of major international problems. Japan was maintaining its well-known 'low posture', avoiding involvement in international controversy as far as possible – an attitude reinforced by its sensitivity about association with the United States and thus with the Vietnam war. Ethiopia was on awkward terms with its Arab neighbour, the Sudan. India was pursuing the Arabs' friendship with rather obvious desperation, in order to avert their siding with their fellow Moslems in Pakistan. Canada and Denmark were reluctant to take initiatives at the UN with which their Asian and African fellow Council members were not associated, since such moves might be seen as catspaw work on behalf of their American and British allies.

If the Russians had been in a mood to work together with the western powers to preserve Middle Eastern peace, Fedorenko would still not have been a good instrument for the carrying out of such a policy through the UN. When he first came to New York his bow-tied, academic, pipe-smoking, slightly raffish image had raised some hopes that he embodied a Soviet intention to improve its UN mission's personal relationships in the Turtle Bay community, but these hopes soon faded as he relapsed into old-style cold war oratory. In any case, Moscow was not in a co-operative mood. Its supreme preoccupation at this time was with its furious contest with Peking.

Mao Tse-tung's regime was presenting itself as the champion of all the world's revolutionary forces, whether communist, anti-colonialist or anti-American. It was urging all these elements to break with the wicked Soviet leaders, whom it accused of conspiring with the

190

Americans to impose on the whole world the hegemony of the two nuclear super-powers. Peking particularly accused Moscow of betraying the revolutionary struggle in Vietnam. Brezhnev and Kosygin were taking pains to avoid being seen in any kind of 'collusion' with the United States, even where there was a common Russo-American interest in preventing a catastrophe – like a new Middle Eastern war. They claimed that the Vietnam war was the main obstacle to 'east–west' co-operation. In fact, the real obstacle was China. (Anybody who imagines that Peking's exclusion from the UN has prevented it from making its influence felt on events there should ponder this evidence to the contrary.) And a specific result of Russia's anxiety about being outflanked by the Chinese was its zeal in backing those Arab regimes, like Atassi's in Syria, which claimed to be more revolutionary than others. If the wilder Arabs even declared that the very existence of Israel was a neo-colonialist crime perpetrated by the sinister Americans, Russia would still play along with them. Moscow's wheel had turned almost full circle since the late 1940s, when it had so eagerly co-sponsored with America the creation of Israel and its recognition by the UN.

These things all contributed to the Council's fateful inactivity in the first months of 1967. The battle on April 7 did not galvanise it into action. On May 8 Thant gave it a prod by publishing a message he had sent to General Bull which showed how seriously he viewed the Syria–Israel confrontation. On May 11, at a press conference, he voiced similar warnings. The only noticeable result was a furious protest from the Syrian representative at the UN, Georges Tomeh. Tomeh went to the Secretary-General's office and spent nearly an hour complaining to Thant about his having told the press that the new guerrilla activity 'is contrary to the letter and spirit of the Armistice Agreements, and menaces the peace of the area'.

The outraged Syrian announced on May 15 that his protest would probably be followed up by a joint Arab request for a Council meeting. A letter to the Council, he said, was being drafted. Thant's spokesman pointed out in reply that his remarks to the press could not possibly be interpreted as 'condoning resort to force by any party' (i.e. as justifying Israeli reprisals). No more was heard of the Arab demand for a Council meeting. Which was perhaps a pity. At this late hour anybody who managed to arouse the dormant Council might have been doing a service to peace, whatever his motives. As it was, Thant was left to take the brunt of the now imminent crisis on his own.

On May 15 Egypt's army was already moving forward through Sinai to Gaza, to the border near Eilat, and to the crucial 'blockading' position at Sharm el Sheikh at the Gulf of Aqaba's narrow mouth. On the 16th and 17th the Egyptians occupied positions along Israel's border and at Sharm el Sheikh, ordering Unef units to hand over their posts, firing shells at some of these and forcing UN detachments out of others. On the evening of the 16th General Mohamed Fawzy, Egypt's chief of staff, sent General Indar Jit Rikhye, Unef's Indian commander, a terse demand for immediate withdrawal of the Unef troops. 'Our troops are already concentrated in Sinai on our eastern borders,' said Fawzy's message. General Eiz-el-Din Mokhtar, who handed this message to Rikhye, particularly insisted that the key post at Sharm el Sheikh must be handed over to Egyptian troops that same day; and he threatened that it might be attacked if it was not.

Rikhye calmly replied that he took orders only from the Secretary-General. Thant, when informed, told Rikhye to stand firm, and summoned the Egyptian representative at the UN, the elegant and dignified Mohamed Awad El-Kony. It was by now after midnight in Sinai, but still early evening in New York. El-Kony, caught on his way to a party, arrived at Thant's office in a dinner jacket and a state of apparently complete ignorance of any demand by his government for a Unef withdrawal. (Fawzy's ultimatum had been worded in such bad English that this alone suggested that it had not been cleared with the foreign ministry in Cairo.) Thant told El-Kony that Fawzy's approach was improper, and asked him to get clarification from Cairo. But he got none for two days.

Early next morning, Wednesday the 17th, Thant heard from Rikhye of a fresh demand from General Fawzy for immediate withdrawal of the thirty-two Unef Jugoslav soldiers at Sharm el Sheikh. Thant called in the UN representatives of the six states then providing troops for Unef – Brazil, Canada, Denmark, India, Jugoslavia and Sweden. The Indian and the Jugoslav indicated that their

THE SIX-DAY WAR

governments would comply at once with any Egyptian request for the removal of UN troops from Egypt. Meanwhile the Cairo press and radio had claimed that Unef was already withdrawing. American and Canadian diplomats in Cairo made representations at the foreign ministry, urging that no irrevocable decisions be taken. The Egyptians were later to claim that this action intensified their fears of a western 'plot' to force them to let UN troops remain in Egypt.

193

After the troop-contributors' meeting Thant called in El-Kony again and gave him an *aide-mémoire* in which he made the particular point that Unef could not make a partial withdrawal to suit the Egyptian army's convenience and then, in effect, cover one of the Egyptians' flanks while they went to war in the sector of their own choice. Fawzy's insistence from the start on immediate possession of the Gulf of Aqaba positions suggests that the Egyptians may have actually expected the UN troops to help them reimpose a blockade of the gulf by getting in the way of any Israeli counter-stroke nearer to Gaza.

From the start Thant accepted the fact that, in the absence of any authorisation from the Council or even the Assembly to do otherwise, he would have to comply with an Egyptian request for withdrawal of the force once the request was made in proper form. At noon on Thursday, May 18, El-Kony delivered such a request from his government, in the name of his foreign minister, Mahmoud Riad. Thant at once expressed deep misgivings about the probably disastrous consequences of a withdrawal. He told El-Kony that he meant to appeal urgently to President Nasser to reconsider the Egyptian decision. El-Kony told him that there was intense resentment in Cairo at what were seen there as attempts to impose Unef on Egypt as an 'occupation force', and that Mahmoud Riad personally advised Thant not to make an appeal to Nasser. Any appeal, he said, would be sternly rebuffed.

Within the hour, Thant convened the Unef Advisory Committee (Brazil, Canada, Ceylon, Colombia, India, Norway and Pakistan), with the representatives of Denmark, Jugoslavia and Sweden in their role as troop-contributors. The views expressed were similar to those at the troop-contributors' meeting of the previous day. No member of the committee proposed convening the Assembly. Later that evening Thant informed El-Kony that he would arrange for 'the orderly withdrawal of the Force' in compliance with Egypt's request, while immediately reporting to both Assembly and Council. Thant again told the Egyptians of his 'serious misgivings' and warned them that Unef's withdrawal 'may have grave implications for peace'.

Before El-Kony delivered the request from Riad, Thant had already called in Israel's representative at the UN, Gideon Rafael, and raised the question of placing Unef on Israel's side of the border. Rafael said this would be 'entirely unacceptable to his government'. On this same day, the 18th, the UN aircraft in which Rikhye was flying to Gaza was fired on by Israeli planes which tried to force it to fly across the line into Israel and land there. But Rikhye's plane flew on to Gaza, where he received Thant's instructions to set in motion a withdrawal which 'must be carried out with dignity'.

Among the more hysterical phenomena at the time were numerous charges that Unef had vanished 'overnight' with panic speed. These statements were made by people who clearly had no idea of the problems involved in extricating a force of 3,400 men stretched out in detachments over 300 miles of very difficult terrain, no part of it being less than 100 miles from a usable port. No UN troops in fact left Egypt until May 29. And then it was only the Canadian unit that was evacuated, in response to a somewhat shrill demand from General Fawzy, in which he said they must go within 48 hours because Canada's 'biased attitude toward Israel' endangered their safety. A large part of the UN force was still in the Gaza zone when the war began on June 5. It then suffered casualties at the hands of the advancing Israelis, whose actions at the time seemed to show that they regarded the UN men as enemies. Unef camps were shelled, ringed by tanks while the Israelis disarmed and manhandled their occupants, and looted.

This UN force had been established by the Assembly, and the Security Council had never concerned itself directly with Unef's activities. But, as Sherlock Holmes might have put it, one of the most 'curious incidents' in the affair of Unef's end was that the Council did nothing. As that sudden night fell, the Council was conspicuous in the role of a non-barking dog. However, in the light of the Council's painful involvement in the immediate consequences, some notice must be taken here of the rather turgid controversy that accompanied the force's withdrawal.

The heat generated by this event mainly reflected the simple fact that many people, shocked and alarmed by the crisis, felt the need of a convenient scapegoat on whom the general sense of guilt could be focussed. Thant was conveniently available. He had himself pointed out, five years earlier, that

195

One of the most important roles of the United Nations . . . is that of the old English institution, Aunt Sally – the large and conspicuous figure at which things can be thrown both with impunity and with almost complete certainty of hitting the target. . . . The United Nations must inevitably accept the risks and insults involved.

The risks and insults were plentiful in 1967. But it was remarkable how few of the pot shots at Thant hit the target at all accurately. For example, he was reproached for not asking whether Israel would let Unef be placed on its side of the line – which he had done.

None of his critics seemed to share his concern for the safety of the UN soldiers, whose governments had never intended that they should be caught in the maelstrom of a full-scale war, and for whose lives he had had to accept responsibility. The critics also chose not to see the plain fact, which he and others had spelt out over and over again, that Unef's effectiveness in its buffer role had always depended on the Egyptians' voluntary restraint in keeping their army well away from the border and from Sharm el Sheikh. Once a large Egyptian army had moved right up to the line, Unef was no longer in any sense 'interposed' between the antagonists. Indeed, at many points the Egyptian troops were interposed between Unef and the Israelis. Moreover, once the host country withdrew all its co-operation, the force could not even survive, let alone perform any useful function. The Egyptians could block its supply lines and even prevent movement between its camps.

Thant's acceptance of the request for withdrawal was nevertheless denounced as 'poltroonery' by Joseph Alsop and as a 'dreadful mistake' by Sir Alec Douglas-Home. Senator Dirksen accused him of acting 'like a thief in the night' – this at a time when the Secretariat was flooding Assembly, Council and press with minutely detailed, blow-by-blow reports of every development. Cy Sulzberger told readers of the *New York Times* that Thant had 'used his international prestige with the objectivity of a spurned lover and the dynamism of a noodle'. None of the guilt-projectors explained how Thant could continue an operation that required the host country's consent and help when both had been withdrawn; when one Unef contingent after another was evidently going to be taken away by the contributors; when the whole thing had ceased to serve any practical purpose.

Stevenson in the 1962 Cuba debate (page 172)

Zorin in debate on Cuba (page 173)

Photographs of Soviet missile sites displayed in the Council chamber (page 175)

UN observers beside the Suez Canal after the Six-Day War (page 219)

Tabor and El-Kony during the
Six-Day War (page 210)

Abba Eban addresses the Council during
the war (page 211)

Unlike his critics, the Secretary-General had the benefit of the close advice of veteran assistants of the calibre of Ralph Bunche, who had been intimately concerned with Hammarskjöld in the creation of Unef in 1956 and understood exactly what was the real basis of its presence in Egypt (and of its exclusion, throughout its ten-year life, from Israel). Bunche, in this time of trial, overcame his instinctively strong discretion about revealing (especially to the press) the more delicate workings of UN mechanisms. He contributed weightily to the impressive defence of Thant's actions that was issued in response to his critics, but not widely read by them. For the Secretariat, which, unlike most participants in the controversy, was concerned about the whole future of the UN as a peace-keeping instrument, there was an over-riding consideration of great importance to that future. If a state that had always understood that the UN force in its territory was there only by invitation suddenly found attempts being made to keep the force there against the hosts' will, what prospect would remain of any state ever again accepting such a peace-keeping force?

No member of the Unef Advisory Committee, nor any one of all the UN member states, exercised the right to call for an Assembly debate – though, by a supreme irony, the Assembly was actually in special session in New York at the time and discussing the general problem of peace-keeping forces. Nor was there any move to invoke the Council. In fact, of course, every member government saw quite clearly that neither Assembly nor Council would approve an attempt to keep Unef in Egypt against Egypt's will. What Thant's critics expected him to do was a thing for which he could not have obtained support from any UN organ.

Later, when the Egyptians found that their insistence on Unef withdrawing had brought catastrophe on their heads, they worked up a whole series of stories to the effect that they had never really wanted it to withdraw. One particular version was that they had not intended to take over Sharm el Sheikh, but that, when Thant pointed out the impossibility of a partial withdrawal, they were 'obliged' to take it over and even 'obliged' to blockade the Gulf of Aqaba. These fabrications were accepted with grotesque eagerness by some commentators who wanted more sticks to beat Thant with; even by those who were passionately pro-Israeli and normally refused to believe a word the Egyptians said. The legend persisted. It was impossible for Nasser and his colleagues to acknowledge – even to themselves, perhaps – that they had made a colossal blunder in May 1967. Nearly three years later the Egyptian president said in the course of a long interview with Eric Rouleau of *Le Monde*, published on 19 February 1970, that:

> 'It was not my intention to close the Gulf of Aqaba to Israeli ships. I had not asked Mr Thant to withdraw the UN troops from Gaza, or from Sharm el Sheikh which commands the mouth of the gulf, but only from the part of the frontier running from Rafah to Eilat. But the UN Secretary-General, on the advice of a high official of the organisation, of American nationality [here Nasser clearly tried to implicate Bunche], decided to withdraw the whole of the "blue helmets", thereby obliging me to send Egyptian forces to Sharm el Sheikh and to impose the blockade. Thus we fell into the trap which had been laid for us.' President Nasser abruptly stopped speaking. He did not want to recall the past, and the Egyptian leaders' mistakes, any more. 'We have prepared a thorough analysis of that dramatic period,' he said, 'but we have decided not to publish it until peace is restored.'

One can see why this analysis has been suppressed, and why Nasser pulled himself up so suddenly after uttering these extraordinary falsehoods. Their total untruth is exposed by the detailed and uncontested public record of events, which is just as available to Egyptians as to others. No Egyptian demand for a withdrawal only between Rafah and Eilat was ever made, either to Thant or to Rikhye. The only demand sent to Thant was for total withdrawal. Before Thant heard anything about any Egyptian demands, in any form, the Egyptian generals had told Rikhye that Sharm el Sheikh must be handed over to them immediately, and had threatened to attack the post if it was not handed over that same day, May 16. Before El-Kony delivered Egypt's withdrawal request to Thant on the 18th, the Egyptian troops that were already at Sharm el Sheikh had given the Jugoslav detachment there fifteen minutes to leave.

If the Egyptians had wanted Unef to stay at Sharm el Sheikh, they had ample opportunity to make that clear; instead they most urgently and threateningly insisted on taking over this key position.

As for Nasser's lurid vision of an innocent but helpless Egyptian army being dragged, kicking and screaming, to the Gulf of Aqaba and there 'obliged to impose the blockade' by the mesmeric powers, extending over 4,000 miles from New York, of Ralph Bunche (who, more than any other man alive, had laboured over many years to avert precisely this kind of danger), this leaves the imagination boggled beyond hope of repair.

As has already been shown, Thant's efforts to persuade the Egyptians to reconsider and modify their stand were repeatedly rebuffed. Undeterred by the warnings from Riad and El-Kony, he nevertheless flew from New York to Cairo on May 22 in a personal bid to save the day by inducing Nasser to accept a face-saving formula, which might have been along the lines of placing a substantial Untso presence on the Israel–Egypt border as a partial substitute for Unef. But while Thant was on his way to Cairo, its radio broadcast a jingo oration delivered by Nasser on the 22nd to his army in Sinai. In this he made the revealing claim that 'On May 16 [sic] we requested the withdrawal of Unef' – nothing about partial withdrawal – and went on:

> A big worldwide campaign began, led by America, Britain and Canada, opposing the withdrawal from Egypt. Thus we felt that there were attempts to turn Unef into a force serving neo-imperialism. . . . It is obvious that Unef entered Egypt with our consent, and thus cannot continue to stay except with our consent. . . . Had Unef ignored its basic mission and turned to achieving the aims of imperialism, we would have regarded it as a hostile force and forcibly disarmed it.

The really fatal words came only a little later in Nasser's broadcast. He announced that Egypt was immediately imposing a blockade on Israel's trade through its port of Eilat on the Gulf of Aqaba, using for this purpose the key position of Sharm el Sheikh at the gulf's narrow mouth.

Up to that point it had been arguable that Nasser really did not want to risk war. By marching his army up to the border very demonstratively (much of it had been paraded through the centres of Cairo and other cities on the way), and by brusquely telling Unef that it could stop being a nursemaid to his country (which was indeed what it had been doing for ten years), he had struck a manful posture that took the edge off the Syrians' taunts and challenges. He had even done something to relieve their fears that Israel was about to swoop on Damascus – if those loudly voiced fears were real. There remains a very reasonable doubt about their reality. Various Arabs had put out various stories about Israel concentrating invasion forces on its border with Syria. But the Untso observers' reports showed that these stories were, to put it bluntly, a lot of bull, and odd bull at that. And Syria, very noticeably, made no appeal for Security Council action to deal with the supposed threat. Its man at the UN, Georges Tomeh, was prominently active there, as we have seen, but he was complaining about Thant's remarks to the press, not about his country being on the eve of invasion.

Russia, for reasons of its own, took it upon itself to assure Nasser that Israel really was about to invade Syria. Nasser may have taken the Soviet stories at full face value. But whether he believed them or not, he was making a gesture that would restore his and Egypt's sagging prestige in the Arab world. And, in moving up his army and ousting Unef, he was acting within his rights – imprudently, no doubt, but quite legally, and without giving Israel a respectable reason for taking a swipe at him.

His announcement of the Aqaba blockade amounted to climbing out on a limb. It changed the whole atmosphere at the UN overnight. Before Thant left for Cairo he had warned members, in his detailed reports on the crisis addressed to both the Assembly and the Council, that Unef's withdrawal confronted them with a 'brutally' dangerous situation. Even on the 21st many of them still did not seem to take the warning very seriously. On Monday, May 22, jaws dropped all round. Nobody at the UN expected Israel to tolerate the resumption of a blockade of its trade from Eilat into the Indian Ocean. 'Israel will fight' was generally agreed; the question in dispute was whether 'Israel will be right'.

On May 24 the Security Council at last creaked into life. George Ignatieff of Canada and Hans Tabor of Denmark had been trying to coax it out of its slumbers. At first they accepted the objection that no debate should be held while Thant was in Cairo trying to make Nasser see sense. Then Nasser's blockade announcement indicated, accurately, that Thant would find no 'give' in Cairo, and it also spurred the Council into meeting before he got back to New York. But even this first meeting of the year encountered objections, notably from Fedorenko, who complained that it was quite unnecessary. The situation was being over-dramatised, said the Soviet representative; and his resistance led the Council to adjourn later on the 24th without fixing a time for resumption, and without taking any vote on a mild Danish–Canadian draft resolution, presented by Ignatieff, that would have simply expressed support for Thant's efforts and asked all states to do nothing that might make things worse.

Fedorenko's distaste for being drawn into debate was understandable. Russia was in a spot. It had admittedly tried to sell Nasser the idea that Israel was about to invade Syria. On the 24th Fedorenko dutifully recited the bit about Israeli leaders threatening Syria which the Council continued to hear from Arab and Soviet lips despite categorical Israeli denials that the alleged statements had been made. But the Russians had not sold Nasser the idea of ejecting Unef; that move took them by surprise. And they were not pleased about the blockade either. The deterioration of Arab–Soviet relations had begun. Within two weeks it was to reach the point where the beaten and bitter Arabs were (with some justice) accusing Russia of having lured them into war and then stabbed them in the back.

Meanwhile Fedorenko fell back on dark mutterings about evil imperialist intentions of intervening in the Arab states' affairs – which didn't really sound like either Ignatieff or his resolution. The Russian expert on China proudly applied one of his many 'old Oriental sayings' to his notional imperialist: 'He points at the moon, but sees his own finger.' This seemed to leave every other Council member, even Liu Chieh, baffled. But it enabled Lord Caradon to raise a general laugh when, saying that he quite understood why Fedorenko had delivered his irrelevant diatribe, he said: 'His motives are as transparent as his proverbs are obscure.' The Russian did not join in the laughter, but he gave ground to the extent of retorting with a more intelligible, though less polished, proverb. He could not tell whether the British representative was smiling or not, he said, because 'when the lion bares its fangs, it is unreasonable to suppose that he is smiling'.

201

El-Kony and the Israeli representative, Gideon Rafael, both addressed the Council on this first day of what was to prove a long series of meetings. As the series rolled on, more and more Arab states were permitted to join in the debates (including non-combatant ones like Lebanon, Saudi Arabia and even Morocco), until most of their spokesmen had to be seated away from the horseshoe table; when each one's turn came to speak, he would come to the table and take the place of one of the happy few among the Arab representatives who had come early enough to get seats there. At various stages several of the non-voting participants were represented by their foreign ministers, who included Abba Eban of Israel.

Much of the Arab oratory was not only repetitious but profoundly retrospective. The Council was reminded at great length of alleged Israeli offences going back over many years, but it was offered little practical guidance about the present crisis. However, it was at least spared the rhetorical flights of Jamil Baroody of Saudi Arabia until the war was over. Baroody did not get back from Europe until June 11. He then made up amply for lost time. At one o'clock in the morning of the 12th he was giving an exhausted Council a history lesson that went back to the Crusades, taking a passing swipe at Robert Kennedy, and declaring that 'with all due respect, the meetings the Council has held in my absence have really been mere delaying actions'. On the 13th he broke off in mid-discourse to demand that the Secretariat should investigate his suspicion that 'numerous television stations have stopped broadcasting this debate since I began to speak', and to ask Arthur Goldberg to ensure that 'the voice of Baroody shall not be silenced' in this manner. The voice of Baroody went on and on. Ralph Bunche, sitting behind Thant, passed him an urgent message from General Bull, and the Saudi spokesman immediately interrupted himself to say: 'Mr Bunche, do not distract the Secretary-General. I want him to hear every word I say'. Next day Baroody again asked to speak, and it turned out that his complaint now was that Bunche had sent him a note protesting at his remarks about distracting Thant. Tabor, as president, tried to bring Baroody back to the agenda. Thant upheld Bunche's action. But Fedorenko saw fit to denounce it as 'a challenge to all the members of the Council'.

Baroody was still going strong when the emergency Assembly began five days later. Leaping in as soon as Kosygin had made the opening speech, he flatly rejected the Soviet prime minister's proposals, declaring that the Arabs could never accept the mere fact of Israel's existence.

The novel development on May 24 was General de Gaulle's call for talks on the crisis between America, Britain, France and Russia. At the time this was, unfortunately, little more than a device for diverting attention from the fact that, while Russia was defending Egypt's right to blockade the Gulf of Aqaba, and America and Britain were denying it, France was undecided about this now crucial question. But the Americans and British promptly welcomed the idea of four-power talks.

In the Council on the 24th, Goldberg said he was authorised to announce that the United States was ready to join in a four-power effort 'both within and outside the United Nations . . . Mr President, all must join in the search for peace, the Secretary-General, the Security Council, and the great powers. Both separately and together, let us work in the common cause.' But the Russians said nothing, even when the French scaled down de Gaulle's first grand design by saying that, if Moscow wouldn't go any higher, it would be enough to hold talks between the four representatives at the UN.

De Gaulle restated his call for four-power talks on June 3, when his man at the UN, Roger Seydoux, also put it to the Council; but it met with the same Soviet brush-off as before. Three weeks later – after the war – the French foreign minister, Maurice Couve de Murville, presented a new version at the Assembly, but in such magnificently arrogant terms that not one of the other 120 delegations could accept it; for Couve's speech suggested that France felt itself uniquely qualified to lead America, Russia and Britain in settling all the Middle East's problems with scant regard for the wishes of the states directly concerned or of the other members of the UN. Only in 1969, at the time of de Gaulle's resignation, was a less overbearing form of four-power consultation on the Arab–Israel conflict devised.

After its first round on May 24 the Security Council retired into silence for another five days. Din raged all around it. Now that the Aqaba blockade had become the point of peril, people all over the world suddenly had to master the tortuous political geography of that straight and narrow waterway, with the two ports at its head, Israel's new-built Eilat and Jordan's sleepier Aqaba; its Saudi and Egyptian shores; and its narrow mouth, easily barred to shipping by guns mounted at Sharm el Sheikh on the Egyptian side. Instant pundits emerged who discoursed learnedly about Tiran Island and the navigability of the waters on either side of it. Legal eagles cited the decisions of the 1958 UN conference on the law of the sea, the relevant parts of the Montreux convention about passage through the Dardanelles, and even Grotius on the question of belligerent powers' rights of action after an armistice. It was a lawyers' field-day. But this was no time for leisurely dissection of grand old texts. Every hour that passed, with Egypt's new hold on the gulf mouth unbroken, brought Israeli restraint nearer to snapping point.

Tension soared in New York almost as visibly as in the Middle East. Things might have seemed bad in the Council chamber, but now that it lay quiet and empty, the surrounding city was buzzing. New York is, among many other things, unchallengeably the world's greatest Jewish city. Not for the first time, it was made clear that it was by no means the ideal site for diplomatic dealings on the Israel— Arab issue. The weekend of May 27–28 brought massive parades of Jewish organisations demonstrating solidarity with Israel in its hour of peril, and rather pitiful counter-demonstrations by small bands of Arabs (New York has everything and everybody, but it must be admitted that it is a bit short on Arabs). The main Sunday rally was addressed by a number of fervent supporters of Israel, including the historian Barbara Tuchman, author of *The Guns of August* and something of a specialist in eve-of-war situations. She told the cheering crowd that the United States should act 'not by futile fiddling in the United Nations, but by straightforward independent action'. She also denounced 'Thant's collapse', with a fine scorn for the Secretary-General and the stricter requirements of scholarship. Her reference to Thant drew hoots and boos from her excited audience, and she was encouraged to repeat herself in a letter to the *New York Times*.

Mercifully the indignation of Israel's local supporters seemed to stop well short of personal assaults on the Arab representatives at the UN. But it was symptomatic of the nervousness of these days that Mahmoud Aboul Nasr, the normally cheerful and easygoing young first secretary of the Egyptian UN mission, when he came home one night to his 12th-floor apartment in the Bronx and found that some unknown hand (presumptively female) had marked his front door with a big Star of David in lipstick, took it seriously enough to report to the police.

The Canadians deserved particular sympathy at this moment. Unef had been created in 1956 on the initiative of Lester Pearson, then foreign minister of Canada. Its first commander had been the Canadian General E. L. M. Burns. 'Tommy' Burns was by now back in his own government's service as its chief negotiator at the Geneva disarmament conference, but Canada was still conspicuously in the lead in UN peace-keeping work. It had troops in the Cyprus force as well as in Unef, and it had sent men to the Congo and Yemen too. The unhappy end of Unef was a particular unhappiness for 'Mike' Pearson, who by 1967 had been Canada's prime minister for four years; but he reacted with great restraint, telling the House of Commons in Ottawa that 'I am not being critical of the Secretary-General. . . . What he did was right, in terms of the documentary evidence.' But worse was to come.

On the newly man-made islands in the St Lawrence river at Montreal, Canada's great centennial world's fair, Expo 67, was going full blast; and its timetable of 'national days' for participating countries was bringing a steady stream of foreign statesmen to Canada. Israel's President Shazar was in Canada from May 21st till the 25th. President Lyndon Johnson visited Montreal for the American day at Expo on the 25th, and went on to Ottawa for a talk with Pearson. Harold Wilson was due in Canada on the 31st; because of the crisis, he sent another minister, Herbert Bowden, to the British day at Expo, but he himself went to Washington and New York, for meetings with Johnson and Thant, three days later.

This nexus of American–British–Canadian–Israeli comings and goings was seized upon by some Arabs as supporting evidence for their fear that a plot was being hatched to force the opening of the Gulf of Aqaba. There had been plenty of talk in Washington and

London about sending ships to challenge the new Egyptian blockade. George Ignatieff's initiative in starting Council debate – despite the objectivity of his words and the mildness of the resolution he introduced – also helped to fuel the fires of Arab suspicion, to the point where the Egyptians insisted on the summary evacuation of Canada's Unef contingent on May 29. They voiced fears that this Canadian contingent might be used to recapture the key position at Sharm el Sheikh from the Egyptians who had occupied it.

It was a compliment of sorts. Egypt had moved an army of 80,000 men into Sinai. Canada had less than 800 men there – who were not even combat troops, but transport and service personnel. But it was hardly a compliment to be welcomed. In New York Ignatieff's brow looked more furrowed than usual. In Ottawa Pearson and his foreign minister, Paul Martin, took pains to emphasise that they were not wholly disenchanted about participation in UN peace-keeping forces; but they made clear that they would insist on a firmer basis for any future operations that Canada took part in.

In the Security Council, when it met again on May 29, Arthur Goldberg took the lead. He was fully aware of the multiple delicacy of his own position. At the time of his appointment as America's councilman two years earlier some disquiet had been voiced at the prospect that, when the Council dealt with Middle Eastern matters, the United States would be personified by a prominent Jewish figure who had shown considerable personal sympathy for Israel. Now he had to act as spokesman for a great power which, however hard it might strive to avoid partisanship, was being branded by the Arabs as Israel's great protector. And he was operating against the background of the New York mood, under the beady eye of the television cameras that were providing more and more coverage of the Council debates every day, and would soon be relaying their every moment to the American mass audience.

Goldberg concentrated on the immediate danger in the Aqaba gulf. He asked the Council to put all its weight behind the appeal Thant had made, in his report on his Cairo mission, that all parties should 'forgo belligerence'. This, said Goldberg, must specifically mean 'forgoing any blockade of Aqaba during the breathing spell requested by the Secretary-General'. El-Kony would have none of this. He could agree with Goldberg only on the need to revitalise the original 1949 armistice agreements. It was part of the Arab case that Israel had occupied Eilat – nearly twenty years ago – in breach of those agreements; and that Israel therefore had no rights in the gulf, which was a wholly Arab waterway. But the Egyptian insisted that, armistice or no, his country was still at war with Israel and thus had the right of a belligerent to blockade the gulf.

Thant's appeal for restraint – which used stronger terms than the Danish–Canadian draft presented on the 24th – was backed in Council speeches on May 29 by Argentina, Brazil, Britain, Canada, Ethiopia and India (and on the 30th and 31st by China, Denmark, Nigeria and Japan). But Fedorenko still questioned whether the Council needed to do anything. He was in a questioning mood. After several hours of unbroken debate on the 29th Liu Chieh, as president, proposed a ten-minute break. Normally a proposal of this kind is accepted without any argument: even councilmen are human. But this time Nikolai Fedorenko formally demanded to know the reason for Liu's suggestion. The president said that a member had requested a brief break. Fedorenko wanted to know who. 'I am the guilty man,' said Arthur Goldberg, 'I thought we could listen with much more attention to the next speakers if we could recess for ten minutes.' Fedorenko again wanted an explanation. Goldberg said his reason was a 'delicate' one. This brought general laughter and made the situation quite clear to all (including the television audience) except, apparently, Fedorenko, who yet again demanded to be told what it was all about. At that, Goldberg called him 'singularly obtuse' and withdrew for a few minutes. This little episode (there is nothing on the public record to show whether it was actually Goldberg or Liu who first felt the call of nature) was not only a small portent of growing strain but also a reminder of the difficulties still arising from the fact that the Russian was not on speaking terms with the president for May.

Much more serious, at this point, was the unexplained failure of those members who backed Thant's appeal to frame a resolution to that effect. Fedorenko might well have abstained, rather than use a veto, on such a resolution, which would clearly have almost all other members' support. But the Council let two more days slip away while it listened to more harangues from the visiting firemen who were still arriving from Arab capitals. Goldberg, who would evidently have preferred some other member to propose a resolution, at last did so himself on the 31st. But Fedorenko said nothing. Or, rather, he spoke three times that day after Goldberg had presented his resolution, but he made no reference to it.

With the clock ticking away ever more ominously, India and France now made moves that regrettably slowed the Council's wheels. Both said that the American proposal would need careful consideration. For India, Gopalaswami Parthasarathi also said that he would ask for a vote on a draft that El-Kony had just presented, which would name Israel as having disregarded the armistice agreement and call for steps to restore that agreement, including Israeli evacuation of the El Auja border area. (Egypt itself could not, of course, move a resolution in the Council, of which it was not a member.) For France, Roger Seydoux asked for, and got, a two-day adjournment to permit study of Goldberg's and El-Kony's texts.

In vain had Goldberg contended that the founders of the UN had meant the Council to be a 'small and compact body', capable of 'prompt and effective action'. Seydoux's two days became three. On Saturday, June 3, the Council held what was to be its last pre-war meeting. No support for Goldberg's draft was voiced. No amendment was proposed. No sense of real urgency seemed to grip the Council on this twelfth day since its first meeting. At 2.20 on the Saturday afternoon it adjourned for 48 hours. But war was less than 36 hours away.

*   *   *

Around three o'clock in the morning of Monday, June 5, the new Council president, Hans Tabor of Denmark, was woken by telephone calls in which Rafael and El-Kony informed him that their countries were being attacked by each other. One of the more extraordinary features of the whole business was that at no stage did either Egypt or Israel ask the Council to meet; not even now that they were both claiming to have been invaded. Both had evidently decided that they could win a war. Yet, while their joint refusal to invoke the UN may have made the Council's earlier sluggishness more understandable, it had not excused it.

Hans Tabor had no doubt about his own duty, not even in the middle of the night. The fact that the belligerents simply wanted to get on with their war was not going to stop him from rousing other Council members from their slumbers. He put in motion the series of further telephone calls needed to bring the Council into session by 9.30 that same morning.

Tabor was a new boy in the Council. He had represented Denmark at the UN since 1964, but it had held a Council seat only since January 1967, and, as already recorded, there had been no meetings that year before May 24. But his lack of Council experience was more than offset by other qualities. Unlike the unfortunate Liu, he enjoyed good political and personal relations with all other members. Denmark, although a Nato member, was in generally good standing with the non-aligned Afro-Asians and even with the communist states. A respected contributor to many UN enterprises, it had sent troops to Egypt and Cyprus and had provided observers for Untso. And Tabor's own large, friendly, energetic personality was another Danish asset at the UN. An athletic 45-year-old, he stood six foot three. An economist by training rather than a diplomat, he showed a political flair in the 1967 Middle East crisis that helped to propel him, a few months later, into becoming his country's foreign minister. The fact that there was a visible element of showmanship in his performance (as there was in Lord Caradon's, and in that of Chief Adebo of Nigeria) did him no harm either.

On that alarming morning, the Council met to hear reports rather than to debate. Thant gave it the information he had already received from Generals Rikhye and Bull. He had to report that Jordanian troops, who had immediately joined in the fighting (as had the Syrians), had occupied the area of Bull's Jerusalem headquarters. Thant at once asked King Hussein to remove these troops; but during the day Israeli forces removed them and took over the former Government House themselves. Egyptian troops, said Thant, had surrounded Unef camps near Gaza, and the Israelis had shelled two of these camps and strafed a Unef convoy, killing nine Indian soldiers.

Far from having vanished 'overnight' on May 18, the UN force had met the fate that Thant had hoped to avert; its lightly armed units were caught in the cross-fire of two large armies and air forces.

Once again, neither El-Kony nor Rafael asked the Council to take any steps to stop the fighting. After they had spoken, Parthasarathi condemned the 'wanton, irresponsible and brutal' Israeli killing of Indian UN soldiers, and at 11.15 the Council, at Tabor's suggestion, called 'a short recess for urgent consultations'. The recess, and the consultations, went on for eleven hours.

Few members strayed far from the chamber during that long day. Those who emerged at all from the privacy of the chamber and its adjoining rooms were at once surrounded by press correspondents desperate for news of what was going on behind the closed doors. Caradon was thus halted on first emerging, and El-Kony, coming out on his heels, caught up with him and said with deep emotion: 'My Lord, I told you we would fight, and we are fighting!' The touch of old-world courtesy was very characteristic of the Egyptian representative, even at a moment of such strain. But as the day wore on Arab confidence at the UN cracked under the impact of the news of Israeli victories. The Jordanians' feat in shelling Tel Aviv's suburbs with Big Bertha guns was hardly as decisive as the fact that Israel had wiped out the Egyptian air force, and was thus in a position to bomb the Egyptian army in Sinai into the desert sand.

On the second day of the war it was already indisputable that Israel had shattered its enemies. Much of the wrangling that had gone on so long on the first day, in Tabor's office and the other private rooms adjoining the Council chamber, now seemed merely academic. In those first hours, Russia and India (and, with some obscurity, France) had pressed for the framing of a demand for a cease-fire linked with a complete withdrawal. Russia had further insisted on a condemnation of Israel as the aggressor. America had proposed a simple cease-fire call, although it had seemed ready to consider linking it with a demand for withdrawals of all forces, not to the positions of June 4, but to those they had held before Egypt moved its army forward in May. But no common ground had emerged.

During Monday evening members had kept drifting back to their seats at the Council table, raising false hopes that something had been agreed; but at last, around 10.30 p.m., Tabor had called it a day, announcing that there would be no formal session that night but that consultations would continue. Next day, Tuesday the 6th, the Council did not return to its table until 6.30 in the evening. Tabor then produced a resolution simply calling for a cease-fire. It was adopted unanimously, by a show of fifteen hands.

Russia had caved in and aligned itself with America and all the others. A storm of Arab fury broke over Fedorenko's head. Adnan Pachachi, the foreign minister of Iraq, told the Council that this was 'an abject surrender to Israel'. Morocco's representative sarcastically noted that 'the club of the four great powers' had reached its first decision − not to brand Israel as an aggressor. The three warring Arab states, which were still losing ground to the advancing Israelis, were less vocal but even more bitter about their betrayal by Russia. The urbane aristocrat El-Kony was heard to say in the corridors that the Arabs would now have to seek aid from communist China. Nor was this all. At midday next day, Wednesday, June 7, the Council was urgently convened again − at Fedorenko's request. Naturally, it was assumed that he wanted to demand an Israeli withdrawal. Instead he asked for immediate adoption of a Soviet resolution which repeated the cease-fire call and set an immediate deadline for compliance. Russia was now desperately trying to stop the war before even worse befell the Arabs; but they saw nothing but a further betrayal in its action.

On Tuesday night in the Council Abba Eban, speaking for Israel, had immediately accepted the first cease-fire call. The Arabs had not. Since then Jordan had informed Thant of its acceptance, but Egypt and Syria had not responded. Now, at Fedorenko's urging, the Council, again unanimously, demanded that they abandon their losing battles. Not until Thursday the 8th did El-Kony tell Thant that Egypt accepted the cease-fire call. He had tried to pave the way for this confession of defeat by telling the Council on the 7th that

> It is proved, without the shadow of a doubt, that the United States and the United Kingdom have participated in the aggressive Israeli air operations. . . . Moreover, they have provided an 'air umbrella' over Israel.

211

The Arabs could not face the idea of having been defeated, once again, by little Israel. They had to claim that they had been crushed by the might of great powers. Georges Tomeh of Syria had made the claim in the Council as early as Tuesday the 6th, asserting that

> we have decisive, irrefutable proofs that the British and American air forces have actively participated alongside Israel's in its aggression. . . . The air forces of the United States and the United Kingdom have . . . joined Israel's air force in its attacks against Arab cities and civilians. . . .

Months were to pass before the Egyptian and other Arab governments admitted that these charges had been unfounded. Meanwhile, the 'revelations' with which El-Kony tried to impress the Council seemed mild when compared with the versions of 'imperialist collusion' that were being pumped out by his government's propagandists for general consumption. Cairo radio was using considerably cruder terms:

> America is the enemy. Gamal [Abdul Nasser] has said it. . . . Arab brethren, your arms have repelled America's flagrant aggression on Arab territory. . . . Arabs, dig graves everywhere, dig a grave for America, dig it, Arabs, dig it, Arabs, dig it, Arabs. . . .

But if the Arabs hoped that their wild inventions would force Russia to make a real military intervention on their side, they were bitterly disappointed. Early on the Monday morning, June 5, the 'hot line' teletype machines in the White House had brought President Johnson an urgent message from the Soviet leaders to the effect that they wanted no part in a Middle Eastern war. The Americans were not, therefore, greatly surprised by the Russians' hasty backing down in the Security Council. Fedorenko ignored El-Kony's and Tomeh's 'revelations' as completely as his masters in Moscow ignored Nasser's.

Egypt and Jordan had now opted out. Syria, whose half-hearted attacks the Israelis had been fending off with, one might say, two fingers of the left hand, was still in the fight. There was a weird logic in this. The Syrians had set off the whole thing, had then played a

212

Michael Stewart in debate on
Rhodesia, 1965 (page 234)

George Brown speaks on Rhodesia,
December 1966 (page 247)

Caradon and Yost vetoing a Rhodesia resolution, March 1970 (page 260)

Irish troops of the UN force evacuating Turkish Cypriots from a danger area in 1964

Rauf Denktash addressing the Council (page 294)

In debate on Cyprus: Kyprianou (page 281) and, to right, Greece's Bitsios

negligible role in the main war, and seemed to feel a need to fight on a bit longer. Whatever they were trying to prove, what they did was to give Israel its chance to oust them from the Golan heights, from which they had long been harassing Israeli border farms by shelling as well as by guerrilla raids.

At one o'clock on the morning of Friday, June 9, Hans Tabor was told that Syria would accept the cease-fire. But at 5.30 that morning the Israelis told him that Syria was still shelling their border villages. At midday the Council met and heard Thant relay Odd Bull's reports of heavy fighting on that border – reports from the undaunted Untso observers, who were still doing their duty wherever they could, despite great difficulties and grave risks. Tabor had spent the morning rounding up support for a new resolution demanding an immediate end to the fighting, which was at once adopted unanimously. By 4 p.m. Thant had been promised the compliance of both governments. During the evening, however, the Council heard each of them complain that the other was still launching attacks. But their representatives, Rafael and Tomeh, united in supporting Goldberg's proposal that Bull's observers should be enabled to find out what was really happening. Thant quickly pointed out that, if Untso was to get back to work properly, freedom of movement must be restored to its observers, and General Bull's Jerusalem headquarters and radio station must be restored to him. Tabor got consensus approval of a request on these lines to the parties concerned. The Council thus made its first contribution to the restoring of the UN's battered presence on the belligerents' borders and cease-fire lines.

A now wearying Council adjourned at 11 p.m. At 2 a.m. Syria demanded an emergency meeting. By 4.30 a.m. on Saturday, June 10, the members were back at their table. Fedorenko, badly needing to offset Russia's abandonment of the Arabs by 'killing Kruger with his mouth', started to rave about 'annexationist Israeli hordes' (later he was to say that the Israelis were imitating their 'Hitlerite masters'). Hard fact broke through around 6.30 a.m., when Thant produced Untso reports of Israeli air raids on Damascus and Syrian shelling of Israeli villages.

The Council gave itself an hour's breakfast break and returned to its table, where, mainly at the insistence of Fedorenko and Georges

Tomeh, it was to remain through much of that day and, eventually, up to 2.30 on the morning of Sunday, June 11. That Sunday members snatched what rest they could during the day. They expected more night work, and they got it – including the ordeal of having to listen to Jamil Baroody's midnight effusions.

After six days the 'six-day war' was effectively over, but the Council laboured on the seventh day and through the seventh night until 3 a.m. on Monday the 12th, when it achieved one more unanimous resolution – its fourth, and Tabor's third – tightening up the cease-fire terms between Israel and Syria. During these later stages of debate the practical part of the talk around the horseshoe table turned on a variety of proposals – American, British, Canadian and Indian – for strengthening the UN machinery for supervision of the cease-fire. The practical talk had to be interposed between such diversions as the belated Baroody's attempts to get in on the act and Fedorenko's tirelessly repeated demands that the Council should proclaim a strictly one-sided condemnation of Israel.

The Russian, supported by Milko Tarabanov of Bulgaria and Moussa Leo Keita of Mali, opposed even at this stage the idea of the Council condemning all violations of the cease-fire. Tarabanov thought it monstrous that the Council should even consider such a move, because it would place both warring parties on the same level. Keita solemnly announced on the Sunday evening that, 'Mali will never associate itself with any – I repeat, any – resolution that treats the aggressor and the victim on the same footing.' Just a few hours later, in the early hours of Monday morning, Keita and Tarabanov and Fedorenko all voted for the fourth resolution, which did precisely that. Seldom does the Council witness such a grotesque example of a councilman eating his words not merely before the ink has dried but, in this case, before there had even been time to set the damning words down on paper at all.

At further meetings on June 13 and 14 the Council agreed on a call to the governments concerned for humane treatment of prisoners and of civilians in the areas of conflict. But in all other respects it found it had run out of unanimity. No agreement could be reached about the next steps.

Goldberg reminded the councilmen of the draft resolution he had presented as far back as June 8 – while Egypt was still fighting. This called for discussions, to be held 'promptly' after the cease-fire and in which the parties might use 'third party or UN assistance', of a peace settlement encompassing the 'withdrawal and disengagement' of forces, the renunciation of force and 'the maintenance of vital international rights'.

He did not press for an immediate vote. Instead he offered the councilmen more time to consider his text, and invited them to propose amendments if they so wished. But Fedorenko would have none of this. Caradon backed two Indian proposals, for strengthening the UN machinery in the war area and sending a special representative of the Secretary-General there. He also suggested that the Council appoint a mediator. Fedorenko would have none of this either. The Soviet representative insisted on a vote on his own draft resolution, which, in Goldberg's words, was 'a prescription for renewed hostilities', since it was a call to set things back exactly the way they had been on the eve of the war. On June 14 the Council rejected Fedorenko's draft. Only four of the fifteen members (Russia, Bulgaria, Mali, India) voted for its paragraph condemning Israel's 'aggressive actions'; only six (the same, with Ethiopia and Nigeria) for its demand for immediate, total and unconditional Israeli withdrawal.

Fedorenko's clear aim was to break off the Council's debate, in spite of its having numerous proposals still before it. For Russia had meanwhile, on the 13th, called for an emergency special session of the UN Assembly. A majority of member governments agreed to this. The Assembly began debate on June 19, and the Council receded into quiescence – but only until July 8, when gunfire along the Suez Canal, the new 'front line' between Israel and Egypt, jerked it back to life.

The Russians made a big production out of the 'emergency' Assembly. The Soviet prime minister, Alexei Kosygin, came to New York, made the opening speech in the Assembly debate and took the opportunity of being in America to accept Lyndon Johnson's invitation to a 'summit' meeting at Glassboro, New Jersey. (Glassboro is a quiet little place which owed its hour in the limelight as a rendezvous

215

for this top-level encounter between the super-powers solely to its geographical position, just halfway between New York and Washington. The fact that neither of the two leaders felt able to travel any farther to meet the other was eloquent of the delicate balance between their wish to meet and their reluctance to show undue eagerness about meeting.)

Kosygin solemnly declared in his opening speech that 'if the General Assembly should find itself incapable of reaching a decision in the interests of peace, this would deal a heavy blow to the expectations of mankind'. He then personally introduced a Soviet draft resolution, along the same lines as the one the Council had rejected five days earlier, which in due course suffered a humiliating rejection. Each of its paragraphs was voted on separately; none received more than 45 out of 121 votes, some only 34. Russia then gave its support to a draft proposed by sixteen Asian and African states, with Cyprus and Jugoslavia, which called for Israel's immediate withdrawal from the occupied areas, but did not condemn or even censure it. It got only 53 votes, and as there were 46 against it, it came nowhere near the required two-thirds majority.

The Russians must have known that they could no more carry the Assembly than they could the Council. In abruptly breaking off the dialogue in the Council, which still had before it several proposals (including the American draft resolution to which Goldberg was inviting other members to offer amendments), Russia's motive was undoubtedly, as Conor Cruise O'Brien has put it, 'to "take the harm" – as we say in Ireland – out of its failure to support the Arab cause . . . by having the General Assembly convened for a propaganda orgy'.* It could, for this purpose, generate more orgiastic sound and heat in the Assembly than in the Council. And, whereas in the Council Russia might well have found itself in the unhappy position of having to veto an amended version of Goldberg's new draft which most members could support, in the Assembly it was reasonably sure that the balance of voting forces would be more even. So it proved. On the same day that the Soviet and Afro-Asian resolutions failed to carry the Assembly (it was the Fourth of July, an appropriate date, in an American city, for both fireworks and

* *The United Nations: Sacred Drama*, London, 1968.

bonfires), a Latin American draft backed by the United States, Britain and most other west European states got 57 votes against 43 – a slightly better score than the Afro-Asians', but again nothing like a two-thirds majority.

The Assembly session ground on for more than a month. One could not say that it lost its 'emergency' character, for it had never had one. The Russians themselves, immediately after demanding that it should meet within twenty-four hours, had sent Thant a second message asking that it should not start work until June 19. By mid-July, when it was quite clear that the Assembly could not agree on any resolution on the main issue, it faced the problem of how to kill itself off. This dilemma was resolved when Sverker Aström of Sweden proposed adjournment of the Assembly with the recommendation that the Council should urgently resume consideration of the Arab–Israel situation. On July 21, over the opposition of the Arabs and thirteen of their keenest partisans (Albania, Cuba and eleven African and Asian states), the adjournment resolution was carried with the combined support of the western members (except France), India and Russia. Thus Russia once more broke ranks with the Arabs. Kosygin in effect told them that he had provided a month's orgy, and that that was all he could afford.

The Assembly had now 'urgently' asked the Council to take over. But the Council did not spring back into life in late July. Nor in August. Nor in September. Not until October 24 did it meet, and that had nothing to do with the Assembly's call. Was this reluctance a sign that the Council members resented that call? Hardly – for they had nearly all voted for it. America, Russia, Britain, China, India, Japan, Canada, Denmark, Argentina, Brazil and Bulgaria had all urged themselves once more to gather at the East River, and fast. France had not voted with them, but Seydoux had explained that he abstained only because there was no need to refer the problem back to the Council, which, he argued, had never parted with it.

With the honourable exception of Mali, which had voted against the Assembly's call, the Council members were thus seen to be flatly ignoring an urgent appeal from most of themselves. Now, it is regrettably common for calls from the Council to be ignored. Its

Glendower rating* is all too high. But it is most deeply regrettable when members of the Security Council choose to ignore an urgent call that they have made to themselves. One is left wondering how they can expect others to take them seriously when they themselves apparently do not.

On this occasion, to be absolutely fair to it, the Council had at least managed to do one piece of useful work during the Assembly session. (In all, the Arab–Israel problem was switched from Council to Assembly or *vice versa* seven times in just over four months, between 14 June and 24 October 1967. This set a new record, but not the kind that people should be encouraged to try to beat.) After the bonfire of ballots on July 4 the emergency Assembly had found itself already at a complete loss; but the delegates were not ready to go home. A procession of Arabs mounted the podium and ritually interred the UN. The Sudanese prime minister said that it 'now lies in ruins' and that the world was threatened with annihilation. The Syrian foreign minister said: 'This is the final funeral of this organisation.' (I liked the neat way he thus reminded his audience how frequently the UN had already been buried. But of course, like all the funeral orators on those earlier occasions, he was wrong about this being the last time.) Then the Assembly's president, Abdul Rahman Pazhwak of Afghanistan, took the only sensible course and gave it a very long weekend off – a six-day one, aptly.

Egypt, not liking the way things were quietening down, opened fire across the Suez Canal on Saturday, July 8; Israel retaliated; and both at once asked the Council's new president, Lij Endalkachew Makonnen of Ethiopia, for a meeting. For the first time in the whole 1967 affair, the Council was being asked to meet by the combatants – a month after the outbreak of the war, and nearly a month after its end. It was rather nice that Egypt and Israel had at last remembered what the Council was supposed to be there for. And all the more flattering when the special Assembly was right there for them to turn to instead, if they chose to.

---

* *Owen Glendower:* I can call spirits from the vasty deep!
  Harry Hotspur: Why, so can I, and so can any man,
                      But will they come when you do call for them?
                                         – *King Henry IV, Part One*

But the first hour or so of the Council meeting on the 8th did not encourage the belief that this body, unlike the Assembly, can be counted on to swing into swift action in emergencies. Fedorenko forced a debate about the agenda. The Council still had on its plate the leftover items from June 14, including Goldberg's draft. The Russian had no wish to get drawn into discussion of that. He insisted that the new breach of the cease-fire was not just priority business but the only business.

Once this fuss was over, Thant jumped in even before Egypt and Israel could speak. (How greatly had things changed since Lie had to fight for the right to speak in the Council at all!) He pointed out that during the war the Council had passed resolutions requiring him to keep it informed about the Egypt–Israel cease-fire, but had omitted to provide him with any means of doing so, in the shape of observers on the Suez Canal. He had taken the initiative himself to remedy this, and was waiting for Egypt and Israel to answer his inquiries as to whether they would accept observers. The Egyptian, the Israeli and the Russian then made speeches that completely ignored Thant's point. But Caradon and Goldberg urged immediate action as proposed by the Secretary-General. Lij Endalkachew suspended the debate so that Thant's proposal could be discussed privately. In the talks that followed, Fedorenko challenged the proposal on the ground that the Council should take wider-ranging action. But his mouth was full of his own foot, for he had just been insisting that the cease-fire breach on the canal was the Council's only business. Late in the evening of Sunday, July 9, Parthasarathi of India induced the Russian not to block Thant's move. Fedorenko was still coy about voting on it, so it was agreed to stage a consensus. Shortly after midnight, Lij Endalkachew was able, without objection, to state 'the view of the Council that the Secretary-General should proceed, as he has suggested', to arrange to place observers on the canal.

This was a good night's work, one of the best the Council could show on its spotty 1967 record. But the main credit must go to Thant and his assistants, including Bunche and Bull. One of the more grotesque aspects of the hue and cry after the Secretary-General that partisans of Israel were keeping up at this time was their claim that he had surrendered to Russian and Arab pressure in agreeing to put

UN observers on the Suez Canal. The record of the Council's work on July 8 and 9 shows how the truth was the exact opposite. Russia, and later Egypt, yielded reluctantly in the face of Thant's western-backed initiative. The public nature of so much of the Council's activity may sometimes impair its effectiveness, but there are times, like this one, when it is good that the truth is made easy for all to see (easy, that is, for all except those who choose to pretend that they can't see).

After July 9 the Council, as such, faded from sight until October, when the cease-fire was sensationally broken by Egypt sinking an Israeli destroyer, in response to which Israel destroyed the oil tanks at Suez. For the second time both sides asked for Council action; the habit was coming back to them. They got more mileage, if that is the right word, this time. Instead of responding with a brief Saturday-and-Sunday session as in July, the Council launched itself into a month of active consultation as well as debate. This brought, on November 22, unanimity on a British resolution that set out guidelines for a peace settlement and asked Thant to send a special representative to coax the parties into agreement. A new phase in the longest-running of UN problems was thereby opened up; and that phase (which may be regarded as still running at the time of writing, for the November 1967 resolution is still the Council's only general statement of position) cannot be considered here. But brief mention must be made of one development late in 1967 which was directly related to the Council's action in July.

On October 25, the second day of the new series of meetings, Thant told the Council that he was going to have to place more observers on the Suez Canal. Fedorenko at once said that the Council must examine this question. On November 10 he presented a draft resolution in which the Council would authorise Thant to carry out his stated intentions. The Council majority could not accept his wording, for it would have meant taking away from the Secretary-General the right to decide for himself what should be the precise arrangements for Untso's cease-fire observation. That right had been fully conceded to Trygve Lie by Council resolutions in 1948 and 1949, and maintained ever since. On November 22, the last day of the series of meetings, Fedorenko said he would not 'at this time'

220

demand a vote on his draft. But the question was left awkwardly hanging in the air over a chamber to which the Council had no wish to return.

Mamadou Kante of Mali, the November president, found no solution to this problem. Simeon Adebo of Nigeria, taking over the presidency for December, consulted privately with all the members and was able to issue on December 8 a statement of consensus in their name. It said nothing about Fedorenko's proposal, but simply announced that the Council members 'recognise the necessity of the enlargement by the Secretary-General of the number of observers in the Suez Canal zone'. Thus the Council got itself off a nasty hook; nobody lost face; the Secretary-General's freedom of action remained undiminished – and Adebo had launched a valuable new precedent. Never before had such a consensus decision been announced when the Council was not formally meeting at all. It is nice to be able to end a survey of the Council's performance on the 1967 crisis on this note.

Chapter Seven

My God, we're in Chapter Seven!

Calling a spade a spade is something the United Nations prefers not to do until it has had the thing in its hands for a while and tried it out. There is always the possibility that, although the tool that was forged was meant to be a spade, the results it produces will be those associated with some other implement: a ploughshare, perhaps, or even a sword. And the first time the tool is used there are almost bound to be complaints, from one quarter or another, that it is bent sinisterly, or that the UN is digging with the left foot, and like that. One way of blunting some of the objections is to avoid being too definite about what the new thing is.

Superstition may even be involved. In some traditional cultures it is thought dangerous to reveal personal names to strangers, or even to utter them at all. This may give evil forces a chance to strike home. True enough, some of the UN's creations which were given names that plainly indicated their purposes (the Military Staff Committee, the Covenants on Human Rights) have withered on the vine. Contrast the 'Special Committee on the Situation with Regard to the Implementation of the Declaration on the Granting of Independence to Colonial Countries and Peoples'. Its proper name is remembered by very few, used by hardly any and only dimly related to its curious activities. It has flourished like the green bay tree (while doing untold harm to the cause it was supposed to promote). And the Secretary-General has been helped through some tight spots by the fact that nobody can quite make out whether he is a secretary or a general.

Whatever the motivation, the habit is ingrained. The UN started to

222

set up peace-keeping forces as far back as 1956, but not until 1964 did it describe one as such from its inception. In the late 1950s there was much inconclusive debate about the definition of a UN 'presence'. Hammarskjöld lifted this on to a higher level of confusion when, at one stage, he contemplated appointing a special representative who would keep an eye on the Middle East but would be based in New York: the 'absent presence' at once entered the Turtle Bay vocabulary.* And somehow these ways of thinking seem to have influenced the way the Security Council reacted in 1966, when to its vast surprise it found itself at last, after twenty years, setting in motion the mechanism of the Charter's famous Chapter Seven. In most minds this 'enforcement' chapter had been so completely identified with the use of the great powers' military force, through the Military Staff Committee and all that, and it had been so widely recognised that no such use of force would be possible for many years, that Chapter Seven had been virtually written off.

What the Council did in 1966, at Britain's request, was to use the 'economic sanctions' article in the chapter – Article 41 – against the illegal regime in Rhodesia, on the ground that a threat to peace existed. A whiff of grapeshot was also provided, when the Council empowered the British navy to use force to prevent tankers bringing oil for Rhodesia to the port of Beira in Portuguese-held Mozambique. But the main emphasis was on the 'interruption of economic relations' under Article 41.

One of the most obsessive ideas of the Three, when they shaped the main structure of the United Nations at Dumbarton Oaks, was the need to create 'a League with teeth'. Meaning military teeth. The League of Nations, both in its Covenant and in its practice, had given special prominence to the use of economic and other non-military 'sanctions' against any state that might 'resort to war in disregard of its covenants'. In the Covenant of the League, all members promised that they would automatically sever trade and other relations with such a war-maker – without the need for any decision by the League

---

* After Unogil, Unipom and all that, it was argued that this rather mystical 'presence' should be named Unicorn. More recently, somebody has come up with Unique; but this name is to be held in reserve in case separatism in Canada necessitates a UN force or presence in Quebec.

Council. In contrast, the possibility of using armed force against the wrong-doer was mentioned only as something that might be recommended by the League Council – which could reach a decision of this kind only if all its members agreed. As to situations involving a threat to peace that fell short of an actual outbreak of war, the League was bound only by its extremely vague obligation, in Article 11, to 'take any action that may be deemed wise and effectual'. The framers of the Charter deemed the League to have been unwise and ineffectual. So they devoted a chapter of no less than thirteen articles (39 to 51) to their 'teeth', under the resounding heading: 'Action with respect to Threats to the Peace, Breaches of the Peace, and Acts of Aggression'.

What is aggression? Jesting Pilate might stay for an answer to this one; but he would still be waiting. In 1952 the UN Assembly set up a committee to define aggression. In 1954 it set up a second committee. In 1957, already in a defeatist mood, it set up a third committee – to determine when the Assembly should come back to the attempt to define aggression. In 1967 it set up a fourth committee 'to consider all aspects of the question'. In December 1969 the Assembly (voting 83 to 1) told this latest committee to keep going. Hope springs eternal. In the eighteenth year of all this pertinacious labour the representative of Ecuador rallied the ranks by pointing out that they had still not concluded that it was impossible to define aggression; and that the mere fact that no definition had yet been agreed did not mean that one could not be found in the future.

But, very fortunately, the 'teeth' job that Chapter Seven gives the Security Council does not require it to plunge into the philosophical and semantic niceties that have baffled the committee men. Here, the Council's assigned task is to decide what should be done to 'maintain or restore international peace and security'; in fact, to stop wars, preferably before they start. And it does not have to consult texts, or lawyers, or entrails, before deciding that peace-and-security is being broken or threatened. This question was settled at San Francisco. As far as the UN is concerned, there is a Threat (or a Breach) when the Council decides that there is one.

When the government of Rhodesia illegally declared itself independent in November 1965 the Council had quite a brisk argument about whether this act had created a Threat (some even saw it as a Breach), and settled for a resolution in which a fine Latin hand had inserted an ingeniously inexact form of words. The 'continuance in time' of the new situation, it said, constituted a Threat. This formula permitted the Council to follow the course the British government preferred at that time, which was to call upon all states to 'do their utmost' to sever economic relations with Rhodesia, without giving this call a 'mandatory', or obligatory, character.

On 9 April 1966 the Council 'determined' that the attempt to deliver crude oil to Rhodesia through Beira, in defiance of its November call, 'constitutes a threat to the peace'. This tauter wording (although there was still no mention of Chapter Seven or any of its articles) provided a basis for the Council's authorisation of the British naval action off the Mozambique coast. But not until its resolution of 16 December 1966 did the Council square up to the main problem. It then flatly determined 'that the present situation in Southern Rhodesia constitutes a threat to international peace and security'. No such words had been in the British draft, presented by George Brown, on which this resolution was closely based. But the Foreign Secretary, in introducing his draft, had said that 'the dangers to peace . . . are acute'. And the British draft in fact made it necessary for the Council to determine that there was a Threat. For, according to this draft, the Council was to act explicitly under Articles 39 and 41, and to require all member states to carry out the Council's decision in accordance with their pledges given in Article 25. This mandatory mechanism could not come into play unless a Threat or Breach was determined, under Article 39, by the Council. In the resolution of 29 May 1968, which broadened the scope of the economic sanctions against Rhodesia, the determination of a Threat was duly repeated and the Council declared that it was 'acting under Chapter Seven of the United Nations Charter'.

It has to be admitted that the Council's record of debate and resolutions on Rhodesia includes some oddities. Oddest, perhaps, was the resolution of 6 May 1965, six months before the illegal declaration of independence, which asked Britain to prevent that act. In a Council still consisting of only eleven members, this was adopted by seven votes to none. The four abstentions were by

225

America, Britain, France and Russia – the substantive permanent members. It was only Taipeh China's alignment with the elected members that got the resolution through. This was an astonishing demonstration of the complete erosion of the strict meaning of Article 27 of the Charter, under which all non-procedural Council decisions require 'the concurring votes of the permanent members'.

However, the 'continuance in time' of the Rhodesian situation did bring the Council, as far back as 1966, to the overt use of Chapter Seven's enforcement mechanisms. Naturally, this was regarded as monstrously unfair by Ian Smith, the head of the illegal regime, who complained in a New Year's Eve broadcast at the end of 1966 that: 'There is more justice where Satan reigns than where the United Nations wallows in its sanctimonious hypocrisy.' His disenchantment seemed very sudden. A few weeks earlier he had assured his followers that: 'The world will give us recognition very soon now.'

It also annoyed his numerous Conservative supporters in both houses of the British parliament and elsewhere. Some of them, especially those who fancied themselves experts in international law, took off on the argument that Smith's regime had not attacked any of its neighbours, or even looked like attacking them; so how could the Council determine that there was a Threat and thus bring Chapter Seven into play? But there was a simple answer to this question: when the Council so determines, a Threat exists, for Chapter Seven purposes. There does not need to be any actual blood on the walls; or even any oil in the tanker. In theory, the Council could say that a Threat had been caused by, say, the Prince of Liechtenstein challenging one of the Co-Princes of Andorra* to a duel with water-pistols. True, the Council must 'act in accordance with the Principles and Purposes of the United Nations'. But there is nothing in them to suggest that the Council cannot tackle a problem like that of Rhodesia – where the Council's action was supported by the only responsible authority of recognised legality, which is the British government.

The critics could get more mileage out of the complaint, 'Why

* No disrespect is intended to the Prince or to the Co-Princes, who are, of course, the President of France and the Bishop of Urgel.

pick on Rhodesia?' They protested that there were states all over the place perpetrating Threats and even Breaches and getting away with it. In Africa itself, most of the independent African governments had vowed to bring down the Smith regime by force, and a few of them were actually doing something about it in a modest sort of way, by helping the Rhodesian guerrillas. Weren't these Breaches, or at least Threats? asked the critics. And what about the rest of the world? Why wasn't the Council imposing sanctions on Israel and/or its Arab foes, on India and/or Pakistan, on Cyprus, Greece and/or Turkey, on America for fighting in Vietnam, on various communist states for various offences? (Sanctions against Portugal because of its wars in Africa were not suggested by these particular critics; for the Portuguese were fighting in the same cause as the Smith regime.)

The explanation – of which some of the critics, despite their seeming naïvety, were well aware – was, basically, that no action under Chapter Seven could be taken if one of the Five opposed it. In specific cases there were also more specific reasons why the Council had taken no enforcement action. India and Pakistan halted their 1965 war, in response to the Council's warning calls, quickly enough to save it from having to frame any enforcement measures (which had begun to take shape in Thant's mind and perhaps in others). Greece and Turkey similarly drew back from their brink, twice in 1964 and again in 1967; and the Council's calls to them to do so were buttressed, after April 1964, by the reassuring presence of the UN force in Cyprus. But in most cases the explanation was the simple one set out on pages 58 and 59. The way the great powers originally designed the United Nations barred enforcement action against any of the five PPs, or against any state that one of them would protect by using its veto.

Before the white-minority government in Rhodesia took its fateful plunge into illegal independence it had enjoyed protection of this kind – provided by Britain. In the early 1960s the Conservative government in London held tightly to the idea that, while Britain itself could not intervene in self-governing Rhodesia's internal affairs, it was still Britain's duty to try to shield Rhodesia from the impact of even purely verbal UN 'intervention'. The only time a British veto was employed in the Council between 1956 and 1970

227

was in September 1963,* when it blocked a resolution under which Britain would have been 'invited' not to let certain powers – and certain military assets – revert to Southern Rhodesia after the breaking up of the federation of the Rhodesias and Nyasaland.

Throughout the later stages of the Rhodesian imbroglio, there were repeatedly clear indications that Britain would use its veto if a Council majority tried to carry a resolution that went altogether too far for Britain's liking. This was an important factor in the production of a series of Council resolutions which, while usually representing a compromise between British and African positions, tended to come out closer to the British than to the African.

In the December 1966 debate George Brown made it clear that Britain would resist any proposal to amend its draft so as to commit the UN to take action against South Africa or Portugal if they violated the Charter (as both did) by refusing to comply with the Council's mandatory decisions. When he introduced his draft he said that the situation 'must not be allowed to develop into a confrontation – economic or military – involving the whole of southern Africa'. He had made this point more bluntly, but privately, a day earlier, when he met the twenty-two representatives of other Commonwealth member states in one of the UN's basement conference rooms. When the May 1968 resolution broadening the sanctions on Rhodesia was adopted, the compromise on this question took the shape of a paragraph saying that the Council

> censures in particular those states which have persisted in trading with the illegal regime in defiance of the resolutions of the Security Council, and which have given active assistance to the regime.

South Africa and Portugal were not even named; still less was it indicated that any action would be taken against them beyond this anonymous censure.

Broadly, the position since 1965 is that PP protection is now extended to the Rhodesian regime only to a very limited degree; but it is still available to South Africa and Portugal in the same context. But this has not been only a simple matter of Britain being prepared,

* This sequence of dates has led some to suppose that Britain suffers from a seven-year itch.

in the last resort, to use its veto. Before any question of vetoing arose, there was in each case the question of assembling the necessary majority of nine Council votes. Next, there was the question whether Britain would be alone in using a veto.

The Council's proceedings in March 1970 were not a model to be recommended in any other respect; but in regard to the questions I have just mentioned they were vividly illuminating (pages 258 to 261). The five elected African and Asian members could count on the two communist votes. They also could, and did, muster nine votes for a draft resolution of sorts by drawing in Taipeh China and Spain. But to win over these two they had to drop from their text not only their proposals for the extension of sanctions to Portugal and South Africa but even their hostile references to those states.

So what Britain and America vetoed in March 1970 (page 260) was not a proposal for action against South Africa and Portugal. There were not nine votes to be mustered in support of such a proposal. But if, on some future occasion, nine votes are thus mustered, it seems quite possible that contrary votes – which would be vetoes – would be cast by three of the PPs: America, Britain and France. Certainly there is no visible prospect of any one of these three actually accepting a move that would seriously disrupt their economic and other links with Portugal and South Africa.

Despite the suggested possibility of these three Council members maintaining a common front, their positions need to be individually distinguished. And, while it is sufficiently well known that the problems involved are most acute for Britain, the reasons for this do not seem to be very clearly understood.

It is not just an export problem. True, Britain is a trading nation which must 'export or die'. True, it sells more than any other country does to South Africa. But it is not true to say – as a South African minister, Ben Schoeman, said at the time of the Council's debate in December 1966 – that South Africa is Britain's 'best customer' and that Britain would therefore be 'fatally' hit if it pursued any idea of UN sanctions. In reality the countries that buy the largest shares of British exports are America, West Germany, Ireland, Australia and Canada. South Africa ranks with Sweden as a country that buys somewhat less than 3 per cent of all British exports. (Nor is this because there has been a catastrophic fall in South African purchases from Britain. These purchases have been rising.)

The boot is on the other foot. It is South Africa, with Britain buying a third of its exports, that has real reason to fear a break with its best customer. And of course it has not been suggested that Britain alone should suspend trade with South Africa, leaving others to take over the trade it abandons. What has been proposed in the Council debates on Rhodesia is that all countries should restrict trade with South Africa and Portugal if they continue to sustain the illegal Rhodesian regime.

Britain also needs to take into account the risk that its trade with, and investment in, other countries might suffer if it became generally identified as the main prop and stay of the white-minority regimes in southern Africa. Moreover, in the longer run (and even businessmen who are primarily worried about next year's dividends must occasionally take the longer view) the explosive potential in white-ruled southern Africa must cast doubt on the wisdom of actually wanting to develop extensive trade and investment relations with it.

The straight commercial argument does not hold much water. A more inhibiting effect on British policy is exerted by the powerful political influence that the white southern Africans have in London. And this is not just a matter of race prejudice; or of Conservative politicians' personal financial interests in South Africa or Rhodesia – though an extraordinary number of them, in both Houses of Parliament, have such interests. And although the City, too, has close links with Johannesburg, the recurring tendency at moments of over-excitement for people in some of London's financial circles to talk as if the City's whole fate was bound up with Jo'burg's can also give a misleading impression. There is a more widely pervasive influence, much of it operating through friendships and family relationships – particularly in business circles, and to a fair extent in official ones too. (It must be remembered that whereas the Afrikaners have long been as cut off from their country of origin as the French in Canada, many of the English-speaking southern African whites still have personal links with Britain.) A Tory MP who has no financial stake in southern Africa may be moved to indignation about UN 'meddling' there mainly because this is the kind of talk he hears among his friends and relatives; he may not even be a racist himself.

The French position is a subtler one, and almost wholly unaffected by personal relationships. The aspect of it that has captured the widest attention is France's refusal to comply with the Security Council's embargo on sales of arms to South Africa. When the Council, on 7 August 1963, called upon all states to stop these sales, France and Britain were the only two members to abstain from supporting the resolution. Rather curiously, a further resolution which Norway presented on 4 December 1963, and which appealed to all states to comply with the one of August 7, was adopted unanimously; this time France and Britain were content to express reservations. In 1964 the change of government in Britain was followed by a pledge that the arms embargo would be respected.* But France, in spite of having voted for the December 4 resolution, clung to the fact that the Council's call had not been a mandatory one; and it rapidly became South Africa's main supplier of arms.

Until 1968, a 'strict constructionist' approach also marked French reactions to the Security Council's moves on Rhodesia. For some time after November 1965 Roger Seydoux insisted, in each Council debate, that the whole thing was Britain's private affair. He abstained in the April 1966 vote on the Beira action. In December 1966 he abstained again, giving the same reason – while promising that France would do its utmost to 'assist the United Kingdom' (not the United Nations), and would comply with the British request for sanctions whether the Council authorised them or not.

One reason given for the French insistence that Rhodesia was a United Kingdom and not a UN responsibility was the argument that, if this point was lost to sight, the Council might appear to be giving the illegal regime a kind of international recognition. In the May 1968 debate in the Council this argument was once again repeated by Armand Bérard, who had succeeded Seydoux as France's

---

* On 20 August 1970 the Council, by a 12–0 vote (America, Britain and France abstaining), called for a tighter arms embargo. This move followed Sir Alec Douglas-Home's appointment as Foreign Secretary in the new Tory government and his display of eagerness to resume arms sales to South Africa.

permanent representative. But this time France felt able to make the vote unanimous. Bérard's only explanation of the change of position was that France now felt it must take account of the intensity of feeling, especially in Africa, that the prolonging of the Rhodesian crisis had created. It would seem that this explanation of the switch was a basically honest one. At the time of this Council debate France was being shaken to its foundations by the outburst of student protest and industrial unrest that made the month of May 1968 so memorable in Paris. Previously, it would appear, the policy of General de Gaulle's government, on this as on so many other UN matters, had been largely shaped by the French president's abhorrence of doing anything that might enlarge the authority of an organisation which he regarded as a tool of the United States – and of Russo-American super-power 'collusion'. This obsession had led him to ignore the mounting resentment of France's policy, particularly its South African arms sales, among independent African states, including the ex-French ones. But the shock of France's May 1968 was instantly transmitted to the Council in the form of a frank admission that a less overweeningly self-confident French government must now recognise the force of African impatience.

Recognition of that impatience has certainly influenced American policy on southern African issues in the UN. But, whereas even de Gaulle's government eventually had to yield some ground to it, and the successor government of France under Georges Pompidou may have to yield still more, the trend of American policy over the past few years has seemed to be, if anything, in the other direction.

'White backlash' has had a less obvious effect on America's foreign policies than on its domestic ones, but its effect cannot be ignored in the international sphere. In the matter of Rhodesia, there has also been a certain American recoil from the discovery that the British had the situation less well in hand than they had seemed to be claiming. In the early stages of the affair the United States was reasonably content to toe whatever line Britain chose to draw. But by the time of the Council's December 1966 session, Washington was no longer quite sure whether London knew what it was doing.

American weight was thrown behind the proposals that George Brown then put forward in the Council. Indeed, the Americans were

232

at that point a step or two ahead of the British, for example in their greater readiness to see oil mentioned in the Council resolution on selective sanctions. When that resolution was adopted, President Johnson lost no time in giving the sanctions binding force in American law. And it should not be thought that he faced no domestic opposition in this matter.

The 'hard core' of that opposition was predictable and not too formidable. Racist elements, mainly in Southern states, naturally rallied to Ian Smith and John Balthazar Vorster as fellow practitioners of white supremacy – and enviably successful ones. (It had been the enthusiastic support of these same groups for Moise Tshombe's Katanga regime that opened a good many other American eyes to that regime's true nature.) But there was a wider, more penumbral but more 'respectable', area of opposition or potential opposition. Many Americans, particularly after the Congo experience, were responsive to the complaint that their country was already too heavily committed in other regions of the world without getting involved in southern Africa too.

Venerable sages like Walter Lippmann shook their heads anxiously over the new commitment. Dean Acheson, who has already figured in these pages as the Damocles man, took time off from writing memoirs to step into the spotlight as a somewhat unexpected champion of the Smith regime, and got into public debate with Arthur Goldberg on the matter. In 1970 Acheson was still at it, denouncing the Nixon Administration for participating in 'an international conspiracy' and 'bare-faced aggression' against the government in Salisbury. Such words from such a normally respected source were, of course, music to the ears of the hard-core 'Smith lobby' men and of certain firms that were feeling the impact of the sanctions.

During the first months of 1970 there was a period when the forces on whose support the Smith regime counted seemed to be gaining ground, particularly when it looked as if the American consulate in Salisbury would be kept open in spite of demands, from Britain as well as from the Africans, that it should be closed when Rhodesia was proclaimed a republic (page 256). But the use of a veto in the Council in March – which was forced upon America, as upon

233

Britain, by a rather sordid little Russo-Spanish–African manoeuvre – was not to be taken as a sign that Washington had surrendered to the Smith lobby in particular or to the white southern African interests in general. For it was accompanied, or soon followed, by the decision to close the consulate; the successful prosecution of an American firm for attempting to evade sanctions; and official steps to discourage American investment in the contested territory of South West Africa (Namibia).

*　　　*　　　*

On 11 November 1965, the day that Ian Smith's government proclaimed Rhodesia independent, the Security Council was inundated with urgent requests for a meeting. One came from the General Assembly, which, interrupting its general debate, adopted a resolution that day recommending that the Council should urgently consider the new situation. One came from the 35 African UN members; another from a group of 22 Asian and African states; and one from Britain. If this was in any sense a race for priority, Britain emerged the winner in that its Foreign Secretary, Michael Stewart, opened the Council debate that began on November 12.

He addressed a decidedly full house, and not only in the public gallery. No less than seventeen states that were not Council members were given permission to join in the debate: Algeria, India, Pakistan, Ghana, Zambia, Sierra Leone, Senegal, Mali, Tanzania, Nigeria, Guinea, Ethiopia, Mauritania, Gambia, Jamaica, Somalia and Sudan. There might have been nineteen. The Council invited South Africa and Portugal to swell the throng too, but both declined. Even without them, the chamber was well filled, and it was a happy chance that the enlargement of the Council itself from eleven to fifteen members, although already approved, did not take effect until the following January.

Michael Stewart said that Britain was making this immediate approach to the Council in order to ask that all UN members should support the steps that Britain itself was taking. Speed was essential, he declared; this 'overwhelming support' should be made clear at once to Rhodesia and the world. Member states should refuse to recognise the illegal regime and should back Britain's decisions to deny it Commonwealth trade preferences, export credits and capital, and to halt imports of Rhodesian tobacco and sugar. He added that while Rhodesia was still a British responsibility, the creation of the illegal regime was 'a matter of world concern'.

The representative of Jordan, Muhammad El-Farra, proposed a brief resolution for immediate adoption, condemning the Smith regime's action and calling on all states not to recognise or aid it. The Council adopted it that same day by a vote of ten to none, France abstaining. Stewart called this 'gratifying'. Next day, Saturday the 13th, he proposed a further resolution asking all states to help Britain make its measures effective. But the African representatives, Council members and non-members alike, heaped reproaches on Britain for not acting earlier and not acting adequately now. In their name, Arsene Usher of the Ivory Coast presented a draft calling on Britain to 'crush the rebellion'; on all states to sever economic and all other relations with Rhodesia under Article 41; and for the Council to invoke military enforcement measures under Articles 42 and 43.

The Council sat throughout that Saturday, and members spent the Sunday in urgent consultations. Stewart, who had planned to spend only a couple of days in New York, stayed on until mid-week. It quickly became clear that the Africans were divided. A majority at their caucus meetings swung to the idea of compromise, and a more moderate African draft resolution was privately circulated on the 16th; but it still went too far for the British, or for a majority of Council members. The two Latin American members, Bolivia (president for that month) and Uruguay, worked up a new compromise draft. Hector Paysse Reyes of Uruguay presented this to the Council on the evening of Friday the 19th. Although the Uruguayan had earlier said that Chapter Seven must be applied, Arthur Goldberg had induced the Latins to word their text with a certain obliqueness. In it, the Council determined only that the situation was 'extremely grave ... and that its continuance in time constitutes a threat to international peace and security'.

Thus the Threat was less of a present than a future one, Chapter Seven was not invoked, and the Council was able to adopt the Latin resolution on Saturday, November 20 (10–0, France again

235

abstaining), the British and African drafts being set aside. While the resolution called on Britain to 'quell this rebellion', its call to all states for economic action was less blunt. They were asked

to do their utmost in order to break all economic relations with Southern Rhodesia,* including an embargo on oil and petroleum products.

Formally, the Council kept the question 'under review'. In fact, it was not to revert to it for more than four months. Meanwhile the council of ministers of the Organisation of African Unity (OAU), in early December 1965, had asked its member states to sever diplomatic relations with Britain if the rebellion was not ended by December 15. Only nine African states did so. But at the UN they continued to demonstrate their dissatisfaction with the Council resolution and with Britain's actions.

It was bad luck on Harold Wilson that, after becoming prime minister in 1964, he had not been able to make an appearance in New York and address that year's Assembly, because the 1964 session was virtually extinguished by the deadlock over voting rights under Article 19. So he came to the 1965 Assembly instead; and when he addressed it on December 16 twenty of the African delegations staged a demonstrative walkout (they included all the Commonwealth African states except Malawi). On November 19 Princess Margaret had visited the UN building while the Council was still debating Rhodesia. The Commonwealth Africans stayed away from the reception Lord Caradon held for her in the 'Indonesian lounge' next to the Assembly hall – so named because it is adorned by two wooden carvings that Indonesia presented to the UN. (These figures are meant to represent the spirits of peace and prosperity. If these benevolent spirits were not much in evidence at the time, this may have been because President Sukarno had withdrawn Indonesia from the UN at the beginning of 1965 in a huff and a cloud of protests at Malaysia's sitting in the Security Council.)

All this posturing and gesturing enabled the Africans to work off some of their indignation, but at a cost. They lost much British goodwill and made it difficult for people to know when to take them

---

* In Council resolutions the name Southern Rhodesia has been retained. The Assembly now prefers Zimbabwe. Continuance in time, yes, in name, no.

236

seriously; even those few states that had brusquely severed relations with Britain maintained offices in London under the wing of 'protecting powers' and carried on much as before. And, while denouncing Britain's voluntary sanctions plan as inadequate and insisting that it should use armed force, the Africans took part in the work of the Commonwealth committee on sanctions that started meeting in London in January 1966. Apparently they also realised that a bad impression had resulted from the way so many African states had piled into the Council's November debate. It was all too clear that many of them had simply joined in from fear of seeming laggard if others took part and they did not. It was noticeable that when the Council took up Rhodesia again in April 1966 only Algeria, Kenya and Sierra Leone sought and obtained permission to participate. For the rest, they were content to be represented by the African members of the Council itself. The Council's enlargement from eleven to fifteen members having come into effect in January 1966, there were now three African members – Mali, Nigeria and Uganda – as against only one in 1965 (Ivory Coast). Nigeria and Uganda being Commonwealth countries, one from West and one from East Africa, the Council's African membership was now both larger and better qualified to deal with the Rhodesia question.

Unfortunately, however, in April 1966 the presidency was Mali's, and its representative, Moussa Leo Keita, proceeded to make a spectacle of himself – by vanishing from view. On April 7 Britain asked for an emergency Council meeting that same day. It explained that one oil tanker had arrived at Beira, and a second was approaching the same Mozambique port, the cargo of both being clearly intended for the new-built pipeline from Beira to Rhodesia's refinery at Umtali, in open contravention of the Council's November resolution. Britain wished to propose action to meet this situation, and no time was to be lost. But Moussa Keita got lost. ('That man,' said one observer, 'is a mousefink.')

Most of the Council members hastily met together, agreed that a Council session should be held at once, and so informed Keita; or rather they sent him word, but got no reply. Around seven in the evening, being still unable to contact their elusive president, they got

237

Thant to send him a fairly crisp reminder that they were waiting for him and were still ready and willing to meet that night. Even then, no word came from whatever mousehole Keita had hidden himself in. Next morning Caradon sent Keita a stiff rebuke for having failed, without any explanation, to call a meeting on the 7th. Pointing out that the rules of procedure clearly obliged the president to call a meeting 'at the request of any member of the Council', Caradon said that his failure created a 'most serious precedent' for the Council's functioning in emergency situations. He insisted that a meeting be called without more delay. But only later that day did Keita tell Thant that he was convening the Council, and then he set the meeting for the next day, Saturday, April 9.

Keita's attitude, which he later explained quite fully in a UN committee, was that Britain was merely pretending to show concern and to ask the Council for action. In reality, he said, Britain wanted to protect the Smith regime from UN intervention. It was making a great fuss about one or two tankers while oil was pouring into Rhodesia from South Africa, and it was refusing to use force in Rhodesia. Mali's general political position at this period was closer to Russia's than to that of most of the African states, and in the Council the Soviet representative, Platon Morozov, took the same line as Keita.

But meanwhile time was indeed pressing. The tankers' appearance off Beira had represented the climax of an intricate, costly, but ultimately unsuccessful plot that the Smith government and its backers in South Africa and elsewhere had long been hatching. Among the well-paid participants were the Greek Vardinoyannis brothers (worth every penny for their sheer entertainment value), who undertook to bring the tankers *Joanna V* and *Manuela* to Beira by devious routes and means. By the time the Council met, the UN representative of Greece, Aristotle Phrydas, who was given special permission to make a statement to it, felt able to assure the members that the *Joanna V* was no longer a Greek ship and that the *Manuela*'s owners (it took some time to work out who they were) had promised that she would not try to get to Beira – though she tried to do just that the very next day. But both before and after he spoke the Vardinoyannis brothers were capturing a fascinated world's attention

238

while they ran a whole rainbow of national flags up and down on their ships (even Panama disowned the *Joanna V* the moment its flag was hoisted on that often renamed, often re-registered, ship whose ownership and captaincy seemed to change with every tide), and eventually revealed that they were taking their orders from a South African, a deft Cape Town operator named Rudolph Rafaely who had a habit of making 'holiday trips' to Beira at interesting moments.

The British navy, well informed but not having authority to open fire on any foreign ships, whatever its doubts about their right to the flags they flew, had intercepted the *Joanna V* as she approached Beira on April 4, but was unable to prevent her entering the port with 18,000 tons of crude oil (this oil had already cost the Smith government, which never got it, at least £1 million). George Vardinoyannis, who at this particular moment seemed to be her skipper, was hailed like a saviour by a crowd of white Rhodesians in Beira. A few days later he told the Greek consul that he wasn't the ship's captain after all, and hastily caught a plane to South Africa. But before ducking out he had moved the *Joanna V* to the wharf from which the Rhodesia pipeline ran (even this little move set off another burst of wild joy among Smith's supporters in Beira as well as in Rhodesia), and had tried several variations on his main theme. Whatever the UN might say or do, he claimed, he would have to discharge some of the oil, in order to lighten the ship so that repairs could be done. He would then have to discharge yet more, since otherwise the ship would not be able to get over the bar outside the port until the next exceptionally high tide, which would not be until September. And so on and on. Meanwhile the *Manuela* had been skittering around the ocean (ostensibly, both tankers had been bound from the Persian Gulf to Rotterdam, but neither of them ever headed for the Suez Canal) waiting to see what would happen at the UN.

At the UN things happened fast, once Moussa Keita had been flushed out. By the end of a long April 9 Caradon had got the Security Council resolution he wanted. It determined that there was 'a threat to the peace'. It called on Britain (be it noted that this was the wording proposed by Britain) to stop ships 'reasonably believed' to be bringing oil for Rhodesia to Beira 'by the use of force if necessary'. It specifically empowered Britain to 'arrest and detain'

239

the *Joanna V* when she left Beira if she had discharged her cargo there.

This was the resolution that carried the United Nations across the threshold into enforcement action under Chapter Seven – without making any explicit reference to that chapter of the Charter or to any of its articles, but conforming to the proprieties by determining that a Threat existed. The Council was told that it was 'making international law this day' by no less an authority than Arthur Goldberg, a former justice of the United States Supreme Court. It was a historic moment. History being the mixed-up thing it is, there was perhaps some aptness in the way this moment had been preceded by the Vardinoyannis antics and Moussa Keita's vanishing act. Shakespeare, with his gift of punctuating heavy drama with clowning interludes, might well have approved.

And Keita's caper may even have contributed to the dramatic dénouement. By the time he came out of hiding, the Nigerian and Ugandan Council members had been able to agree with other African representatives on amendments to be proposed to the British resolution; to get authority to vote for the resolution when their amendments had been rejected (as they knew they would be); and to ensure that Caradon was aware of this. Which simplified things considerably. There was no real argument in the Council about the need for swift action, and no attempt to filibuster. Argentina dickered briefly with a compromise between the British and African texts, but did not press its arguments when it saw how things were going.

The African amendments requested South Africa to stop sending oil to Rhodesia, and Britain to use force both to prevent any supplies reaching Rhodesia and to bring down the Smith regime. Seven members voted for the first point (the three Africans, Jordan, Argentina, Russia and Bulgaria), six for the second (the same minus Argentina). Nobody voted against the amendments, but both lapsed by failing to get the nine votes now needed in the enlarged Council. The British resolution was then adopted by a vote of ten to none. Russia, Bulgaria and Mali abstained on the ground that the resolution was ineffective, Uruguay because its representative had not been able to get instructions from his government, and France as usual. But Caradon had got the authorisation he had sought for immediate action; and he had got it with the backing both of America and of Nigeria and Uganda, the Commonwealth African members of the Council. After the rejection of the amendments these two Africans voted for the British text without more ado. So did Jordan, Argentina, China, Japan, Netherlands and New Zealand.

A few hours later the *Manuela*, making her last-minute dash for Beira in hope of reaching it before the British naval patrol got new orders, was halted by the frigate *Berwick*. As the newly Panamanian tanker's Greek captain insisted that his orders were still to head for Beira (contrary to the assurance that Aristotle Phrydas had given the Council a day earlier), the *Berwick* put an armed boarding party on the *Manuela* and escorted her out to sea. Another frigate, the *Puma*, waited outside Beira to seize the *Joanna V* if she unloaded her oil and came out. But the *Joanna V* never discharged her cargo at Beira, although she stayed there a good deal longer, undergoing a small mutiny; the Greek crew resented the way they had suddenly become Panamanian, and had to be paid off and flown home. The *Manuela* then tried to unload her 15,000 tons of oil at Durban, where George Vardinoyannis reappeared and again played a brief role as skipper. But by now he was having trouble both with the Greek authorities (the *Manuela* being Greek that week) and with the South Africans, who flatly refused to take his oil. As far as Hendrik Verwoerd's government was concerned, the game was over. It did not wish to invite further UN action by openly dealing with Rafaely and Vardinoyannis. The object of the exercise had been to get crude oil into Rhodesia, to be refined at Umtali, rather than moving refined products in by overland transport at much greater cost. This having failed, Verwoerd did not want to play any more.

Predictably, the Portuguese government was outraged by the Council's action. Its foreign minister, Alberto Franco Nogueira, wrote to Thant arguing that the resolution was invalid. It conflicted, he said, with the principle of the freedom of the seas, and with the principle of a land-locked country's (i.e. Rhodesia's) free access to the sea; it meant that the Council was abdicating its responsibilities by empowering one state (i.e. Britain) to ensure compliance with a resolution; it had been improperly adopted without the concurrence of France and Russia. At a press conference, Franco Nogueira accused Britain of fostering hostility to Portugal in the Council. The resolution, he said, was useless, discriminatory and intended to pin guilt on Portugal. The Council had acted with 'injustice, ineffectiveness, and inelegance'. Britain had pretended to be acting under strong African pressure, but 'all our information showed us' that there was really no such pressure.

If this last point had been true, things would certainly have gone easier for Britain in the Council than they did in the next few weeks. On May 10 the African group at the UN asked for another Council meeting on Rhodesia. The Africans had already prepared a long draft resolution, which they handed over that day to the Dutch acting president, Jonkheer Leopold Quarles van Ufford. They said they had drafted their text so that its calls for a stoppage of all supplies to Rhodesia, which could be seen as coming under Chapter Seven's non-military Article 41, were separable from its calls for the use of British armed force to 'abolish the racist minority regime'. They explained that this had been done to ease matters for those Council members who shied away from the idea of force. But the separation was unfortunately incomplete, for the draft also called for Britain to use force to ensure the stoppage of supplies.

In the event, the Council did not begin debate until May 17. On the 16th the Smith government asked to be allowed to participate. Since November 1965 it had maintained an office in Washington run by Henry Hooper, who had formerly been attached to the British embassy there. Hooper had been registered as a Rhodesian government agent in Washington, but had been officially told in March that since the United States recognised no independent state of Rhodesia he could not remain in America 'on the basis of a purported official capacity'. At one stage or another he and other emissaries of the Smith regime appeared at the UN to try a little lobbying. But at no time did the Council agree to give a hearing to any spokesman for the regime. This was a point about which Smith's supporters in Britain repeatedly complained; but neither the Charter nor UN practice required the Council to grant a hearing to representatives of an unrecognised and illegal regime.

In seeking a new Council meeting so soon, the Africans had

largely been moved by disquiet at the sight of 'talks about talks' being initiated between London and Salisbury. This led the OAU to depute Algeria, Senegal and Zambia to seek participation in the debate as additional spokesmen for the African states. India, Pakistan and Sierra Leone also piled in. The first speeches were in fact made by Simon Kapwepwe (Zambia's foreign minister), Doudou Thiam (Senegal's), and representatives of India, Pakistan, Algeria, Nigeria and Sierra Leone. It was thus the second day, May 18, before any non-African Council member got a word in. Caradon then reassured the Africans about the talks with the Smith government, urged them not to force the Council into a deadlock that would damage the UN's authority and the cause of the Rhodesian people, and recalled how Britain, at great cost to itself, had not only cut off all its own trade with Rhodesia but also helped Zambia to import oil and other essential supplies by new routes after the break with Rhodesia had disrupted Zambia's trade channels. The British position was at once supported by America, Japan, New Zealand and Uruguay.

Goldberg privately urged the Africans not to press their resolution but to have the Council send a deputation to London to try to clear up their doubts. But they insisted on a vote. At one stage they seemed hopeful that something like their draft could secure the necessary nine votes. Argentina, Uruguay and Japan appeared to be wavering. There were, however, many qualms among the Africans themselves at this point. Some of them privately acknowledged that their draft could not muster more than six votes (this proved correct). These Africans complained that an unrealistic draft had been forced upon them by the 'extremists' in the group. But it was not really clear who were the extremists, for even the apparently chastened Keita of Mali was now privately urging his African colleagues to settle for the more restrained parts of the resolution.

Up to May 21 the Africans planned to have their text voted on clause by clause, in hope of getting nine votes for a good part of it. Then even this hope faded. Although the Latin Americans and Chinese were willing to support a few of the clauses, little would have been left of the original text if the clause-by-clause procedure had been followed. So on May 23 the sponsors put it to the vote as a whole, and thus at least got their defeat over quickly. The draft

243

received only the three African votes, the two communist ones and Jordan's. New Zealand voted against it and there were eight abstainers (including America, Britain and France). The whole affair left a bitter and distrustful mood unhappily prevalent at the UN.

As the summer months of 1966 wore on, attention became focused on the approach of the London meeting of Commonwealth heads of government that had been set for September 6 to 15. And when September came, the Commonwealth conference duly fulfilled all the expectations that it was going to witness a knock-down, drag-out fight over Rhodesia. At the two previous London meetings in the series, in 1964 and 1965, the African member states' pressure on the matter had already been visibly building up. There had also been a special meeting held in Nigeria in January 1966 which was devoted entirely to the Rhodesian crisis. (Three days after it ended, its host, the federal prime minister, Sir Abubakar Tafawa Balewa, was murdered during a *coup d'état* that brought a military regime to power in Lagos.) The Lagos meeting had led to the creation of a Commonwealth committee, meeting in London and serviced by the new Commonwealth Secretariat that had been set up in 1965, to review the effect of the voluntary sanctions that Britain and other states were imposing on Rhodesia.

At the September 1966 meeting all but one of the twenty-three Commonwealth countries were represented, fourteen of them by their presidents or prime ministers. They spent nearly all their time on Rhodesia. The eight African members and the majority of the fourteen others kept up unrelenting pressure on the British prime minister to take swift and decisive action to end the rebellion, preferably by armed force. In the words of a sympathetic non-Commonwealth journalist covering the conference, it seemed to be 'Bash Britain Week'. Yet the bashing was, with only one or two exceptions, not just a matter of sound and fury but one of persistent argument that the Commonwealth relationship between white and other members simply could not be maintained if Britain was going to allow the Rhodesian white minority, in effect, to carry off five million Africans into perpetual captivity. At one stage complete deadlock, with all its obvious consequences, seemed very near. And

244

the atmosphere was in no way relieved by the coincidence that, on the eve of the London debates, the South African prime minister, Hendrik Verwoerd, had been murdered in Cape Town and swiftly replaced by an equally 'tough' successor, John Balthazar Vorster. While South Africa itself had been eased out of the Commonwealth in 1961, its shadow now hung even more heavily over the whole Rhodesian problem.

Some desperate bridge-building by Lester Pearson of Canada and others at last brought the Commonwealth meeting to a dramatic but not disastrous end with a late-night communiqué which, to many people's surprise, had been agreed by all members. The joint communiqué frankly set out the conflict of views. But it also recorded that, if the rebellion continued, the Commonwealth heads of government were agreed that there would have to be 'stronger and mandatory economic sanctions under Chapter Seven of the United Nations Charter'. It stated that Britain favoured selective sanctions, while most other members wanted comprehensive ones to be 'applied under Articles 41 and 42'. The nub of the statement, however, was a declaration of British intentions which was incorporated in the communiqué. Harold Wilson's government said it would immediately inform the Smith regime that, if it was not prepared to submit to a return to legality on terms that had been set out, Britain would withdraw all its previous proposals for a settlement, and would not accept any settlement that gave Rhodesia independence before majority rule; and that, 'given the full support of Commonwealth representatives at the United Nations', Britain would sponsor in the Security Council 'before the end of this year, a resolution providing for effective and selective mandatory economic sanctions against Rhodesia'.

Many participants in the conference went straight from London to New York for the opening of the 1966 UN Assembly, in whose proceedings Rhodesia also loomed large. Wilson sent Herbert Bowden, his Commonwealth Secretary, to Salisbury to expound the new terms to Smith and other Rhodesians. Bowden's visit yielded no results, and in early November he was telling the House of Commons that, 'Unless the matter can be resolved in the next few weeks, the undertakings which we gave to the Commonwealth

245

will be carried out in full. . . . There is now a time limit.' The time limit was closer even than the end of the year. The British government recognised that a Council move for sanctions would have to be made early enough to get it through before the Assembly adjourned (and that year's Assembly, under the brisk presidency of Abdul Rahman Pazhwak of Afghanistan, already looked like completing its work by its target date of December 20 – which it duly did).

On December 1 Wilson flew to Gibraltar for last-minute talks with Ian Smith, which were held at sea on the British navy's *Tiger*. This somewhat melodramatic rendezvous, coupled with the difficulty of getting any clear idea of what exactly was being discussed on the *Tiger*, sent a wave of nervous anxiety across the Atlantic to New York, where there was feverish speculation at the UN. (As on some earlier occasions, part of this speculation turned on the question whether Lord Caradon would feel. bound to resign his post at the UN – in this case, if the *Tiger* talks produced an agreement that conceded too much to Ian Smith.) But by December 5 the suspense was over.

On that day Wilson told the House of Commons that the Smith regime had rejected his latest proposals, and that Britain would fulfil its commitment to UN sanctions. In New York, Caradon asked the Security Council president, Pedro Berro of Uruguay, for an urgent meeting. There were at once mighty rumblings among British Conservatives, and Lord Salisbury declared in the House of Lords that to submit the matter to the UN would amount to 'a great disaster'. Vorster announced, in a press interview published on the 5th, that South Africa would in no circumstances co-operate in UN sanctions against Rhodesia.

George Brown, who had succeeded Stewart as Foreign Secretary, arrived in New York on December 7 for the Council debate just as the Council members received another request from the Smith government for representation in 'any meeting in which Rhodesia may be involved'. In London that day the Commons plunged into a fierce two-day debate on Bowden's motion supporting the government's decision 'now to implement the undertakings given in the

246

Commonwealth Prime Ministers' communiqué'. Leading for the Conservative opposition, Reginald Maudling outdid Lord Salisbury by accusing Wilson of 'leading this country to one of the greatest disasters it has known'. Wilson drew wild cheers from his Labour benches when he bluntly accused the Tories of 'voting in support of the illegal regime in Salisbury'; their party leader, Edward Heath, threw the whole House into uproar by accusing Wilson of 'hypocritical cant'; and the motion was carried at the end of the second day in a division on straight party lines.

The Security Council debate that Brown opened on Thursday December 8 was less disorderly than that, but its atmosphere was one of high tension. This time only five visiting firemen sat in with the Council members: Algeria, Senegal, Zambia, India and Pakistan. But the Council chamber was jam-packed for the opening of the debate, and with a very distinguished audience. It seemed that representatives of at least a hundred states had torn themselves away from their Assembly duties to watch the George Brown show. Most of them had to stand, and they formed such a dense mass on the floor of the chamber that late-comers who tried to get in failed because the crowd was pressed back tightly against the doors. Every seat in the press gallery was full. This is a singularly rare phenomenon at UN debates, even at times of excitement, because important debates are relayed to a good number of the press rooms, and many correspondents can thus hear the speeches without leaving their telephones and typewriters. But this was a day when journalists had actually had to queue up to be sure of getting places in the gallery. Many had been disappointed, and great scandal had been caused by the discovery that the wife of one of the Council members had pre-empted a press gallery seat.

The often ebullient George Brown wore, as the *New York Times* accurately reported, 'a look of unwonted gravity'. He said that the voluntary sanctions had already had the effect of cutting Rhodesia's exports by 40 per cent. 'Quite frankly, we had expected a greater economic and political impact. But do not let this lead us to underrate what we have in fact achieved.' Britain had been trying to maintain economic pressure while seeking to persuade 'the rebel regime' to accept a settlement on terms that would be fair to 'the

247

population of Rhodesia as a whole'. But the regime's rejection of the *Tiger* terms had 'created a new situation'; clearly it meant to persist in its rebellion and in 'defiance of civilised opinion'. The Council should now, under Articles 39 and 41 of Chapter Seven of the Charter, take decisions that would be binding on member states by virtue of Article 25.

He introduced a resolution under which all members would prevent imports of, shipments of and trading in Rhodesian tobacco, chrome, copper, iron, asbestos, sugar, meat and leather – 'the most important Rhodesian exports which can be identified and controlled' (these items had accounted for about 60 per cent of Rhodesia's 1965 exports); and would ban arms sales to Rhodesia. Hewing closely to the line of Britain's September pledge to the Commonwealth, Brown said that if such a Council resolution were approved with full Commonwealth support, Britain would withdraw all previous proposals for a settlement and would contemplate no settlement involving independence before majority rule. He would not oppose a move to include oil among the sanctions items if it were made 'in acceptable terms'. By this, he made clear, he meant that sanctions must not 'escalate into economic confrontation with third countries' (i.e. South Africa and Portugal). 'We are proposing selective sanctions against Rhodesia only.'

American support for the British proposals had been assured in talks held in Washington a week earlier during a visit by Sir Saville Garner, the Commonwealth Office's senior official. The Americans were ready for a mandatory oil embargo, and indeed had helped to ease the British over that hurdle. But, as Brown had told the Commonwealth representatives at the UN the day before the debate opened, Britain would not accept a wording that implied the taking of any action to prevent South Africa or Portugal passing on oil to Rhodesia.

Nobody else spoke on that first day of debate. Next day, Friday the 9th, Zambia's cadaverous and fiery foreign minister, Simon Kapwepwe, bitterly reviled Britain for its 'perfidious plot' with Smith and Vorster, 'motivated by racism'; its 'patronising handouts' (i.e. its emergency aid to Zambia); and its 'unworkable and ineffective' proposals. The Wilson government's aim, he said, was to expand white

248

THE AFRICAN DIVIDE

supremacy 'from the Cape to the Congo and, if possible, to Cairo, as was the dream of Cecil Rhodes'. The western countries' abstention on a Rhodesia resolution in the Assembly on November 17, he said, had shown Africans that the West was

> only interested in exploiting us. In Africa we have a proverb: 'Lunshi ukukukonka nipacilonda', which means that a fly is your best friend only when you have a sore on which it feeds, and when the sore heals you see the fly no more.

Kapwepwe reeled off a long list of alleged violations of the voluntary sanctions by Britain itself (his charges were at once rebutted in detail by British spokesmen in New York), and demanded 'comprehensive

249

sanctions in which South Africa and Portuguese Mozambique would be forced to comply'. This might have been more impressive if he had explained how he wanted them forced to comply, and had not admitted, when questioned after his speech, that he had not even tried to draft an amendment. All he seemed to have achieved was to goad a remarkably restrained Brown into retorting that the Zambian's attacks on Wilson had been 'both unworthy and untrue' and that abuse was no substitute for argument. Brown then flew back to London, but not before having a last private talk with the representatives of Nigeria and Uganda, Chief Simeon Adebo and Apollo Kironde. These two were the crucial Council members in terms of the stated British condition about 'the full support of Commonwealth representatives at the United Nations'.

The Council gave itself a full two-day weekend without speeches (though there was plenty of consultation), and met only briefly on Monday December 12, when Arthur Goldberg gave full American support to the British proposals. The African caucus had by now formed a committee of seven (Algeria, Mali, Nigeria, Senegal, Sierra Leone, Uganda, Zambia) to draft amendments; but its meetings, like those of the full caucus, revealed serious divergences, especially over the question of oil, and the amendments appeared only on the 13th. The one on oil turned out to be acceptable to Britain, now represented by Caradon, who himself amended the British text on the 16th, adding cars and aircraft to arms as prohibited exports to Rhodesia.

On the evening of Friday December 16 (a year to the day since the Africans' Assembly walkout on Wilson) the Council at last produced its resolution. There was an avalanche of voting, during which only Roger Seydoux of France took the restful course of abstaining in all the fourteen votes. Eight of the African group's amendments were approved, but of these only the oil one meant very much, though another one inserted the ritual words determining a Threat. The most immediately significant of the five defeated African amendments would have added coal to the list of banned Rhodesian exports. It received only seven votes (the three African and the two communist ones, Jordan and Argentina), as did three other amendments; one got only six. The vote on the whole British resolution as amended was eleven to none, the abstainers being France, Mali, Russia and Bulgaria.

There had been some fairly vivid last-minute fears that even the necessary nine votes for the whole resolution might not be mustered. Frank Corner of New Zealand, whose government tended to share the British Conservatives' distaste for the whole operation, had not committed himself during the debate, and even the British were not quite sure that he would not, in the end, abstain. El-Farra of Jordan would have abstained if the Nigerian and the Ugandan had joined Keita of Mali in doing so. But Adebo and Kironde came through with their crucial votes for the resolution – just as had happened in April – despite the defeat of so many of the amendments they had proposed. (Four days later they were rewarded for this. Wilson duly announced the withdrawal of all previous British proposals for a settlement.) And Japan, the Netherlands, the two Latin Americans and China swelled the majority.

Although the April 1966 vote on the Beira tankers had carried the Security Council into Chapter Seven 'enforcement', it had not laid far-reaching obligations on all states. The resolution of December 16 did, and thereby broke wholly new ground. Over the years the General Assembly and lesser UN bodies had already adopted scores of resolutions deploring racist rule in southern Africa, calling upon member states to do something about it, urging boycotts and economic embargoes; but none of these had mandatory force, nor (as the French had been quick to point out) did the Council's own 1963 call for a halt to arms sales to South Africa. Now the Council was being wholly explicit about the mandatory nature of its new resolution.

Citing Article 39, it determined that there was a threat to peace. Citing Article 41, it used its Chapter Seven authority not just to urge member states to act but to '*decide* that all States Members of the United Nations *shall* ... [act]' while at the same time, citing Article 2, it urged all non-member states to follow suit. To underline the point, a further paragraph in the resolution said that the Council

> *Reminds* Member States that the failure or refusal by any of them to implement the present resolution shall constitute a violation of Article 25 of the Charter.

251

That is the article in which members 'agree to accept and carry out the *decisions* of the Security Council in accordance with the present Charter'.

To comply with this Charter obligation, new legislation was required in a good many capitals where the government did not have executive authority to order trade embargoes. An important factor was that this was not required in the United States, the country from which many others might be expected to take their lead. Under its United Nations Participation Act of 1945, its president was empowered to take the necessary steps by executive order. Exercising this power for the first time, Lyndon Johnson signed the order on 5 January 1967. The corresponding British order had been made on December 22, when the vote in the House of Commons was marked by the disarray of the Conservative opposition. Its leaders and most of their followers abstained, while 50 Tories voted with the government for the order and 31 voted against it. The immediate effect of the Council's decision was, in point of fact, relatively small for Britain, since it had already imposed extensive embargoes unilaterally. Indeed, one of the arguments used in Britain at this time by supporters of the new move in the Council was that it would spread the sanctions burden more evenly. Critics who had been complaining that Britain, by giving a lead in sanctions, was merely letting other countries take over its trade, had to find another line.

Ignoring a call from the 1967 Assembly to take further action on Rhodesia under Chapter Seven, the Council remained quiescent until March 1968, when the hanging of five Africans by the illegal regime (which denied them the right to appeal to the Privy Council in London) provoked a call for a Council meeting from 36 African governments. The Council began debate on March 19, with two non-member participants, Jamaica and Zambia (the African Council members for 1968 being Algeria, Ethiopia and Senegal). Tewfik Bouattoura of Algeria and Lij Endalkachew Makonnen of Ethiopia called for the imposing of comprehensive instead of selective sanctions. Resort to armed force was additionally urged by Keith Johnson of Jamaica, Reuben Kamanga of Zambia (who had succeeded Kapwepwe as foreign minister), Parthasarathi of India and

Ousmane Diop of Senegal. The idea of an extension of sanctions was supported by George Ignatieff of Canada, Otto Borch of Denmark, Geraldo de Carvalho Silos of Brazil and Agha Shahi of Pakistan.

For Britain, Caradon urged the Council to concentrate on effective and practicable steps rather than on sweeping demands that could not be met. He invited both Council members and others, such as Kamanga, to join in consultations. On March 27 the British government announced its readiness to support a move to make the sanctions comprehensive, and the Council broke off its formal meetings and embarked on some lively consultation. The background to these included a series of clashes between the Smith regime's forces and Rhodesian guerrillas, which made the atmosphere at the UN even livelier – especially when it emerged that South African armed forces had been sent to Rhodesia to fight alongside the regime's troops.

Caradon's hopes that the consultations would produce an agreed draft resolution were disappointed when, on April 16, the three African Council members, with India and Pakistan, presented their own draft. It called for the use of British force to end the Rhodesian rebellion, and for 'resolute' (but unspecified) UN action against South Africa and Portugal. A week later Caradon introduced a British draft that set out a plan for comprehensive sanctions in great detail, including the prohibition of all Rhodesian exports and imports apart from a few humanitarian exceptions such as medicines and educational materials. In presenting it, he particularly asked the Council not to resort to 'empty threats' that might raise among the Rhodesian population hopes that it could not satisfy, but to take effective and united action that would convince 'everyone, especially the illegal regime', that the Council 'means to go on'. His draft provided for the setting up by the Council of a committee to watch over the implementing of the new sanctions.

While the Council retired again for consultations that were to last for over a month, the British government ran into another storm of Conservative protest. Sir Alec Douglas-Home protested in the House of Commons that the proposed new sanctions were vindictive and futile, and that if there were any victims they would be the 'African labourers' who, he claimed, 'are the people we are trying to help'.

253

Edward Heath said the proposed move would exacerbate the situation. He urged the government, instead, to offer the Smith regime a settlement on lines that Douglas-Home had been expounding since he visited Rhodesia and talked to Smith a month earlier.

On May 29 the Council returned to its horseshoe table, was presented with an anonymous draft resolution that looked remarkably like the one Caradon had introduced on April 23, and adopted it unanimously within a few hours – even France, in the person of Armand Bérard, at last finding it possible to join in with only minor reservations. Only one amendment was proposed, by Yakov Malik of Russia. A paragraph in the resolution asked all states to help Zambia solve the special economic problems that would arise for it. Malik proposed, instead, that Zambia's losses should be compensated by America, Britain, West Germany, Portugal and South Africa, the states which he branded as responsible for the Rhodesian regime's existence. His amendment was defeated, and was described by Caradon (who was Council president for May, but had handed over the chair to Arthur Goldberg) as a 'misinformed, misleading and mischievous, not to say malicious, last minute intervention'.

Even Malik, having decided to go along with the Africans in voting for the resolution, admitted grudgingly that it was 'a step forward' and 'could to a certain extent promote the attainment of United Nations purposes'. Agha Shahi of Pakistan said it had been thought better to compromise on a text that Britain and all other Council members could accept, rather than seek to get a majority vote for a resolution that Britain would not implement. Senegal's representative likewise stressed the need to 'choose the possible'. The Algerian said nothing. Arthur Goldberg vigorously supported the resolution, but he also noted that it contained some non-mandatory paragraphs, including the one in which the Council emphasised the need for withdrawal of consular representation in Rhodesia.

In Salisbury Piet van der Byl, Ian Smith's 'information' chief, commented that the resolution showed that some UN members were 'criminal warmongers'. Douglas-Home, too, complained about a paragraph urging member states to give 'moral and material assistance to the people of Southern Rhodesia in their struggle to achieve their freedom and independence'. Caradon rejected the argument that these words amounted to endorsement of the use of violence by guerrillas against the Smith regime.

Once again, as after the December 1966 resolution, member governments all over the world were now obligated under Article 25 of the Charter to put the Council's mandatory embargoes into effect. This time it took longer in some cases: the comprehensive sanctions were more complicated, and where parliamentary action was necessary things were delayed in certain countries by the summer recess. Italy, for example, did not issue its decree until October 1968. In West Germany the Kiesinger coalition government decided this time to get more closely in line with the UN member states, but even so its decision did not take legal effect until November. Allowing for goods in transit and in bond, and for administrative time-lags, it seemed doubtful whether even the 1969 trade figures would fully reflect the impact of the 1968 resolution. But some of the cuts were quite visible. In the first two months of 1969 German imports from Rhodesia were reported at only $50,000, against $3½ million in the same months of 1968.

In June 1969 the Council was again called into session, on the eve of a referendum that the Smith regime was staging on its plan for a new constitution (voting in this referendum was, of course, limited to the almost entirely white electorate). A Council meeting was requested by Cyprus, Jugoslavia, Turkey and 57 African and Asian member states ranging from Senegal to the Philippines. Debate began on June 13 with the non-voting participation of Burundi, Guinea, India, Mauritania, Saudi Arabia (represented by Jamil Baroody), Somalia, Sudan and Tanzania. The Council's own African members for 1969 were Algeria, Senegal and Zambia. As in May 1968, the Algerian led off, and in a long series of African and Asian speeches the failure of sanctions was denounced and the use of force demanded. Baroody proposed that Rhodesia should be 'cordoned off' by African troops who would prevent any goods crossing its borders, the cost of this rather dreamlike operation being shared by America and Russia.

Caradon expounded his government's view that Britain could not stand the economic shock of a break with South Africa; and he reminded the Council that using British force against Rhodesia was not a matter of maintaining order in a colony where Britain had troops, but one of invading a territory which had been self-governing, controlling its own armed forces, for half a century, and where there had never been a British army or a British administration. Malik, for Russia, claimed that Britain had made only a 'miserly reduction' in its trade with Rhodesia. Caradon emphasised the sacrifices that Britain had in fact made, and told Malik that he had an obligation, like any other Council member, 'to keep a civil tongue in debate'. Baroody lightened the atmosphere somewhat by envisaging a descent on Salisbury by parachute troops who would put Ian Smith and his colleagues into straitjackets and take them to London.

Rejecting pleas from Caradon and other members that the Council should maintain unity and not give the illegal regime comfort by falling into deadlock, the Council's five African and Asian members – Algeria, Nepal, Pakistan, Senegal and Zambia – forced a vote on a draft resolution that would call for sanctions against South Africa and Portuguese Mozambique and would urge Britain to end the rebellion by force. On June 24 this was defeated; but narrowly, for it got eight votes, those of its five sponsors and those of Taipeh China, Hungary and Russia. It might have got the necessary nine if the sponsors had not, by specifically bringing in Portugal's territory, forced Spain to join six other Council members in abstaining. If nine votes had been mustered for it Britain might have had little option but to use a veto. As it was, the outcome was unhappy enough. 'We have not gone forward, we have gone backward,' said Caradon at the end.

In March 1970 the Council was brought back to its table by the Smith regime's proclamation that Rhodesia was now a republic. As the regime was recognised by none of the world's governments, and its new republican constitution was designed on the same white-supremacy lines as it had already marked out, there was no great substance in the change. Ian Smith might as well have proclaimed the restoration of the Holy Roman Empire. But one practical point was involved for the international community. Without recognising the regime in Salisbury, several countries had kept open their consulates there, which had originally been opened by agreement with Britain. In May 1968 the Council had 'emphasised the need' to close these

256

consulates; but, as Arthur Goldberg took care to note at the time, it had not made this a mandatory point. Now that it could no longer be claimed that the consuls were still in theory accredited to a legitimate authority (i.e. Britain), their continued activity in Salisbury would imply at least a degree of *de facto* recognition of the Smith regime. And, as Caradon told the Council on March 6, the main reason for its proclamation of a republic was that

> what that regime wants more than anything is to be recognised . . . without international recognition it cannot escape from the isolation in which it slowly sinks. . . . In the long haul it has no hope without recognition.

But there had been reports that the United States meant to keep its consulate open, and indications that the American lead on this question would be followed by most of the other countries concerned — Austria, Belgium, Denmark, France, West Germany, Greece, Italy, the Netherlands, Norway, Switzerland, Portugal and South Africa (the last two being, of course, the least likely to close their offices). It was common knowledge that the Secretary of State, William Rogers, who had just made an extensive African tour, wanted to close the American consulate, but that President Nixon's 'national security' adviser, Henry Kissinger, favoured keeping it open. On February 27 — three days before Smith's new constitution came into effect — the White House spokesman first announced that the consulate would stay open, and then, four hours later, issued a 'clarification': no decision had yet been taken, he said.

Within a few hours of the proclamation in Salisbury, Caradon called urgently for a Council meeting. He presented a draft resolution making it mandatory for UN members not to recognise the illegal regime and urging non-member states to toe the same line. Simultaneously Britain made strong representations to the governments concerned. A notably forceful reminder was given by the Foreign Secretary, Michael Stewart, to the American ambassador in London. The British pointed out that no country that agreed that Rhodesia was still British territory in law could properly maintain a consulate there against Britain's wishes.

Norway and Denmark announced the shutting down of their

Salisbury offices on March 4 and 5. Security Council debate began on Friday the 6th, but was then adjourned. By the time the Council returned to its table on the 11th, Rogers had come out on top in the Washington tussle. On Monday March 9 the closing of the American consulate was announced. On the 10th Italy and the Netherlands followed suit, on the 11th France, on the 12th Germany, on the 16th Austria, Belgium and Switzerland and on the 17th Greece. This left only the two expected diehards, Portugal and South Africa. (During April British pressure brought the withdrawal of the Portuguese consul-general from Salisbury; but it seemed that the Portuguese meant to keep some kind of consular office open there if they could get away with it.)

It is doubtful whether the Security Council's rather lamentable performance during March contributed much to these developments. It did not manage to adopt a resolution until the 18th. Caradon had begun by urging that, as the members evidently agreed that the Smith regime must not be recognised, they should immediately adopt a resolution in that sense. He made clear that he was not trying to cut debate short, but to obtain a swift demonstration of the Council's unity. 'If we were to disagree now, and fail to take the action which seems to me essential, we should merely give comfort to a regime which all of us detest.'

The African, Spanish and Russian councilmen proceeded to give that regime considerable comfort. The Burundi, Sierra Leone and Zambia representatives first obtained a three-day delay in starting the Council session, on the ground that the Organisation of African Unity's council of ministers was still discussing the Rhodesia problem in Addis Ababa. When the Council met on the 6th they insisted on a further adjournment because, they said, the OAU had decided that the foreign ministers of Algeria, Senegal and Zambia should go to New York to speak on its behalf in the Security Council debate. Yakov Malik got in on the act with an all too obvious attempt to misrepresent the position, which led Caradon to remark that 'the Soviet representative finds the temptation to make mischief irresistible'. Despite yet another postponement, no Algerian or Senegalese minister appeared. Zambia eventually sent a junior minister, and the visiting firemen who joined in the debate included a Jugoslav and,

258

naturally, Jamil Baroody. As so often, the African spokesmen made a long series of long speeches (in the course of making one, the Algerian notably declared that 'the time for long discourses is past') in which they vied with one another in clamouring for the use of armed force in Rhodesia and denouncing all idea of taking less violent steps. This time the hollowness of their oratory was doubly apparent. Not only did they eventually help to carry a resolution that did not call for armed force; they themselves presented a draft resolution that likewise did not.

Nsanzé Terence of Burundi accused the British government of 'shedding crocodile tears', of having 'hatched the Machiavellian scheme' of which Ian Smith was only the executor, and, among many other things, of having 'stifled nationalist movements' in America in 1776 and in Anguilla in 1969. While Davidson Nicol of Sierra Leone admitted that Britain had made considerable sacrifices in imposing sanctions, Malik tried to better Burundi by alleging that Britain's active support of sanctions was 'only for show'; and the Zambian visitor, Moto Nkama (who seemed to be doing his best to sound like Simon Kapwepwe), claimed that sanctions had merely strengthened the illegal regime's position. A few days later both Malik and Nkama were to vote for a call for strict compliance with these 'simulated' sanctions that 'strengthened' Ian Smith.

Baroody again said his piece about America and Russia financing and organising an African-manned cordon 'all around' Rhodesia. Caradon must have been almost relieved by the Saudi representative's intervention, for Baroody argued that Britain could not be expected to send troops to Rhodesia or to go bankrupt on Rhodesia's account. But most councilmen must have been bewildered when Malik proceeded to take Baroody's wilder visions seriously – though he pretended he hadn't heard Baroody name Russia as one of the powers who should carry out his plan.

Joaquin Vallejo Arbelaez of Colombia, presiding, and Max Jakobson of Finland pleaded with the Council to maintain its unity; and Jakobson began to draft a resolution that all members might accept. But on March 17 Malik and the Africans – who had earlier prevented the Council from even getting down to debate until the

11th, eight days after Caradon's call for swift action – insisted that members must vote that day on the British draft and the one that had later been presented by the five elected African and Asian members (Burundi, Nepal, Sierra Leone, Syria, Zambia). Caradon and Charles Yost asked for time so that the Finn's draft, which all members had seen informally, could be formally presented. They asked for one day's delay; or even for a half-hour break for consultations. The communist, African and Asian members combined to block even a slight delay. Caradon expressed regret that these members 'having swallowed the camel of two weeks, had strained at the gnat of half an hour'.

The British draft was then voted down by abstentions. Nobody voted against it (its substance was, in fact, included in the Council's resolution adopted the next day). But only America, Britain, Taipeh China, France and Nicaragua voted for it. Now came the big moment for Jaime de Pinies of Spain. He had privately promised the Africans and Russians his vote if they would let him remove the nasty bits about Portugal from their text. At his request, these paragraphs were voted on separately; by his abstention and that of Taipeh China, they were deleted. Then the rest of the Afro-Asian draft was given the nine votes of the African, Asian, communist, Spanish and Chinese members. It would have been adopted as a Council resolution but for the veto, which this time was jointly used by Caradon and Yost.

Caradon said he had hoped never to have to use a veto on an African issue, and he deeply regretted that some members had chosen to force him to do so; those who had insisted on an immediate vote knew very well what they were doing, and had deliberately produced a deadlock. Malik had the nerve to say that it was 'a sombre page in the annals of the United Nations' when the veto was thus used. When Yost pointedly recalled Russia's 105 vetoes, the last of which had been used after its invasion of Czechoslovakia in 1968, Malik claimed that in that case he had used it 'to prevent the imperialists from occupying Czechoslovakia', and that the 50 vetoes he had personally cast were all used 'exclusively for just causes'. (The Soviet news agency, Tass, pushed fantasy still further. In a commentary on the day's events, it said there was 'no precedent' for the simultaneous use of the veto by two states. This ignored not only the Franco-British 'Suez' vetoes in 1956 but also the fact that the first simultaneous vetoing had been done as far back as June 1946, jointly by France and Russia – page 83.)

The Council's Colombian president described the outcome of its meeting on the 17th as 'tragic'. Max Jakobson deplored the insistence on voting that day, and said the situation thus created served the interests only of the Smith regime. Outside the chamber, Charles Yost was asked why he had not merely abstained, if Britain was going to use the veto anyway. He said it was better 'to stand up for what you believe, rather than hide behind British skirts'. This first American veto (in conjunction with Britain's fourth) was evidently meant to have significance. It may be noted that no vetoing would have been necessary if Taipeh China had not provided a ninth vote for the Afro-Asian draft. Arguably, if the Americans had felt it was intolerably embarrassing either to use their veto or to abstain while Britain used one, they might have been able to induce the Taipeh man to abstain. Yost gave the impression that the American intention was to make a point. In the words of a *Washington Post* editorial, the United States meant to indicate

that there are limits to its acquiescence in meaningless, unenforceable and potentially harmful resolutions, whose passage can ultimately only undermine the reputation and integrity of the UN.

Jaime de Pinies had, by his deal with the Africans and Malik, obtained the removal from the Afro-Asian draft of the paragraph seeking to extend the application of sanctions to Portugal and South Africa. In what was left of the draft, a specific point which Yost had already stated to be unacceptable would have made it mandatory for all communications with Rhodesia to be cut. Not only would this mean that several hundred American missionaries in Rhodesia would be cut off from contact with the outside world, but it would give the Smith regime more complete control over all Rhodesians' access to information. Max Jakobson had suggested a ban only on transport, not on communications; and this was generally acceptable (though, since it would require action by Zambia which Zambia had no intention of taking, Nkama voted for it with his tongue in his cheek).

On March 18 the Council found no difficulty in adopting Jakobson's resolution, which incorporated the British draft and parts of the Afro-Asian one, by a 14–0 vote. The Spaniard, with an irony that Cervantes might have found excessively heavy, pointed out that in this case his vote was 'not decisive', and abstained. He gave exquisitely obscure reasons for doing so, which did not disguise the fact that he had pleased the Africans by helping them to force the vetoing of their text, and had then pleased the Portuguese by not voting for a considerably milder text. The communist and African councilmen all found plausible reasons for voting for the Finn's resolution, despite their previous categorical condemnations of any idea of a resolution that did not demand the use of armed force.

So in the end the Council – thanks largely to the hard work done by the Finnish and Colombian councilmen – had produced a new show of unanimity (apart from Spain). Unlike the session of June 1969, this one had not been simply abortive. But the revelation of disunity during the unhappy debate had given great pleasure to the Smith regime and its backers. And the openly insincere manoeuvrings of the African, Spanish and Russian councilmen had lost the African cause a good deal of sympathy. Cynicism about the African representatives' real motives was the more widespread at the UN at this time because they had already, with Terence of Burundi giving a lead, paralysed the working of the Security Council's committee on sanctions for several months by getting into a silly little squabble about its membership.

*   *   *

As George Brown told the Council in December 1966, the selective sanctions that were then to be imposed would affect items representing about 60 per cent of Rhodesia's exports. In 1965, the last 'normal' trading year – in that the illegal declaration of independence came near its end – the Rhodesian economy had yielded $400 million in exports.* The items embargoed under the Council's

* Figures in this section will be given in US dollars. Because of the 1967 devaluation of the British pound, sterling equivalents of other currencies cannot be shown on a comparable basis for the period 1965–9.

December 1966 resolution made up some $235 million of the 1965 total, including (in US $ millions):

Tobacco	132
Asbestos	30
Meat, skins, leather	20
Copper	18
Iron (pig and ore)	12
Chrome	11
Sugar	11

In 1965 Rhodesia had sold $125 million worth of its products to its African neighbour states, Zambia, Malawi and Botswana; $84 million to Britain; $41 million to South Africa, Mozambique and

EXPORTS FROM RHODESIA (in US $ millions)

	1965	1966	1967	1968	Jan.–June 1969
Exports to:					
Britain	84	13	—	—	—
West Germany	35	31	16	13	0·5
Japan	26	14	1	1	—
Italy	17	9	—	—	—
United States	14	9	6	2	—
Switzerland	6	4	4	3	1·5
Others outside southern Africa*	54	30	8	2	0·5
Totals outside southern Africa †	235	110	36	22	3 †
Zambia, Malawi, Botswana	125	82	61	45	22
Totals of all above †	360	192	97	67	25
Portuguese territories	6	8	10?	8?	4?
South Africa	35	60?	80?	80?	40?
Overall Totals †	400	260?	187?	155?	70?

*In 1965 this included (in $ millions): India 6, Netherlands 6, Austria 4, Malaysia 4, Australia 3, Belgium 3, Canada 3, France 3, Greece 3, Spain 3, Hongkong 2, Norway 2, Singapore 2, Sweden 2, Denmark 1, Egypt 1, New Zealand 1, Nigeria 1.

† Totals shown are rounded figures.

263

other Portuguese territories; and $151 million to all other countries. The table shows how, in later years, its recorded exports were progressively affected by the imposing of sanctions. One can see that many countries reduced or ended their purchases from Rhodesia in response to the November 1965 call for voluntary sanctions – the largest reduction during 1966 being that of Britain itself.

During 1967 the trade figures still showed continuing imports of some embargoed goods by several countries that had in fact imposed embargoes, because goods had already started on their way before the bans took effect, or, on arrival at the importing countries' ports, had remained in bond there for some time before passing through customs and being recorded as imports (a common procedure with tobacco). The 1967 figures showed continuing large imports of Rhodesian copper by West Germany, which, not being a UN member, was not formally bound to comply with the Council's resolution: it chose to let existing contracts run their course. And Switzerland, another non-member, undertook only to ensure that it would not actually increase its imports from Rhodesia.

The full effect of the December 1966 decision was not to be seen until the 1968 figures became available. These indicated that the total loss to Rhodesia of export markets other than in South Africa and Portuguese territory had reached nearly $300 million – equivalent to three-quarters of all its 1965 export trade. It was notable that even its African neighbour states, although unable to sever immediately or completely the tight economic ties that bound them to it, had cut as much as $80 million off its export earnings.

The Smith regime, of course, claimed that sanctions were not hurting it at all, or hardly at all. Its claims were eagerly accepted at face value both by its supporters in Britain and elsewhere and by some of its most loudly vocal opponents, who used these claims to support their argument that sanctions were useless and that military action was the only way of bringing down the illegal regime. Yet even the figures issued at intervals by the regime itself showed a severe drop in export earnings – instead of the steep rise from 1965 onward that would have been produced, in normal conditions, by the then swiftly expanding Rhodesian economy. And there is every reason to suppose that the regime's figures were the highest ones it could

264

plausibly issue. It was careful to publish no detailed breakdowns of its trade statistics.

It was abundantly clear, however, that South Africa and Portugal were enabling the regime to survive by not merely refusing to comply with their Charter obligation to impose the sanctions ordered by the Council, but also actively assisting the regime's efforts to evade sanctions. South Africa ceased to publish figures for its trade with Rhodesia, and such figures as the Portuguese issued became suspect. Between them, they were estimated to be pushing their own consumption of Rhodesian exports up to perhaps $100 million a year. There were also indications that they were helping the Smith regime to sell goods in the world market by passing them off as South African or Mozambique products. The fact that Rhodesia's normal export outlets were through their territory facilitated this.

The trick was more easily worked with certain minerals and raw materials than with, for instance, tobacco, whose origin can normally be identified by experts. Due allowance must be made here for the fact that South Africa's own mineral exports have been expanding in a growing world market, in which Japan has loomed ever larger as a buyer of materials for its booming industries. But, due allowance duly made, eyebrows were still raised by the size of the increase in asbestos exports recorded by South Africa in 1967 and 1968. The eyebrows rose even farther when it appeared that in those two years South Africa said it had shipped 63,000 tons of the stuff to Japan and 18,000 tons to Spain, whereas Japan and Spain said they had imported respectively 133,000 and 56,000 tons from South Africa. A discrepancy of 108,000 tons was hardly to be accounted for by technical differences in recording procedures.

The Smith regime and its South African patrons came up against a particular difficulty in attempting to market Rhodesia's chrome ore. The United States, which had been the chief customer, took its Charter obligation seriously, testing imported ore to establish its origin, hauling into court and fining an American firm that had imported chrome after the imposing of the embargo, and holding down its purchases from South Africa. American imports of chrome from South Africa were in fact smaller in 1967–8 than they had been in 1964–5.

Again there were eye-catching discrepancies in the Japanese figures. Japan's chrome imports from South Africa had averaged 50,000 tons a year in 1964–6. In the two years 1967 and 1968 South Africa declared exports of 246,000 tons to Japan. Japan declared imports of 362,000 tons from South Africa. However, it is possible that no Rhodesian ore reached Japan or any other market except South Africa itself. In recent years South Africa had not only overtaken Rhodesia as a producer of chrome ore but had used an ever-growing amount of the ore in its own industry. One theory was that South Africa was buying and using as much Rhodesian ore as it could, and thus freeing more of its own output for export.

Tobacco, formerly Rhodesia's great export staple, proved very hard to unload. Before 1965 an annual output of over 100,000 tons had brought in one-third of all Rhodesia's export earnings. By 1970 the regime had been forced to restrict the annual crop to under 50,000 tons, and also, each year since 1965, to buy the greater part of the crop from the farmers itself – at prices which, the farmers complained, did not cover their costs – and stockpile it at great expense. There were indications of a certain amount of Rhodesian tobacco being passed off on world markets as being of South African, Mozambique or Malawi origin. But here allowance had to be made for the undoubted fact that Malawi had vastly increased its production in order to capture as much as it could of Rhodesia's former markets. And even if the evidence of clandestine trade was viewed in the most suspicious light, it was evident that the Smith regime was not managing to dispose of more than a small fraction of its tobacco.

It must also be noted that clandestine operations seldom yield the same returns to the original seller as legal trade would provide. The full market price cannot be obtained for goods that even the shiftiest dealer is wary of accepting. Many palms have to be greased along the way. A number of smooth operators certainly made private profit out of the Smith regime's elaborate and devious 'sanctions-busting' efforts; but the Rhodesian economy benefited far less than might be suggested by the scale of the activity. One example may be cited of the more spectacular type of attempt to beat the embargo, whose failure must have involved the regime in heavy loss.

266

In January 1969 a Liberian-flag Greek-operated motor vessel, *Blue Sky*, left the Mozambique port of Lourenço Marques with 4,000 tons of ferro-chrome purportedly bound for Salonika. The British mission at the UN warned the Council's sanctions committee that this cargo was of Rhodesian origin and was mainly destined for a French firm. The committee chairman and the Secretary-General alerted various governments concerned. *Blue Sky* turned up first at Salonika; then at Bar in Jugoslavia, where the authorities prevented her from trans-shipping her cargo to another vessel; then at Lisbon; then at another Jugoslav port – empty. The British learnt that 1,000 tons of her cargo had been reloaded at Lisbon into the French *Atlantique*, which left on April 1, ostensibly for Bordeaux, but actually for Split in Jugoslavia, where her. master showed papers alleging that the ferro-chrome was of Portuguese origin and belonged to an Italian company. This time the Jugoslavs allowed it to be unloaded and reloaded into the Italian *Hierax*, which then headed for a French port. The French refused to let her unload, but she tried Barcelona with more success.

In June a fourth ship, the Italian *Massimoemme*, picked up the 1,000 tons from Barcelona. Meanwhile the rest of *Blue Sky*'s cargo had been collected from Lisbon by the Greek *Archon*. But by now the stuff was apparently too 'hot' for anybody to touch. In July both *Massimoemme* and *Archon* took the long trail back again – to South Africa, where the Rhodesian ferro-chrome found a resting place after its visits to Spain and Portugal, and after what must have been one of the most unprofitably expensive round trips in maritime history.

In the *Blue Sky* case it appeared that the operators' obsessive wish to whisk in and out of Jugoslav ports arose from their plan to sell the mineral in Western Europe as originating from Eastern Europe. But the Smith regime, which insists that it is defending Rhodesia against communism, has also made desperate efforts to trade with communist Eastern Europe. In May 1969, for example, the Danish-chartered and Cyprus-registered *Goodwill* left Mozambique with Rhodesian tobacco valued at over £200,000 for the East German port of Rostock. When her movements were detected the ship was hastily diverted to Szczecin (Stettin), the Polish frontier port. This, too, became known, and the embarrassed Poles at first said she had left there for Rotterdam in July without unloading. But it was later revealed that the tobacco had been discharged at Stettin. The Poles claimed that it had gone into the East German sheds there.

The illegal regime's backers, in Britain and elsewhere, veered rather wildly in their efforts to persuade the world to end sanctions. One line they propagated was that sanctions were hurting only the five million Africans of Rhodesia by depriving them of jobs, while the whites were so unscathed that white immigrants were 'pouring in'. But it emerged that the Africans were strongly in favour of continued sanctions, which at least showed that they had not been forgotten; and that African employment in Rhodesia was actually rising, because many small but labour-intensive enterprises had to be started to make local substitutes for goods that could no longer be imported. As to the alleged flood of white immigrants, the regime tried to maintain this fiction by publishing statistics claiming that the white population had risen buoyantly. But it then blundered into disclosing a new census figure which, allowing for natural increase, revealed that a net loss of whites by emigration had replaced the former net inflow – even though, after 1965, many Rhodesian whites who had been working in Zambia returned home. Meanwhile, with African natural increase (3·4 per cent per year) much higher in Rhodesia than white (less than 1 per cent), it was predictable that within twenty years the black/white population ratio would rise to around 30 : 1.

The opponents of sanctions – whether they loved the Smith regime or loathed it – relied heavily on the argument that evasion was easy, massive and, above all, increasing. But it was remarkable how little evidence they showed in support of their claims. Usually they cited irrelevant facts and figures: for instance, figures about Rhodesian imports in 1967 and 1968, before any mandatory embargo had affected most of them. They chose to ignore the obvious fact that time-lags are inevitable before the effects of this kind of operation can be seen. And they generalised wildly from isolated cases. In 1970, for example, a London newspaper passionately opposed to Rhodesia sanctions and strongly sympathetic to the illegal regime published an apparently extensive 'survey' which, it claimed, proved that sanctions were completely futile. But the few actual cases of evasion that it cited turned out to be familiar ones, several of which had been frustrated, and each of which revealed the risky and costly nature of the evaders' activities.

On the other hand, the list of firms successfully prosecuted for attempting evasion grew longer. It included the American firm already mentioned; a Malaysian company fined for importing Rhodesian copper; a Danish firm which was fined $26,000 as well as having its shipment of ten tons of Rhodesian mica confiscated; and a British textile machinery firm that was fined $240,000 for shipping prohibited goods to Rhodesia. In 1970 prosecutions were initiated in Italy and Finland, while a shipload of copper was denied entry to Japan because its purported Mozambique origin was suspect.

The Smith regime itself, while assuring the world that it was doing fine and did not need to take sanctions seriously, in practice took them so seriously that in 1969 it introduced draconian penalties for any disclosure of commercial or economic information that might jeopardise the evasion effort or reveal the true state of the economy. Worried businessmen who could see how badly things were going were unable to cite facts and figures in challenging the regime's claims. Such an authoritative spokesman for industry as Harry Oppenheimer could not be prevented from declaring in Salisbury that it was 'idle to pretend that sanctions were not affecting the economy seriously'; but even he could not quote the detailed evidence. It was known, however, that minerals as well as tobacco were having to be stockpiled; that sugar production was running at no more than a third of the normal level; and that the 'friendly' South Africans and Portuguese, while taking their cut on all the clandestine trade they handled, were becoming difficult about buying more Rhodesian products for their own use.

Chapter Eight

Peace is too serious to be left to civilians

On a steep mountain ridge in a Mediterranean island, one day in 1969, soldiers of the Black Watch of Canada took over a chain of lofty observation posts from another Canadian regiment, the Royal 22e (widely known as the Van Doos). Looking northward from their eyries, the newcomers saw across forty miles of water the coastline of Turkey. But if they lowered their gaze they saw, between their range of hills and the sea, blue-and-white flags marking positions held by Greek Cypriot troops. It was when they turned to look south that they saw the red Turkish flag with its white crescent flying over hilltops and armed camps, all the way from the Kyrenia range to Nicosia, the divided capital of divided Cyprus.

Even in this pattern, so paradoxical in itself, there were untidy exceptions. The crescent flag also flew boldly from one of the most eye-catching summits along the northern edge of the range, the ancient hilltop castle of St Hilarion, a ruined fantasy perched high above the port of Kyrenia. And this was only one small part of the kaleidoscopic confusion of an island considerably smaller than, say, Yorkshire or Connecticut, and boasting only 600,000 inhabitants. The United Nations peace-keeping force in Cyprus has not been simply strung out along a single border or cease-fire line, like Unef in Egypt or the UN observer group in Kashmir. As U Thant said in 1964, it has been placed in

> the most delicate position that any United Nations mission has ever experienced, for it is not only in the midst of a bitter civil war but it is dangerously interposed between the two sides of that war.

270

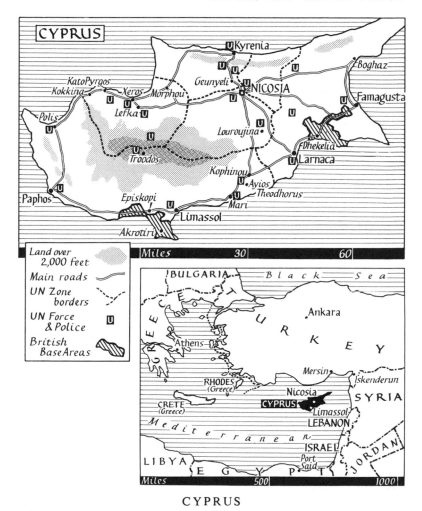

CYPRUS

The bitterness and the danger were not immediately apparent to most of the 120,000 tourists who came in 1969 to sun themselves on the beaches of Cyprus, to drink its wine and contemplate the rich store of antiquities bestowed on it by Ottoman Turks, Venetians, Crusaders, Byzantines, Greeks of the classical age, Assyrians and even earlier masters of this much colonised island. The average holiday-making visitor saw soldiers of the UN force only when they took time off to swim or explore the pleasures of the coastal resort

271

towns. He was apt to think their peace-keeping an enviably cushy job, and to suppose that their main function was to keep the Cypriot bars, restaurants and night clubs comfortably supplied with 'permanent tourists'. He knew nothing of the less pleasant side of their service in an island where, for all its climatic delights, the hills can be bitter cold in winter, the inland plains baking hot and dusty in summer; where the unending task of curbing silly little spats before they led to bloodshed still required the peace-keepers, in this sixth year of their work, to combine permanent vigilance and patience with occasional courage.

Yet it was only because of these soldiers' presence and tireless activity that the tourist could, if he chose, wander in and out of the Turkish Cypriot 'enclaves' which no Greek might enter; or be welcomed to St Hilarion by soldiers who seemed as eager to expound the old castle's history as to defend it; or swim in the pool at Nicosia's Ledra Palace Hotel, in a Greek-held salient almost ringed by Turkish strongpoints which, a few years ago, was the scene of fighting as fierce as that at St Hilarion.

Only under UN protection, in a twice-daily convoy of cars, buses and trucks, could Greeks use the road between Nicosia and Kyrenia. Only the UN men's efforts had brought back to cultivation many tracts of farmland abandoned since 1963 because the villagers were exposed to sniping fire, or because their enemies had cut off the irrigation water. It was not seriously disputed in any quarter that a withdrawal of the force would be followed by a renewal of violent conflict in the island, which would at once revive the risk of full-scale war between Turkey and Greece.

No two UN peace-keeping operations have been alike. The one in Cyprus is in no sense 'typical'. But there are several reasons for focusing a chapter of this book upon it. It is, at the time of writing, the largest continuing UN peace-keeping operation. (When it began, early in 1964, there were two other sizeable UN forces in the field, in the Congo and Egypt.) It has the distinctive characteristic of the participation of British troops; this, among other things, is a noteworthy exception to the rule that permanent members of the Security Council do not provide contingents for these forces, a rule that had seemed to be becoming established in the early 1960s. In various ways the Cyprus operation has taken a form which (although one would hesitate to speak of it as more advanced) might at least be called 'fashionable'. It is widely thought that, if yet another UN force were created in the fairly near future, it would resemble the Cyprus one more than those that served in Egypt until 1967 and in the Congo until 1964.

And a particular point related to the theme of this book is that, whereas the force in Egypt was authorised by the Assembly, and the Assembly several times took a hand in the Congo operation, the Security Council has maintained its authority over the Cyprus operation throughout the years – at least in form. As we shall see, there have been limits to the effectiveness of that authority. But the solitary attempt made, in 1965, to bring the Assembly to bear on this operation turned out to be a flop.

The circumstances of the birth of the force in Cyprus (Unficyp) were even more complex than in the cases of the two other UN forces then in the field. Both of the latter had been authorised and installed remarkably quickly. (The speed with which the Assembly authorised Unef, the Egypt force, in 1956 disproved the idea that this 'unwieldy' body could never move as fast as the Security Council. Given an exactly adequate dose of panic, it was very wieldy.) But although the Greeks and Turks of Cyprus started to kill each other in large numbers in December 1963, and the conflict became international only a few days later with the involvement of the armed forces of Greece and Turkey, it was not until March 1964 that the Security Council authorised the creation of the force, and few of the troops reached the island before mid-April.

The simple explanation is that there was at first only one thing on which all parties were agreed. None of them wanted a UN force in Cyprus. It must take a little longer to explain how they were all eventually obliged to agree that the installing of precisely such a force was the only way of preventing the spread of war.

Before taking up the Cyprus end of the story it is important to recall the general atmosphere of that period at the United Nations end. The Cypriot slaughter began in the last days of a year whose first days had seen the UN Congo force succeed in ending the tenacious attempt, initiated in 1960, to keep the Congo's mineral-rich Katanga province on the 'white' side of the African divide – within the orbit of white-ruled South Africa and its Rhodesian and Portuguese associates. History may eventually conclude that this remarkable (and remarkably bloodless) achievement saved Africa and the world from a looming disaster. But hardly anybody seemed to feel that way at the time. The Congo operation had been messy, infuriating and expensive. It had brought Dag Hammarskjöld first into Russia's black books and then to his death. It had involved soldiers of a UN 'peace force' in battle. It had built up, in countries that duly paid their shares of the force's costs, resentment against those that did not. And at the end of 1963 the Congo force, although much reduced, had not yet been wholly extricated.

The major powers – America and Britain on one side, Russia and France on the other – were starting to lock their horns in the struggle that was to paralyse the 1964 Assembly: the argument about defaulting member states losing their voting rights under Article 19 of the Charter. Bound up with this was the dispute over the control, as well as the financing, of future peace-keeping operations. The one element of agreement was the general disinclination to contemplate any such operations. And in the case of Cyprus each of the governments concerned had particular additional reasons for disliking the idea of installing a UN force there.

*   *   *

The Security Council was first introduced to the Cyprus conflict on 27 December 1963. Six days earlier large-scale fighting had broken out between Greek and Turkish irregular forces in the island. Throughout the year these forces had been arming themselves and getting ready for battle, as the governmental machinery ground to an almost complete halt. This machinery had been imposed on Cyprus by the agreements reached in 1959 between Britain, Greece and Turkey, on the basis of which it became independent in 1960. Never had independence been granted by Britain to a former colony with such a cat's cradle of strings attached.

Although Turkey had ruled Cyprus from 1570 to 1878 (during most of which time Greece, too, was under Turkish rule), nearly

274

four-fifths of the population is Greek, only one-fifth Turkish. The Turkish community is scattered across the island – few villages, and no towns, are wholly Turkish – yet there has been very little blending between the two groups in four centuries, although it would be as impossible to draw a clear 'ethnic' dividing line between them as it would in the case of Indians and Pakistanis (or Catholic and Protestant Irishmen). The traditional aspiration of Greek Cypriots is for union with Greece (*enosis*). The traditional concern with the island felt in Turkey is not a simple anxiety about the fate of the Turkish Cypriots but also a wish to ensure that this offshore island shall not pose any threat to Turkey itself.

The British, who took over Cyprus in 1878 to strengthen their imperial life-line through the Mediterranean and the Suez Canal to India, in fact found little strategic interest in it until the 1950s. Successive Conservative governments were then persuaded that a base there would be vital for British influence in the Middle East after the abandonment of the base built up alongside the Suez Canal during the Second World War. This stiffened British resistance to the post-war revival of Greek Cypriot demands for *enosis*. By 1954 the Greek government was bringing the case for Cypriot self-determination before the UN Assembly, which at first shelved the question and in subsequent years limited itself to voicing the hope that negotiation would lead to a solution.

In 1955 Greek Cypriot impatience flared up into a campaign of terrorist attacks launched by the EOKA (National Organisation of Cypriot Struggle) organisation against both the British and other Cypriots, whether Greek or Turkish, who were supposedly identified with the colonial regime. The direction of the campaign was largely in the hands of George Grivas, a Cyprus-born ex-officer of the Greek army, who had returned to the island after playing a part in violent right-wing extremism in post-war Greece. Grivas used the pseudonym of 'Dighenis' – a giant hero of local legend whose feats included leaping across the straits between Cyprus and Turkey, and leaving the mark of his hand on the Kyrenia range (where, to this day, a conspicuous grouping of five small peaks in a row is called Pentadaktylos, the five-finger mountain).

Political leadership among the Greek Cypriots, during the four

centuries of Turkish and then British rule, had become the preroga-
tive of the island's 'autocephalous' (independent) Orthodox or Greek
church. The Turks' system of 'indirect rule' had encouraged this.
They broke the power of the long dominant Catholic hierarchy,
restored that of the Greek one and preferred to deal with the Greek
Cypriots largely through their Archbishop and Ethnarch ('head of
the race'). In 1950 the astute Myriartheus Makarios, then only 37,
was elected Archbishop and Ethnarch as Makarios III. He rapidly
became the unchallenged leader of the *enosis* movement; and in 1956
he was deported to the Seychelles on the ground that he had, in Sir
Anthony Eden's words at the time, 'not only countenanced but
actively fostered terrorism'.

A year later Harold Macmillan allowed Makarios to leave his
Indian Ocean place of exile (but not to return to Cyprus, which he
did not see until 1959), to the fury of Lord Salisbury – who, thinking
he could bend the new British prime minister to his will, forced the
issue too far and was thrust into outer darkness himself. The
Macmillan government began to try to wriggle off the hook on which
its predecessors had impaled themselves. But each sign of British
yielding to the Greeks now inflamed the Turks. They, it must be
admitted, had received some encouragement from such leading
British politicians as Alan Lennox-Boyd (who remained Colonial
Secretary until 1959) to maintain their demand that the island should
be partitioned.

During 1958, as well as anti-British demonstrations in Turkey,
there were increasingly violent collisions between Greeks and Turks
in the streets of Cypriot towns. Late that year the prime ministers of
Greece and Turkey, Karamanlis and Menderes, decided that the drift
towards catastrophe must be halted, and they initiated serious
bilateral talks about a settlement. Early in 1959 they reached agreement with Britain on a formula for Cypriot independence which
Makarios and the Turkish Cypriot leader, Dr Fazil Kuchuk, were
induced to countersign.

The Zürich and London agreements provided that Cyprus should
become independent in 1960, although Britain would retain sovereignty over two coastal base areas. Cyprus would renounce all idea
of *enosis*, while Britain, Greece and Turkey would undertake in a

Treaty of Guarantee to prevent either *enosis* or partition ('double *enosis*', as the Turks liked to call it) and would retain the right to 'take action', jointly or individually, to maintain the whole new *status quo*. Greece would station 950 soldiers in Cyprus, Turkey 650. The Turkish Cypriots would have 30 per cent of all seats in parliament and of police and civil service posts. Each of the five larger towns would be split between Greek and Turkish municipalities. There would be two communal chambers, each with powers of taxation. Veto power over parliamentary or ministerial decisions on foreign affairs and defence would be wielded by a president and vice-president, elected respectively by the Greek and the Turkish Cypriots. In 1960 Cyprus duly became a republic on this basis, with Makarios as president and Kuchuk as vice-president. The agreement got Britain off its colonial hook, and bought time all round by halting the violence. But it proved unworkable. By 1963 an accumulation of deadlocks was paralysing the government, and violent talk and action were reviving in the island.

In November Makarios proposed sweeping constitutional changes. These included abolition of the veto powers, unification of town councils and reduction of the Turks' civil service quota. This precipitated a crisis, as the president must have intended it to do. The taciturn and by no means volatile Kuchuk might have agreed to negotiate about some of the proposals, but the Turkish government rejected them outright. This action reflected the fact that the government in Ankara was then in a shaky state, as was the government in Athens. Neither was in a position to make concessions over Cyprus that its domestic opposition might exploit.

On 21 December 1963 heavy communal fighting broke out. The Turkish Cypriots suffered most, but there were hundreds of casualties on both sides and thousands of people were driven or fled from their homes. There are still 'ghost town' sectors in Nicosia whose inhabitants have not been able to return; there are still refugee camps and settlements in various parts of the island.

On December 25 Turkish warships sailed towards Cyprus, and planes of the Turkish air force flew low over Nicosia; and the 950 Greek and 650 Turkish soldiers stationed there under the 1959

277

agreements came out of their barracks, occupied commanding positions and joined in the fighting. They did not accept invitations to join British troops from the base areas in helping to restore peace. The British then acted alone, securing local cease-fires wherever they could. Meanwhile the Cyprus government broke apart. Contact between Makarios and Kuchuk ceased; the Turkish ministers took refuge in the Turkish-held zones.

At the United Nations, where a good many of the permanent representatives had dispersed for Christmas holidays after the annual Assembly session, a meeting of the Security Council was urgently requested on December 26 by the Cyprus representative, the elderly and often loquacious Zenon Rossides. The Council met late in the evening of the 27th. Rossides spoke at some length about the threat of a Turkish invasion of the island and asked the Council to 'take steps' to ensure maintenance of the cease-fire; but he did not say what steps. For Turkey, Adnan Kural said the invasion threat had been invented to cover up the Greek Cypriots' attempts to destroy their Turkish fellow citizens. The representative of Greece made a notably mild statement. When these three invited participants had spoken there was a deafening silence. Not one of the Council's own members wished to say anything at all.

One reason for hesitation on the part of some of them was doubt about Rossides' right to appeal to the UN without Kuchuk's approval. There was also Kural's reassuring insistence that 'the situation is improving'. And none of the three parties represented had asked the Council to do anything specific. At one o'clock in the morning of December 28 the Council was adjourned, without the fixing of any time for it to meet again, by Francis Plimpton of the United States, who was presiding in the absence of Adlai Stevenson. This first bid to involve the UN in the conflict had fizzled.

Not until 18 February 1964 was Council debate eventually started. In the interim there was furious activity – outside the UN. The British were desperate to spread the load of a peace-keeping task that was seriously straining their military manpower (then simultaneously involved in propping up the newborn East African states in the face of mutinies among their own troops) and earning them illwill among both Greek and Turkish Cypriots. But they were not so desperate as to want a UN force. While the Foreign Secretary, 'Rab' Butler, got himself storm-bound on the isle of Mull, the Commonwealth Relations Secretary, Duncan Sandys, convened an unsuccessful London conference with Greek, Turkish and Cypriot leaders, and then plunged into the shaping of plans for an international, but non-UN, force.

The first British objection to the idea of a UN force was that this would mean Russian and Afro-Asian meddling in the affairs of an island of strategic importance to Britain, and in a dispute that intimately concerned Nato because, although Cyprus was not a Nato member, three members were embroiled – Britain, Greece and Turkey. The British government, still smarting from its implication in the Katanga affair, also argued that the UN would be automatically prejudiced against the Turks because they had sought partition; and it recoiled from the thought of another UN force of the Congo type, from which British troops would be excluded by the rule barring great-power contributions, while other Nato members might be excluded by their alignment. Britain wanted to spread the load, but not to lose control of the operation.

So, late in January 1964, the British, with American agreement, proposed that a force of about 10,000 men, under British command, should be provided by Nato member countries, and be given political guidance by a committee of contributing governments meeting in London. The Americans indicated a readiness to provide 1,000 to 1,200 men. Britain would contribute about 8,000. It was hoped that the Germans would provide a sizeable number. Greece and Turkey accepted this plan, but Makarios turned it down flat. Rather than Nato contributors, he would prefer Commonwealth countries; but above all, he insisted that 'any force stationed in Cyprus should be under the Security Council'.

George Ball, the American Under-Secretary of State, made a hasty round of London, Athens, Ankara and Nicosia with a revised formula under which non-aligned countries as well as Nato ones would be asked to provide troops, the Security Council would be asked to 'take note by consensus' of the arrangements for forming the force, and the UN would also receive reports on the operation. But even Ball's habitually forceful approach failed to persuade the archbishop-president. And meanwhile it emerged that there was little enthusiasm for the plan among the members of Nato themselves. The French would not play at all, and the Germans backed away. And from Moscow came a strong note to the interested governments in which Khrushchev denounced the 'attempt to place this small neutral state under the military control of Nato' as a plan for 'armed invasion'.

But the fact that Makarios now appeared to be holding out for a UN force did not mean that he actually wanted one. He did not want any kind of international force. What he wanted, as he made extremely clear, was that the UN should guarantee Cyprus against the threat of a Turkish invasion, and thus give the Greek Cypriots a free hand to get on with making the Turkish Cypriots knuckle under. For that purpose he was rapidly recruiting a large Greek Cypriot armed 'national guard', in violation of the constitutional limit on Cyprus's armed forces, and importing both arms and soldiers from Greece. Among the 1964 imports, or rather re-imports, was George Grivas, who soon took control of the new Greek Cypriot forces.

In early February, while violence continued to rage in Cyprus despite the British peace-keeping efforts, Greece and Turkey mounted naval, army and air force manoeuvres on an alarming scale. The British prime minister, Sir Alec Douglas-Home, talked with President Lyndon Johnson on the 13th; and on the 15th Britain called for an early meeting of the Security Council to discuss 'the deterioration of security in Cyprus'. This was a kind of procedural pre-emptive strike, and it succeeded. Makarios had been contemplating a new appeal to the Council, but the British move, made on a Saturday, caught him off balance. Rossides quickly put in his own request for an emergency Council meeting to consider the 'obvious and imminent' danger of a Turkish invasion. But Rossides' request was supported by only four members of the Council, and its Brazilian president gave the British request priority – enabling Sir Patrick Dean to present his case first.

In London, Sandys was pressed to explain the sudden British switch from the previous policy of keeping the Cyprus problem well away from the meddlesome UN. He did his best, by evoking the obligation that Article 33 of the Charter lays on parties to a dispute

280

to try 'at first' to settle it by negotiation or other peaceful means before going to the Council. The underlying fact, however, was that both the British and the Americans now saw no way of averting disaster other than by letting the UN take a hand, and the Americans at least had concluded that an appeal to the organisation would be less risky than they had at first feared.

When debate began in New York on February 18, Patrick Dean still held to the idea that the Council should simply call on the 'parties concerned' to secure the formation of their own peace-keeping force, 'in consultation with the Secretary-General'. The Norwegian representative, Sivert Nielsen, backed this up, arguing that the Council 'would not be well advised to prescribe in detail how this task should be carried out'. The way the unanimous resolution of March 4 eventually came out was quite different. It was the Secretary-General who would determine the force's size and composition, in consultation with the parties (Britain, Cyprus, Greece and Turkey); he would appoint its commander and report on its work. The force was to have much more of a UN character than the British government had wished.

But at least the British were able to vote for every part of the resolution. It was the Soviet representative, Nikolai Fedorenko, who insisted on a separate vote on the paragraph authorising creation of the force. In this vote Russia, Czechoslovakia and France abstained. Fedorenko explained that Russia did not really like the idea of sending any troops to Cyprus, and particularly disliked the idea of giving U Thant such a wide measure of authority over the operation. France likewise argued that the Council should not delegate so much power to one man.

Much of the audible part of the two-week debate was devoted to the argument voiced by Makarios's foreign minister, Spyros Kyprianou, that Turkey could no longer claim a right to intervene in Cyprus. Kyprianou contended that the 1960 Treaty of Guarantee had lost its validity now that Cyprus was a sovereign UN member state. But the British view that the Council could not abrogate the treaty was upheld by most of the Council's own members, including the Arab and African members (Morocco and Ivory Coast), on whose support Makarios had counted, and even by Greece.

Behind the scenes, while the public debate seemed to be bringing agreement no nearer, Thant and some of his chief assistants were busily shaping up an acceptable text in close co-operation with the Council president for February, Carlos Bernardes of Brazil – who was later to play another hand in the Cyprus operation as Thant's special representative. Bernardes was able to present on March 2 a draft resolution jointly sponsored by five of the six non-permanent Council members (Brazil, Bolivia, Ivory Coast, Morocco, Norway). Two days later it was unanimously adopted with hardly any further debate. The only noticeable discord was the Russian and French criticism, already mentioned, of the scope allowed to the Secretary-General. The resolution's preambular paragraphs were so delicately balanced as to save face all round.

The resolution of March 4 asked the Secretary-General to appoint a Mediator (who, like the Force Commander, would report to him) to tackle what was, discreetly, called simply 'the problem confronting Cyprus'. It proposed that the 'peace-keeping force' should seek to 'prevent a recurrence of fighting and, as necessary, to contribute to the maintenance and restoration of law and order and a return to normal conditions'. The force would have an initial life of only three months. Its costs would be met by Cyprus, by the states providing troops and by voluntary contributions from others.

The fact that no attempt was made to levy financial contributions from all UN members revealed that, although the showdown in the Assembly over Article 19 was yet to come, it was already being accepted as a fact of life that peace-keeping costs could not be extracted from an unwilling great power like Russia, and therefore could not be obtained from all the smaller members either. There were also newly established precedents. In 1962 it had been agreed that the costs of the small UN force then being sent to West Irian (New Guinea) would be shared between the parties concerned – the Netherlands and Indonesia. In 1963 a similar sharing arrangement was made (between Egypt and Saudi Arabia) to cover the costs of the UN observer mission that was sent to Yemen. In the Cyprus case there were, fortunately, certain states which, although not directly parties to the dispute, were interested enough to be counted on to make voluntary payments: they were the United States and most other Nato members. In the event, over 90 per cent of the funds provided for the Cyprus operation in its first five years came from America, Britain and other Nato countries. France was a notable non-contributor, Australia and Sweden ranking high among the non-Nato contributors, and Germany even higher among the non-UN ones.

The March 4 resolution was an important step forward. But its immediate aftermath was tragic. Fighting at once became fiercer in Cyprus, as the Greeks seized their last opportunity to wrest territory from the Turks before the arrival of the UN force, and the Turks fought back in desperation. On March 12 Turkey notified the Council of what amounted to an ultimatum. If there was not an immediate cease-fire, it said, it would use its rights under the Treaty of Guarantee and send a Turkish force to protect the Turkish Cypriots until the UN force reached the island. Makarios's government at once requested an emergency Council meeting in the light of this 'imminent invasion'.

On a grim Friday the 13th the Council found itself in session again, and once more hearing the by now familiar exchange of charges and counter-charges. A wider war seemed nearer than ever. All that the Council itself could do was (unanimously) to urge Thant to 'press on' with his efforts to raise a force. There never was a clearer illustration of the danger of assuming that, once a Council resolution has been adopted, something has actually been done. In the March 4 resolution the Council had set out a framework, but it had left Thant to fill it in. And he (unlike Hammarskjöld in 1956) had found no crowd of eager governments beating on his door, demanding to be allowed to offer troops for the new force. Apart from the problem of how it would be paid for, there were two other special factors that made potential contributors of troops hesitate. The Cyprus crisis had not set off such a general panic as the one that brought people running in 1956. At the same time, fighting was still going on in the island, and no government wanted to see its troops caught in cross-fire immediately they landed.

Credit for saving the day should be given to the Canadian foreign minister, Paul Martin. When Turkey issued its ultimatum Martin swiftly contacted Thant, the Swedes, the Irish and the Finns, as well

283

as the Turks. By the evening of the 13th Thant was able to announce that Canada, Sweden and Ireland would provide troops. That same evening Turkey reduced the tension by issuing a statement welcoming the progress made towards forming a force; and the Canadian House of Commons met in emergency session and approved the sending of a contingent to Cyprus. The Security Council thankfully retired from the scene, muttering 'over to U'. It did not resume consideration of Cyprus until it was summoned in June to extend the force's life at the end of its first three-month period.

*   *   *

Six years later the UN Force in Cyprus (Unficyp), whose existence had thus been originally authorised for only three months, was still on the island – and still needed. Nor had its unforeseen long life been an undisturbed one. Apart from many moments of less critical danger, there had been two occasions – in August 1964 and November 1967 – when Greece and Turkey once again seemed to have reached the brink of war. Each such threat of escalated conflict brought the Security Council into session. The Council also found itself having to hold a more regular series of meetings on Cyprus, at intervals of three or six months, because it could neither authorise the indefinite extension of Unficyp's life nor end it.

Before each of these 'regular' meetings Thant issued a report on the operation, in which he also recorded relevant political and economic developments in Cyprus and expressed, sometimes forcefully, his views about what was happening and what needed to be done. His reports, formally addressed to the Security Council, were published without restriction, and this gave him a certain leverage. But the Council paid little more than lip service to the idea that its duty was to examine Thant's reports, debate them in detail and maintain control over Unficyp by keeping up a flow of instructions about the operation. Many of its meetings were largely taken up with repetitions of the usual charges and counter-charges made by the parties. The Soviet representatives in the Council monotonously repeated their statements that they had disliked the idea of the force at the start; that they still thought it unnecessary and undesirable; that they would reluctantly go along with yet another extension, because the Cyprus government seemed to want one; but that the Council must take great care not to let Thant have too much of a free hand. Yet even the Russians failed to produce a clear version of what they thought the Council should tell Thant to do.

Thant himself repeatedly pointed out, in his reports and elsewhere, that the Council's original instructions about Unficyp's role had been extremely vague, and that it had done nothing later to remedy this. The mandate the Council had provided in March 1964 was even vaguer than those that had been given to the UN forces in Egypt and the Congo. As early as September 1964 Thant told the Council that 'if Unficyp is extended, there will be serious need for at least some clarification as to actions that the Force may take in the discharge of its mandate'. Even this straightforward nudge did not produce a clarifying resolution. What Thant did obtain at that time, however, was a quite usable tacit approval of his actions and intentions. He in effect challenged the Council by telling it in his report that 'I intend to proceed on certain assumptions and to instruct the Commander of the Force accordingly'. He said he would assume it was the Council's wish that Unficyp should have the right to defend itself, the right of freedom of movement, the right to dismantle fortifications erected by the combatants and the right to establish buffer zones where these were needed. He simultaneously rejected the Cyprus government's demand that the UN troops should help it to suppress the Turkish Cypriots, and the Turkish Cypriots' demand that the troops should use armed force to restore the constitutional structure that had been shattered in December 1963.

At least the subsequent Council debate yielded some reactions to Thant's assumptions. His general approach was approved by the French and the African and Arab members of the Council as well as by the Americans and other westerners. For Russia, Nikolai Fedorenko put in a routine warning that Unficyp must stick to careful compliance with the March 4 resolution. But Fedorenko said nothing at all about Thant's specific 'assumptions'. And Thant, of course, was arguing that his assumptions were quite compatible with the original resolution (as indeed they were). There was not much bite to the Russians' insistence on 'strict compliance' with such an obscure mandate when they themselves could offer no response to Thant's request that it should be clarified for him.

Orhan Eralp, the Turkish representative, later argued that the Council, by noting Thant's proposals and then granting an extension of the force's life, had in effect given him permission to act on his proposals. In outward form the Council had not done this; and Thant was careful not to make any explicit claim that it had. But the Council's action, or rather its inaction, had left Thant in a position to recall that his assumptions had not been challenged. Like Dag Hammarskjöld before him, and in a similar situation, he had learnt that a Secretary-General can often get better results from a UN organ if he does not ask for a formal vote.

In outward form, practically the only thing Thant got from these 'regular' Council meetings on Cyprus was approval of the series of extensions of Unficyp's life which he recommended. In June, September and December 1964, and in March 1965, he proposed and got three-month extensions. After that the Council met and the force was renewed every six months, and this cycle was still running in 1970 (with the exception of the first halves of 1966 and 1968, which had each been split into two three-month phases). Ritually, the extending resolutions mentioned the Council's expectation that by the end of the next period 'progress toward a final solution will make possible a withdrawal or substantial reduction of the Force'. Privately, Council members seldom voiced any such expectations.

It was rare for Thant to address the Council during these renewing sessions. Each time he had said what he wanted to say in the written report that he presented to the Council several days before it met. One occasion when he was moved to speak at the table came in September 1964. He had already warned the Council, in his report earlier in that month, that voluntary contributions were not coming in fast enough, and that if they remained inadequate he would be forced to pay some of Unficyp's bills out of general UN revenues. No member of the Council commented on this warning directly; but the French and Russian members said their usual pieces about the need to stick to voluntary financing more loudly than usual. After the debate and the resolution, Thant spoke up quickly and told the Council that, since the use of general UN funds had been opposed, he would be obliged, if the voluntary contributions did not come in faster, 'to withdraw the Force before the end of the three-month period'. (After which, more money came in.)

At that meeting the dispute about financing gave the proceedings a distinctly waspish tone. Two days before the Council met, the Soviet government newspaper *Izvestia*, in one of that staid daily's odder ventures into gutter journalism, had printed a photograph of UN soldiers watching a blonde belly dancer in a Cyprus night club, under the outraged headline: 'And they want us to pay for this?' (*Izvestia* had 'lifted' the picture from a German magazine, without attribution and without some of the anatomy that the original photograph had revealed. But presumably the Soviet reader, although thus deprived, took the point.) In the Council debate, Adlai Stevenson made a neat jab at France and Russia by drawing attention to the strange position of member states that insisted that only the Security Council could authorise peace-keeping operations, yet did not think it necessary to contribute to the cost of the Cyprus operation – which the Council had authorised. The French government (as an editorial in *Le Monde* pointed out at the time) never came up with any convincing explanation of this paradox. The Russians have been foolish enough to attempt an explanation. Belly dancers apart, their line was (and in 1969 it still was) that the whole UN operation really served the interests of Nato, so why should they help pay for it? Yakov Malik told the Council in 1969 that the UN force was 'composed mainly of armed contingents of the Nato countries' (which was not true), and that

> the Soviet Union from the start did not consider the presence of these forces in Cyprus as justified, and it will continue to adhere to that view. . . . The arguments put forward in that connection [about financing] are of course completely unacceptable. . . . Those who have been responsible for many years for this problem must pay for those expenditures and cover the deficit.

Incredibly, the Soviet government was solemnly casting its vote, every three or six months over a period of six years, for the continuance of an arrangement that enabled the wicked Nato powers to impose their armed forces on poor little non-aligned Cyprus, under

287

the banner of the United Nations. Russia rejected the idea that Unficyp served the cause of peace; it regarded the operation with dark suspicion; yet it went on and on down the years voting for it, when a Soviet veto might have halted the evil thing in its tracks, and even an abstention might have helped to cleanse Soviet hands of the taint of complicity.

The clashes over Unficyp financing in 1964, of course, took place against the background of the mounting crisis over the financing of all UN peace-keeping operations which reached its climax in the abortive Assembly session at the end of that year. Later, the exchanges in the Council about Cyprus costs tended to become more ritualised, and ceased to attract much attention outside the Council chamber. But they did not stop altogether, nor were they limited to jousts between the great powers.

At the Council meeting in June 1969 it was Max Jakobson of Finland who brought the subject up. The Finns have good reason not to get into unnecessary rows with Russia; but, with their own soldiers standing guard along the 'Green Line' through divided Nicosia, and their Swedish and Danish neighbours also providing troops for Unficyp, they have equally good reason to want to see the force properly sustained. Jakobson told the Council that

> My government shares the view of the Secretary-General that reliance on voluntary contributions from a relatively small number of Member States is quite unsatisfactory. We firmly believe that a peace-keeping operation based on decisions that the Security Council has taken on behalf of all Member States should be paid for by all.

'We share Mr Jakobson's concern,' said Charles Yost, the American representative; and he gave the thorn in Malik's flesh another twist by stressing the 'special obligation to carry a fair share of the burden' that lay on those powers that had 'a particular responsibility for international peace and security'. The Russians have always harked back to this 'particular responsibility' when defending their privileges as a permanent member of the Council. In reply, Malik repeated the familiar Soviet axioms that I have already quoted; while the French, as usual, clung to the narrowly legalistic argument that Unficyp was financed voluntarily and that they didn't feel like either volunteering or explaining why they didn't.

So the Council, as such, did nothing to relieve Thant of the endless task of going around, like a Buddhist monk with a begging bowl, pleading for funds to sustain a UN operation which the Council had authorised and kept on extending. He lived with a permanent deficit. Up to the end of 1969 the total amount that the UN had paid for the operation was about $110 million (£46 million). Contributions received totalled $93 million, including (in $ million) 40 from America, 21 from Britain, 8 each from Germany and Greece, 2 each from Sweden and Turkey, and over 1 each from Australia, Belgium, Denmark, Italy, Norway and Switzerland. The real total cost of Unficyp also included a further $30 million that states contributing troops had spent without asking for reimbursement from the UN; this included $14 million spent by Canada and $11 million spent by Britain. The force lived 'from hand to month', as the slightly adapted saying went. Inevitably, it therefore cost more than it need have done. For one thing, supplies often had to be bought in small quantities limited by the availability of funds, when the placing of long-term contracts would have saved the UN a lot of money.

The Council also left it to Thant to determine, within the limits set by hard fact, how large a force should and could be kept in Cyprus. At the start, Unficyp was over 6,000 strong. By 1969 it was down to 3,650 men, of whom 175 were civilian policemen. Late that year Thant sent out to Cyprus a Secretariat team (including Colonel Louis Monteagle, the wakeful liaison officer of the sleeping Military Staff Committee) to take a fresh look at the force 'with particular attention to the possibility of reducing its cost'. The team found it difficult to see how the force would be able to do its job at all effectively if its numbers were cut much further. The only heartening feature of the scene it surveyed was the fact that the states contributing troops – Austria, Britain, Canada, Denmark, Finland, Ireland and Sweden – did not now, despite occasional murmurs of impatience, seem desperately anxious to get their contingents out. Yet none of these states – not even Britain – had contemplated such a long commitment when they made their original contributions to the force in 1964.

And it should not be supposed that the Unficyp troops have spent six years in Cyprus tranquilly standing about in the sun. They have all too often had to intervene when firing broke out between Greek and Turkish Cypriots. They have been shot at; threatened; man-handled; exposed to the dangers of booby-traps and mined roads. When obstructed in doing their duty they have usually negotiated their way patiently past angry, nervous and often trigger-happy Greeks or Turks; but on occasion they have had to concentrate superior force to make the combatants give way.

Recorded 'shooting incidents' in the island were down to 55 in 1969, as against 171 in 1968 and over 600 in 1967. (The UN has found roughly half of these attributable to each side; the force has never opened fire itself.) Indeed, in 1969 the most worrying source of tension in Cyprus was the new campaign of terrorist attacks launched against Makarios and officials of his government by right-wing extremist Greek Cypriots who could not forgive him for admitting, realistically, that *enosis* would remain impossible as long as the Turks barred the way to it.

*   *   *

Walk into the UN building in New York by the delegates' door, and you see before you the escalator up which the councilmen ride, past a huge and gay tapestry presented by Belgium, to the second floor (in British usage, the first) where the Council meets. But if you walk round behind the escalator you find stairs going down to the basement level where the UN's many committees lead their teeming subterranean life. Near the foot of those stairs a large wallboard indicates the day's meetings.

One December day in 1969 two acquaintances happened to meet beside this notice-board, and were heard to speak as follows:

'The Security Council's meeting today? Good God, what's up? Nobody told me!'

'It's Cyprus – one of those.'

'Oh, that! For a moment they had me worried. . . .'

This little exchange was revealing, but it should not be misunderstood. The Cyprus problem itself is not taken lightly at the UN. But the 'regular' Council meetings held to renew the life of the force in Cyprus had become so ritualised by 1969 that they stirred only a small ripple of interest among those not directly involved. It was understood that the holding of such a meeting meant that the extension of Unficyp's life had already been agreed off-stage. What would arouse interest and anxiety would be the news that a 'regular' meeting was *not* going to be held.

Very different have been the occasions when the Council was called into urgent session because a worsening of the Cyprus situation had again presented the threat of war between Greece and Turkey, despite the presence of the UN force in the island. On the first such occasion, in August 1964, when the force had been at work for only four months, the Council was moved to make what, so far, has been its only specific assertion of direct authority over the force.

The one part of Cyprus's north coast held by the Turkish Cypriots is a stretch running westward from near Xeros. In the first week of August the Greek Cypriot and Greek-Greek forces attacked the Kokkina sector of this coastal beachhead. The Turkish air force came to the Turkish Cypriots' rescue and blasted several Greek positions around Kokkina, Kato Pyrgos and Polis. The Security Council (Russia and Czechoslovakia abstaining) called for an immediate cease-fire. Two days later, on August 11, the Council met again because there had been reports of violations of the new cease-fire. But Thant was able to give it a more reassuring report. The Council did not adopt a further resolution, but Sivert Nielsen of Norway, as president, announced a 'consensus' in which, among other things, the Council asked the Commander of the UN force, General Thimayya of India, 'to reinforce its units in the zones which were the sphere of the recent military operations, so as to ensure the safety of the inhabitants . . .'

The Russian councilman, who at this point was going through a strongly anti-Turkish phase, was only grudgingly willing to accept Nielsen's statement, which he thought was altogether too balanced. However, the fact that these words were addressed directly to Thimayya, by-passing Thant, made it easier for the Russian to go along with it. But this small concession to the Soviet distrust of the Secretary-General was not to be repeated. Since then, the Council

291

has accepted as a fact of life Thant's authority over the Commander of the force as well as over the Mediators and Special Representatives in Cyprus. (Earlier in 1964, Thant had quietly weathered a storm of British Tory indignation at his refusal to let Britain, or any other PP, tell him what his orders to the Commander should be.)

The first Mediator, Sakari Tuomioja of Finland (who had previously served as Hammarskjöld's representative in Laos in 1959, page 150), died suddenly just after the August 1964 crisis, and Thant found a successor in Galo Plaza Lasso, the former President of Ecuador, who was already acting as Thant's Special Representative with Unficyp. Plaza, then 58, was no stranger to the UN; he had been at San Francisco, and in 1958 had worked alongside General Odd Bull as chairman of the UN observer group in Lebanon. When he became Mediator the post of Special Representative was filled by Carlos Bernardes of Brazil, who as Council president had done so much to get agreement on the first Cyprus resolution. Thant had a good team, for Thimayya, too, was widely respected. But Thimayya was to die a year later, while Plaza had to resign as Mediator after the Turks had violently denounced the proposals he made in 1965. One might call it ironic that the very points in Plaza's proposals that were then rejected by both parties were later accepted by both as their basis for negotiation. But this is merely one of the recurring experiences of UN representatives.

One reason why the Turks became so intransigent in 1965 was that the Russians had unexpectedly swung over to their side – a shift that earned Moscow bitter reproaches from Akel, the Cyprus communist party. Makarios thus found that he could not count on the backing of any one of the great powers. He had rebuffed the American mediatory approaches of Dean Acheson (the former Secretary of State whom President Johnson had recruited as a special envoy); and General de Gaulle was developing a habit of bracketing Cyprus with Canada as an example of the error of forcing two different nationalities to share one government. Makarios had already thought of trying to mobilise the mass of UN Assembly members in his support, but had been frustrated by the paralysis of the 1964 session. In December 1965, however, he managed to get the adoption of an Assembly resolution calling on all other states not

After Russia's 1968 invasion of Czechoslovakia. From top: Bouattoura of Algeria, George Ball, Caradon and Malik (pages 306 and 309)

Jan Muzik of Czechoslovakia telling the Council about the invasion (page 307)

Ireland's Hillery addressing the Council in August 1969 (page 326). At right, Finland's Jakobson (page 364)

to intervene in Cyprus. The Greek Cypriots hailed this as a tremendous diplomatic victory.

In reality it was a classic example of a 'hollow voting victory' of the kind that Hammarskjöld used to beg UN members to eschew. Only 47 delegations voted for it. True, only 5 voted against; but these included the United States as well as Turkey. And there were no less than 65 abstainers and absentees, who included the other western powers and Russia. This was the kind of non-event that devalues all the Assembly's resolutions, but is unfortunately permitted by the absurd voting rules which the Three at Dumbarton Oaks devised for the Assembly – and which the Fifty at San Francisco swallowed whole, apparently because they were obsessed by the battle over voting rules in the Council.*

The supposedly dramatic Greek Cypriot triumph in the Assembly had no noticeable effect on either the Council's or Thant's approach to the Cyprus problem. In 1966 Thant told the Council that, as the Turks refused to deal with a Mediator, he was simply going to widen the scope of Bernardes' activity. (In 1967 Bernardes was succeeded as Thant's Special Representative by Bibiano Osorio-Tafall, an energetic Mexican who had already worked for the UN in various capacities for some sixteen years.) And General Ilmari Armas Martola of Finland, who had been Hammarskjöld's military adviser in the first months of Unef's life, took command of the force after a five-month period following Thimayya's death during which Brigadier James Wilson was acting commander – the first occasion on which a British officer commanded a UN peace-keeping force. Martola was to serve in Cyprus for three and a half years, and to be succeeded at the end of 1969 by another Indian officer, General Prem Chand, who had already held a UN command in the Congo.

While the UN force held the ring and Thant's emissaries carried on coaxing, the two sides in Cyprus remained obdurate, dealing with each other only through the UN. Then the 1967 military *putsch* in Greece changed the situation. Greek Cypriot enthusiasm for *enosis*

* The Assembly itself has compounded this felony by agreeing that a mere majority of members is enough to make a quorum. There are now 126 members; in nightmare theory, a resolution could be adopted with the support of only two members, 1 voting against, 61 abstaining and 62 absent (or, of course, with 1 vote for, and 125 abstentions in a full house).

cooled, while the colonels who were now in control in Athens, feeling in need of friends, made overtures to the Turks. Makarios swayed with the wind, and thereby became suspect in the eyes of those who were still passionately bent on *enosis* – including George Grivas, now the chief of the officers from Greece who commanded Makarios's 'national guard'.

Grivas felt he must precipitate a new conflict before Makarios could make some real deal with the Turks. He had fresh supplies of arms for his guardsmen brought in by night through the port of Boghaz, north of Famagusta. In November 1967 he found his moment. Rauf Denktash, Kuchuk's chief lieutenant, who had been in Turkey since 1964, was caught trying to enter Cyprus by sea; but Makarios released him after representations from the UN. His release enraged the extremists, and it was in this satisfactorily turbulent atmosphere that Grivas, three days later, chose to launch 2,000 guardsmen against Turkish Cypriot positions at Ayios Theodhoros, south of Nicosia. The fighting spread to other parts of Cyprus. Greece and Turkey massed troops on the border between the two countries. Turkish forces moved to the south coast opposite Cyprus, and Turkish aircraft flew over the island. The Turkish parliament went into secret session and authorised the government to land forces in Cyprus. The Turkish foreign minister, Ihsan Caglayangil, sent Athens a stiff demand for the removal from Cyprus of Grivas and the Greek soldiers who had been secretly introduced into the island since 1964.

The Athens regime made appeasing gestures, but the Turks were not to be easily appeased. Thant sent one of his under-secretaries for special political affairs, José Rolz-Bennett, on an urgent pacificatory mission to the three capitals concerned; President Johnson sent Cyrus Vance (instantly nicknamed Cyprus Vance) on a similar mission. And the Security Council came back to its table in some alarm.

The Council had been called to special meetings on Cyprus several times since 1964, but not in such menacing circumstances as this. It did not, however, match up to the occasion in the first days of the crisis. Thant had reported the Ayios Theodhoros battle to it on November 16, within a few hours of Grivas launching his offensive. The Council did not meet until the 24th. Then, as well as the usual

294

exchange of accusations between Greeks and Turks, the Council had to endure two rambling speeches by Fedorenko in which he seemed mainly concerned to pin the blame for everything on the wretched colonels in Athens (whose anxiety to conciliate Turkey was really the one bright spot in the grim situation). After consultations on the 25th the Council president, Mamadou Kante of Mali, announced a consensus in which the members merely issued a call for restraint to 'all the parties concerned', and left the rest to Thant. (And, of course, to Vance; but they did not refer to him.)

Thant's appeals to Greece and Turkey had specifically included an appeal for the removal from Cyprus of the troops they had illegally sent there. On December 3 they both agreed to withdraw these troops. This was really a purely Greek concession, for Turkey had sent only a few officers and student volunteers to Cyprus, whereas Greece had smuggled into the island whole battalions of its regular army, with a total strength estimated at various times as ranging between 6,000 and 10,000 men. But Greece's face was saved by the pretence of a Turkish withdrawal. The Greek troops began to leave on December 8, and their withdrawal was complete by 16 January 1968. Some 1,000 Greek officers and non-commissioned officers remained, however, with Makarios's Cypriot guards – who were now no longer Grivas's guards, for Grivas was packed off to Athens and kept there under surveillance.

At the 'regular' meeting held in December to renew the life of the UN force the Council authorised only a three-month renewal – with the idea of focusing the antagonists' minds on the need to get down to real negotiations. The meeting was marked by the participation on a Rule 39 basis (page 126) of Osman Örek, who had been defence minister in the Cyprus government from 1960 to 1963 and was now a prominent figure in Vice-President Kuchuk's *de facto* government of the island's Turkish Cypriot areas. A week later, on December 29, Kuchuk announced the formalising of a 'Provisional Cyprus Turkish Administration'. This move, which Kuchuk made after a visit to his headquarters in the Turkish part of Nicosia by an official from the Ankara foreign ministry named Professor Bilge, was little more than eyewash; for he and his colleagues had been effectively administering all the Turkish Cypriot areas since 1964. But it was enough to set off a long series of complaints and counter-complaints from both sides, during which the Council and Thant were informed that Makarios and Kuchuk would have themselves re-elected as president and vice-president in separate elections to be held in February 1968 on their respective sides of the dividing lines; which they duly did.

Thant and Osorio-Tafall pressed on regardless. In March 1968 Makarios's men dismantled their barricades on the dividing lines and thenceforth allowed Turkish Cypriots to pass freely from one side to the other. There was no matching Turkish move, despite Thant's appeals for one; but in April Thant and his representative were successful in persuading the Greek and Turkish Cypriots to agree to start talks at last.

These talks – the first contacts between the two warring leaderships since 1963 – began on May 23 with a private and secret meeting at Osorio-Tafall's house between Rauf Denktash and Glafkos Clerides, the president of the Greek Cypriot assembly. The same two met more openly on June 4, but in Beirut. Only on June 24 was Osorio-Tafall able to get them embarked on a series of meetings in Nicosia, the first being held in the Ledra Palace Hotel adjoining the UN headquarters, while the subsequent meetings took place alternately in the Greek and Turkish sectors of the divided capital.

By 1969 considerable progress had been made both in these talks and in the restoration of stability and even a kind of normalcy in Cyprus. In effect, both sides were now admitting that Galo Plaza's rejected 1965 ideas had been right. The Turks dropped their demands for partition or federation; the Greeks recognised that there could be no *enosis* as long as the Turks opposed it. By September 1969 attitudes had so softened that the president and vice-president of Cyprus could actually meet and shake hands – for the first time in nearly six years – at the conference then held in Nicosia by the World Federation of UN Associations. Meanwhile Unficyp not only kept the peace but also ironed out many little local difficulties, thus permitting buildings to be reoccupied and repaired, derelict land to be cultivated again and irrigation water to flow across dividing lines.

Things looked brighter in the Council too. At one of its 1969 meetings the representative of Turkey, Orhan Eralp, ended his remarks by voicing the hope that the contending parties might yet 'out of this nettle, discord, pluck this flower, safety'. Caradon promptly took up the Shakespearean quotation and, gently reminding the Council of his earlier service as the last British governor of Cyprus, suggested that

> we may say to Mr Clerides and Mr Denktash what the people cried out from the walls of Famagusta as the ship of one of my predecessors, Governor Othello, was sighted:
> 'Bring renewed fire to our extincted spirits,
> And give all Cyprus comfort!'

Unfortunately, as one recalls, Othello fell prey to fear, hatred and suspicion in an old Cypriot tradition, and proceeded to destroy himself and all that he best loved. The signs of sanity and reconciliation returning to Cyprus in 1969 brought out the familiar Iago syndrome. Plots were hatched among ultra-rightists who shared Grivas's views – including some of the Greek officers still commanding the national guard. Acts of violence against officials of Makarios's government were followed in March 1970 by a spectacular attempt on the life of the Cypriot President himself. Mixing the modern with the traditional in his own remarkable manner, he had just taken off by helicopter from his archiepiscopal palace in the old walled city of Nicosia, when shots were fired from a nearby rooftop: the pilot was wounded and Makarios narrowly escaped with his life.

Two weeks earlier General Gerakinis, who had taken command of the national guard, had been recalled to Athens and disciplined after making a speech in which he called for the achievement of *enosis* by force. Two weeks after the attack on Makarios the Turkish government declared that it had discovered a plot by the enotists to overthrow him; and Turkish Nicosia was placed on 'red alert' for several nights. In April George Grivas, still in Athens, broke a long silence by violently accusing Makarios of having 'betrayed the cause of *enosis*' and calling on young Cypriots to fight for that cause in the manner of the EOKA struggle against the British. Meanwhile the Denktash–Clerides talks seemed to have become deeply bogged down; and the pro-*enosis* groups were adding to the tension by their actions in the campaign for the elections that were to be held in July

297

to renew, at long last, the Greek Cypriot part of the assembly originally formed in 1960.

For the UN force in 1970, it still seemed that a policeman's lot was not a happy one. There are, of course, always those who complain that peace-keeping activity limited to 'holding the ring' merely freezes a bad situation and enables the parties to evade responsibility for reaching a real settlement. Action under 'Chapter Six and a Half' of the Charter is particularly vulnerable to his charge. Lacking the enforcement power of Chapter Seven, but drawing the UN in deeper than the mere recommendations that are all that can be made under Chapter Six, these operations expose the UN in general and the Council in particular to many accusations – of both recklessness and pusillanimity, of being both meddlesome and ineffective.

These charges, at least, could be avoided if the UN were to do nothing at all. But it will be recalled how Trygve Lie, at the start of the 1948 Palestine war, reproached the great powers for sitting in the Council and leaving the rival forces to fight it out. Can it be seriously contended that it would be better to leave the Cypriots to kill each other until the neighbour countries are dragged into a wider war? The UN operation in Cyprus is easy to criticise – until you give a little thought to the alternatives.

Many people still seem to need to learn everything the hard way. The argument that, if the force were only taken away, everything would sort itself out, reminds me only too vividly of one of the episodes immortalised by the Marx Brothers. Harpo was leaning against a wall. Groucho asked him sarcastically if he thought he was holding it up. Harpo nodded vigorously. Groucho jeered at him and made him move away. The entire building collapsed.

Chapter Nine

The day before yesterday

Nearly eighteen years after its intense but brief involvement in the first stages of the Korean war, the Security Council was drawn into a Korean problem again in 1968. The *Pueblo*, a small American naval vessel used for monitoring radio communications and similar purposes, was seized by North Korean patrol boats on January 23 and taken into the port of Wonsan. On the 25th the United States asked for an urgent Council meeting to consider this and other recent 'increasingly dangerous and aggressive military actions by North Korean authorities'.

The communist regime in Pyongyang had at this time been stepping up its harassing action against South Korea for more than a year. Its chief, Kim Il Sung, had publicly launched this new aggressive policy in October 1966. During 1967 his forces had attacked South Korean fishing vessels on several occasions, capturing four of them, and had stepped up their hit-and-run raids across the demilitarised zone separating the North from the South, as well as landing infiltration parties on South Korea's coasts. It was assumed that Kim Il Sung wanted, among other things, to warm things up on his 'front' so that he would be restored to Peking's favour (which he had lost by taking Moscow's part in the quarrel between the communist powers), and to reduce South Korea's ability to send troops to fight in Vietnam. In January 1968 he sent a specially trained infiltration commando of thirty-one young officers to Seoul, the southern capital, with orders to kill South Korea's President Park. They were detected on the 21st, and most of them were killed or captured in the running battle that ensued.

The Council met on the 26th in an extremely tense atmosphere. President Johnson was under great public pressure to take immediate

299

forceful action to rescue the *Pueblo* and her crew of eighty-three. He had moved warships to waters near North Korea, called up air force and naval reserves, and launched urgent diplomatic approaches to Moscow and other capitals through which pressure might be brought on Pyongyang to release its prisoners. In approaching the Security Council, the American administration did not expect to obtain a resolution demanding that North Korea should return the ship and her crew. It did not even plan to present such a resolution. Russia would undoubtedly block it, and would thereby be forced to line itself up behind Kim Il Sung more solidly than it was inclined to do. As things stood, although the Sino-Soviet quarrel prevented the Russians from imposing their will on North Korea, they wanted to keep the *Pueblo* affair from escalating. For one thing, they themselves made extensive use of *Pueblo*-type ships for gathering intelligence – though usually theirs were ostensibly fishing vessels. In 1967 three of their ships had been caught violating American waters off Alaska but were released on payment of fines.

Their representative in the Council, Platon Morozov, opposed any acceptance of the American complaint for debate. Echoing the North Koreans' claim that the *Pueblo* had been seized inside their territorial waters, he argued that the Americans had no right to appeal to the UN about it. But the Council voted 12 to 3 (Russia, Hungary, Algeria) to accept the item on its agenda. Arthur Goldberg then presented convincingly detailed evidence, from North Korean as well as American sources, to show that the *Pueblo* had been in international waters when she was captured, that the North Koreans knew this, and that the attack on this virtually unarmed vessel had been a wilfully aggressive action. He reminded Morozov that 'Soviet ships engage in exactly the same activities as the *Pueblo* and sail much closer to the shores of other states. One such Soviet ship . . . currently is not far from South Korean shores.' Goldberg urged the Council to help to secure the prompt return of the *Pueblo* and her crew. But he did not propose a resolution; nor did any other Council member.

Goldberg and Morozov exchanged, at some length, accusations about responsibility for the recent increase in tension in Korea. Next day, Saturday the 27th, George Ignatieff of Canada pointed out

300

that at least it was agreed that this increase in tension was very dangerous. He thought it would be best for Council members to start private consultations, in which it might be arranged to appoint an intermediary or intermediaries to provide 'good offices'. Lij Endalkachew Makonnen of Ethiopia asked the parties to make 'gestures of conciliation and goodwill' that would reduce the risks of the situation. He also suggested that the North Koreans should be invited to present their case to the Council.

The idea of inviting the North Koreans to New York was naturally supported by Morozov, and it was not flatly opposed by Goldberg. But he argued that the *Pueblo* and her crew should first be released. In any case the Pyongyang government, far from welcoming the possibility of an invitation, put out a strong statement in which it refused to have anything to do with any Council decision. It must be remembered that, to the North Korean communists, the UN had not only been 'the enemy' in the 1950–3 war; it was also still 'the other side' in the continuing series of meetings at Panmunjom, on the north–south border line, at which allegations about breaches of the 1953 armistice were regularly exchanged.

Ignatieff's proposal to switch from public Council debate to private consultations was more readily accepted. The Council meeting set for Monday the 29th was cancelled; in fact, the Council never came back into formal session on the *Pueblo* case at all. The weekend saw a lively round of private talks. The Canadians canvassed views on the idea that a special envoy, who might be a representative of a non-aligned state, should go to Korea to seek to obtain the release of the ship and crew and perhaps lend his good offices to other matters in dispute between the two Korean governments. In view of Pyongyang's hostile attitude to any formal dealings with the UN, this envoy need not be officially authorised by the Council, although he would in fact be acting on its behalf. Ignatieff drew attention to an offer of 'such assistance as may be possible' made by the Swedish foreign minister, Torsten Nilsson. Sweden had been appointed in 1953 to the four-nation neutral supervisory commission for Korea, and still maintained at least a formal position there.

It seemed more likely, however, that Pyongyang might accept an Asian or African intermediary. Agha Shahi of Pakistan, the Council president for January, lost no time in calling together the other Asian and African members – Algeria, Ethiopia, India and Senegal. Of these, Algeria and India had direct links with Pyongyang in the shape of embassies there. Then the Afro-Asian members joined the five other non-permanent Council members (Brazil, Canada, Denmark, Hungary and Paraguay) in what developed into a series of meetings. Shahi himself had talks with each of the permanent members. On the evening of Sunday the 28th Morozov and Goldberg had a private talk; and UN connoisseurs of these matters noted with particular interest that it was the Russian who immediately made public the fact that this meeting (which Ignatieff had successfully promoted) had taken place.

On Wednesday the 31st Shahi put to Goldberg and Morozov a proposal, already endorsed by the non-permanent Council members, that the five Asian and African members should jointly act as intermediaries, inviting North Korea to send a delegation to meet them at Geneva. But this suggestion was promptly rejected by the North Koreans. At the same time, however, the secretary of the North Korean communist party, Kim Kwang Hyup, said in Pyongyang that the *Pueblo* case could be discussed at the Panmunjom armistice commission meetings. The Americans at once agreed to this, and the matter was taken up at Panmunjom within the next two days. Consultations continued for a while at the UN, but the focus had now shifted away from New York. The eventual release of the *Pueblo*'s crew in December 1968 followed a series of twenty-eight Panmunjom meetings on the subject.

Recourse to the Security Council in this case had served two purposes. It helped President Johnson to withstand the wave of angry American demands for armed action against North Korea that the seizing of the *Pueblo* immediately evoked. It also enabled the United States to emphasise publicly that it wanted to resolve the matter by diplomatic means, and that its case was reasonable enough for the non-aligned Asian and African states to offer to help – even though at this period there was strong feeling in many of those countries about the American role in the Vietnam war. On the other hand, there was never any prospect of North Korea complying with a Council call for the return of the *Pueblo* and her crew, or of Russia consenting to the Council making such a call; and indeed there was little prospect that nine votes could have been mustered in support of a resolution on those lines. In the circumstances it made sense for the Americans to bring the matter to the Council, but it also made sense for them not to try to push it any further there than they did. The *Pueblo* affair provided an illustration of the fact that, in cases where the Council's proceedings seem to taper off to a quite inconclusive end, this may in reality be a great deal better than the forcing of an apparently dramatic climax which yields no results in actual substance.

*   *   *

As Russian military pressure on Czechoslovakia built up during the summer of 1968, anxiety mounted at the United Nations. The first open portent there came on July 19, one month before the Soviet invasion. At the regular daily press conference held by the Secretary-General's spokesman, the UN correspondent of Ceteka (or CTK), the official Czechoslovak news agency, Karel Kral, put a question prefaced by the remark that it was generally felt that the situation in central Europe was 'serious or even critical'. Kral asked if U Thant thought that the current attitudes and activities of 'certain states' neighbouring on Czechoslovakia were in accordance with the 1965 Assembly resolution on the inadmissibility of intervention in states' domestic affairs. The spokesman replied, as Kral knew he would, that Thant did not wish to make any comment at that time. Milan Klusak, the Czechoslovak permanent representative at the UN, who was on the point of leaving New York to take a post in the foreign ministry in Prague, formally disavowed any responsibility for Kral's action. Klusak talked with Thant several times before he left New York on the 22nd, but on the 23rd Thant's spokesman said that in these talks Klusak had never suggested the existence of a threat to international peace involving his country.

Nevertheless, Kral's question had served to remind many people at the UN that the 1965 resolution had resulted from a Soviet initiative. This had been part of the Russians' curiously crablike technique of obtaining Assembly debates on general principles,

CZECHOSLOVAKIA

during which they could make some propaganda against American actions in Vietnam, while they still insisted that the Vietnam war was none of the UN's business and must not itself be debated. In September 1965 they urged the Assembly to declare that 'armed or any other type of intervention in the domestic affairs of states' must be 'halted forthwith and not permitted in future'. They hailed the resultant resolution as a very important one. In November 1967 Vasily Kuznetsov, initiating another Assembly debate of the same kind, commended the 1965 resolution as a valuable 'guideline' for the conduct of all states. That resolution had condemned not only acts of intervention but also the use of threats of intervention. Now, in 1968, a threat was already ominously apparent in the massive Soviet concentrations of armed forces all along Czechoslovakia's northern border – in East Germany and Poland as well as in Soviet territory; and the act of armed intervention itself was to follow very soon.

During the night of August 20–21 Soviet airborne troops seized Prague while huge Soviet forces poured across the frontier at many points, bringing with them (as distinctly unenthusiastic accomplices in the aggression) East German, Polish, Hungarian and even token Bulgarian military units. Only a few days earlier, at Bratislava, the Soviet leaders and the heads of the East German, Hungarian, Polish and Bulgarian regimes had given solemn assurances of 'respect for sovereignty, national independence and territorial integrity' to the members of Czechoslovakia's communist government. And that government had never indicated any intention of renouncing communism, or even of withdrawing from the Soviet-dominated Warsaw Pact alliance. All it had been trying to do, in response to massive popular demand, was to 'give socialism a human face' by freeing the Czechoslovak people from the familiar tyranny of the political police and permitting some degree of democratic discussion. Now its members were seized by the invaders and subjected to brutal pressures to induce them to legitimise the invasion by declaring that they had invited the Russian army to take over their country.

The Security Council was called into urgent session on Wednesday the 21st at the request of six members – America, Britain, Canada, Denmark, France and Paraguay. Four days of intensely acrimonious debate followed, in which representatives of Czechoslovakia, Bulgaria, Poland and Jugoslavia were permitted to join. The Russians' demand that an East German spokesman should also participate was refused; only Russia and Hungary voted in favour of it. Thant did not speak in the Council. But before it met he had already denounced the Soviet invasion, describing it as striking a 'serious blow to the concepts of international order and morality which form the basis of the Charter', and had urged the Russians to 'exercise the utmost restraint' in their dealings with Czechoslovakia.

For the first two hours of the meeting that began at 6.30 on the evening of the 21st, Yakov Malik struggled to prevent the Council

305

from debating the invasion at all. He kept repeating the claim that the Czechoslovak government had asked the Russians to occupy the country, but the only 'evidence' he could give for this was a handout from Russia's own press agency, Tass, which alleged that the reason was a 'threat emanating from counter-revolutionary forces in collusion with foreign forces hostile to socialism'. Malik could hardly have been vaguer when he tried to explain what this supposed threat amounted to. In the first of a series of rambling filibusters, he spoke at length about Israel, Vietnam and even Bolivia, but cast no light on what he thought was really happening in Czechoslovakia. However, he was more revealing when he pronounced the first version of what was to become known as the 'Brezhnev doctrine'. The events in Czechoslovakia, he claimed, were a matter only for the states of the 'socialist community'.

Malik, who on this occasion resorted to wearing dark glasses at the Council table, gave many observers the clear impression that he was reading out texts which even he could not believe. Caradon offered him the Council's sympathy, 'because it realises his disgust at having to defend such a disgraceful act. No wonder he carried so little conviction.' The British representative pointed out that Malik's justification of the invasion conflicted even with the terms of the Warsaw Pact, which bound its members to settle their disputes without using force. 'When we see what the Soviet Union can do to an ally,' said Caradon, 'we shudder to think what it could do to anyone else.'

George Ball, who had newly succeeded Arthur Goldberg as America's permanent representative at the UN, made very effective use of quotations from official Czechoslovak statements to demolish Malik's claims, which, with characteristic bluntness, he described as 'feeble and futile' and as 'an inept and obvious fraud'. 'The voices that the Soviet leaders heard calling on them to invade were – if they existed at all – the voices of a new breed of quislings.' (Next day Ball was to say, referring to Malik's claim that Russia was giving Czechoslovakia 'fraternal assistance', that this was 'exactly the same kind that Cain gave to Abel'.)

Every Council member except Russia and Hungary voted in favour of debating the invasion. In practice, debate had already begun, for Malik's way of arguing the procedural question had been to open up the one of substance. But now it was permissible for a Czechoslovak representative to address the Council. This was Jan Muzik, a lean young man who, after Klusak's departure, had become acting chief of his country's UN mission. Speaking with intense but controlled emotion, he told the Council that he was carrying out his foreign ministry's explicit instructions. He read out the texts of statements, declaring the invasion illegal and demanding the withdrawal of the Soviet army, that had been issued by the members of his government, the presidium of their Communist Party, the national assembly and President Svoboda. Jan Muzik described the Dubcek government's efforts to 'retain the human rights and liberty which are an integral part of any truly socialist system'. While scrupulously avoiding any direct attack on the Soviet representative's statements, Muzik added: 'I want to convince Ambassador Malik that my government's only aim is to protect the rights of the workers of Czechoslovakia and the security of the socialist camp.'

The Canadian, Danish, Ethiopian and French representatives, and the Brazilian, who was presiding, voiced strong condemnations of the invasion, while the Hungarian, Jozsef Tardos, claimed that it would prove beneficial to the 'commonwealth' of socialist countries. Around midnight the Council broke off, to meet again on the morning of Thursday the 22nd. When it then reassembled, Otto Borch of Denmark presented a draft resolution. The eight sponsors were America, Brazil, Britain, Canada, Denmark, France, Paraguay and Senegal. The draft condemned the invasion, called on Russia and its associates to withdraw their forces at once and stop intervening in Czechoslovakia's internal affairs, and called on other UN members to 'exercise their diplomatic influence' on the invading states to bring about compliance.

Malik continued to read out Tass 'reports' that he had received from Moscow, which claimed that all was calm in Czechoslovakia except for attacks on some Soviet army units by 'counter-revolutionaries', and that 'Czechoslovakia' would not agree to Security Council discussion of the situation. Caradon poured scorn on them, paid tribute to the courage shown by Jan Muzik and by the Czechoslovak leaders, and asked Malik: 'Where are those leaders

307

now?' Let Ambassador Malik tell the Council, said Caradon, that President Svoboda, the Czechoslovak Communist Party's First Secretary, Alexander Dubcek, and other 'acknowledged leaders' of the Czechoslovak people, were free and safe, that they 'will not be arrested and will not be molested', and would be allowed to go on speaking and working for their people. Malik's only response was to talk of 'the repulsive comedy' in which, he complained, 'a representative of the American monopolies and a British lord pose as defenders of socialism'. George Ball replied that what he was defending was freedom. He noted that Malik had claimed that the Soviet invasion was opposed and deplored only by imperialists. These included, he pointed out, such 'imperialists' as the prime minister of India, the presidents of Jugoslavia, Rumania and Tanzania, the Pope and the leaders of the French and Italian Communist Parties.

It became clear, as this second day of debate grew longer and longer, that the Russians, who were making desperate efforts in Prague to put together something that would look like a new Czechoslovak government and yet be a docile instrument, were trying equally hard to stall the proceedings in New York until they could produce in the Council some new evidence in their favour: something less ludicrous than the alleged 'appeal' from an anonymous Czech source which Malik had already read out, and which Ball had derided as 'a document in search of authors'. Malik and Tardos embarked on an evident filibustering tactic, with the aid of the guest speakers from Poland and Bulgaria, Leszek Kasprzyk and Milko Tarabanov, exploiting points of order and the customary 'right of reply' to the full. Their hopes had seemed to rise when Jan Muzik did not appear in the Council chamber on the Thursday morning. The Hungarian openly voiced his expectation that this meant that, when Muzik or another Czechoslovak representative did appear, he would prove to have been given new instructions. But this hope was quickly dashed. Later in the day Muzik took his place, crisply restated his government's demand for the immediate withdrawal of the occupying armies, and told the Council that his foreign minister, Jiri Hajek, was on his way to New York to take part in the proceedings. (Hajek had been in Jugoslavia when the invasion came, and had thus escaped the fate of other members of his government.)

Hammarskjöld in the Council shortly before his death

Thant at the table with, behind him, General Rikhye (page 192) and
Ralph Bunche (page 199)

Foreign Ministers at the table in 1956: from left, Shepilov, Selwyn Lloyd, Dulles and Fawzi (page 366)

Left to right, Pineau, Selwyn Lloyd and Dulles at the 1956 meetings

In succession, the Senegalese representative, Ibrahima Boye, George Ball, George Ignatieff of Canada and Caradon called for a vote on the draft resolution without further procrastination. Ball called the Soviet delaying tactics 'shameless, shoddy and desperate', and warned that the Hungarian's words indicated that 'an *ersatz* government of political hacks' was at last being put together in Prague. He said he would not even be surprised if Malik's filibustering led him 'to read us excerpts from the Moscow telephone directory', where he might indeed 'find the names of those who will be in the new Czechoslovak government'.

The Russians got some help from Tewfik Bouattoura of Algeria, who thought the Council should adjourn for private consultations, since things were changing so rapidly in Prague. Ignatieff thought this was precisely the reason why the Council should vote without delay. Caradon said doughtily that he, for one, was prepared to stay at the meeting until the vote was taken. He had to stay through long hours of the night, while Malik dredged up various scraps of unimpressive 'evidence' of sinister western intentions towards Czechoslovakia. Some time after midnight Malik even claimed that American arms had been brought into Czechoslovakia from Germany, to be used 'to bring back the old order'. (Much more was to be heard of this tale before it was finally exploded.)

At three o'clock in the morning of Friday, August 23, the founts of Russian, Hungarian and Bulgarian eloquence ran dry, and the Council voted. Ten of the fifteen members – America, Brazil, Britain, Canada, China, Denmark, Ethiopia, France, Paraguay and Senegal – backed the draft resolution. Only Russia and Hungary voted against it, but the Soviet vote constituted a veto – Russia's 105th. Pakistan's Mohammad Yunus abstained, saying that he had received no instructions from his government. India's Parthasarathi abstained, saying that he could not vote for condemning the invasion, although he supported the demand for withdrawal. (The underlying Indian motive was evidently to avoid any loss of Russian goodwill that would work to the favour of Pakistan in the two neighbours' continuing quarrel.) The Algerian, like the Indian, insisted that the invaders should withdraw; but he abstained on the ground that the resolution was a propagandist move, and supported this argument

309

with a singularly confused attempt to attribute the invasion to events in the Middle East.

There had never, of course, been any doubt that Russia would use its veto. The eight sponsors of the resolution had not expected it to do anything else. Their concern had been to place on record as clear an expression as possible of the majority's view of the invasion. They were ready now – even at 3 a.m. – with a further move to keep up the momentum. On behalf of all eight, George Ignatieff at once introduced a second draft resolution. In this, the Council would ask Thant to send immediately to Prague a special representative 'who shall seek the release and ensure the personal safety of the Czechoslovak leaders under detention'. Malik described this as 'a new trick' and an attempt to drag the Secretary-General into 'the dirty business of intervening in the affairs of a socialist state'. He indicated that he would use the veto again if the new draft came to a vote. And he then kept the weary Council at its table until 4 a.m., partly by delivering an uncompromising defence of the veto power in general. 'The veto,' he said, 'will continue to afford, as long as the United Nations exists, the possibility for the Soviet Union to defend a just cause.' He then developed at some length the not too relevant argument that the United States was seeking to subjugate Asia, Africa and Latin America.

The Council's president for August, João Augusto de Araujo Castro of Brazil, adjourned it until the afternoon of the same day, Friday the 23rd. When debate was resumed at 6.30 p.m., Malik and Tardos launched their expected attacks on the draft that Ignatieff had presented, but, perhaps because of loss of sleep, perhaps because of the unreality of the case they had to argue, they got out of step. While the Russian denounced the Canadian's move as a 'repugnant' attempt to violate the Charter, the Hungarian accepted Ignatieff's argument that it was, above all, a humanitarian proposal; Tardos therefore claimed that it should be transferred from the Council to one of the UN bodies concerned with humanitarian questions.

Armand Bérard of France, who had previously taken little part in the debate, strongly backed the Canadian, pointing out that world opinion was deeply disturbed about the fate of Dubcek and the other Czechoslovak leaders, about whom Malik still found nothing to say to the Council. Caradon again pressed the Russian for news of them. The aim of the new draft, he said, was to get answers to the questions that Malik had refused to answer. The draft's sponsors were putting a simple question and hoped for a straight reply; but all they got was insult and a show of contempt both for themselves and for the democratic process. Malik interrupted himself in the middle of another long stalling speech, in which he incidentally dwelt on the 'crimes of Cuban reactionaries in the United States', and priced the cost of 'the four years of the Second World War' to Russia at 1·89 billion roubles, to provide one crumb of apparent information: some of the Czechoslovak ministers, he said, had gone to Moscow with their president to 'negotiate'. George Ball, noting press reports about such negotiations, said that if this meant the Russians were having second thoughts and the Czechoslovaks could regain their freedom, the Council should do nothing to interfere; but it must still, as things stood, remain concerned about the missing men.

A forceful statement came at the end of Friday evening from Jugoslavia, a non-member of the Council represented by Anton Vratusa. He said that the government headed by President Tito saw the invasion as a gross violation not only of Czechoslovak sovereignty and territorial integrity but also of the UN Charter, and as an act that threatened world peace and the independence of other states too. Jugoslavia fully supported the demand for an immediate withdrawal that had been made by Czechoslovakia's legitimate representatives. 'No socialist principle whatsoever' could be used to justify the occupation.

On Saturday the 24th the Council witnessed an even more desperate Soviet blocking operation than the previous three days had seen. Jiri Hajek, the Czechoslovak foreign minister, had arrived and was waiting to address the Saturday meeting. Malik evidently still clung to the hope that the captive Czechoslovak government could be compelled to send orders to Hajek forbidding him to state its case. So he presented a demand that the East German regime should be allowed to join in the Council's debate. It took three hours to beat this off. During the procedural wrangling the Ulbricht regime's pretensions were rebuffed with particular indignation; this was, indeed, hardly the most tactful moment the Russians could have chosen to advance them. To hear 'the person who asked to be heard', said Caradon, would merely cause delay and confusion, which was doubtless the purpose of the request. Ball said that the East German representative would simply be 'a proxy for the Soviet government', which was attempting a diversionary manoeuvre. Borch of Denmark clinched the matter with the biting comment that 'participation in an invasion does not confer the right to a passport for the United Nations'. The Soviet proposal was rejected by nine votes to two.

Jiri Hajek was at last able to address the Council; and it was noticed that while he spoke Malik kept his face averted. Hajek minced no words, but he spoke, as he himself said, 'with sadness, but without hostility' towards the five states which had occupied his country on the night of August 20–21 despite all their many pledges of goodwill and respect, most recently reaffirmed at Bratislava on August 9. No Czechoslovak constitutional organ, he said, had ever asked the Russians and their associates to occupy the country. The occupation could not be justified by claims that Czechoslovakia was not fulfilling its Warsaw Pact obligations, for it was doing so conscientiously; and even the five occupiers did not claim that the country had been in danger of aggression from elsewhere. Far from there having been any danger of counter-revolution, the course which the Czechoslovak Communist Party had set since January 1968, under the new leadership of Dubcek and others, had won it a genuine popular authority such as had not existed before. The presidents of socialist Jugoslavia and Rumania had visited the country in the week before the occupation and had attested to the truth of its socialist regeneration.

If anything seriously endangered the socialist cause in his country, said Hajek, it was the insensitive and illegal actions of the occupiers. The Czechoslovaks' natural feelings of friendship towards the peoples of the five occupying states had been deeply hurt and gravely damaged – whereas they greatly appreciated the Jugoslavs' and Rumanians' help and understanding. The occupiers were responsible for acts that could have fatal effects on world peace. His government demanded that the foreign troops must leave Czechoslovakia without delay; its full sovereignty must be restored – only on this basis would it be possible to heal the deep wounds and restore friendly relations.

The Czechoslovak people and government hoped that the occupiers, seeing their unity in the face of the occupation, would 'grasp the enormity' of their mistake, and correct it. They hoped President Svoboda's negotiations in Moscow would contribute to this end.

The end of the Council's formal proceedings came quickly after Hajek's historic speech. Agha Shahi, who had now taken Pakistan's seat, made its first and only statement on the occupation, in which he called for a speedy withdrawal. Malik read out some more bits from Tass and *Izvestia*, but made no reference to Hajek at all. (This omission was, correctly, seen as indicating that the Russians had still made no headway towards shaping up a 'stooge' government; if they had, Malik would have been able to respond to Hajek's damning revelations by branding him as an ousted counter-revolutionary.)

The meeting of the 24th was then adjourned on the understanding that there might or might not be another one on Monday the 26th. But when that Monday morning came, Araujo Castro announced the cancellation of the next meeting, while Hajek and Muzik let it be known that, as long as there was hope of progress at the Moscow talks, they did not want any more public debate in the Council. The western states' representatives took the same line.

On Tuesday the 27th Hajek talked with Araujo Castro, with Thant and with the Rumanian foreign minister, Corneliu Manescu, who had just arrived in New York – ostensibly in his capacity as outgoing president of the UN Assembly (which, however, was not due to start its new session for another four weeks). In the evening Araujo Castro received a letter from the Czechoslovak UN mission, signed by Muzik, asking that the Council should remove the question of Czechoslovakia from its agenda in view of the fact that 'substantial agreement' had now been reached at the talks in Moscow. Lively consultation between members ensued. It emerged that the request for removal was one of the points on which the Russians had insisted at the Moscow talks. The Council was in no way bound by the request. Czechoslovakia had not even initiated the debate. Even if it had done so, the decision whether to take the item off the agenda rested not with the initiator but with the Council members as a whole. Any such procedural move would require the support of at least nine of the fifteen.

In practice, the public debate was simply allowed to lapse. The item was not removed from the Council's agenda. This at least kept the Russians aware that another storm in the Council might be set off if they resorted to new violence against their victims. It may fairly be argued that they might have summarily disposed of Dubcek and his closest colleagues, whom they had treated with contemptuous brutality immediately after the invasion, if there had not been first the Council's painfully revealing debate and then the uncomfortable possibility that it might at any moment spring to life again. The Council's practice of breaking off an unfinished debate (in this case no vote had been taken on the proposal about seeking the captive leaders' release), yet leaving the unfinished item on the agenda, sometimes for very long periods, has an untidy and illogical look; but it can sometimes serve a thoroughly practical purpose.

Just three weeks after the invasion, on September 11, the Security Council met on quite different business, which should have been merely brief and formal. The fifteenth African state to emerge from British rule, Swaziland, was being unanimously recommended for admission to the UN by the Assembly. Caradon could not resist the opportunity to say: 'I like to reflect, and to remind my Soviet colleague, that my country has done more to end imperialism than any other country in the history of the world.' Malik rose like a fish to the bait, insisting that it was Russia that had done the most to this end, and, in reference to Britain, adding that: 'The one who has taken the most from others has to do the most to return it.' The British representative promptly took him up, saying: 'These words will be heard with happiness in Czechoslovakia.'

George Ball noted that Malik had spoken of 'the downfall of the imperialists', and suggested that the Soviet government would be wise to 'take his own dark prophecy very much to heart'. Malik protested that the British and American representatives were raising 'a question that has absolutely nothing to do with the matter under discussion, or for that matter with the United Nations'. The Czechoslovak question, he repeated, was entirely the affair of the socialist states. To Ball, he said bluntly: 'Don't stick your nose into other people's affairs.' And he went on:

Any further attempt to drag this organisation into a discussion of such a problem will only deal a grievous blow to its authority and prevent its normal operation.

This was taken by many people as a threat that the Russians would seek to disrupt the UN's 'normal operation', perhaps by reverting to their old boycotting tactics, if the question of Czechoslovakia was raised again either in the Council or at the next session of the Assembly, which was due to open in two weeks' time on September 24.

The prickly Soviet reaction to the rather slight affair in the Council on the 11th certainly showed how sensitive Moscow was about the training of the UN spotlight on events in Prague. This tended to confirm the feeling among the western countries' UN representatives that the Council's four-day session in August had been a worthwhile effort, despite the Russians' predictable refusal to let any resolutions go through or to accept any UN authority in the matter. Apart from the two communist 'occupier' members themselves, every Council member, including all five of the Asian and African states, had publicly called on the occupying powers to withdraw their forces. Jiri Hajek's address to the Council had not just been a moving occasion; it had also, while completely destroying the Russians' argument, held the door to negotiation open for them if they wished to moderate their position. What the Council could do for the unhappy Czechoslovaks, it had done. It had helped to illuminate both the reality behind the Russians' veils of illusion and the extent to which world opinion had been outraged by the invasion. Its proceedings had certainly not made things worse for the Czechoslovaks, and might have done something to inhibit Soviet ruthlessness.

The Russians' discomfort at finding themselves so prominently pilloried was also reflected in their continuing search for distractions. One of these took the shape of an attempt to revive a hoary claim that the UN Charter entitled Russia to intervene in West German affairs. Soviet propaganda had been doing its best (not a very good best) to justify the invasion by allegations that Czechoslovakia was in some vague way threatened by German 'militarism and Nazism'. In July, while the Soviet pressure on the Czechoslovaks was building up,

Moscow had advanced its claim about the Charter in a note to Bonn. In September the theme was given much more prominence in articles in *Pravda* and *Izvestia* and broadcasts from Moscow.

The Soviet claim referred to Articles 53 and 107 of the Charter. Article 107, under the heading 'Transitional security arrangements', says that:

> Nothing in the present Charter shall invalidate or preclude action, in relation to any state which during the second world war has been an enemy of any signatory to the present Charter, taken or authorised as a result of that war by the governments having responsibility for such action.

Article 53 forbids regional agencies to take any enforcement action without Security Council approval, but 'with the exception of measures against any enemy state . . . provided for pursuant to Article 107 or in regional arrangements directed against renewal of aggressive policy on the part of any such state. . . .'

The Soviet press and radio insisted that these Charter articles were still fully valid and that, in accordance with them and with the 1945 Potsdam agreement, 'the Soviet Union is still ready to take, if necessary, effective steps together with other peace-loving states to halt the dangerous activity of neo-Nazism and militarism' in West Germany. This was a notable bit of bogey-raising. It evoked a chorus of crisp retorts from all three of the western allies which, with Russia, had occupied Germany in 1945 and were 'the governments having responsibility' for post-war transitional security action in regard to the defeated Axis powers.

In Washington the State Department's spokesman declared that Articles 53 and 107 gave neither Russia nor any other Warsaw Pact members any right to intervene by force in West Germany's affairs. He also took the opportunity to remind the Russians that it was their own East German protégés whose military activities had contributed to the latest alarms. While the West Germans threatened nobody, the East Germans had actually invaded Czechoslovakia. In Paris the Quai d'Orsay spokesman said that to interpret the articles as giving 'certain countries the right to intervene unilaterally by force in the Federal Republic of Germany, without Security Council agreement' was 'misleading and incorrect' in both letter and spirit. In London the Foreign Office spokesman called the articles 'irrelevant'.

It was widely held that Charter articles that lent themselves to such dangerous misinterpretation would be better deleted. However, since Russia would obviously veto any amendment that removed them from the Charter, no move was made in that direction. The official statements by western spokesmen, denying that the Charter gave Russia any such right as it claimed, were accompanied by commentaries emphasising that the 'enemy states' articles were in any case quite obsolete. They had indeed become meaningless as soon as such states as Finland, Hungary, Italy, Japan and Rumania joined the UN. From then on, the key words 'any state which during the Second World War has been an enemy of any signatory to the present Charter' could be applied to every country that had fought in the war, on either side.

Soon after the opening of the Assembly session on September 24 it became clear that there would not be a special debate there on Czechoslovakia. Originally, eagerness for such a debate had been particularly shown by Jugoslavia and Rumania, which feared that they might be the next victims of a Soviet campaign to impose a newly tightened discipline on the whole of eastern Europe. As their immediate fears subsided, they swung over to the argument that a special Assembly debate would only reduce the chances that Russia might show more restraint. The Czechoslovak delegates to the Assembly, while reiterating that the occupiers must withdraw, asked other member states not to prejudice the prospects of further agreement with Russia by giving the Czechoslovak question prominence during the session.

This, however, did not prevent many members from taking opportunities to condemn the invasion and demand a withdrawal, either in their speeches in the Assembly's general debate or on other occasions. Trenchant criticisms came not only from the Americans and their west European allies but also from numerous other states ranging from Sweden to Ceylon and Tanzania. And the sharpest words of all were used by Halim Budo of Albania, who denounced 'the armed aggression against Czechoslovakia, an act of banditry of the fascist type'. One notable silence interrupted the series of protests. The

317

Spanish foreign minister, Fernando Castiella, contrived to make no mention of Czechoslovakia at all. It was universally recognised that he was in dire need of Russian support both for his campaign against Gibraltar and for Spain's ambition of winning a seat on the Security Council for 1969–70. In the latter respect he was successful.

*   *   *

On 12 August 1969 Northern Ireland witnessed its most serious outbreak of violence for many years. On August 20 the Security Council met to take up a request from the Irish government that a UN peace-keeping force should be sent to the area. This was the first time that the historic 'Irish question' was broached by any United Nations organ.

The partitioning of Ireland in 1921 had amounted, in constitutional terms, to a partitioning of the United Kingdom (of Great Britain and Ireland, until then). The 1921 treaty, which ended three years of virtual civil war, created an Irish Free State on the territory that is now the Republic of Ireland. It also created a new border in Ireland, dividing that territory from Northern Ireland, which remained within the United Kingdom (of Great Britain and Northern Ireland, thenceforth). This partition was an acknowledgment of the fact that a million Protestants in Belfast and the surrounding northeastern counties were determined to resist being transferred to the control of the new Catholic-dominated Irish government in Dublin.

The conflict between Ireland's Catholic majority and Protestant minority has been in fact not so much a quarrel over religious doctrine as an old struggle for economic and political ascendancy, in which the confessional division has served to harden the line between the two contending groups. During the centuries of British rule successive waves of English and Scottish colonists were 'planted' in Ireland, particularly in the northeast, where many of the settlers were Scottish Presbyterians, and where they formed a local majority. While earlier colonising groups had been absorbed into the Irish Catholic community, the Protestants of the northern province of Ulster remained a people apart. Their separateness was intensified by the 1688–90 war – an English civil war mainly fought out in Ireland.

318

IRELAND

The Catholics followed James II to defeat. The Protestants fought for the victorious William III (who, however, was backed and even financed by the Pope – because France was sponsoring James).

Although the eighteenth century saw some closing of Irish ranks in common cause against England, few Protestants joined in the eventual struggle that brought about the creation of an independent Irish government fifty years ago. The Ulster Protestants rejected all idea of Irish 'home rule', organised a Unionist party (forming part of the British Conservative party) and maintained their morale and discipline through semi-masonic Orange lodges. These were named

319

after William III, Prince of Orange, whose victories were ritually recalled in the Orangemen's parades, though one could not say that his memory was kept evergreen, for the Irish green was the colour of the opposing faction.

The 1921 partition left only a small Protestant minority in the Free State; but in the Northern Ireland that was formed out of six counties of Ulster and retained within the United Kingdom, a third of the population was Catholic. No line could possibly have been drawn so as to separate the two communities entirely. A quarter of the population of Belfast itself is Catholic, and elsewhere in the north-east 'Prods' and 'Micks' are intricately intermingled. But Catholics are numerically predominant in the western half of Northern Ireland, in the counties of Fermanagh, Tyrone and Londonderry, whose inclusion in Northern Ireland in 1921 reflected the Protestants' political and economic, rather than demographic, domination of these areas. A particularly contentious issue was the inclusion in Northern Ireland of the little city of Londonderry (population 65,000). Two-thirds of Derry's inhabitants are Catholic, but the Unionists kept control of its city council by ingeniously gerrymandering the electoral boundaries, and maintained a historic mystique derived from this Protestant stronghold's success in withstanding siege by James II's army in 1689.

The Unionists' demand had been simply to remain within the United Kingdom. While they secured this in 1921, the British government also endowed Northern Ireland with a parliament and government of its own, sited at Stormont on the outskirts of Belfast. The British motive for taking this unprecedented step to provincial devolution of political power, which introduced a federal element into the otherwise unitary British system, was a wish to get the 'Irish question' out of the Westminster parliament, which had so long been bedevilled by it; and, perhaps, to keep ajar the door to an eventual reunification of Ireland. The effect, however, was to give the Ulster Unionists unchallenged control of the province. The Westminster parliament's ultimate authority to intervene in Northern Irish affairs was unused for nearly fifty years.

To the beat of the Orangemen's big Lambeg drums, the Protestants rallied in each Stormont election campaign to give the

320

Unionist party victory not only over the Catholic-backed Irish Nationalists but also over the local Labour party, which had similarly incurred the taint of 'disloyalty' by having too much truck with Dublin. The Unionists' simple 'no surrender' appeal to communal loyalty was strengthened by the alarm and anger caused in Ulster by recurrent cross-border raiding campaigns (the last ended in 1962) by intransigently violent elements in the republic such as the 'Irish Republican Army' (IRA).

Legally, there was no discrimination against Catholics in Northern Ireland as such. Elections to Stormont as well as to Westminster were played straight. And the Catholics' meagre representation in government service and, particularly, in the Ulster police force was in large part the result of their own reluctance to serve a permanently Unionist government. But they had plenty of legitimate grievances. The Protestants, descendants of colonists who had taken the best farming land away from the native Irish, now controlled not only the modern economy but also the Stormont and (almost everywhere) the local governments, and used this power to maintain their ascendancy and relative prosperity. Unemployment, nearly always heavier in Northern Ireland than in any other part of the United Kingdom, was particularly heavy among Catholics. In the public as well as the private sector they could seldom expect promotion. Discrimination was particularly obvious in the allocation of public housing by local councils, and in the gerrymandering of local election boundaries to keep as many of these councils as possible in Unionist hands. On the other hand, in education generous state subsidies were paid to the separate schools which the Catholics insisted on maintaining. Thus this most liberal aspect of Northern Ireland's treatment of its minority had the unhappy effect of helping to reinforce the communal division, for nowhere below the university level did the children of the two communities study and play together.

In 1963 the Unionists acquired in Captain Terence O'Neill (now Lord O'Neill) a new leader who eventually proved too enlightened for them and was ousted from the premiership early in 1969. But during his years in office the Stormont government began to try to catch up with the modern world and break out of the straitjacket of communal politics in which it had encased itself for forty years. In

321

the teeth of furious protests from many other Unionists, and from the extremist faction led by Ian Paisley, the founder of an exceptionally bigoted breakaway presbyterian church, O'Neill joined hands with the prime minister of the republic in initiating a series of Belfast–Dublin talks on co-operation of a very practical kind. (In reality, there has never been any complete severance between the republic and Northern Ireland, or between the republic and Britain, in commercial, financial, ecclesiastical and many other matters. But much progress towards sensible co-operation had been slowed by the Dublin and Belfast politicians' reluctance to be seen even meeting together.)

O'Neill ousted Londonderry's entrenched Unionist council, and put the contested city in the hands of a fairly balanced and non-party development commission. He announced plans to enforce fair allocation of housing, to stop local councils from gerrymandering boundaries and to have these councils, for the first time, elected on a 'one man, one vote' basis. O'Neill attacked the Orange order's more pernicious political activities, made personal and public gestures of goodwill towards the Catholics and in effect invited them to back him with their votes against his own Unionist party's intransigent elements.

This last appeal came too late. In the Stormont elections that O'Neill called at the beginning of 1969 few Catholics rallied to his support, and so many anti-O'Neill Unionists won seats that he was forced out of the premiership soon afterwards. The tension that had shown itself in a number of street conflicts in 1968, but had abated while discontented Catholics watched to see if O'Neill would succeed in his final bid to reform his own party, was now revived. It was foreseeable that there would be a particular risk of trouble in Londonderry in August if the Orangemen were allowed to stage once again, in this mainly Catholic town, their annual parade celebrating the raising of the siege of 1689. But O'Neill's successor as prime minister of Northern Ireland, Major James Chichester-Clark, let the Orangemen go ahead with what, in the circumstances, was an invitation to violence.

The fighting that duly broke out in Derry during the August 12 parade developed into a three-day battle between the police and the people of the Catholic Bogside sector of the city, lying just below its ancient walls. Guns were not used, but the Bogsiders threw petrol bombs ('Throw well, throw Shell' was their exultant slogan), the police used CS tear gas with a partisan excess of enthusiasm, and both sides threw all the stones they could lay their hands on. At the end of the third day British troops were sent in and a truce was made. The soldiers were welcomed by the Catholic rioters, who saw their intervention as marking the defeat of the police – and particularly of the hated 'B' special police reserve, a wholly Protestant force, originally raised and armed for use against raiders of the IRA type, which (much like the IRA) had an unsavoury reputation for ill-disciplined partisan violence.

But communal fighting on a bigger scale now developed in Belfast, where guns were used, whole streets were burnt out, casualties were heavy and a much larger military force had to be brought in to restore order. Again the soldiers were made welcome by the inhabitants of the city's Catholic areas, who in this case felt that the police had not protected them against attacks by Protestants bent on driving them from their homes. On August 19, with the army in control of both battered cities, the British and Northern Ireland prime ministers, Wilson and Chichester-Clark, agreed that the control of the province's police should be transferred from its government to the British army commander in Northern Ireland, General Sir Ian Freeland; that the 8,000 'B' specials should be kept away from areas of potential conflict; that the regular police should be reorganised; and that senior civil servants from London would go to Belfast to help ensure that reforms already promised by the Stormont government would be implemented.

This was the background to the Security Council meeting on August 20. An urgent meeting had been requested by the government of the Republic of Ireland in a letter sent on the 17th. The Dublin government, very fortunately, was at this moment in quite a strong domestic position. Under Jack Lynch's leadership, the ruling Fianna Fail party had not merely maintained itself in office in the general elections held two months earlier but had won 75 seats in a Dail of 144, gaining a little ground at the expense of the opposition Fine Gael and Labour parties, which had failed to combine against it. A weaker government might easily have been forced into making unwise moves by the naturally intense reaction of the republic's Catholic population to the sight of their fellows in the North undergoing such ordeals.

Although in practice all responsible republican politicians (and even the leaders of the vestigial Sinn Fein group) had renounced the idea of bringing about the reunification of Ireland by force, the question of the North remained powerful 'mood music' in Irish politics. And by tradition Fianna Fail, the party formerly led by the now 88-year-old President Eamonn De Valera, is the particular heir to the insistence on all-Irish unity that led him in 1921 to reject the treaty with Britain and plunge Ireland into a second civil war, this time between the 'Free Staters' who accepted the treaty and the purist republicans who rejected it. So Lynch had to resist demands from powerful elements inside his own party for a more forceful reaction to the events in the North.

In principle, the Fianna Fail leaders had never accepted the British government's right to exercise any jurisdiction over Northern Ireland (although, in practice, Lynch and his predecessor as prime minister, Sean Lemass, had repeatedly asked British governments to exercise their authority there a bit more, for the benefit of the Catholic minority). In principle, they denied the United Kingdom's right to station its troops in this part of the British Isles, let alone to use these troops to maintain order there (although, in practice, the Dublin government was as relieved when the British army went into Belfast and Derry in 1969 as were those cities' Catholic communities). On August 13 Lynch declared in a broadcast that it was clear that the Stormont government's police were no longer either able to maintain order or accepted as an impartial force, but that the use of British troops in the North was not acceptable. He asked the British government to request the United Nations to send an international peace-keeping force to Northern Ireland.

The idea of a UN force had a certain appeal to the Irish, who are legitimately proud of the sizeable contribution their republic of barely three million people has made to the organisation's peace-keeping work. (There is an Irish contingent in Cyprus today.) Lynch's proposal also enabled him to mobilise his small army's equally small first-line reserves, a move that helped to satisfy the public demand for some sort of loin-girding action, without conjuring up the absurd idea that the republic was going to war with its big neighbour; for he could say that the purpose of this preparedness was merely to equip Ireland for participation in any peace-keeping operation that might be agreed. He moved a few troops up to the border, where refugee camps and field hospitals were set up to receive Northern Catholics who had been driven from their homes or, being injured in the fighting, would not go to Northern hospitals for fear of coming into the hands of the police. Apart from these humanitarian purposes, the military reinforcing of the border mainly served to make it more difficult for IRA-type hotheads to slip across from the republic and exacerbate the North's troubles.

As Jack Lynch had doubtless foreseen, the British government promptly rejected the idea that it should ask for a UN force. (As the subsequent months went by without any sign of Britain being able to extricate its troops from the costly and wearisome job of keeping Northern Ireland's peace, some people in London and elsewhere came to suspect that it would have been a very good bargain for Britain if the UN had been induced to provide a force. But no such rational move was politically possible.) Keeping the ball in the air, Lynch then suggested that, if the British wanted the UN kept out of it, a joint British and Irish peace-keeping force should be constituted. Neither to his surprise nor to anybody else's, this, too, was rejected by the government in London.

The Dublin government now felt that it had sufficiently respected the Charter obligation, under Article 33, for states to try to resolve disputes by 'peaceful means of their own choice' before approaching the Security Council. On August 17 it asked for a Council meeting, announcing that it felt obliged to appeal to the Council to send a UN peace-keeping force to 'the Six Counties of Northern Ireland'. In view of the Irish people's feelings, it said, it could not stand by and watch Irish men, women and children suffer injury or worse in the six counties. 'Serious disturbances in our own state' might arise out of the events in the North, which had produced tension along the border that 'separates part of Ireland from the area of our present effective jurisdiction'.

The use of such mood-music phrases, which had been notably absent from Dublin's diplomatic language for years, was meant to blunt the obvious British objection that the United Nations had no right to concern itself with a wholly domestic United Kingdom problem. Since Ireland joined the UN in 1955, it had been often remarked how differently its spokesmen there behaved from those who had represented Ireland in the only international political forum previously available to its government, the Council of Europe. At Strasbourg the Irish had said their bit about the injustice of partition, and the Dublin government's aspiration to extend 'the area of our present effective jurisdiction' to embrace the whole island, so often that even sympathetic delegates were bored to tears. In New York they kept quiet about it, and got on with the job of making Ireland a respected source of constructive international initiatives.

Frank Aiken, the republic's foreign minister from 1957 to 1969, presided over this impressive performance and became personally identified with such elements in it as the 1961 Assembly's 'Irish resolution' from which the 1968 nuclear non-proliferation treaty eventually derived. Aiken, the Lynch government's 'grand old man', relinquished the foreign ministry after the June 1969 elections to a younger man, inexperienced in diplomacy, Patrick Hillery. When Hillery appeared in New York in August some UN veterans wondered whether the new man's arrival meant a reversion to the old policy of tireless, emotional evocation of Ireland's historic wrongs – with matching British counterpoint.

But it did not come out that way. The welling up of violence and passion in Northern Ireland brought the Security Council one of the most intelligently conducted confrontations in its record. Pat Hillery, who as a newly installed foreign minister was undergoing a gruelling baptism of fire, kept his cool. He had already met two personal rebuffs from British ministers. When he went to London before the outbreak they rejected his plea that the Derry parade should be banned. When he went there again they turned down his request for Britain to open talks with his government in view of the new situation created by the intervention of British troops. But in New York Hillery got together with Caradon for a quiet talk in which he and the British representative evidently found that, while their positions could hardly be reconciled, they could trust each other to play their parts in the Council with dignity and what may be termed style.

Caradon opened the Council's public proceedings by arguing that it must not accept the proposed item for its agenda, since Northern Ireland was an integral part of the United Kingdom, whose government was restoring order there and did not want any UN intervention. Any such intervention against its wishes would be in violation of the Charter's Article 2(7), which bars the UN from intervening in 'matters which are essentially within the domestic jurisdiction of any state'. Council members should therefore confine their speeches to the procedural question. But Caradon accepted a proposal by Max Jakobson of Finland that, as a matter of courtesy, the Council should invite the Irish foreign minister to address it before it took any decision about its agenda. This, Jakobson pointed out, need neither prejudge the question nor create a precedent.

Hillery then made what Caradon later acknowledged to have been a restrained statement. He briefly restated the historic objective of Irish unity, but he also argued that if the Council members accepted the agenda item they would not be merely taking sides in a territorial dispute; for the denial of civil rights to the six counties' Catholics was also involved, as was, too, the risk of friction between Britain and Ireland. Hillery held that British troops had been accepted in Belfast and Derry only as 'the lesser of two evils', for their mere presence in Northern Ireland was 'a basic factor in the perpetuation of partition'. In replying, Caradon departed smoothly from his own declared intention of sticking to the procedural question, and, as well as cataloguing the reforms now 'under way' in Northern Ireland, he made the point that whatever the republic's constitution contained about Irish unity in theory, its political leaders had long recognised partition in fact; while the present agitation for civil rights in the North was not focused on Irish reunification, but on reform within the United Kingdom framework.

The Zambian representative, Lishomwa Sheba Muuka, then formally proposed that the Council should simply adjourn; and it did. More than a year later, the Council had not recurred to the Northern Ireland situation; nor was any debate on it staged at the 1969 Assembly. Caradon, on August 20, had said that he agreed to the adjournment on the understanding that the Council did not in fact wish to accept and consider the agenda item proposed by Ireland; and his understanding was well substantiated by the Council's subsequent inaction.

A superficial judgment might well be that the whole August 20 affair was a solemn farce. Hillery knew that the Council's members were far too sensitive about Article 2(7) to show any enthusiasm for plunging into a substantive debate, whatever the attractions for some of them in any opportunity to pull the British lion's much-tweaked tail. Why, then, appeal to the Council at all?

A second look at the situation is enough to show that in this case the 'defusing' potential of an airing in the Council was exploited with unusual deftness. The Irish government, at home, faced a general demand that it should do something, and a specific demand that it should take the matter to the United Nations. Its action enabled it to claim that it had responded to both these demands; that it had pushed its case as far as the Council would allow it to go; and that it had thereby added to the pressure on the British government to put the right kind of pressure on the Ulster Unionists. Yet it could not be accused, by any level-headed person, of having further inflamed an explosive situation. The brief and measured exchanges in the Council (and the marked silence of no less than eleven of its fifteen members) had the opposite effect.

The only clumsy move on August 20 was made by Alexei Zakharov, the Russian, who, ostensibly speaking in support of Hillery, addressed the Council in terms that must have made the Irish minister wonder 'with a friend like this, who needs enemies?' The Soviet spokesman, of all people, complained of the restriction of civil liberties in Northern Ireland. Only Protestants, he said, had the 'right' to form a government there. Inevitably, his audience reflected on the rather more glaringly sectarian set-up in the Soviet Union, where only the communists, a privileged minority, could hold office; whereas in Northern Ireland, whatever the Protestant politicians' faults, they had to win genuinely free and democratic parliamentary elections to retain power.

Apart from Caradon and the Russian, the only Council members who spoke were the Finn and the Zambian. Both limited themselves

328

to proposing sensible moves which, as we have seen, enabled the Council to avoid futile squabbling or procedural deadlock. Even the August president, who happened to be Jaime de Pinies of Spain, resisted the temptation to prod Britain; this was the more remarkable in view of the fact that at this point General Franco had not yet dropped the foreign minister, Fernando Castiella, whose Gibraltar policy mainly consisted of exploiting any opportunity to cause Britain embarrassment. England's difficulty was not, it seemed, Spain's opportunity this time.

With the solitary exception of Zakharov, no Council member failed to co-operate in making the August 20 meeting a model from which students of diplomatic technique can learn much. Precisely because it passed off smoothly and quickly, it does not loom large in the Council's record, and it may well be wondered why notice should be taken of it in these pages. The answer is that it admirably illustrates the way in which an apparently empty exchange of words in the Council, leading to no formally identifiable agreement or action, can sometimes help to stabilise a dangerous situation – if the trick is worked neatly, by people who understand how to operate the UN mechanism without letting it get out of hand. And there are few instances of comparable neatness on the record.

*   *   *

Three million square miles of the Pacific Ocean are, at least in theory, the special province of the Security Council. True, the 2,000 Micronesian islands scattered across this great waste of water add up to only 700 square miles of land. Only 95 of them are inhabited, and by only about 90,000 people. But this Trust Territory of the Pacific Islands – often known as Micronesia for short, or as the Marianas, Marshalls and Carolines for less short – was classified as 'strategic' when, having been taken from Japan by the Americans in the Second World War, it was brought under UN trusteeship. And the Charter (Article 83) ordains that, whereas other trust territories are the concern of the Trusteeship Council and the Assembly, in strategic ones 'all functions of the United Nations . . . shall be exercised by the Security Council'.

The large, if empty, Pacific territory has loomed larger in the trusteeship system as the UN gradually ran out of other trust territories. Originally there were eleven of these, with some twenty million inhabitants; but by 1968 nine of them – Cameroon (British and French), Nauru, Ruanda-Urundi, (Italian) Somaliland, Tanganyika, Togo (British and French) and Western Samoa – had become independent states or parts of such states, and there remained only the Australian-administered northeast part of New Guinea and American-administered Micronesia. The Trusteeship Council, which enjoys the use in New York of a chamber similar to and alongside that of the Security Council (but much more attractively decorated), was left with very little to do. Fortunately for its disconsolate members, the Americans were agreeable to arrangements by which the Trusteeship Council would in practice exercise most of the UN's functions in regard to Micronesia, under the Security Council's fairly remote control. It is therefore the Trusteeship Council that receives and discusses the Americans' annual reports on the territory, hears statements by petitioners and elected representatives of the inhabitants, and sends out visiting missions (one of which went to the Pacific in 1970). At the 1969 hearings in New York the vice-president of the Micronesian senate, Olympio Borja, told the Council that his people wanted to confer with the Americans about the early termination or revision of the trusteeship agreement, and that their most likely approach would be to seek self-government combined with some 'loose association' with the United States. A report based on an Anglo-French draft, welcoming the Americans' intention to enable the Micronesians to make an 'act of choice' about their future status, under the surveillance of UN observers, was duly transmitted to the Security Council.

*   *   *

Since the Assembly can admit states to UN membership only if the Security Council has already approved their applications, it is not only in regard to maintaining peace that the Council has the 'primary responsibility': the same applies to admissions. Naturally, most of the Council's activity in this matter has concerned individual requests for admission to the UN (page 96). But in 1969, a year marked by the absence of any new applications, the Council addressed itself to the question in more general terms.

U Thant, in his annual reports in 1965, 1967 and 1968, had suggested that it was time for the organisation to review its criteria for admissions, in the light of the emergence to sovereignty of states so small and weak that it was very doubtful whether they could qualify, under Article 4 of the Charter, as being 'able and willing to carry out' their Charter obligations. His first warning about these 'micro-states' had not prevented Council and Assembly from admitting the Maldives, an Indian Ocean island group with a population of only 100,000 and very few resources. The Maldivians found themselves unable even to man an adequate Assembly delegation. They did their ingenious best to maintain a mission at the UN by combining it with their New York office for the sale of postage stamps, which was one of their main sources of foreign currency. But this best was visibly not good enough to ease their plight. The Maldivians' chief role at the UN became that of providing an awful object lesson to other potential micro-members. The 3,000 people of Nauru, at least, got the message. When this Pacific island became independent in 1968 its President Hammer DeRoburt announced that it would not seek membership. He received heartfelt thanks from relieved UN delegates.

On American initiative, the Council's members began general consultations about the micro-state problem early in 1968, but their talks lapsed when new applications for membership arrived later that year. In 1969 anxiety was quickened when the Caribbean island of Anguilla (population 6,000) tried to break away from St Kitts (60,000) and sent spokesmen to the UN to plead its cause. In July the United States suggested that the Council should consider the problem in formal session. Debate began on August 27.

Charles Yost, the American representative, asked the Council to set up an expert committee to study the problem and report within two months, so that the Council could make recommendations to the Assembly during the 1969 Assembly session. He gave warning that there were nearly fifty small territories with populations of under 100,000 that might gain independence in future years, and he endorsed Thant's view that 'the line has to be drawn somewhere'. Yost questioned whether some of the potential micro-members could even afford the $160,000 a year needed to pay their basic dues and maintain adequate representation at the UN, let alone contribute in any real sense to the organisation's work. The American government thought the Assembly should create a class of 'associate members'. These states could be invited to take part, without voting, in UN debates that involved their interests. They might also have access to the International Court at The Hague, as well as to UN regional economic commissions and specialised agencies.

In American working papers that had been circulated among Council members it was suggested that full UN membership should require at least 100,000 inhabitants, 100 square miles, a $15 million annual budget and $10 million in annual foreign trade, or at any rate several qualifications of this kind. Another document available to Council members was a report by the UN Institute for Training and Research (Unitar), which suggested that, after admitting Iceland with 130,000 inhabitants and the Maldives with 100,000, the UN would presumably not deny membership to any future applicants that had populations of over 100,000. The Unitar report listed forty-four potential applicants that would thus be qualified for full membership. But, noting that Western Samoa and Nauru had already chosen not to seek admission, it commented that the actual number of small applicants might be fewer than was commonly supposed.

All members of the Council agreed to Yost's proposal that an expert committee should examine the problem; but there was no support for his idea of completing the study quickly and putting the matter to the 1969 Assembly. Caradon agreed with the Russian representative, Zakharov, that extensive consultations would be needed. For France, Armand Bérard argued that the creation of 'associate member' status would involve amending the Charter (Yost had suggested that it could be done by simpler procedural moves). The French point was backed by the representatives of Hungary, Nepal and Senegal, while Jaime de Pinies of Spain contended that, unless the Charter were to be amended, the UN could not categorise applicants: it could only offer them a free choice between full and associate membership.

While the Council's experts went to work on the problem, most public discussion of it remained strikingly unexpert and ill-informed. It is not generally appreciated that several forms of association between small states and the UN system already exist. Two of Europe's oldest micro-states, Monaco and the Vatican, maintain permanent observer missions at the New York headquarters. Brunei, Belize and other still dependent territories are associated with the UN's regional economic commissions for Africa, Asia and Latin America. A number of little states that are not members of the UN itself are members or associates of some of its specialised agencies.

Clearly there is a case for systematising arrangements that have developed in piecemeal fashion. A generalised associate member status would offer many practical advantages, both to the micro-states and to the organisation. But this should not be seen as a startling innovation. It need amount to little more than a tidying up of existing practices. With all due respect to the French and Spanish arguments that were voiced in the Council in 1969, it is hard to accept the contention that a Charter amendment would be necessary. The Charter says nothing about permanent observers, or associate membership of regional commissions or specialised agencies; but these things exist. And to establish a 'threshold' for admission to full membership, all that is really needed is some informal understanding between the Security Council's permanent members, to the effect that they will take Article 4 seriously.

What looms conspicuously in the emotional background to the micro-state question is the major powers' resentment at the un-biddability of so many of the relatively small states in the existing UN membership. But the real unbiddables are not in the 'micro' (or 'mini', or even 'see-through') category; and no new threshold can be devised to keep them out of the organisation, for they are already in. The notion that a provision for associate membership would in some way help to 'tame' the UN is suggestive of shutting the stable door after the wild horses have got in – and thereby keeping out a few decidedly tame pussy-cats. Very few of the potentially emergent micro-states are really likely to want to take on either the financial or the diplomatic burdens of full membership. And, not surprisingly, the UN's experience has shown that the littlest members are very

333

easily influenced by major powers. Indeed, in this light it should perhaps be set to the credit of some of the major powers that they have at least shown some concern about checking the entry of too many micro-states. If, instead, they simply encouraged the largest possible inflow of these tiny entities, they could hope to make the Assembly both more docile and more easily disregarded, to their own obvious advantage.

*   *   *

The Security Council's rules of procedure, after twenty-four years, are still only provisional rules. (This little anomaly reflects the fact that, back in 1946, members failed to agree on the spelling out of voting procedures.) But the rules have not become wholly unchangeable like the laws of the Medes and Persians. In January 1969, for instance, it was unanimously agreed to amend the rules so as to make Russian and Spanish 'working languages' of the Council alongside English and French.

These four languages, and Chinese, were already 'official languages' of the Council, as of the UN as a whole. The change was not a revolutionary one; but it was potentially costly. The Council is distinguished by the fact that its procedures involve both simultaneous and consecutive interpretation. While a speech is being made, everybody in the Council chamber can listen through headphones to versions of it in all the official languages, coming from the wondrously skilled simultaneous interpreters who look down on the chamber from sound-proofed boxes built into the north wall. When the speech is finished, consecutive interpretation may follow.

In practice, speakers have very often waived the right to consecutive interpretation. When they have not done so the consecutive interpretation may sometimes have ensured that certain subtle nuances in a speech came across more precisely than was possible in even the most accomplished simultaneous rendering. But the main function of the consecutive interpreting has been to provide a gap in the sequence of speeches which Council members can use for private consultation, or for a visit to the washroom.

When English and French were the only working languages this

334

was a fairly practical device. A speech made in either English or French would be consecutively interpreted only into the other of these two languages; a speech in some other language would be rendered into English and French. The new rules, however, opened up the tedious prospect of three or sometimes four consecutive renderings. While not opposing the change, the American representative said at the time that he hoped the Council would soon agree that consecutive interpretation should be provided only if it was requested in advance; and that the several consecutive interpretations should be given simultaneously. (If that sounds like a contradiction in terms, I'm sorry; that's the way it was.)

The representative of Nepal put in a plug for Chinese, which he described as one of the world's richest and most precise languages. But the Chinese member did not support him, and other members recoiled in quiet horror from the idea of acquiring yet another working language. (If and when communist China is represented in the Council, even this last dyke seems likely to give way. The Taipeh Chinese have usually said their pieces in English; the Peking ones would almost certainly use Chinese on principle.) It was also somewhat noticeable that, while the Council meeting on languages had been requested by Russia and Spain, and the resolution that was adopted had been sponsored by these two members and six others, including Spanish-speaking Colombia, the sponsors did not include the other Latin American Council member, Paraguay. It was obviously gratifying to the status-minded Spaniards that the change in the rules should be secured in the very first month of their membership of the Council; but Hispanic America appeared to be less than unanimous in its enthusiasm for the change.

*   *   *

In June 1968 the Council was drawn back, although rather obliquely, into the field of arms control and disarmament – a field from which it had retreated, leaving the Assembly in possession, more than a decade earlier (see page 81). On June 12 America, Britain and Russia asked for a Council meeting. In a joint letter addressed to the Council's president (who, in fact, happened to be the

American representative, Arthur Goldberg) they pointed out that the Assembly had adopted a resolution on that same day commending the newly agreed nuclear non-proliferation treaty (NPT), after a debate during which the three powers had said they would sponsor a Council resolution designed to meet many member states' wish that steps be taken to safeguard their security in connection with their adherence to the NPT. The three jointly presented a draft Council resolution which they had prepared for this purpose.

In the Assembly, the NPT had been commended by a vote of 95 to 4, with 21 abstentions. The majority looked impressive, and the four states voting against the resolution – Albania, Cuba, Tanzania and Zambia – were of no great significance in this context. But the abstainers included Argentina, Brazil, France, India, Portugal and Spain – a much more substantial group, even though Spain could offer no better explanation for its abstention than its failure to take over Gibraltar. And among those who voted for the Assembly resolution there were a number of states that were evidently still hesitant about actually adhering to the new treaty: these included Australia, Israel, Italy, Japan, Pakistan and South Africa – all of whom were regarded as capable of 'going nuclear' in the alarmingly near future. One of the most widely voiced complaints about the treaty had been that states adhering to it, and thereby renouncing the right to acquire nuclear arms, would remain exposed to nuclear attacks by non-adherents – among whom communist China loomed large. For this reason the three nuclear powers sponsoring the NPT had promised to accompany it with certain 'security assurances', to be provided through the mechanism of the Security Council.

The UK–US–USSR draft resolution which the Council was invited to adopt stated that, if there was any threat of (or resort to) nuclear aggression against a non-nuclear-armed state, the Council 'and above all its nuclear-weapon state permanent members' would have to 'act immediately' in accordance with their Charter obligations. In identical declarations that were also presented in the Council, each of the three powers said it would 'seek immediate Security Council action to provide assistance' to any non-nuclear-armed NPT adherent that was threatened with or subjected to nuclear aggression.

This was as far as the three powers felt they could go towards a commitment to protect states that renounced the right to make or procure their own nuclear arms. Goldberg, Caradon and Vasily Kuznetsov argued in chorus that the assurances offered, in conjunction with the treaty, would greatly enhance the security of adherent states; and they urged the Council to adopt their resolution and thus automatically bring their accompanying declarations into force. On June 19 the Council duly adopted the resolution, but only by a 10–0 vote. Algeria, Brazil, France, India and Pakistan abstained. (The votes for the resolution were those of the three sponsors and of Canada, Taipeh China, Denmark, Ethiopia, Hungary, Paraguay and Senegal.)

France stuck to the bizarre position into which General de Gaulle had got himself locked by his refusal to take part in the disarmament negotiations of the previous six years. Armand Bérard had announced in the Assembly that France would not sign the NPT, but would behave exactly like those nuclear powers that did sign it. Now, in the Council, Bérard said that France could not join the resolution's sponsors, or offer a declaration like theirs, but it would not obstruct the passage of the resolution and would in practice conform to its provisions.

The other abstaining Council members took a tougher, but a more logical, line. The representatives of Algeria, Brazil, India and Pakistan insisted that the Council's nuclear-armed permanent members were already bound by their Charter obligations to join in protecting any member state that was attacked or threatened with attack. They had, therefore, no right to limit this protection to states that adhered to the NPT; that was discriminatory and contrary to the Charter. Moreover, they were now offering no more than declarations of intention, whereas their obligations under the Charter were definite ones; and who knew how they would interpret the word 'aggression'?

It was rather noticeable that the sponsoring powers did not make any serious attempt to reply to these criticisms. In a sense, the best pleas made on their behalf were those made by the Ethiopian representative, who echoed the abstainers' point about the universality of security obligations under the Charter, but called for support for

337

both resolution and treaty despite their flaws; and by the Chinese, who pointed out that Charter obligations had not been very consistently respected in the past, and that it was of real importance that these obligations should be jointly reaffirmed by three states that commanded an overwhelming preponderance of nuclear power. This new solidarity, most notably between the two nuclear super-powers, was indeed a remarkable feature of the whole UN handling of the NPT and the related assurances. Yet it was equally remarkable how much opposition was shown, in the Council as elsewhere, to the projects jointly sponsored by America and Russia.

Kings and other heads of state, prime ministers and other heads of government, and presidents who may or may not be heads of both, have all too often addressed the Assembly when visiting New York. When such a personage wishes to harangue the captive audience of delegates there is not much the UN can do to discourage him. Much time and manpower is wasted on these occasions, for the exalted visitor may spout nothing but platitudes, yet protocol requires that a respectable number of delegates should sit and suffer him; the UN cannot employ the technique familiar to the House of Lords, in which a noble old buffer may be left droning away to a virtually empty Chamber. Of course there are exceptions. Some of the eminent guest speakers have delivered important statements. But one often detects a sense of heartfelt relief in the UN corridors when it is made known that a visiting dignitary is dropping in merely to have a few quiet chats with the appropriate people, without exercising his semi-divine right to make a speech.

The Security Council is spared these ordeals. But in its 24th year it was surprised to find itself, in June 1969, being called into session for the sole purpose of listening to a speech by a visiting head of state – President Carlos Lleras Restrepo of Colombia. President Lleras was visiting New York at a time when the Assembly was not in session; Colombia was a current Council member;* so the Colombians had the bright idea of asking for a Council meeting which would provide a forum for their head of state and government.

* For the fourth time. It has shown a very special attachment to the horseshoe table.

Other Council members were not too happy about it, fearing that Lleras might be the thin end of a wedge of unwanted oratory. But it seemed that the only way they could express their apprehensions was by refusing to give his meeting a serial number (it would otherwise have appeared in the record as the Council's 1,477th meeting).

Lleras let them off quite lightly, speaking for only twenty minutes. With minimal ceremony, he simply spoke from the seat assigned to Colombia near one end of the horseshoe table; this was the first time that a head of government had occupied one of these seats. And it turned out that he had something relevant to say. He recalled how the Council had been charged, in Article 26 of the Charter, with the duty of drawing up plans for the regulation of armaments; and how this article had virtually passed into oblivion. Since 1956 the Council had not even professed to be taking any part in the struggle to restrict and reduce armaments, except on the one occasion in 1968 when, as we have just seen, it played a supporting role to the Assembly in regard to the nuclear non-proliferation treaty. Lleras made a particular appeal to the small and middle powers to take initiatives in the direction of making the Council revert to its duty under Article 26.

Chapter Ten

Second generation

When will the Chinese seat in the Council be occupied by a representative of the government that actually controls China? I have suggested elsewhere (page 12) that back in 1950 it was a close-run
thing. The prospects of a transfer of the seat during the first year
after the proclamation of the new communist government in Peking
were first reduced by the Soviet withdrawal from the Council, and
then 'frozen' when the Chinese army, thinly disguised as a 'corps of
volunteers', went into battle against the United Nations in Korea.
Each year from 1951 to 1960 a ritual move by Russia or India to
raise the question in the Assembly was blocked by a majority decision, at the suggestion of the United States, not to consider the
matter.

In 1961 the Assembly accepted the question for debate for the
first time. At each Assembly during the 1960s it was debated and
voted on. Both Russia and India ceased to act as sponsors for Peking,
and its claims were advanced by a group of smaller member states
which varied from year to year, but often included Albania, Algeria,
Cambodia, Cuba, Guinea, Mali, Mauritania, Rumania and Syria.
Each year they lost their fight. But the voting figures are worth
recording, for they reveal how Peking's chances were affected both
by its own conduct and by that of other powers.

In the early 1960s the majority against Peking was reinforced as
Russia ceased to sponsor its claims and the 1962 Chinese invasion of
India brought a further reaction against it. Then, at the 1965
Assembly, there was a swing in its favour, which in part reflected
smaller UN members' resentment of the way the 19th regular
Assembly session (1964) had been reduced to a nonsense by the
conflict between the other major powers – America and Britain on

340

	Total UN membership	For Peking	Against Peking	Majority against
1961	104	36	48	12
1962	110	42	56	14
1963	111	41	57	16
1965	117	47	47	0
1966	121	46	57	11
1967	122	45	58	13
1968	126	44	58	14
1969	126	48	56	8

(There was no voting, on this or any other question, at the abortive 19th Assembly that began in December 1964.)

one side, Russia and France on the other – over voting rights and contributions to peace-keeping costs. In the débâcle of the 19th session Halim Budo of Albania, who was in effect serving as Peking China's interim representative at the UN, had struck some responsive chords when he denounced Russo-American 'collusion', arguing that although the two super-powers purported to be at loggerheads over Article 19 of the Charter, they were really united in treating the UN's smaller members with contempt and paralysing the 19th Assembly by their quarrel.

After 1965, however, Peking's score slipped again. The 'cultural revolution' and the savage excesses of Mao's young Red Guards, which included attacks on embassies in Peking, alienated some potential supporters. The Chinese got nowhere with their call for the formation of a 'rival United Nations' after Indonesia's withdrawal from the UN. Peking remained rigid in its opposition to any kind of 'two Chinas' formula under which the Taipeh representatives might be allowed to retain an Assembly seat while the Peking men took over the privileged role of permanent member of the Council as well as of the Assembly. And, as the Sino-Soviet conflict flared into open border fighting, the Russians, who had long ceased to initiate moves in Peking's favour in the UN, swung even farther into hostility. While Fedorenko and later Malik dutifully voted each year for Peking's admission, they made it abundantly clear to other members that they had no desire to see the transfer of the seat actually made.

Meanwhile the fact that France had swung over to Peking's side seemed to affect the Assembly vote remarkably little. Even the ex-French African states failed to follow the lead from Paris.

Not until 1969 did the score for Peking start to pick up again. The worst ravages of the 'cultural revolution' were over. Growing weight was attached to the argument that communist China must be drawn into the world community because of its status as an emerging nuclear power and its involvement in the conflicts in Indo-China. Belgium, Canada and Italy were among the nations now seeking to establish diplomatic relations with Peking. The Americans themselves, while still leading the opposition in the Assembly to any immediate transfer of the UN seat, had for some time been stressing the importance of restoring communication between Peking and the wider world. But the improvement in Peking's score in 1969 was still made without any help from the Russians, who distinguished themselves by not making any speech at all in that year's Assembly debate on the question.

One factor that has worked against any early transfer has been Peking's plonking insistence on clearly unacceptable conditions for its acceptance. These conditions were most notably set out by Chen Yi, the foreign minister, in September 1965. Before his government would take a seat at the United Nations, he said, not only must the UN expel the Taipeh representatives, it must also expel all those members who in Peking's eyes rated as 'imperialist puppets'. It must 'rectify its mistakes and undergo a thorough reform and reorganisation', which would include the revision of the Charter. It must cancel the resolutions the Assembly adopted in 1950 and 1951 which charged China and North Korea with aggression, and must adopt a resolution condemning America as an aggressor. Formally, these conditions still reflect Peking's attitude to the question. In practice, however, nobody doubts that they would lapse into oblivion if Peking received an offer of the UN seat in circumstances that would suit its book.

A rather more substantial obstacle is the fact that a good many members, while genuinely favouring the admission of representatives from Peking, are also quite genuinely opposed to the expulsion of those from Taipeh. To expel the Taipeh men might involve opening up a whole new set of dilemmas; for it would strengthen Peking's claim that the Taipeh regime is illegal and that any American support for it amounts to illegal intervention in Chinese domestic affairs. And the Taipeh men at the UN represent a government that has, for the last twenty years, ruled a population of thirteen million – which is larger than the population of some 90 of the UN's 126 member states. The rational solution would be to transfer the Chinese seat to the government that rules China and create a Taiwan seat for the government that rules Taiwan (Formosa). But no Assembly majority has ever been mustered in support of such a solution. Unfortunately, there is just one thing the two Chinese governments agree on: that there is only one Chinese government.

We have seen that in one year, 1965, the Assembly votes cast for and against a transfer were equal; and also that the margin against a transfer was halved in 1969. But one more vote for Peking in 1965 would not have brought it victory; nor would a transfer of the seat automatically follow if, during the next year or so, a small majority in Peking's favour were to emerge. For, each year since 1961, before the vote on the seat, the Assembly has adopted, at the instance of the United States and other members, a procedural resolution defining the China seat question as an 'important question'. It is hard to deny its importance – although the Guinea delegate at the 1965 Assembly made his mark by declaring that: 'This is too important a question to come under the heading of an important question.' But, under Article 18 of the Charter, an Assembly resolution on an important question requires a two-thirds majority. (This is not quite the same as the distinction that applies in the Council, under Article 27, between 'procedural' and other questions.)

On this basis, so long as at least 42 members remain opposed to a transfer, they could be out-voted only if all the other 84 lined up in favour of one. On the other hand, the preliminary procedural resolution requires only a simple majority. In each of the last few years it has been carried by a comfortable margin: 69 votes to 48 in 1967, 73 to 47 in 1968, 71 to 48 in 1969. But in 1965 it was carried only by 56 to 49. If something like the 1965 voting balance were to reappear within the next few years (with the procedural resolution

343

passing only by a small majority, and the voting on the substantive proposal then coming out roughly equal) Peking's opponents might have difficulty in holding the line. The Americans already seem to go about the annual rounding up of floating voters rather less zestfully than they used to do. And if there were close votes in two or three successive years a member like Britain, which has customarily voted for Peking only after helping to carry the procedural resolution (thus making reasonably sure that its vote in favour of a transfer would not have any effect) would be placed in an even more embarrassingly exposed position. (This British ploy has never won much of a following. In 1966 it was imitated only by Indonesia; in 1969 only by Mauritius.)

It is clearly worth while to consider not only the voting trends but also the composition of the tallies. In November 1969 the 48 members voting for Peking on the substantive resolution were: all the 12 communist members, including Cuba, Jugoslavia and Mongolia; 30 Asian and African states; and 6 West Europeans – Britain, France, and 4 Scandinavian countries. The 48 voting *against* the procedural resolution were the same except that Britain and Mauritius were replaced by Singapore and Tunisia. The 56 voting against Peking were: 28 Asian and African members; 17 Latin American ones; in Europe, Greece, Ireland, Luxemburg, Malta and Spain; and the United States, Australia, New Zealand, South Africa, Barbados and Israel. All of these, except Malaysia and Barbados, voted *for* the procedural resolution; and so did Britain, Mauritius, Canada, 4 more Asians, 2 more Latins, 3 more Caribbean states and 5 more European ones (Belgium, Cyprus, Iceland, Italy and the Netherlands).

Abstaining or absent members were, in the substantive vote: 9 Asian and African, 2 Latin and 3 Caribbean members, Canada, and in Europe, Austria, Belgium, Cyprus, Iceland, Italy, Netherlands and Portugal; in the procedural vote, Indonesia, Malaysia, Kuwait, Equatorial Guinea, Barbados, Austria and Portugal.

It is not easy to see the line-up as a simple one of the Americans and their friends versus the rest. In the substantive vote only 4 Nato allies (America, Luxemburg, Greece and Turkey) voted against Peking; 4 voted for it and 6 abstained. Even in the procedural vote 1

Nato ally abstained and 3 voted against the resolution. The Asian and African states split on the substantive vote into groups of 30 for Peking, 28 against and 9 abstainers or absentees; on the procedural vote, into corresponding groups of 31, 32 and 4.

The Assembly, of course, cannot lay down the law for the Council; or vice versa. Over the years there has even been speculation about the idea that the Assembly might decide to seat the Peking men while the Taipeh ones hang on grimly to the seat in the Council. But this is the kind of international lawyer's nightmare that only an international lawyer could dream up.

If and when an invitation to occupy the Chinese seat finds the Peking government in a mood to accept, all the 'conditions' that Peking has stated are likely to vanish in a puff of smoke. For a government that has totalitarian control over every word that its subjects may hear, read or utter, it is no problem to flush away previous statements down the memory hole. But it is a certainty that no Peking regime is going to accept an Assembly seat until it is assured of a Council one too. This would be unthinkable, even for rulers less obsessed with 'face' than China's present government.

If and when the Assembly's voting balance shifts clearly to Peking's side, it will become politically impossible for the Council not to fall into line. Either the Americans will have stopped using their influence against Peking in the Assembly, in which case they will not use it in the Council; or they will have found that they cannot prevail on this issue in the Assembly, in which case everything indicates that they would not be so unwise as to attempt a last ditch stand in the Council. And although at such a moment the Russians may well be even more troubled than the Americans by the prospect of the Peking man's appearance in the Council, a Russian bid to prevent that appearance would evoke even more humiliating mockery than an American one.

There remains, admittedly, the question of what the Taipeh representative in the Council would do. In the first instance, this would depend on what kind of a deal had been arranged. For all the lack of success that has hitherto attended the various attempts made to muster support for a 'two-China' formula, the possibility of some such deal cannot be excluded. As has already been pointed out, a fair number of UN members have argued that the satisfying of Peking's claims should not and need not mean the expulsion of the Taipeh men from the Assembly. If, after the eating of many words by many people, there was general acceptance of a deal that ensured continued seating in the Assembly for Taipeh's representatives, they would have good reason to withdraw from the Council without more ado.

If, on the other hand, the circumstances were such that only Taipeh China remained bent on blocking a transfer of the Council seat, the first question to arise would be how much pressure its American patrons could apply to induce it to give way; the second, how effectively the Taipeh men could protect their position by skilful use of Council procedures. The likely answer to the first question is that the Americans, having got this far, would feel that they must finish the job, however painful the implications. As for the second – assuming that the Taipeh Chinese held out even against intense American pressure – it is sufficiently clear that they could not, in the end, rivet themselves into the Council seat by using the 'double veto' or any other device.

When the Council first (and, so far, last) grappled with the question in 1950, the first move was a Russian proposal that the Council should reject the credentials of the sitting Chinese representative. The American councilman at that time, Ernest Gross, said that the question was procedural and that his vote against it should not be rated as a veto. The French councilman took the same line. The man from Taipeh, of course, insisted that it was more than a procedural question; but as the Soviet proposal failed anyway to win seven votes, no veto needed to be used against it. There followed Malik's withdrawal from the Council for six months.

Malik returned to the Council at the beginning of August, a month in which it was his turn for the presidency. As president, he immediately ruled that the 'Kuomintang representative' could not occupy the Chinese seat. The Council overruled its president. Two days later it also rejected Malik's proposal to include in its agenda an item on the recognition of the Peking government.

While John Foster Dulles was Secretary of State he told a press conference on 8 July 1954 that the United States would use its

Council veto 'if necessary' to prevent Peking taking over the Chinese seat. But this isolated remark has not been reinforced by any subsequent pronouncement in the name of the American government. In fact, while the threat of an American veto might well have been enough to discourage other members from trying to push through a transfer of the seat, at least at the time of Dulles' statement, there does not seem to be any watertight method of blocking a transfer merely by the use of a veto – either by an American or by a Taipeh representative.

True, in their 1945 San Francisco Statement the Big Five had claimed the right of veto on the point whether a specific decision was procedural (and therefore not subject to veto). This is the so-called 'double veto'. But that Statement was never endorsed by the San Francisco conference or by the whole UN membership. And the Statement itself clearly indicated that veto-free 'procedural' voting should apply in general to Council decisions unconnected with threats to the peace or with disputes that might endanger peace. Among several examples of this, the Statement mentioned that changes in the Council's own rules of procedure could not be vetoed.

In April 1949 the Assembly recommended that the Council should treat as procedural a number of types of decision; the list included 'Approval of credentials of representatives of members of the Security Council'. America, Britain, France and China had all sponsored and voted for this Assembly resolution. In October 1949 the American representative, who was then president of the Council, informed it about consultations that the five permanent members had held about the resolution, and confirmed that, except for Russia, they all adhered to the position set out in it.

In September 1959 America, Britain and France proposed that the Council should appoint a sub-committee to inquire into the situation in Laos. The president, Egidio Ortona of Italy, declared that the proposal was a procedural one. Arkady Sobolev protested vigorously, and there was a lively midnight debate about the San Francisco Statement. But ten of the eleven Council members backed Ortona's ruling; he declared the proposal to have been adopted despite Sobolev's contrary vote; the sub-committee was set up and went to work. In this particular case it appeared that Sobolev had some good grounds for his objection (see page 149). Nevertheless, Ortona had set a significant precedent. He had not strictly followed the lines of the San Francisco Statement (and why should he have? it was only a declaration by five states, none of which he represented). He had used instead the weapon of a presidential ruling.

A presidential ruling can be challenged, it can be overruled, but it cannot be vetoed. As the eagle-eyed Sydney Bailey has pointed out,* one of the defects in the Council's still 'provisional' rules of procedure is a discrepancy between the French text and the English, Spanish, Russian and Chinese texts of these rules (which are all equally valid) in regard to votes on rulings. If a president is using the French text, when his ruling is challenged he will ask the Council to vote yes or no to the challenge. If he uses one of the other texts he will ask for a vote on his ruling. In the present Council of fifteen a president using the French text will prevail if less than nine members support the challenge; but a president using another text needs to find nine members to uphold his ruling. Not surprisingly, presidents show some tendency to play this one by French rules. A ruling can then prevail even if nobody, not even the president himself, votes against the challenge. Seven mere abstentions will frustrate it.

Suppose that, after the Assembly has voted decisively for the transfer of the Chinese seat, there is a proposal in the Council to reject the Taipeh representative's credentials and accept those of a Peking man. The Taipeh government (like those of America, Britain and France) has been committed since 1949 to the thesis that approval of credentials is a veto-free procedural question. Its representative will not, therefore, be able to make much play with the San Francisco Statement. Since Ortona's 1959 ruling (which had the backing of Taipeh's councilman, and of all the others except Russia's) there has been a precedent for acceptance of a presidential ruling in such a case; indeed, even the arguments in support of the 'double veto' that Sobolev found in 1959 would not be available to the Taipeh man.

If the shift in voting alignments has been big enough to swing the Assembly, a presidential ruling that the transfer of the Council seat is a procedural and thus veto-free question can hardly fail to

* *Voting in the Security Council,* Indiana University Press, 1970.

have the backing of nine members. Should it somehow fail to muster so much backing, the Council could simply *reculer pour mieux sauter* and try again *à la française*. It would be inconceivable, in the circumstances, that nine Council members would actually support a challenge to the president's ruling. There would therefore be no need to resort to the ultimate weapon and dislodge the Taipeh incumbent by invoking the San Francisco Statement's dictum that the Council can alter its rules of procedure by a procedural vote. His position would be quite pregnable enough without that.

*   *   *

Not since the classic case of Frankenstein and his Monster has there been a love–hate relationship to match that which exists between the Secretary-General and the permanent members of the Security Council. The office is in the gift of the five PPs. It is a unique, challenging, exalted office. The Five tend to feel, quite naturally, that any man on whom they bestow this extraordinary status ought to be grateful, loyal, docile and above all not bothersome. But, just as befell the wretched Frankenstein,* it is their fate to find that their creature develops an unexpected and uncontrollable will of his own.

After each such painful experience the great powers do their best to find a new man who can be trusted to keep quiet. Each time, they find their nice tame monster eventually breaking away and finding himself forced by circumstance to rear up and defy one or more of his original patrons. The five PPs picked Lie and Hammarskjöld and Thant because, one after another, they looked 'safe'; but, one after another, these monsters stood up on their hind legs and talked back, causing grief and woe in Washington, Moscow, London, Paris and Taipeh.

We have already seen (page 69) how in 1944–5 the Three and later the Five, attaching little importance to the Secretary-

---

* It is hardly surprising that so many people have got the idea that Mary Shelley gave the name Frankenstein to the monster rather than to his creator. The first encyclopaedia I opened to verify the references contained only one entry under the name. Here it is, in full: 'Frankenstein: *see* Zabkowice Slaskie.'

Generalship, neglected to spell out clearly the limits of its scope. Among other things, they had been misled by the experience of the League into assuming that the last thing a Secretary-General would try to do would be to intervene publicly in the Security Council. Trygve Lie soon opened their eyes.

As early as 16 April 1946, Lie presented the Council with a controversial statement of his views on the question whether the case of Iran's complaint against Russia should be dropped. At first it seemed that the Council president, Quo Tai-chi of China, would simply ignore Lie's document. In the event, Quo had it read out to the Council, but then proposed an immediate vote on the question without further consideration of Lie's argument (which was couched in strictly legal terms).

Iran had withdrawn its complaint. Andrei Gromyko, who had staged the first Soviet walk-out on this issue, had returned to the Council. But Secretary of State James Byrnes, backed by a majority, argued in the Council that the item should remain on the agenda. Lie thought it would set an undesirable precedent if the Council thus hung on to a complaint that had been withdrawn by the complainant. Naturally, Lie's intervention annoyed Byrnes, who accused him of exceeding his powers. Just as naturally, it pleased Gromyko, who specifically cited Article 99 of the Charter in support of his argument that

> the functions of the Secretary-General . . . are more serious and more weighty than was indicated just now. . . . The Secretary-General has all the more right, and an even greater obligation, to make statements on various aspects of the questions considered by the Security Council.

In the committee that was then trying to draft rules of procedure for the Council, the Australian and Russian members backed Lie's claim to a right to intervene in the Council whenever he chose. The Americans were 'not at all sure that the Charter can be construed as authorising the Secretary-General to make comments on political and substantive matters'. But first the British and then the whole group swung in Lie's favour, and it was agreed that he should be empowered 'to make oral or written statements to the Security Council concerning any question under consideration by it'.

In September 1946 Lie pushed his boat out farther. Russia had indicated that it would veto a proposal that the Council should send an investigating mission to Greece's northern frontier, where rebel guerrillas were being aided by the neighbouring communist states. Lie promptly cited his duty under Article 99 to inform the Council of threats to peace, and declared that even if the Council itself could not act, he must reserve his own right 'to make such inquiries or investigations as he may think necessary'. No Council member challenged him. Moreover, Gromyko gave him another helping hand, saying that

> Mr Lie was right in raising the question of his rights. . . . In this case, as in all other cases, the Secretary-General must act.

The Russians, and Gromyko personally, were later to have cause to regret the part they had played in setting the monster loose. But at the time they seemed to think that a Secretary-General with fairly wide powers would serve to moderate the western preponderance in the Council. Thus do great pines from little acorns spring.

Gromyko already knew that Lie's Council interventions would sometimes add his weight to the western side of a controversy, for in August Lie had backed an American move on admissions to UN membership (page 97). A year later, in August 1947, Lie made another proposal to the Council about admissions; this time it was the Chinese who declared it unacceptable.

By July 1948 Lie was exercising, without challenge, the right to present his own amendments to a resolution before the Council. His first such amendment, which provided for the Mediator in Palestine to be given 'the necessary staff and facilities', was denounced by Yakov Malik as 'directly contravening the Charter'. But the Council accepted it, Russia and Syria abstaining. Soon afterwards it became accepted practice that the Council would allow Lie considerable freedom in regard to the activities of the Palestine truce observation missions.

Dag Hammarskjöld's achievements have been deservedly well recorded. But it is important to recognise not only that he, unlike either Lie or Thant, was able to settle in slowly during a quiet period of almost two years (in 1953–4), but also that he was able to exploit

351

a position that Lie had built up from scratch. It was Lie who won the right to beard the Council members – in public or private, collectively or individually – with demands for action and specific proposals on matters of real substance; the right to hit back when attacked and publicly expose falsehoods uttered by members, even if they were PPs; the right to ask the Council to adopt his own resolutions, and, in some cases, even the right to act himself when the Council failed to do so.

The five PPs chose Hammarskjöld because they thought he would keep quiet, unlike Lie. They chose U Thant because they thought he would keep quiet, unlike Hammarskjöld. Thant proceeded to surprise them as much as his predecessors had done. And by 1966, when the time came for them to renew his term or find a successor, the permanent members of the Council found themselves reduced to having to beg openly for the acceptance of a new term by a man who had already given pain, at one time or another, to each of the Five.

In August 1961 Hammarskjöld had served for nearly eight and a half years. He had received remarkably widespread support against Khrushchev's assaults on him and his office; but he was now in de Gaulle's bad books as well as being boycotted by the Russians. The decision about his successor would in any case have to be taken not later than the 1962 Assembly session, and first soundings about it were likely to be made during the imminent 1961 session. Speculation began to turn in the direction of the Asian member states, most of which were at that moment sending delegations to the first nonaligned summit conference, due to open on September 1 in Belgrade.

Journalists, too, were naturally converging on the Jugoslav capital; and it happened that four of them found that their journey involved changing planes at Zürich. In the transit lounge there, one of the four revealed that his initial assignment was the tricky one of filling half a page with conference gossip which he would have to file very soon after reaching Belgrade. His colleagues, sympathetically suggesting a few paragraphs that could be written right away, came up with the thought that the next UN Secretary-General might well be among the Belgrade delegates.

One of the four happened to have specialist knowledge of southern

Asia, another of the UN. A fairly logical process, largely of elimination, led them to name U Thant, then Burma's UN representative, as The Man Most Likely. So it came about that, just after the cónference opened, a widely influential newspaper ran a piece, written by a man who had never heard of Thant before, saying that he was being spoken of in Belgrade as a likely successor to Dag Hammarskjöld. After which, of course, U Thant was so spoken of in the conference corridors. And less than three weeks later he and many others who had been in Belgrade were back in New York at an Assembly that opened to find itself facing the shocking news of Hammarskjöld's death.

Hammarskjöld's second term would have run until April 1963. Already looming over the question of the succession to him was the fact that in September 1960 – just one year before he died – the Soviet attack on him had been extended to the office as well as to the man. Nikita Khrushchev, addressing the UN Assembly in the maximum glare of the world's spotlights, had tossed aside everything Moscow had said about the sanctity of the Charter and demanded its amendment in order to abolish the office of Secretary-General. No one man, said Khrushchev, could be trusted with the power of that office. It must be replaced by a 'troika' team of three men chosen respectively by the communist, neutralist and western-allied states, each able to veto the others' decisions.

The Russians never even got near to demanding an Assembly vote on their plan. They saw clearly, from the way the mass of smaller members rallied in defence of Hammarskjöld, that they could not run their troika through the Assembly session of 1960–1. But it was already envisaged that, during the 1962 Assembly, they might wheel the troika out again and refuse to agree to the appointment of any new Secretary-General at all. After all, Khrushchev had staked his personal prestige on the matter.

Now the void left by Hammarskjöld's sudden death, at a moment when the UN operation in the Congo faced pressing perils and could not be left without firm executive direction, seemed to give Khrushchev a dazzling opportunity to get his way. All the Russians needed to do was simply to veto any new appointment. They could keep the Secretary-Generalship vacant until the other UN members

353

were forced to agree to its abolition; or at least to some modified *troika* formula. Gromyko did in fact haul the *troika* round the Assembly hall once or twice just after Hammarskjöld's death. But it was so badly received that he lost his nerve and pushed it back into the carriage house. The Russians saw UN opinion starting to swing to the argument advanced by Secretary of State Dean Rusk, that the Assembly by itself had 'full authority' to make a provisional appointment to the vacant office. If the Assembly did that and got away with it a large hole would be blown in the PP veto. Gromyko hastily accepted the idea of a single acting Secretary-General; but he stipulated not only that the man must be chosen by the Five in the usual way, but also that he should be required to act in agreement with three deputies – a Russian, an American and an Asian or African – and to define his policy publicly before he was appointed.

By now U Thant (whether blown forward by the puff from Belgrade or identified by much the same logical analysis as had been used at Zürich airport) had emerged as something more than The Man Most Likely; quite early in October he was accepted to be The Man. The question was no longer who, but how. Thant made it clear that he would insist on having the same authority as previous Secretaries-General. He was not to be pinned down to precise policy statements in advance of appointment; he would choose his own chief assistants – though he was quite willing to retain, among them, the American and Russian under-secretaries who had been working for Hammarskjöld – and the most he would promise was to consult them 'in a spirit of mutual understanding'.

The Russians could get no more than this. Their attempt to tie Thant's hands by surrounding him with a second-level *troika* failed. By the end of October Thant had the blessing of the Five. On November 3 the Council formally (and unanimously) recommended him and the Assembly accepted him with the same unanimity, as Acting Secretary-General until April 1963. Adlai Stevenson told the Assembly that

> There will be no veto in the Secretariat, and no weakening of the office. . . . He will have the full powers of that office. . . . He will appoint his own staff and consult them entirely as he decides, as he has told you. . . .

354

Stevenson cited a news item he had seen that told how, when a scientist described his experiments to his colleagues, 'a wave of guarded enthusiasm swept through the audience'; and he added: 'I think we delegates might be permitted a wave of unguarded enthusiasm.'

A year later the Council and Assembly, again both unanimous, gave Thant a term as Secretary-General running until November 1966. His 'acting' year had been an active one. A little too active, it seemed, to please the Russians. *Pravda* trotted out the *troika* again in September 1962, and in October Gromyko told a press conference at the UN that the *troika* system must come some day. But what came that month was the Cuba missile crisis. When the dust cleared, Russia was seen to be united with America in offering Thant another four years.

Before that four years had passed he was exhibiting his reluctance to take another term. In September 1966 he said he would not offer himself for reappointment. He was disheartened by his inability to prevent the escalation of the Vietnam war, by the UN's continuing financial difficulties, by lack of progress over peace-keeping operations, disarmament, economic development and the representation of China in the UN. He said that

> I have found it increasingly difficult to function as Secretary-General in the manner in which I wish to function. . . . I do not subscribe to the view that the Secretary-General . . . should be a glorified chief clerk.

He asked the Council to look for a successor, but promised that he would stay in office until the end of the year if no successor was found before then. The Council, far from canvassing alternatives, closed in around Thant with cries of anguish. During September its members first had him to a lunch at which Fedorenko, as their president, told him that they wanted him to accept another term; and then they repeated this in a formal, and unprecedented, consensus statement.

Thant began to feel that, if the world was going to beat a path to his door, it ought to let him build a better mousetrap. After a great deal of pleading, particularly by Arthur Goldberg and Vasily Kuznetsov, he yielded. On 2 December 1966 he was reappointed for five years by a unanimous Council and an Assembly whose unanimity (in the usual secret balloting) was marred by only one spoiled vote.* In its anxiety to get him to stay on, the Council had gone to the length of issuing a second consensus statement that catalogued his virtues, promised him every consideration and virtually pleaded with him from a kneeling position. It referred to his

> demonstrated capacity to evoke the co-operation and confidence of all Members . . . his proven qualities . . . the great positive role played by the Secretary-General, U Thant, in the activities of the United Nations . . .

It appealed to his 'dedication to the Organisation', and said that the members of the Council

> fully respected his position and his action in bringing basic issues confronting the Organisation and disturbing developments in many parts of the world to their notice, as he has done in his statement of 1 September 1966, to which they accord their closest attention.

But Thant had been around long enough to know that all these fine words would butter few parsnips. Admittedly the UN's founding Three, back at Dumbarton Oaks, could hardly have dreamt that a mere Secretariat official would ever be addressed in such terms by the governments of the great powers. It was all quite gratifying. But it was also quite clear that the mud would soon start to fly again; as it duly did less than six months later when Thant served as scapegoat for the Council's inability to avert the Arab–Israeli 'six-day war'.

*   *   *

Many things have changed since the Security Council was born. It is larger; it is more representative of the world's regions; it is no longer numerically dominated by western allies or associates; instead of the mighty sword-arm that was to be its Military Staff Committee, it has

---

* One observer reported that the Taipeh China delegation did not join in the Assembly's ovation for Thant. If the Chinese deliberately spoiled their Assembly vote, this was in rather ludicrous contrast with their support for the Council's paean of praise for the Secretary-General.

that Damoclean or Achesonian sword hung from the ceiling of its chamber. But the changes have not been as extensive as many people seem to think. It is often said, for example, that there are now only two real great powers in the Council instead of 'the original five'. But there never were five.

When the Council was born France was still flat on its back and China was passing through chaos to collapse. Britain had rated as one of the wartime Big Three, but was already heavily dependent on America, both economically and, as the Council's first years were to show, militarily; and probably only the removal from office of Churchill saved it from the utter disaster that would have been involved in an attempt to cling to an empire which, in 1946, still included India. Britain's real strength in the Council's early years was no greater than it is today; France's was less; so was China's if one measures the recognised government of 1946 against the actual government of China today. (But it should not be imagined that, if Peking China takes its place in the Council in the near future, it will represent a power on the same level as Russia and America.)

Neither France nor China was able to play any significant part in the great-power talks that shaped the Council's framework. If General de Gaulle had had his way at that time, it is arguable that he would have stressed, even more than the Three did, the simple idea of a 'concert' of only a few major powers. The idea that the Council should also include a representative group of lesser states was not one that appealed to him, then or later. After his return to power in Paris in 1958 he manifested his objection to the participation of small states in disarmament talks by leaving France's seat at the Geneva conference empty. In the 1967 Arab–Israel crisis he called for 'Big Four' talks before the six-day war began, and again just after it. But in the end it was two years later, at the time of his departure from office, that four-power meetings on the Middle East got under way, and then on a less exalted level than he had contemplated: it was the councilmen of the Four, Yost, Caradon, Malik and Bérard, who held a sporadic series of private talks, taking turns to meet at each other's offices in New York.

And it was the Four, not the Five – though these meetings were often incorrectly described (for instance, by the French councilman on 15 May 1970) as meetings 'of the permanent members of the Council'. The Taipeh Chinese had been quietly faded out, over the years, to the point where they joined the Four only in those consultations that formally required the presence of all five permanent members – for example, consultations about appointing or reappointing the Secretary-General. (They objected to Thant's reappointment, as to Lie's, but, as we have seen, they prudently did not exercise their right to block it.

As the Council enters its second quarter-century it is not yet clear how far General de Gaulle's successors will depart from the very distinctive positions which (see page 29) made the French image mainly one of aloofness in regard to the UN as a whole and the Council in particular. *En principe*, de Gaulle's cry was 'all power to the Council!'; in this, he was more than Soviet. In practice, he disliked the Council's activity – but expressed this dislike by dissociation rather than open opposition. No French veto was used in the Gaullist decade between 1958 and 1969; but no major Council decision enjoyed wholehearted French support.

The voting records, of course, show Britain aligned with the United States more often than any other combination of the major powers occurs. But it would be a misleading over-simplification to interpret this as merely reflecting a British readiness to serve as an American echo. What particularly distinguishes Britain, not only among the powers but among the whole UN membership, is the fact that it has furnished the UN with far more problems to grapple with than any other country.

The vast British imperial withdrawal has provided almost one-third of the UN's total membership of 126 states – and a still higher proportion of the business on its political agenda. Palestine, India–Pakistan, Cyprus, Rhodesia and South Africa have all loomed large in the Council's affairs, and must indeed be reckoned as major items of still unfinished business. Over the years the Council's records (to say nothing of the Assembly's) have also included such names as Bahrain, Kuwait, Oman, Jordan, Hyderabad, Malaysia and Northern Ireland, to name but a few. One is almost left wondering what the UN would have found to occupy itself with if the British had not kept up a steady supply of problems. And in strict truth there might be added a number of situations in which there was a special, if less formal, British involvement, such as the Congo and Goa.

Some of these cases represented a successful British dumping of a problem in the UN's lap; others appeared on the agenda because Britain had failed to disengage completely. Nowhere does the imperial penumbra still loom over Britain as thickly as at Turtle Bay. And in a fair number of the line-ups on these questions, in the Council and other UN bodies, it is the British who have thankfully found the Americans willing to keep in line with them, rather than the other way round. The British relationship with the world organisation has, in fact, to a degree surprising at this late stage in the twentieth century, been a function of the progress of British disimperialism.

It is true that Britain's relations with the Assembly (and its committees) have been more extensively strained by these things than its relations with the Council. In the Council the British have often been able to sit quite comfortably. They could take pride in the fact that in Cyprus they were making the only great-power contribution of troops to a UN peace-keeping force. The British-sponsored resolution of November 1967 remained, nearly three years later, the only basis the Council had for an approach to an Israel–Arab settlement. The whole Rhodesia sanctions operation proceeded on the lines of British-sponsored Council resolutions, produced by British-initiated Council debates, until March 1970 – when the third extension of sanctions was embodied in a resolution that represented, with exactness, the limits to which Britain was prepared to go without using a veto.

As to the Soviet record, the essential thing to be said is that Russia, while insisting almost as firmly as General de Gaulle on the privileges of power, has signally failed to play a part in the Council (and the whole UN) worthy of one of the super-powers. The fact that it has used 105 vetoes is not, in itself, particularly relevant here. Most of those vetoes merely reflect the fact that, especially in the early years, Council majorities could be mustered for admissions to UN membership and other proposals when the western powers backed them, but not when Russia backed them. Russia abused its right of veto on some occasions, but it was not alone in this, and in most cases its vetoes merely amounted to 'working the Charter as it

359

was meant to be'. The responsibility for the way the Charter had been framed was not only Russia's.

Much more deplorable, in the circumstances, was Russia's failure to make positive contributions. Behind all the arm and leg work involved in vetoes and walkouts, it was the negative sterility of Russia's attitude to the UN that did most damage. Soviet diplomats – at least until quite recent years – showed no talent for the kind of informal consultation that is the real nervous system of the Council and other UN bodies. Terrified of stepping out of line, they shunned private talk altogether or, if persuaded to converse, recited the same dreary litanies that *Pravda* had already printed. They threw away countless opportunities by holding to stiff dogmatic positions on many issues where a little flexibility could have brought benefits to Russia as well as to the UN.

At bottom, I think, the Russians found it hard to believe that the UN was going to survive the first great-power quarrels of its early years. When they saw that, despite these quarrels, the UN was still there, they simply dubbed it an American-operated mechanism – and, by sticking to a strictly negative and defensive posture, they proceeded to make it more of one. Later, with cries of joy, they hailed the admission of the 'new nations' who could, of course, be counted on to take their lead from the great anti-imperialist Soviet Union; and they were repeatedly shaken to find that when the Asians and Africans called themselves non-aligned they quite often meant it.

It must be admitted that the Russians' original mistake was an understandable one. The great powers had devised a UN that was going to be effective only if they jointly made it so. How could it survive when those powers fell into bitter hostility? The extraordinary thing is that it has survived – and has shown a remarkable capacity for development.

At this point let us bring back that useful device of the preinterplanetary age, the Man from Mars, and suppose him to visit Earth at twenty-five-year intervals. Having seen the way the UN was originally set up, and having returned in 1970 to find the UN still in being, he would naturally assume one of two things to have happened. Either the founding great powers must have quite forgot their quarrel, like Tweedledum and Tweedledee, and agreed to co-operate after all in working the mechanism they had shaped; or those powers must have fallen into complete impotence, so that others could operate the UN mechanism without them – indeed to some extent against them.

But in fact neither of these alternatives provides an accurate description of what has happened. The super-powers have reached accommodations on certain issues – enough, at least, to evoke charges of 'collusion' from Peking – but they are nowhere near getting Article 43, and the Military Staff Committee and all that, into working order. On the other hand, they are still unrivalled in military might; and there is no question of the main UN mechanisms having been actually 'captured' by the smaller members – least of all in the Council. Yet it is true that some of the UN's activities have been carried on quite effectively without the great powers' unanimous backing, and sometimes in the face of the visible disapproval of one or more of those powers.

A large part of the credit for this must go to the Americans. I notice that even Conor Cruise O'Brien, who is no slouch when it comes to denouncing their manifold machinations, has been generous in conceding that they have made more enlightened use of their pre-eminent position in the UN than Britain and France made of theirs in the League. They have also, I think, shown considerable ability to adjust to their steady loss of pre-eminence. They have weathered the successive buffets of finding that the UN could not be rallied to support them in the 1964 tussle over Article 19 and peace-keeping costs; that it would not keep its fingers out of the Dominican pie in 1965; that it would not endorse their action in Vietnam; that it could do nothing to prevent the Arab–Israel war in 1967 or the Russian invasion of Czechoslovakia in 1968. They seem in fairly good shape even to stand up to the sight of Peking man in the Council. Already they have taken in their stride the traumatic experience of having to use their first Council veto.

American support for the UN has undoubtedly been the organisation's greatest prop and stay. The United States is the host country, the largest contributor, still the most influential single member state and much more. But the fact that the Americans could at any time

361

have sunk the UN by pulling out is not, in fact, the most distinctive feature of their relationship with it (for a Soviet withdrawal would have been almost as certainly destructive). The most distinctive thing is that the Americans alone have had the power to crush the United Nations by embracing it too closely.

The fact that the Americans have learned that it is not the end of the world when they find themselves on the losing end of a UN vote, and have made certain moves whose apparent effect is to 'downgrade' the UN among their diplomatic priorities, need not mean the end of the world for the organisation. It could mean a healthy new beginning. Indeed, it is probably essential for the UN's long-term future that it should not always be able to count on massive and enthusiastic American support.

The American expressions of unmitigated enthusiasm in earlier years contributed to the fact that far too many other member states, far too easily, acquired the habit of leaving it to Uncle Sam both to call the tune and to pay the piper. No international body that claims to act in the name of the world community can afford to remain crucially dependent on the goodwill of even the most benevolent of great powers. As Hammarskjöld told the UN (and as Thant reiterated), it is primarily the smaller members' organisation in the sense that they need it more than the major powers do. But the only way they can make the assertion that it is theirs a reality is by putting more into it themselves – so that it need not become paralysed just because a great power has lapsed, not even into hostility, but merely into indifference towards it.

Something in this direction has already been achieved during the first quarter-century. It has become an accepted practice – in glaring contrast with 'the Charter as it was meant to be' – that the smaller members provide not only mediators and good offices but military observers and even armed contingents for UN forces. While the top brass of the five PPs' Military Staff Committee exist only in fortnightly fantasy on the 35th floor of the UN building in New York, the UN finds real live generals from India, Finland, Ethiopia, Canada, Chile, Ireland, Australia, Pakistan or Norway who serve it in the field. And who, for the most part, carry out operations that have been approved by the great powers in the Council.

But the charmed circle of the PPs still divides these five in a quite artificial way from the mass of what, for brevity, I have been calling the 'smaller' members. Among these 'smaller' members no distinction is made between, say, Japan and Nicaragua. At the time of writing Nicaragua is a Council member: Japan, with the world's third largest gross national product and a real 'weight' greater than that of Britain or France, has been a Council member for only four years of its fifteen in the UN. Indeed, there has lately been some murmuring in Tokyo about a claim to a permanent Council seat; and the Japanese have had to be told that there is no early prospect of one for them.

The League of Nations was perhaps excessively flexible in this matter. It not only granted new permanent Council seats but permitted a category of 'semi-permanent' members who were regularly re-elected – there being no such absolute bar to immediate re-election as the Charter prescribes for the UN Security Council. The League's practice could not easily be applied to the much larger membership of the UN. But the organisation, which since 1966 has been able to give its enlarged Council a more 'equitable geographical distribution', badly needs to pay more heed to the other words in the Charter's Article 23, which requires that in elections to the Council due regard should be

> specially paid, in the first instance, to the contribution of Members of the United Nations to the maintenance of international peace and security and to the other purposes of the Organisation.

To formalise a new category of 'middle powers' and provide for them to occupy seats at the horseshoe table more often than others might be beyond the present limits of political possibility. But some remedy must surely be found before long for a situation which permits Council seats to be occupied simultaneously (in 1970) by Burundi, Nepal, Nicaragua, Sierra Leone and Syria – while, for example, neither Australia nor Italy nor Sweden has held a seat during the past decade, Indonesia has never held one, and Jugoslavia now seems unlikely ever to hold one again.

*   *   *

In April 1970 Max Jakobson, the Finnish councilman, who was also the Council's president for the month, formally presented his fellow members with a suggestion that they should at long last do something about Article 28(2) of the Charter. This is a part of the Charter that the Security Council had persistently violated ever since it was born. It provides for 'periodic meetings' at which each member state may be represented by 'a member of the government or by some other specially designated representative'.

The Council had held no such meetings. Yet Article 28(2) is no mere authorisation: it is a direct order to the Council. It says flatly that the Security Council *shall* hold these meetings. The Three agreed on this at Dumbarton Oaks. The Fifty at San Francisco swallowed it whole. Thus the great-power PPs, and the other member states that fill the other Council seats, both told themselves that they must hold these periodic high-level Council meetings. Twenty-five years later, they had yet to hold one. A quarter of a century is admittedly a 'period', but there is ample evidence that in 1944–5 it was not supposed that the Council would operate this part of the Charter in quite such a sempiternal spirit.

At Dumbarton Oaks it was Stettinius and his team who first emphasised the need for the Council to operate continuously. Sir Alexander Cadogan accepted this, but drew attention to the value of arranging matters so that foreign ministers themselves, or other Cabinet ministers, could attend the most important meetings. The British felt that the League's experience had shown the usefulness of regular ministerial gatherings, and they did not want to see these vanish. Andrei Gromyko took a similar line and specifically proposed 'periodic meetings', to be attended by 'responsible members of governments'. The Americans' only worry was that the status of the permanent representatives might be reduced by these recurrent appearances of their superiors. No great difficulty was found, in the end, in providing for both continuous Council operation and special 'periodic' meetings.

But it turned out that nobody was in a hurry to start off the periodic series. Ernest Bevin of Britain, Georges Bidault of France and James Byrnes of the United States each appeared for a while at the Council table in early 1946, but there was neither a formal move

364

for a meeting at the foreign-minister level, nor even an informal coming together of several of these ministers at any one time in the Council. As 'east–west' relations rapidly worsened in the later 1940s, and the four-power contacts and meetings about Germany and related issues ran into bitterness and breakings-up, it was plausibly argued that a high-level confrontation in the Security Council would only end in tears.

In the early months of 1950 Trygve Lie blew five years' dust off Article 28(2) and personally approached Harry Truman, Joseph Stalin, Clement Attlee, Bidault (by then Prime Minister of France) and their foreign ministers, with a 'peace programme' in which the first of ten points was a call for semi-annual Council meetings at ministerial level. These meetings, Lie urged,

> should be used for a general review . . . of outstanding issues. . . . They should not be expected to produce great decisions every time; they should be used for consultation – much of it in private – for efforts to gain ground toward agreement . . ., to clear up misunderstandings, to prepare for new initiatives that may improve the chances for definite agreement at later meetings. They should be held away from Headquarters as a general rule.

Stalin told Lie he would be agreeable, if the UN China seat was given to the Peking government – as, at that moment, there seemed a fair chance it would be. In the western capitals the coldest reaction came from Ernest Bevin, who told Lie that he would not take part in any new talks with the Russians until they had shown by their actions that they were worth negotiating with. This, of course, was the period when Russia was boycotting the Security Council; the boycott was one of the main reasons both for Bevin's reluctance and for Lie's anxiety to get talks going between foreign ministers.

However, Lie's proposals were still being chewed over in the great powers' capitals when the invasion of South Korea destroyed all hope of bringing the ministers together for quiet, wide-ranging talk. Article 28(2) went back into the Secretary-General's desk drawer for another five years. Variations on the theme nevertheless recurred, and from surprisingly different sources. In the November 1950 'Uniting for Peace' resolution the same Assembly majority that adopted Dean Acheson's contingency plan for meeting situations in

365

which the Council could not act (page 90) added a call to the permanent Council members. They were urged to

meet and discuss . . . and, if necessary, with other States concerned, all problems which are likely to threaten international peace . . . with a view to their resolving fundamental differences. . . .

And in January 1952 Russia proposed that the Assembly should ask the Council to hold an Article 28(2) periodic meeting 'without delay'. The Assembly amended the Soviet text so that the call was for a meeting to be held when it could be of use in removing the existing tension.

There was a tide in the affairs of Article 28(2) which usually came every five years (and was then missed). In 1955 and again in 1960 – both great-power 'summit' years, when things seemed to be looking up for a moment – Hammarskjöld dug in the desk drawer and pulled out the old article. In between his two unsuccessful initiatives there had occurred the pulling and hauling over a 'summit' meeting on the Arab crisis in the summer of 1958 (page 94). At one stage, on August 1, this brought a formal request for an Article 28(2) Council meeting from the American, British and Canadian governments. But that, too, proved abortive.

Yet there had meanwhile been held the only Security Council session on record that almost looked like an Article 28(2) affair – though nobody suggested that it was one. The series of Council meetings on the Suez Canal crisis that began on 5 October 1956 saw foreign ministers occupying six of the eleven seats around the horseshoe, including all four of those of the substantive PPs. France was represented by Christian Pineau (who presided), America by John Foster Dulles, Britain by Selwyn Lloyd and Russia by Dimitri Shepilov. Belgium and Jugoslavia were also represented by their foreign ministers, Paul-Henri Spaak and Koca Popovic; and the Egyptian foreign minister, Mahmoud Fawzi, appeared as a visiting fireman.

This was emphatically not a 28(2) gathering of the kind that all three Secretaries-General have wanted to see. It was not attempting a 'general review of outstanding issues' on the firm understanding that nobody would think it disastrous if the ministers failed to

366

'produce great decisions'. It represented an urgent search for means of averting a specific disaster. On the other hand, it conformed with the 28(2) approach in that the ministers and the five other council-men soon went into a series of closed meetings, during which there also developed a separate series of wholly informal and private meetings of a smaller group – Lloyd, Pineau and Fawzi. The British, French and Egyptian ministers met as Hammarskjöld's guests in his office and with the benefit, which they all later acknowledged, of his 'able and tactful assistance', as Lloyd put it.

It is now widely known – but it was not, of course, known at the time – that the impressive amount of agreement yielded by these talks in New York was meaningless because, in the immediately following series of talks held in London, Paris and Sèvres between Guy Mollet, Pineau, Anthony Eden, Lloyd, David Ben-Gurion, Moshe Dayan and others, agreements of a very different kind were reached. A week after the crucial British–French–Israeli meeting at Sèvres on October 22, the invasion of Egypt was launched; and the Security Council was faced with a new situation, whose ramifications included the first British veto and the first fall of Acheson's Damoclean sword. It may be argued that this outcome did nothing to encourage the general idea of making a reality of Article 28(2).

But the old article kept coming back like an old song. Thant, particularly after his reappointment, made it one of his recurrent suggestions. In September 1969 Gromyko included it in his 'general debate' contribution to the 24th regular session of the UN Assembly. The Russians had at least achieved a more positive attitude during the nineteen years since Lie first tried out Article 28(2) on Stalin and Molotov; for the one thing that Gromyko very noticeably did *not* stress in his September 1969 speech was the need to put a Peking man into the China seat either before staging a 28(2) meeting or, indeed, at all.

There was, however, no subsequent Soviet move in the Security Council itself. Jakobson's initiative in the spring of 1970 might admittedly be – and in some quarters inevitably was – taken to be a move made on Russia's behalf. Yet the Finns' diplomatic record, in the Security Council as elsewhere, really has not borne out the idea that they are content simply to act as mouthpieces for Russia when it wants to vent a proposal through a respectable 'neutral' blow-hole. In this case it could hardly be said that Gromyko had tried to keep his enthusiasm for Article 28(2) a secret (unless one assumes that speeches in Assembly general debates pass quite unnoticed; this can happen, but rarely to Russians). Anyway, by 12 June 1970 the Finnish councilman's patient coaxing had produced a Council consensus statement endorsing his general approach.

Jakobson's proposal was essentially the same one that Trygve Lie had made in 1950: periodic meetings twice a year, at which there would be general (and private) talk about general questions, and a firm refusal to let any specific immediate problem dominate the whole exchange. Indeed, it could be understood that any such meeting would probably be postponed if a preoccupying major crisis blew up just when it was due. In this way, the timetable for meetings within the Council framework would have more flexibility than the existing custom that brings many foreign ministers to New York during the first weeks of each regular Assembly session; for that September season has often been over-shadowed by some urgent international problem or conflict. (In September 1970 it was the Jordan conflict that cast such a shadow over both the Assembly opening and the immediate prospects for a first-ever Article 28(2) meeting.)

There are always plausible reasons for putting off meetings of this kind until some later year. Perhaps the Russians fear that Peking's accusations about Russo-American collusion will gain credibility. Or the western powers fear that Russia is simply trying to push its suppression of Czechoslovak freedom under the rug. Or the Europeans fear that the super-powers will jointly pressure them into agreements they will later regret. Or there is unease among certain small states at the sight of the great powers getting too chummy. But the trouble with these plausible arguments is that their logic points to the impossibility of ever getting high-level exchanges of views at all.

The Security Council is not the ideal setting for such exchanges. Its non-permanent membership may be more representative than it was a few years ago, but it is still something of a random selection. Apart from the absence of communist China (whose presence might or might not prove an asset during the first years after its appearance) and of Germany, it is also a matter of chance whether in any one year the Council includes countries of such significance as Japan and India. But the trouble with this argument is that there is *no* ideal setting for high-level exchanges. The Council, with its crude balances between great and small, east and west, rich and poor, is as good a setting as there is likely to be in our time.

And it does present the very great advantage that nobody expects much from it. The curse that has hung over so many of the 'summits' and other majestic international occasions of recent years has been the fact that such gatherings arouse quite unreal expectations. Statesmen become terrified of returning from these meetings 'empty-handed'. So they fake 'achievements' – a device that leads to later disenchantment. Or they are led to make unwise concessions in order to prevent the conference from breaking down. Or they are forced to accuse other governments of obstinacy, illwill and deceit, in order to explain away the failure of the whole enterprise. But nobody sees the Council's horseshoe as a guarantee of good luck. Ministers could safely drop into the chairs around it once or twice a year without panicking about coming away 'empty-handed'.

The Security Council is no Everest; but it is there. The manner in which I have written about it will, I think, convey my feeling of confidence that it will continue to be there – and for a second quarter-century, if the rest of us manage to get that far. It will continue to irritate some of our elder statesmen by its 'impotence', and to infuriate them when it actually does things. It will continue to disappoint the hopeful; but from time to time it will also have a healthily discouraging impact on various people who need discouraging. It will continue to have good moments and bad ones, good members and bad ones, good and bad relations with the Secretary-General, the Arabs and Israelis, the General Assembly and the press. It may acquire a new interest in disarmament, a Peking representative, a regular series of 28(2) meetings, and even women. It may undergo such further changes as to make it unrecognisable by its original founders. But I think it will still be there.

Index

371